DISNEP PRESENTS
A STUDIO GHIBLI FILM

The Secret World of
Arrietty
Picture Book

Planning by **Hayao Miyazaki**
Based on *The Borrowers* by **Mary Norton**
Original Screenplay by **Hayao Miyazaki** and **Keiko Niwa**
Directed by **Hiromasa Yonebayashi**

VIZ Media
San Francisco

MEET THE CHARACTERS

Arrietty

A fourteen-year-old Borrower girl who lives with her mother and father beneath the floor of an old country house. Cheerful and active, Arrietty looks forward to helping her father on his "borrowing" trips.

Homily

Arrietty's mother. She tends to be a worrier, and Arrietty's recklessness makes her anxious.

Pod

Arrietty's father. When his family needs things, he "borrows" them from the humans who live above the floorboards. He is a man of few words, but is a dependable, protective head-of-the-household.

Spiller

A young Borrower man, Spiller wears a cloak made of mole hide, carries a spear, and proudly fends for himself.

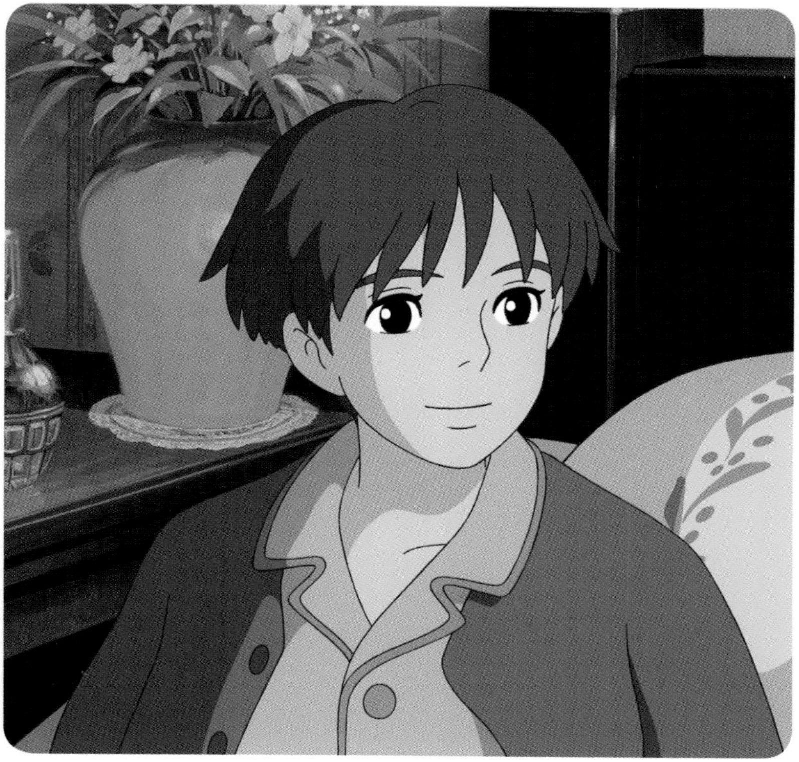

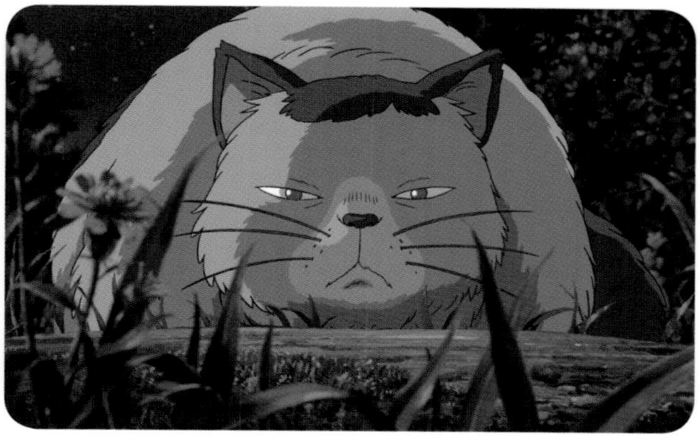

Nina

A big cat who is fond of Shawn, but not fond of the crow. Nina knows that tiny people live under the floorboards of the house.

Shawn

A twelve-year-old human boy with a weak heart. Shawn is scheduled to have an operation, and has come to stay at his mother's childhood home to rest and collect his strength before the procedure.

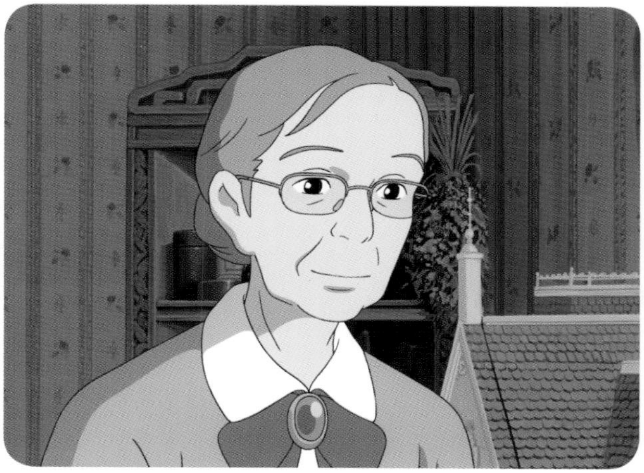

Jessica

Shawn's aunt, and the owner of the old house. She has a gentle personality.

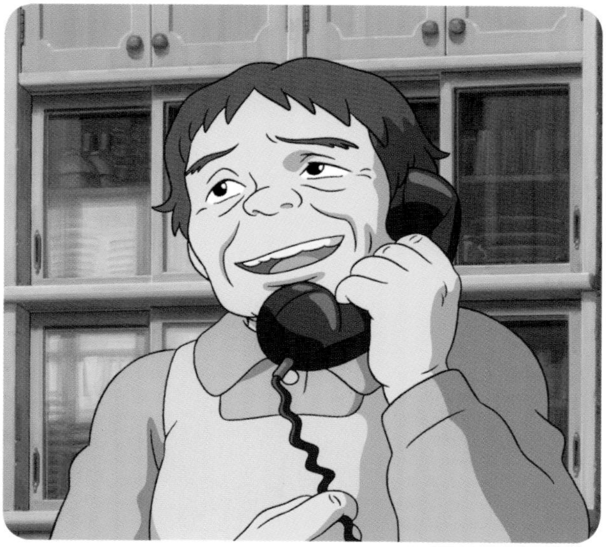

Hara

A live-in housekeeper who has worked in Jessica's house for decades. She is full of curiosity.

"It's funny how you wake up each day and never really know if it will be one that will change your life forever. But that's what this day was: the day I left the city to spend a week in the house where my mother grew up. A day I'll never forget."

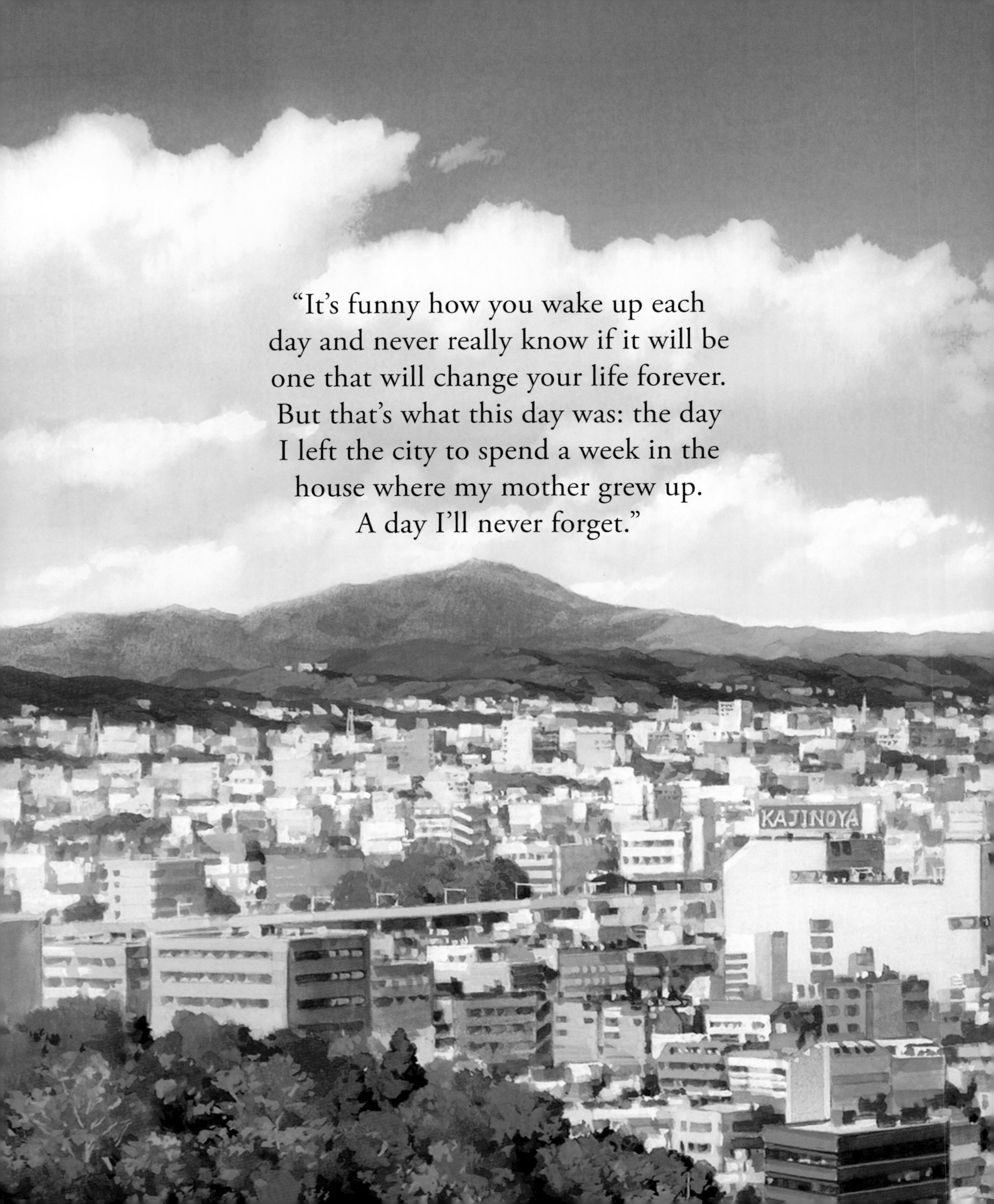
KAJINOYA

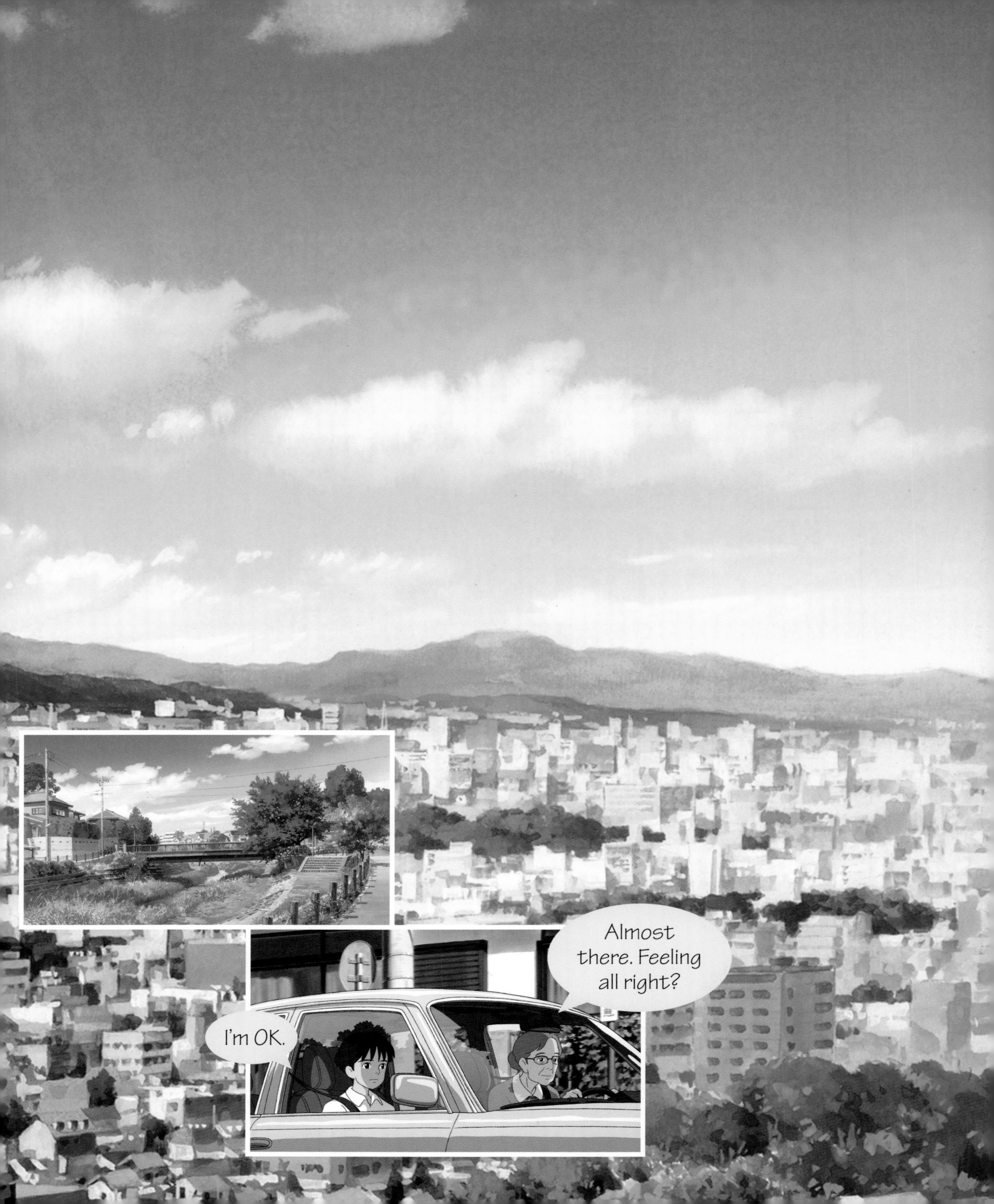
Almost there. Feeling all right?
I'm OK.

The House Where the Borrowers Lived

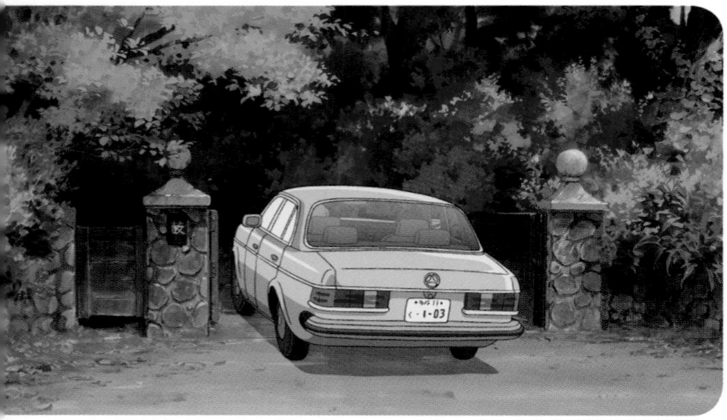

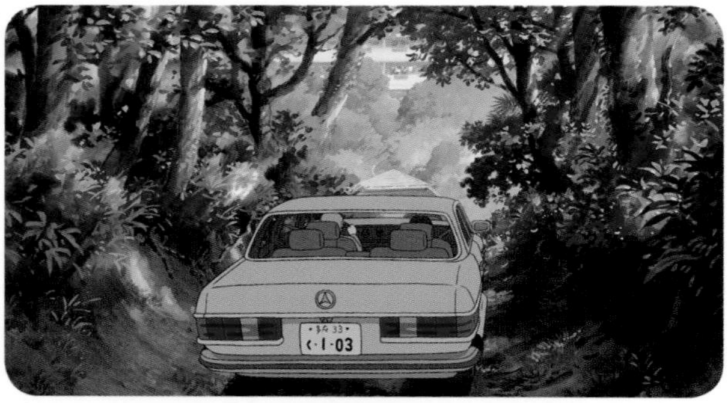

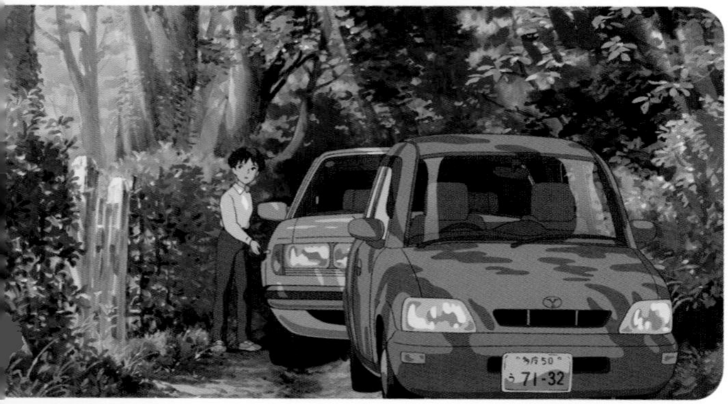

The car carrying Shawn turned into an entrance marked with stone pillars, and continued along a dark driveway that led to the old house.

Further along the driveway, a parked red car blocked the road.

"Oh, Hara," Jessica sighed. "How many times have I told her? Wait here, Shawn."

Jessica got out of the car and walked toward the house.

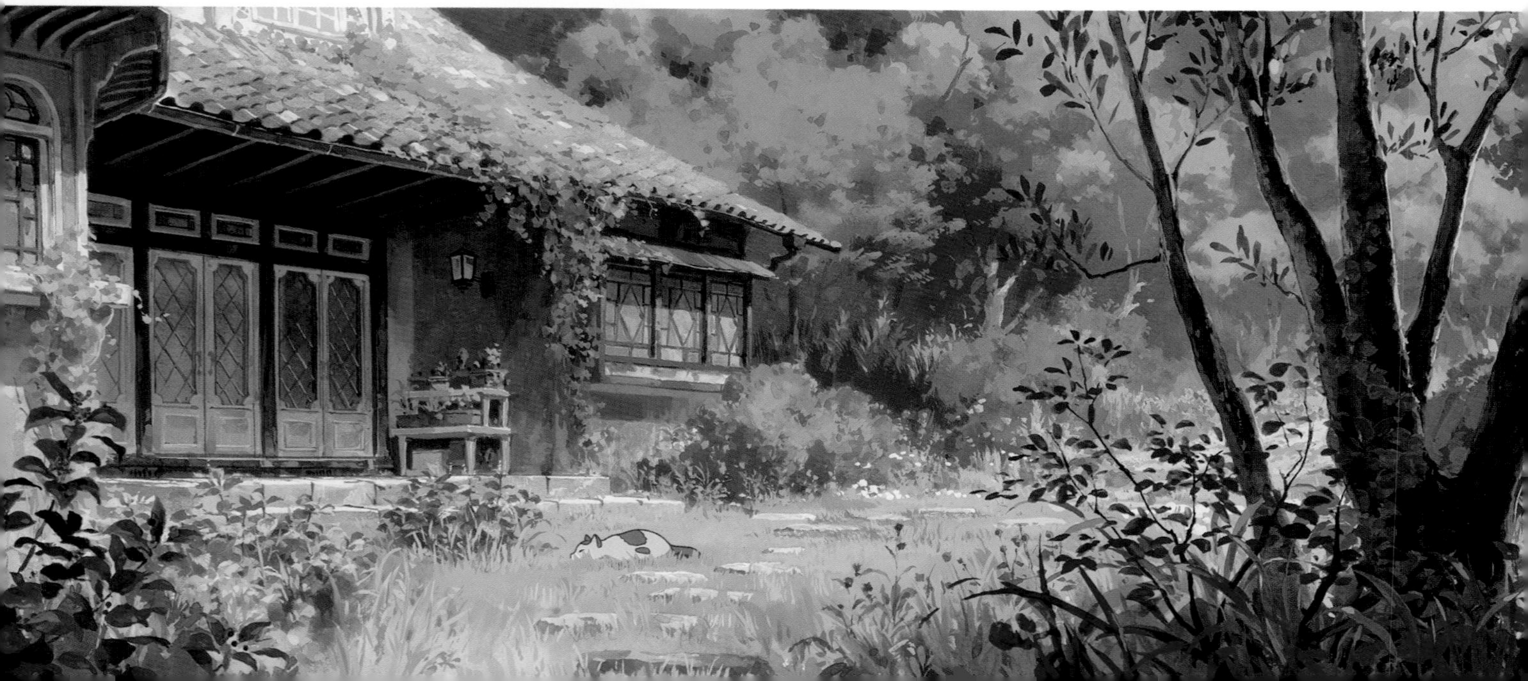

"Hara! Your car's blocking the driveway again!" Jessica called.

Shawn got out of the car and stood in front of the wooden gate.

He looked around and saw beams of sunlight peeking between the branches of a tree so big it blocked the sky. Beyond the trees lay a spacious green garden that looked like something from another world.

Half-hidden in the grass, a cat snuck by, as if stalking prey.

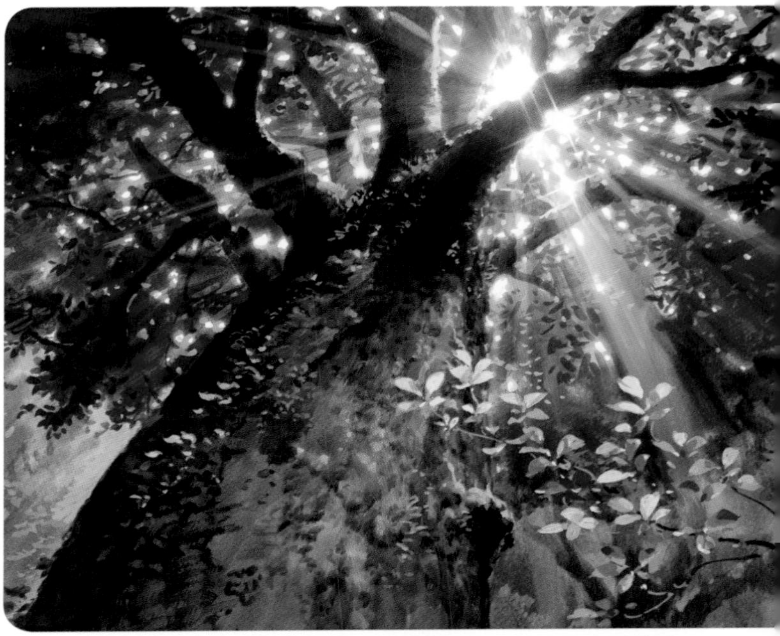

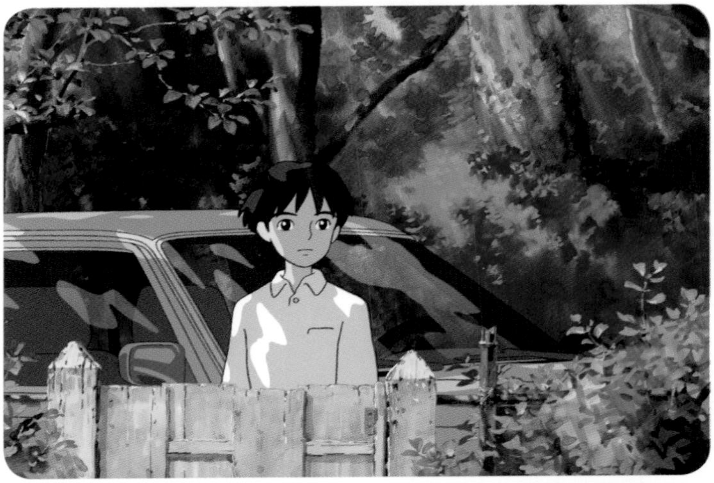

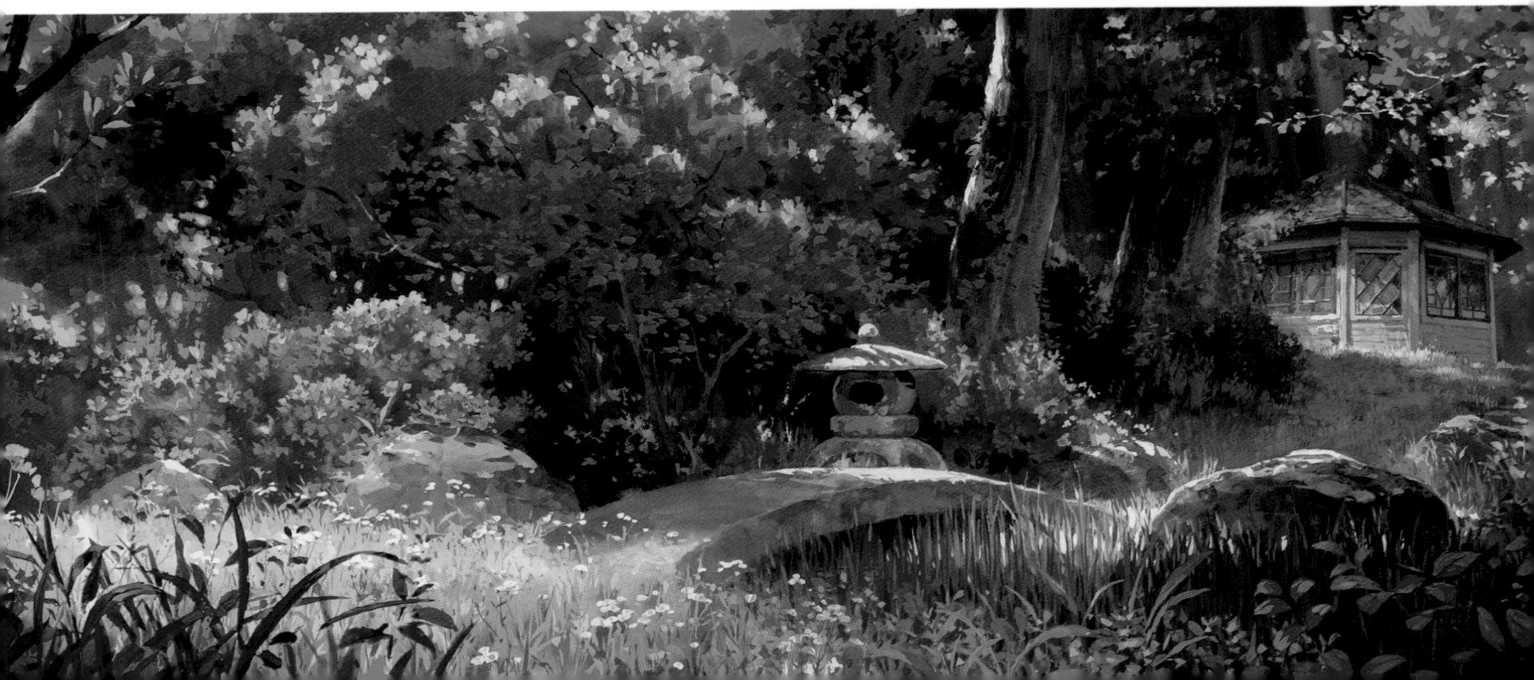

Flap flap flap!

"Caw, caw!" Suddenly a crow flew down and attacked the cat.

"Hey!" Without thinking, Shawn opened the gate and rushed into garden.

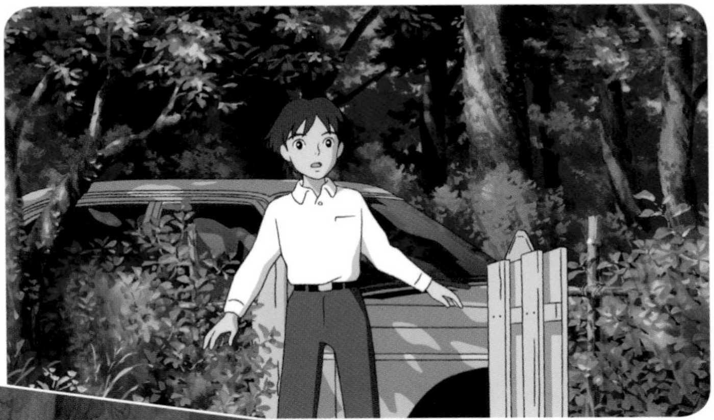

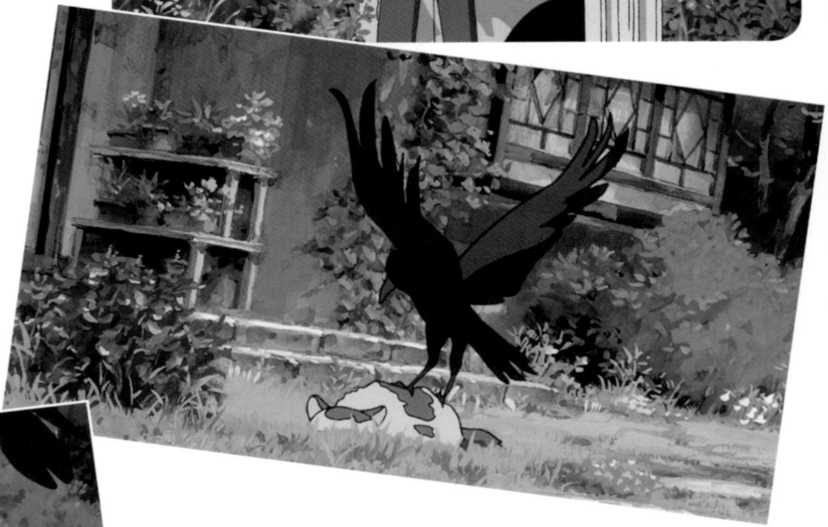

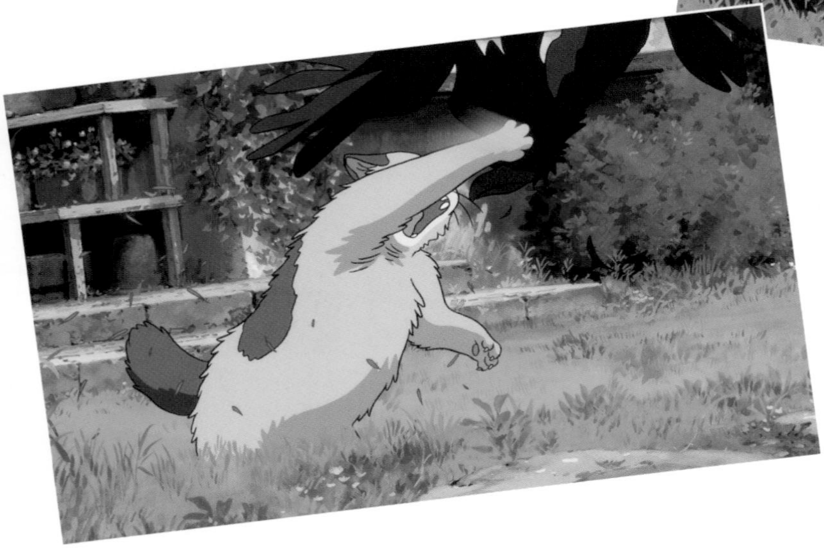

"Mrrreowww!" The cat bared its claws and swiped at the crow.

Shawn crept closer to make sure the cat was okay. For a moment, the cat paused, fascinated by something in a bush. But it soon lost interest and turned away.

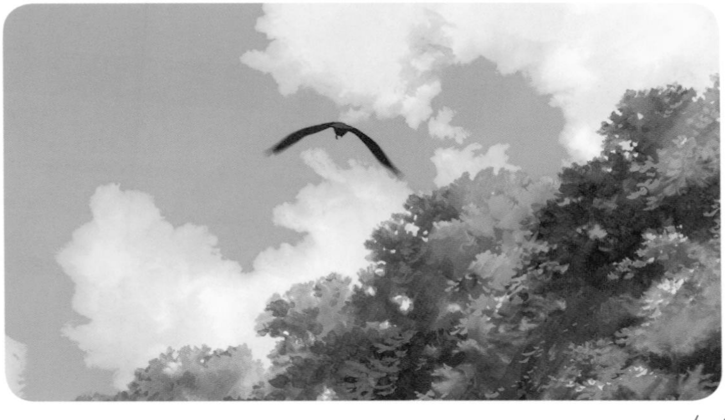

What could the cat have been staring at?

Shawn peered into the bush.

Suddenly, a leaf sprang back and revealed a small girl not four inches high! She nimbly stepped across the leaves of the bush. Before Shawn could blink, she disappeared.

"Shawn?" Jessica called. "Where are you?"

Shawn returned to the wooden gate, but he kept looking back at the bush.

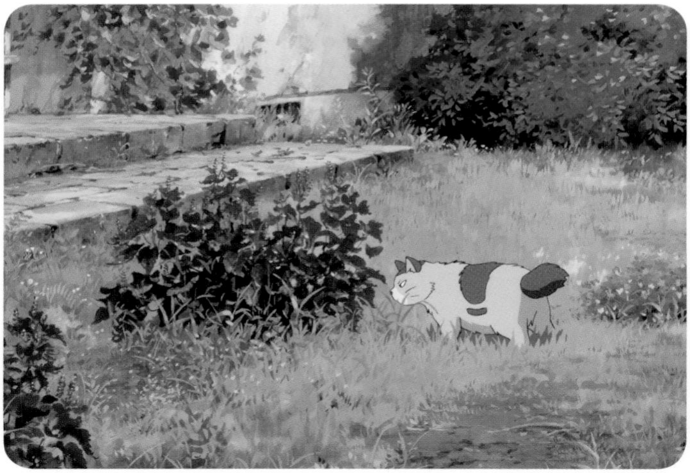

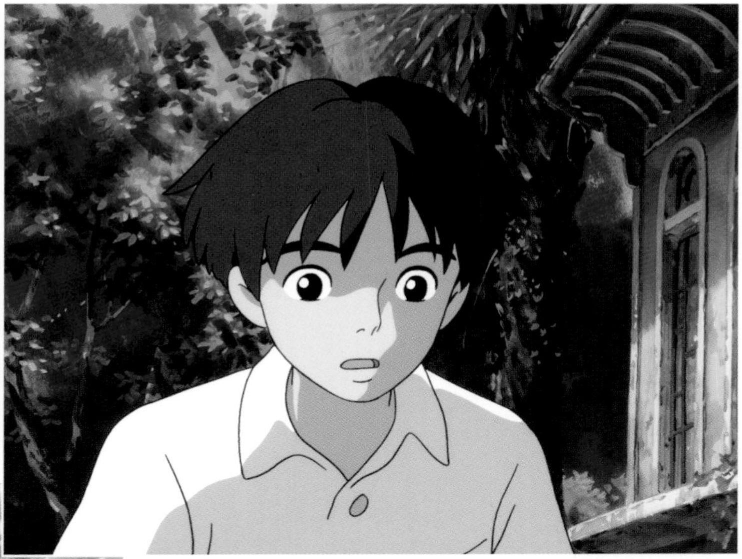

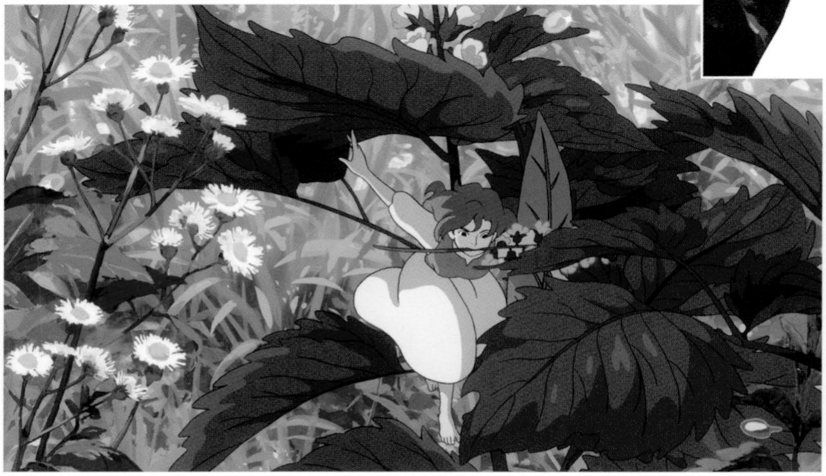

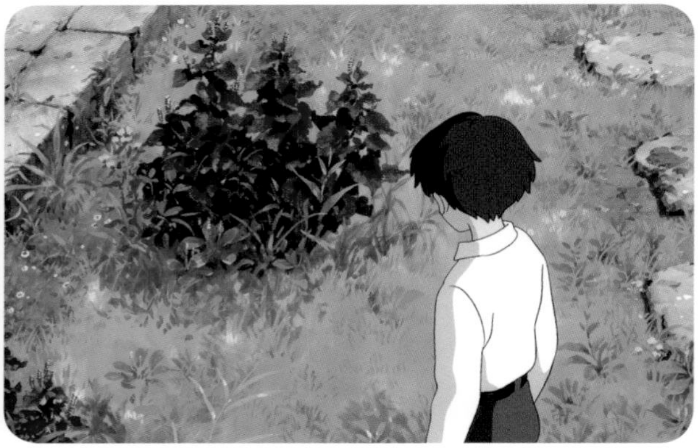

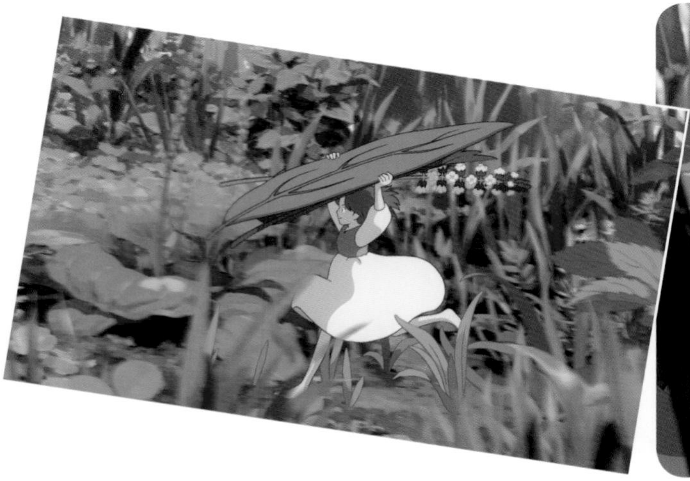

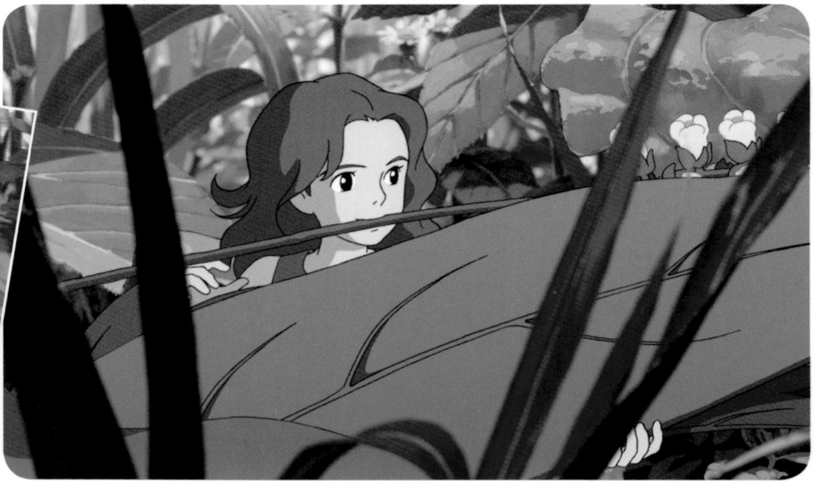

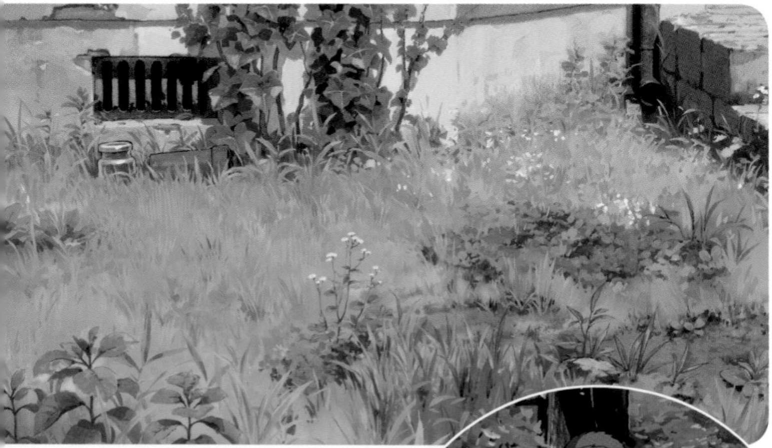

Arrietty looked around to make sure the coast was clear. When it was safe, she ran gracefully, holding a perilla leaf and a bay leaf over her head.

She forgot about the cat!

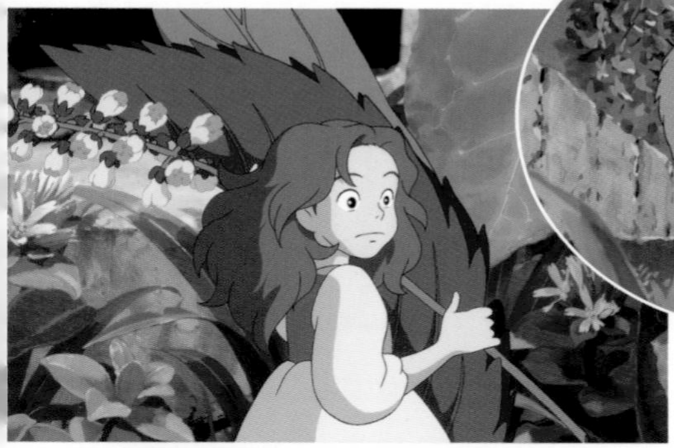

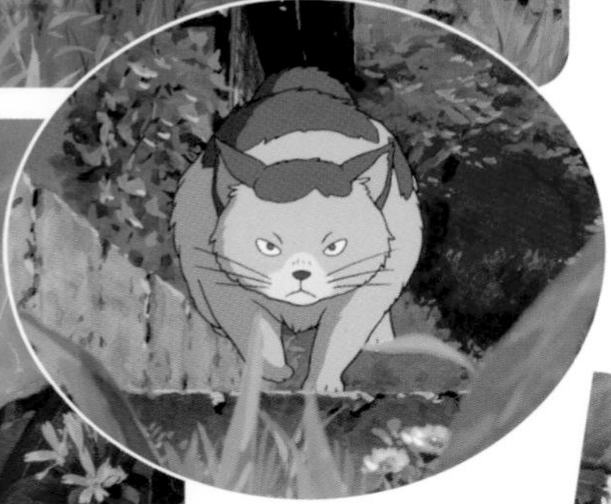

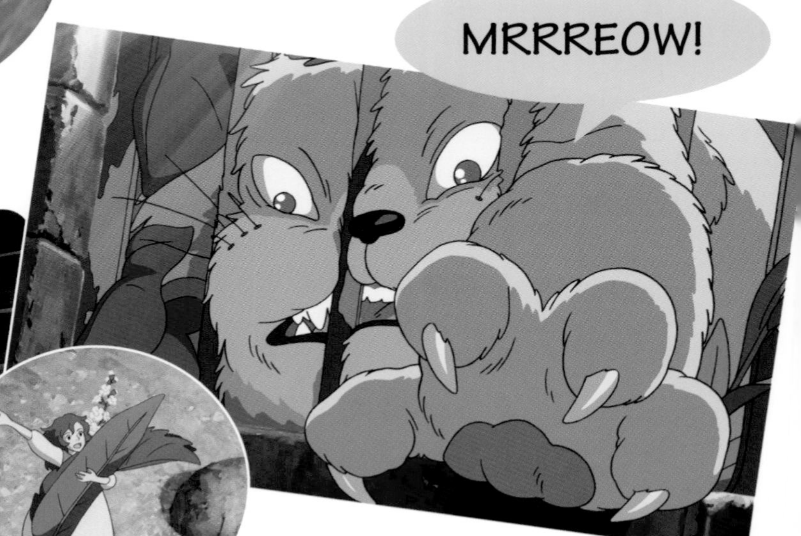
MRRREOW!

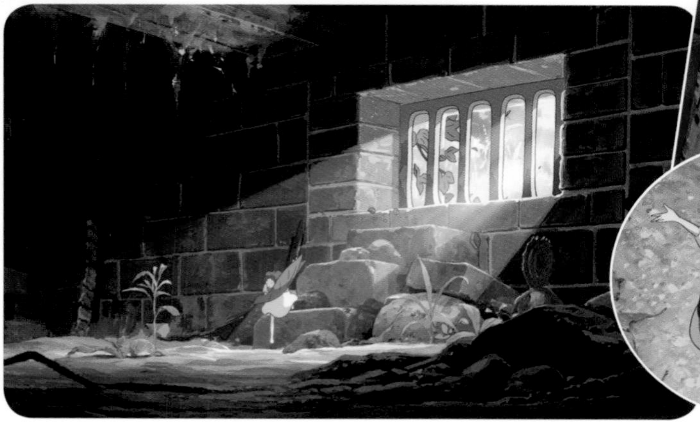

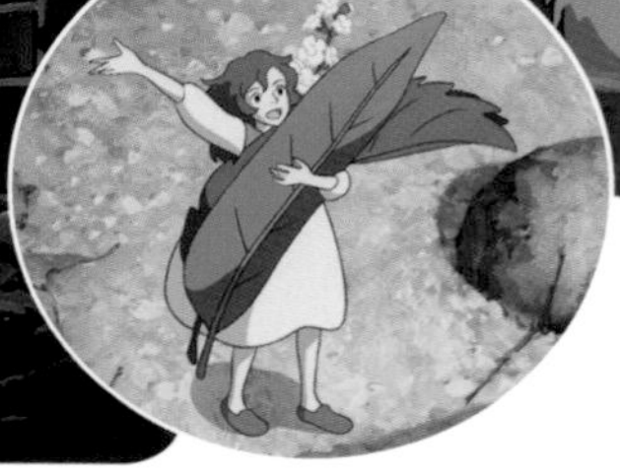

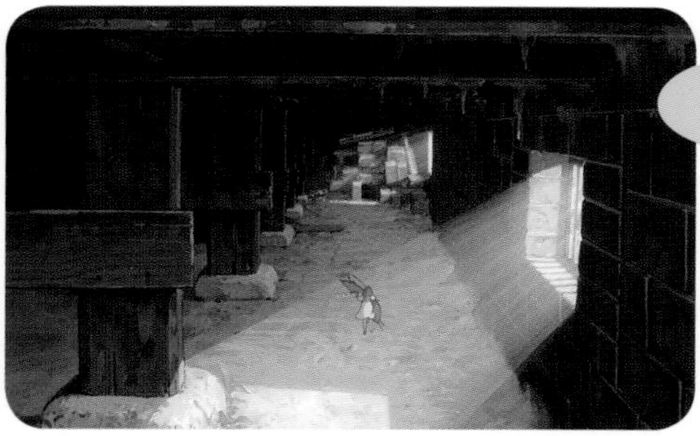

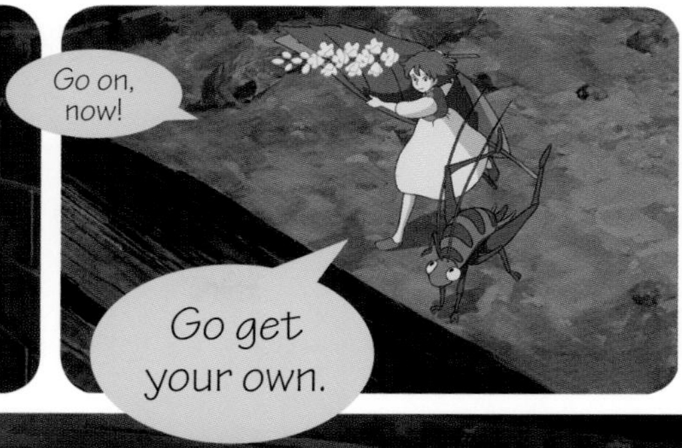
Go on, now!
Go get your own.

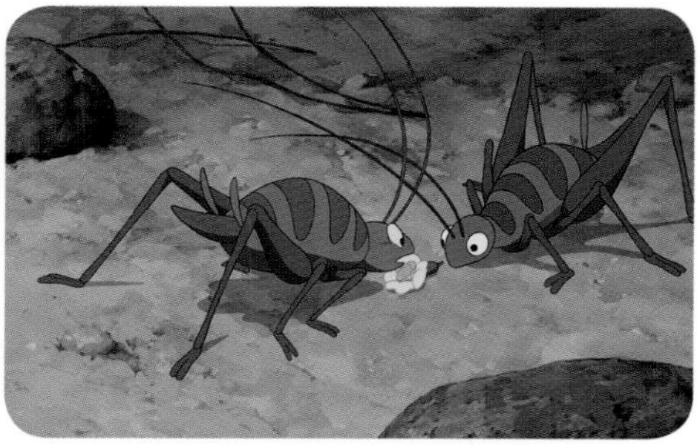

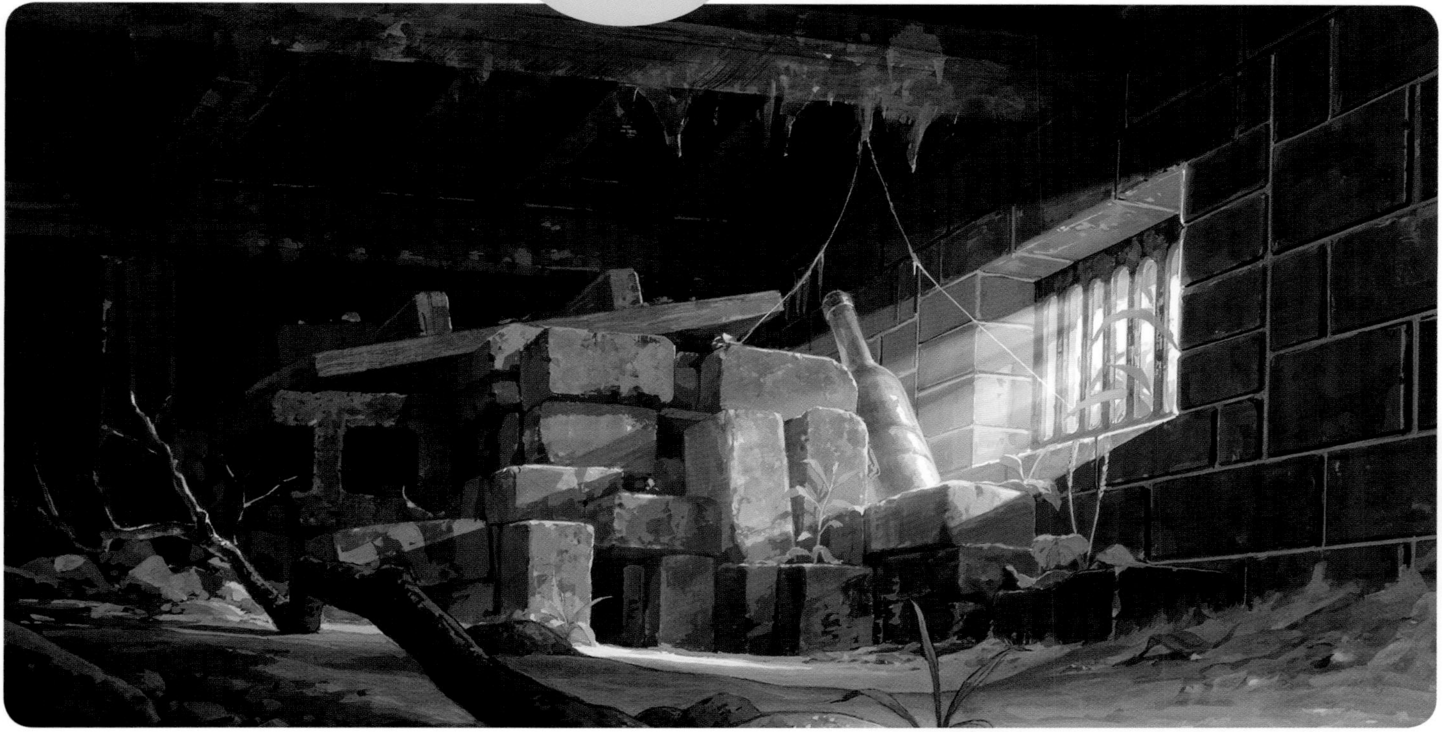

Arrietty hurried into a grate under the house and waved goodbye to the cat.

Sunlight shone through the grate into the space under the floorboards. It lit the bricks and rubble that made up Arrietty's home.

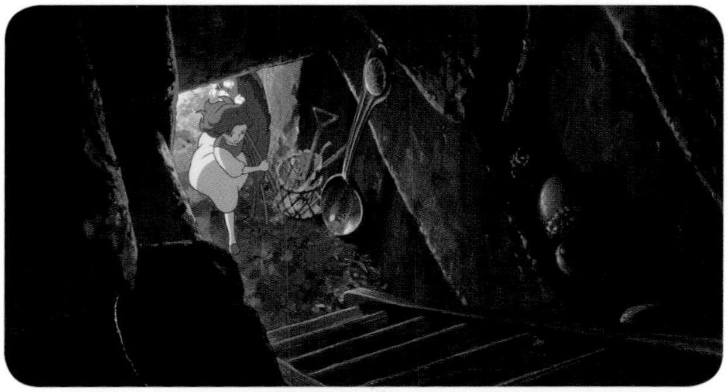

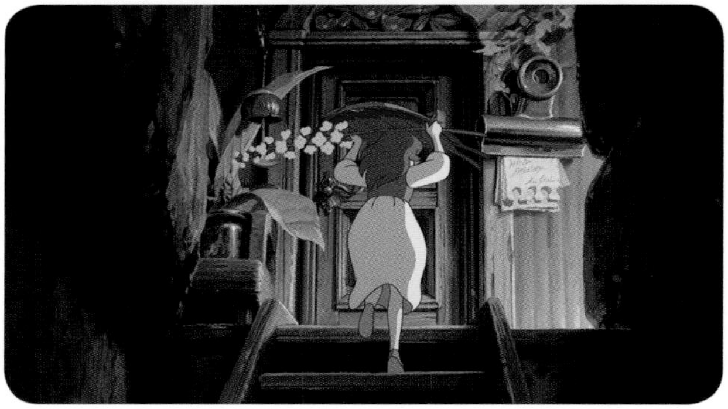

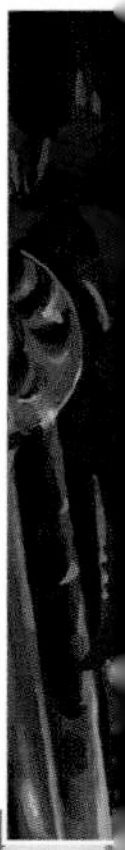

Arrietty snuck in through a window just as her mother came in.

"You went outside again, didn't you?" Homily scolded. "Oh! Is that a bay leaf?"

"I wanted to wait and give it to you on your birthday, but…happy birthday!" said Arrietty, offering her mother the leaf.

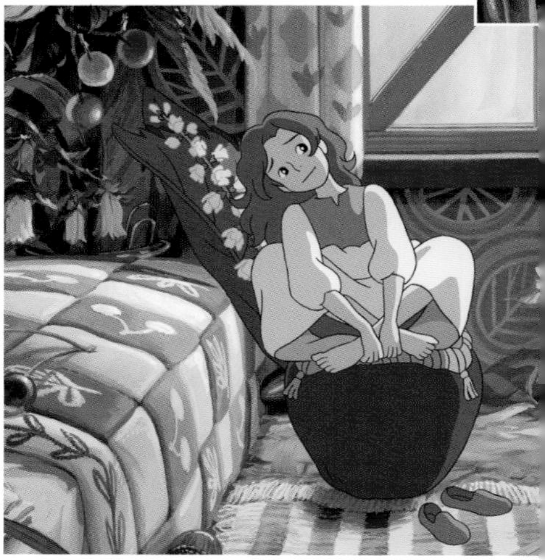

Homily lifted the bay leaf to her face. "It smells wonderful. But the bay tree is so far away. If a beans saw you…"

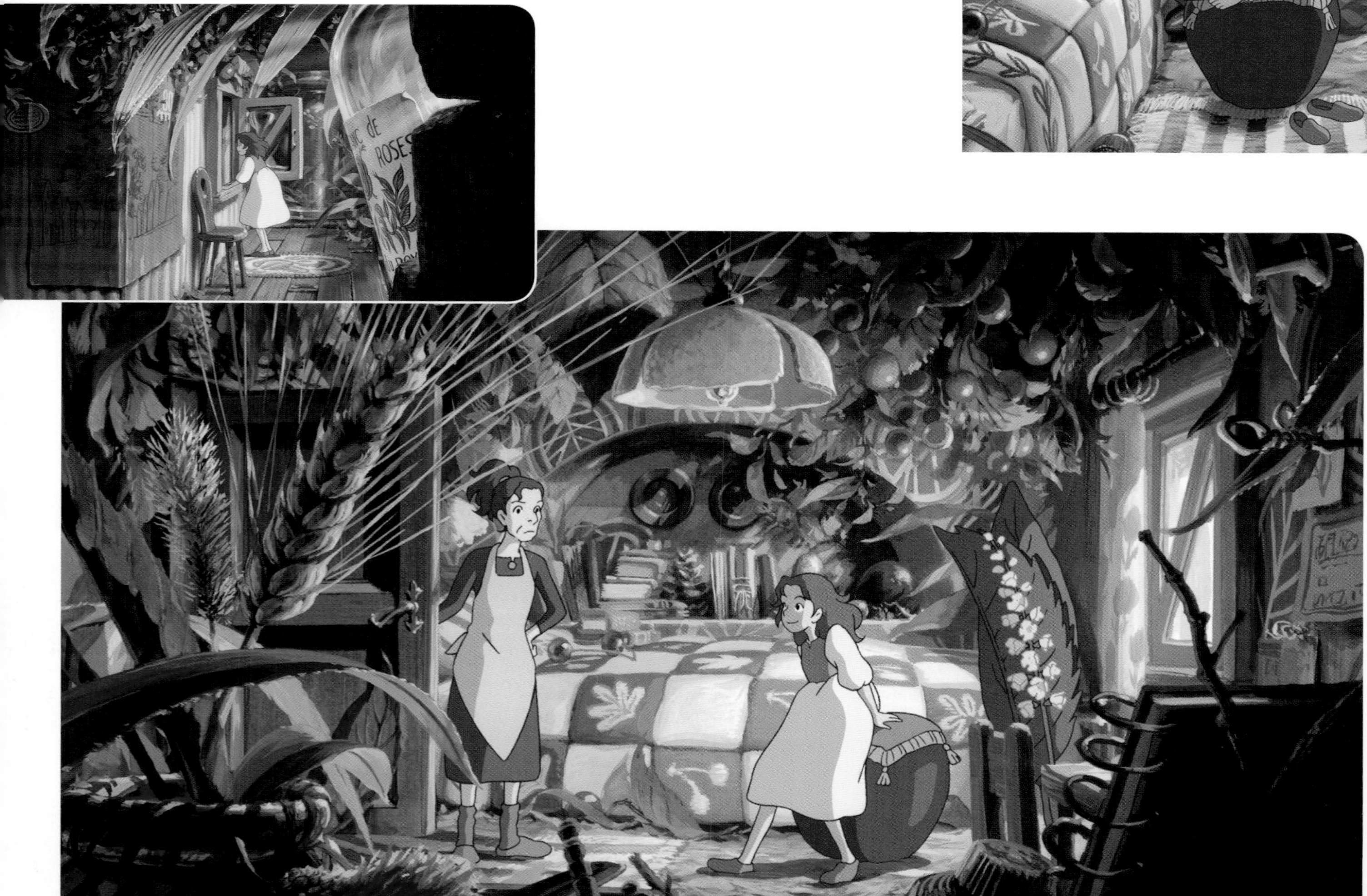

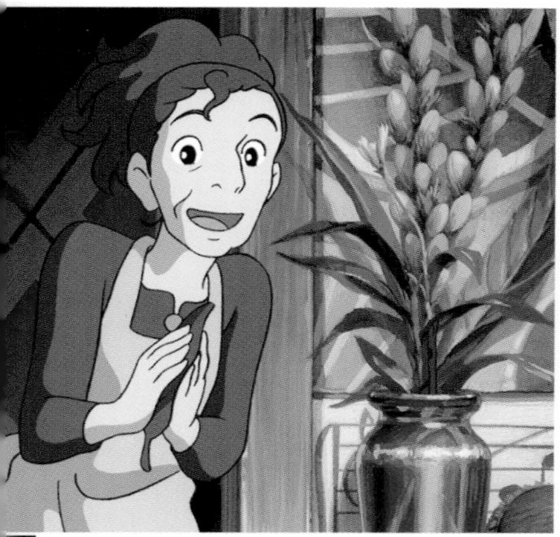

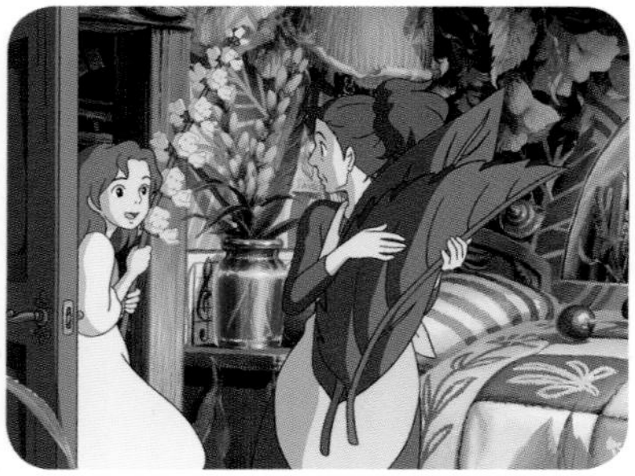

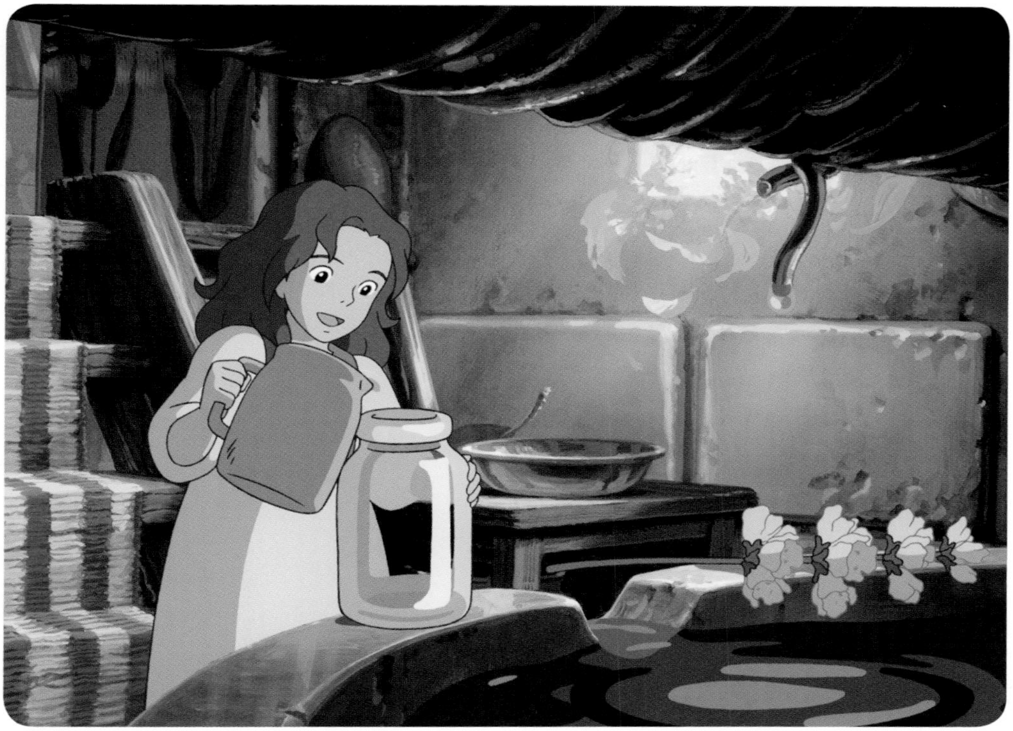

“The beans don’t scare me,” Arrietty replied.

“That’s what worries me! The world is a dangerous place for a Borrower, Arrietty. Your Aunt Eggletina wasn’t scared either, and she—”

“—was eaten by a toad, I know, I know,” Arrietty finished. “If you don’t like your gift I can put it in my room—”

“No, no. I should keep it. I have just the recipe for these. I’ll have your father borrow some sugar.”

“Oh, you don’t have to—because tonight, I’ll borrow some for you. Don’t you remember? Tonight’s my first borrowing!”

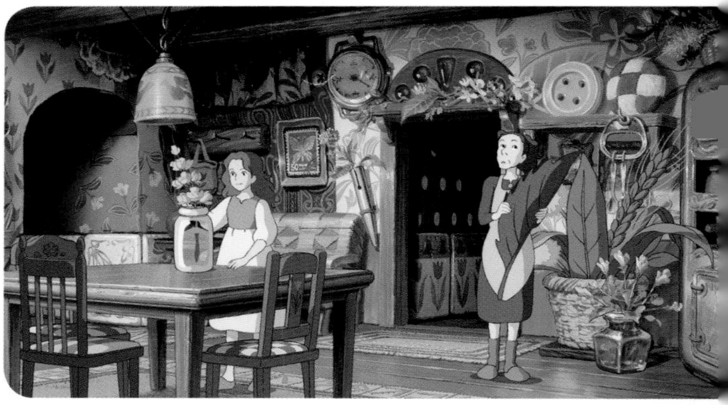

Just then, the door opened.

"Look, Papa's home!" said Arrietty. "Papa, I made it all the way to—"

Her father looked stern. "There's a new bean in the house."

"I know. I saw him," Arrietty said.

"Arrietty, I told you to be—" her mother started.

"Yes, Mama, I was careful and he didn't see me! And he's much smaller than other beans. Papa, I can still go borrowing tonight, right?"

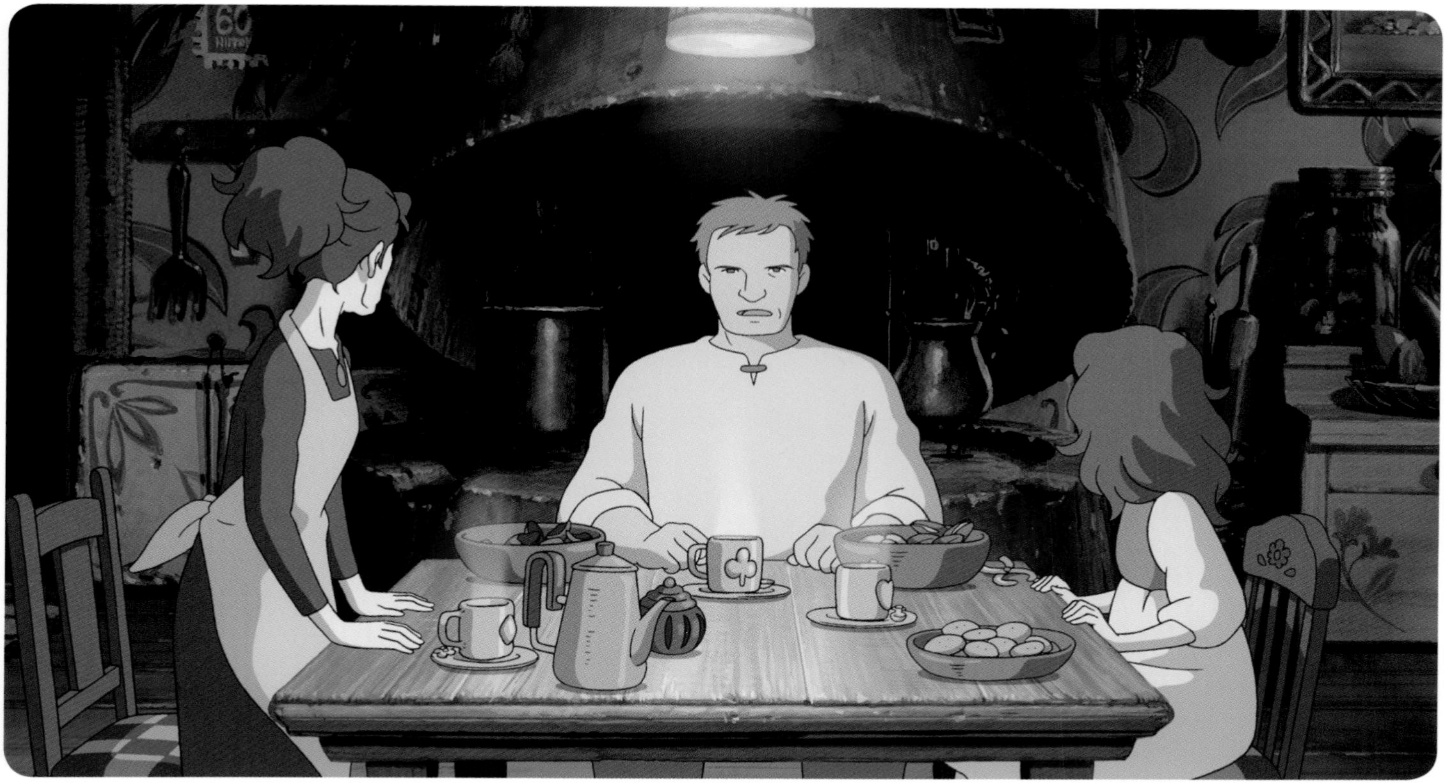

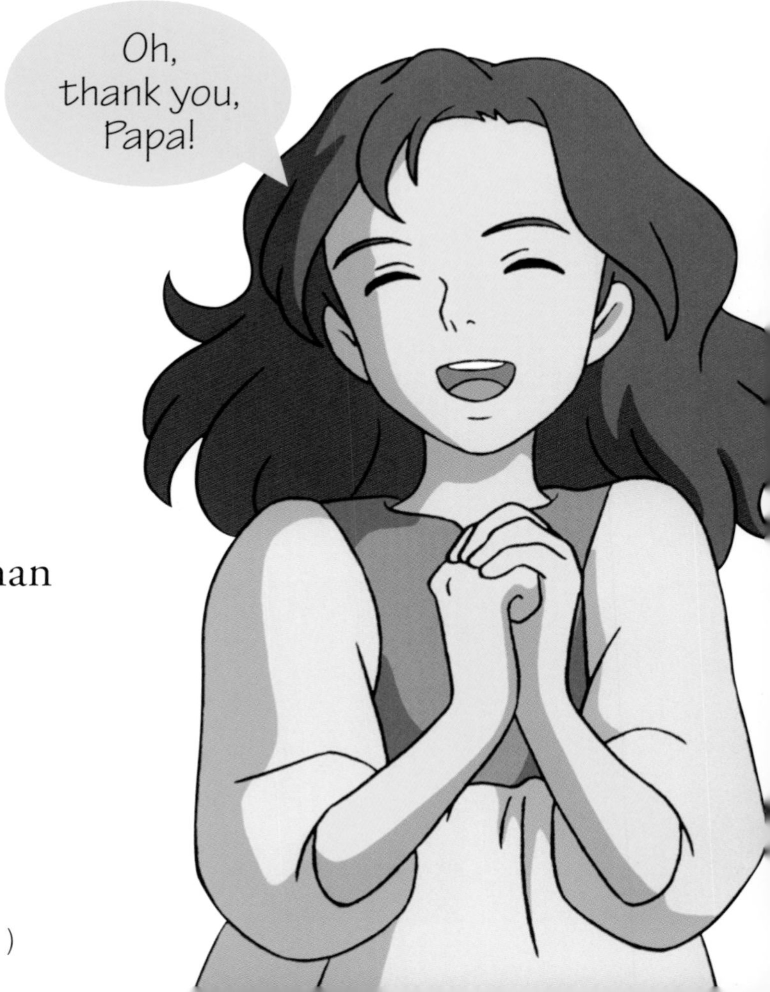
Oh, thank you, Papa!

“No,” said Homily as she poured some tea. “We know nothing about this new bean.”

“But he’s just a child!” Arrietty pleaded. “Please, Papa, I’ve been looking forward to this night for such a long time!”

“The children are more vicious than the grown-ups,” warned Homily.

“But,” Pod sighed. “The young beans do go to bed early.”

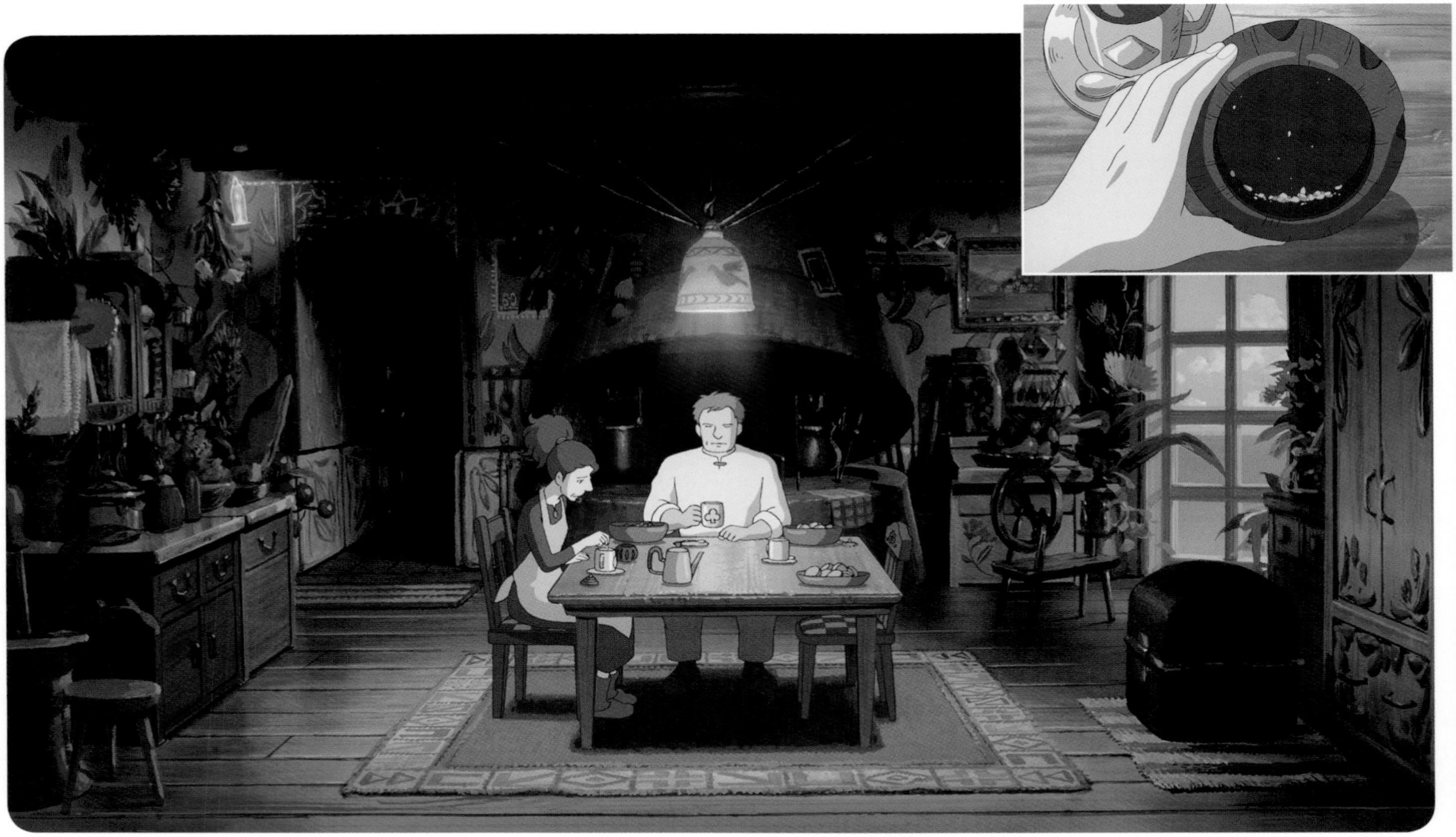

"But…" Homily protested, still worried.

"The boy is sick and very weak. She'll be fine," Pod said.

When Arrietty left the room Pod said, "Arrietty will be turning fourteen soon. She needs to know how to take care of herself out there…without our help."

"Sometimes I worry that we are the only Borrowers left," said Homily as she stirred the last of the sugar into her tea.

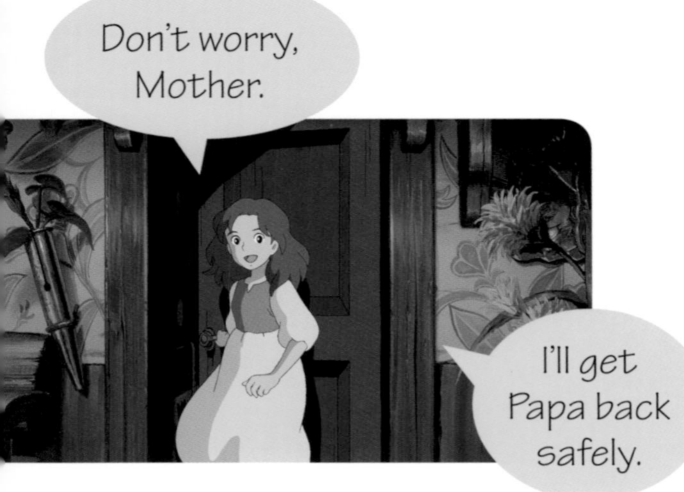
Don't worry, Mother.
I'll get Papa back safely.

A small light shone
inside the grate.
In the house above, Aunt
Jessica and Hara were
preparing Shawn's room.

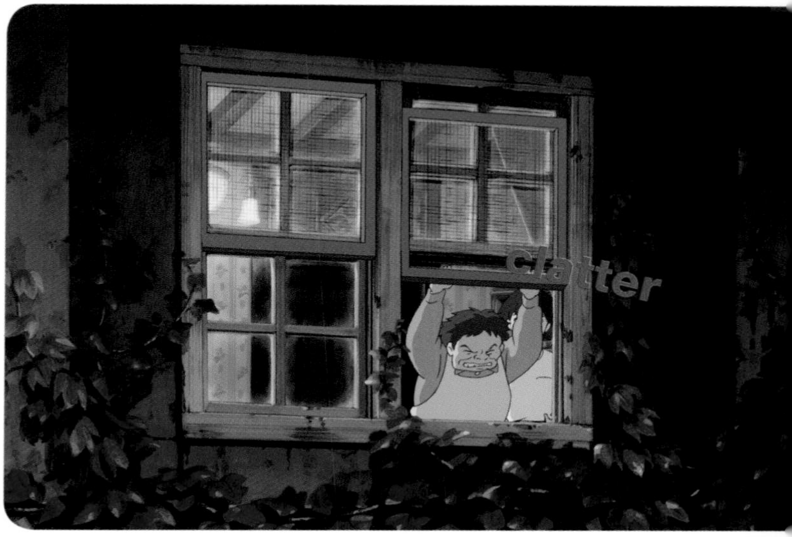
clatter

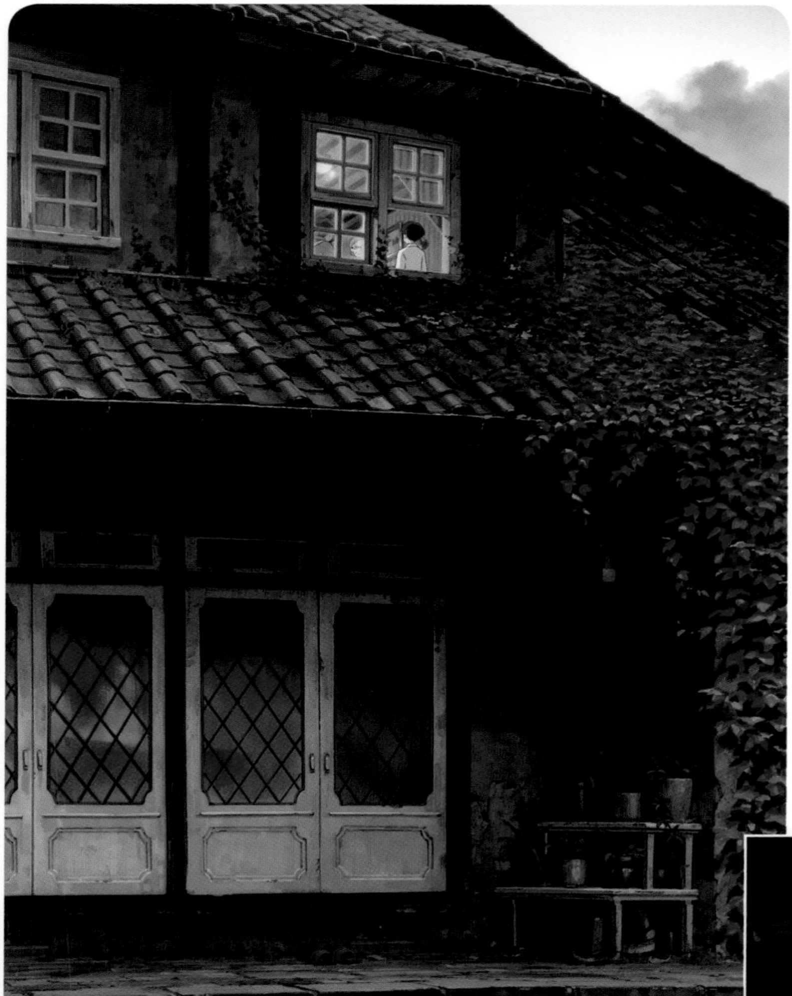

"Whatever you need,
Shawn, you ask Hara and
she'll get it for you, all
right?" said Aunt Jessica.

"Make him feel at
home, Hara."

"Yes, ma'am. We'll start
by keeping the bugs out."
The poorly fitting screen
rattled noisily as Hara
struggled to close it.

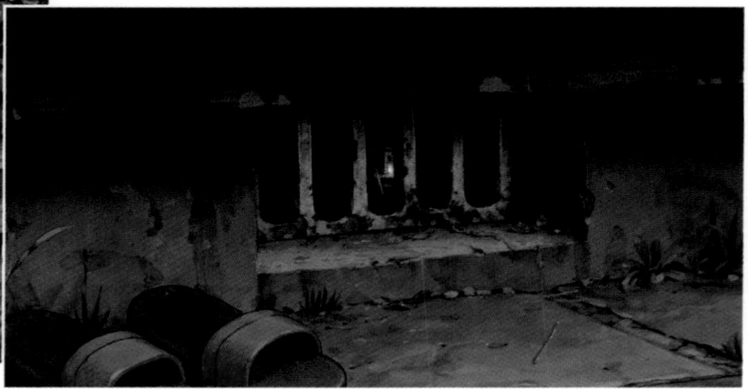

The First "Borrowing"

With great excitement,
Arrietty got ready.

She chose her clothes carefully, and put on the soft shoes Pod had made her especially for borrowing. She put her hair up with a small clip and twirled around in front of the mirror. Now she was ready!

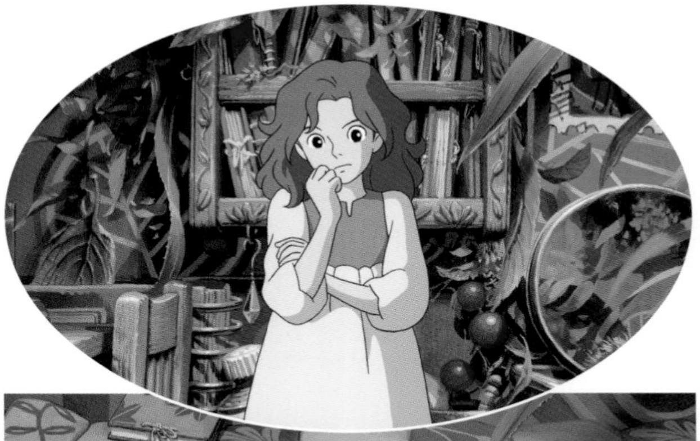
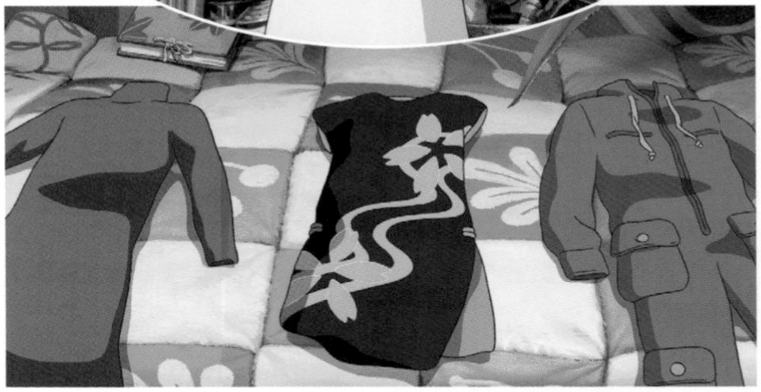
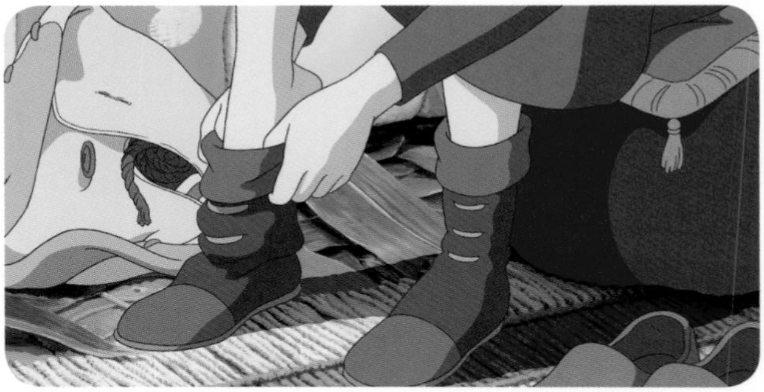
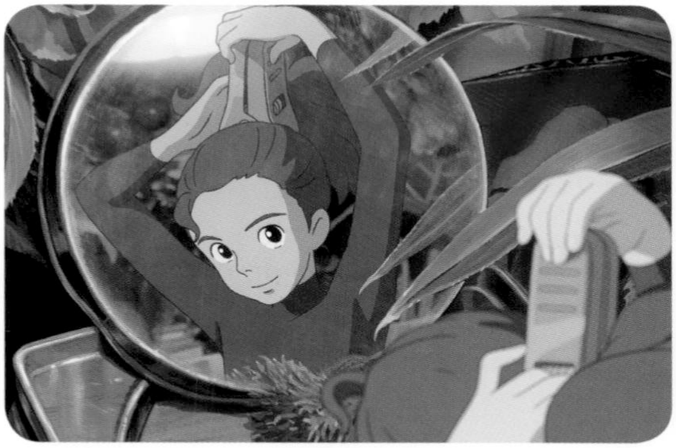
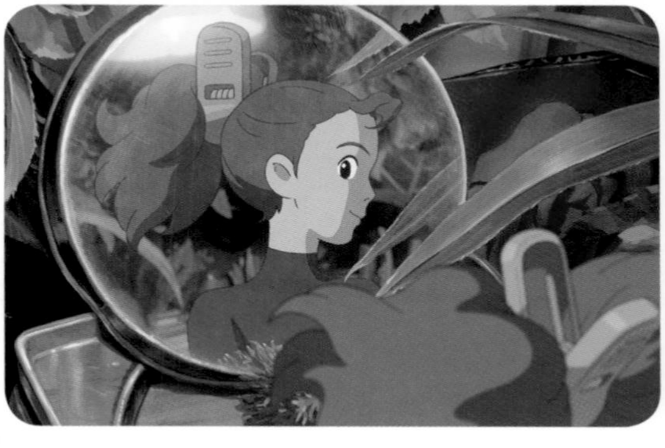
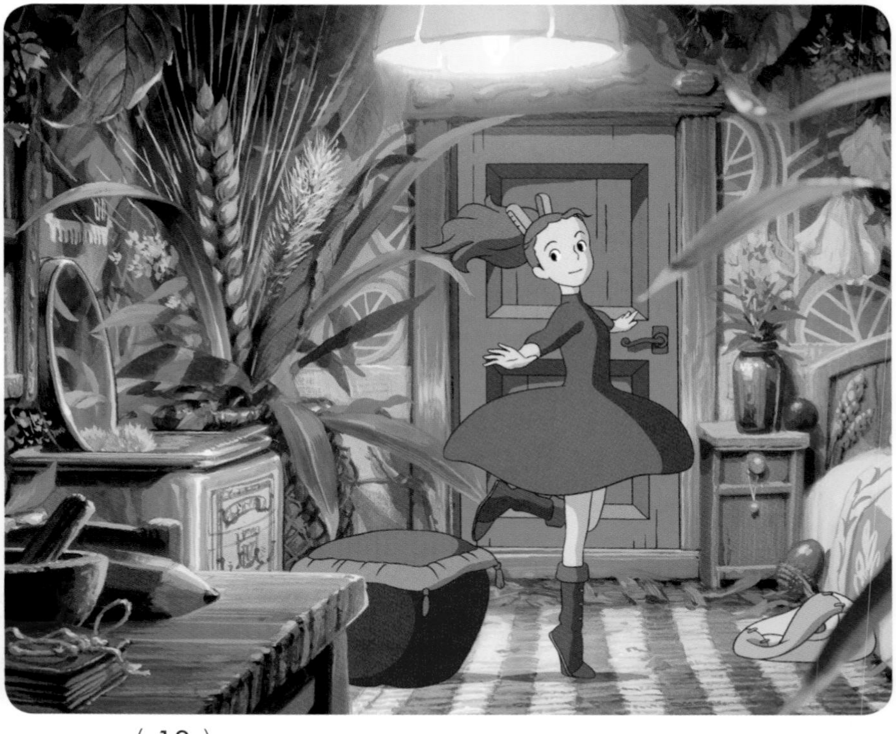

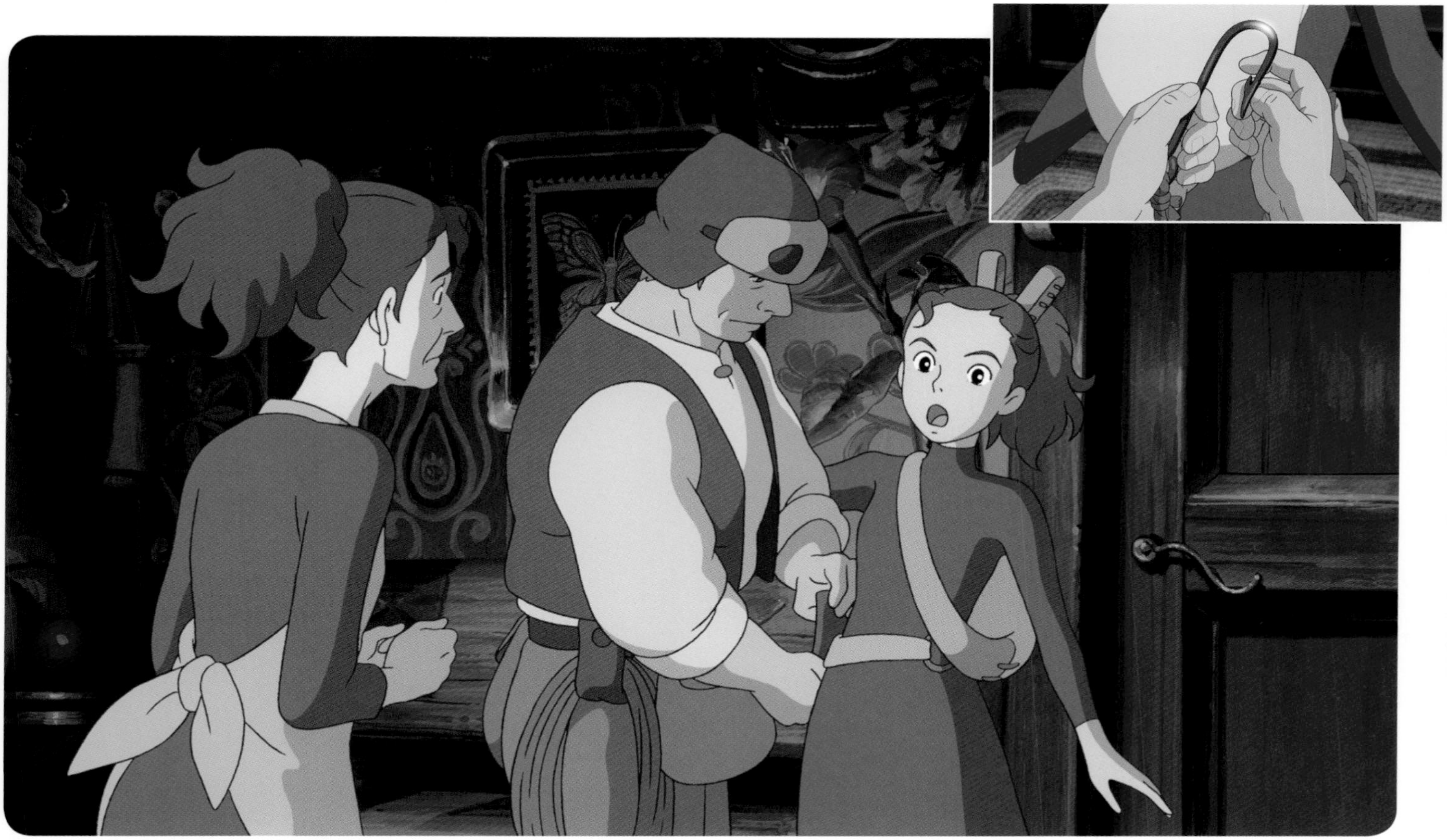

Homily looked on anxiously as Pod checked Arrietty's gear.

"Don't you think you should wear something
a little darker?" Homily suggested.

"No, I think this is perfect!" replied Arrietty.

Homily watched and worried as the two
prepared to head out.

"All right then. I need some tissue
paper and a sugar cube, if you can
manage it," Homily said. And don't
worry about me, I'll be just fine."

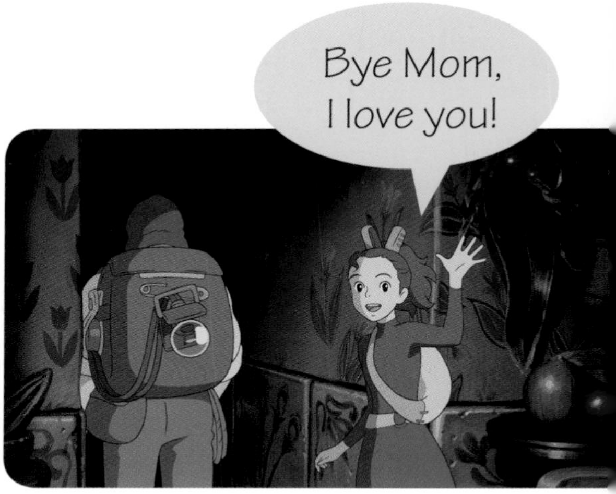
Bye Mom, I love you!

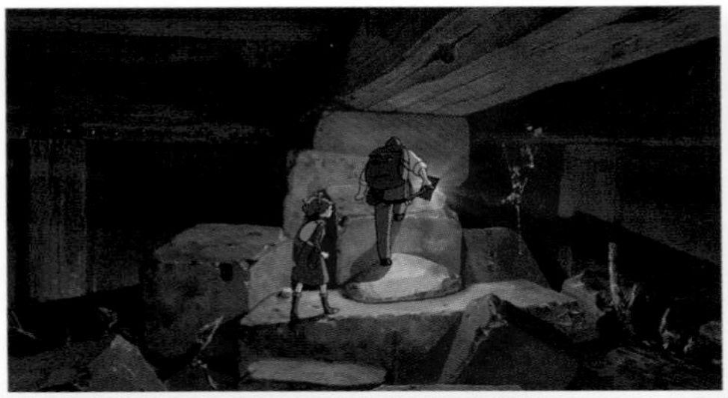

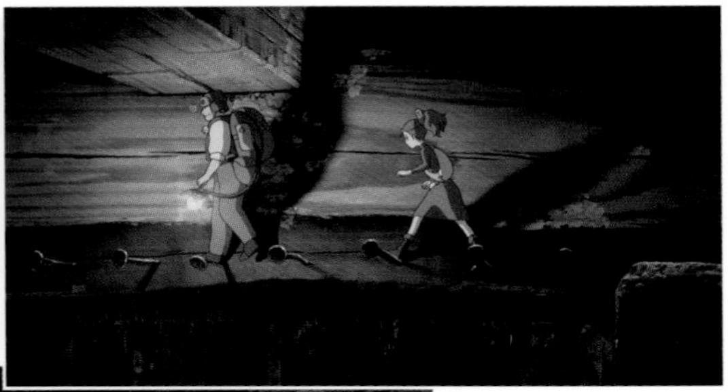

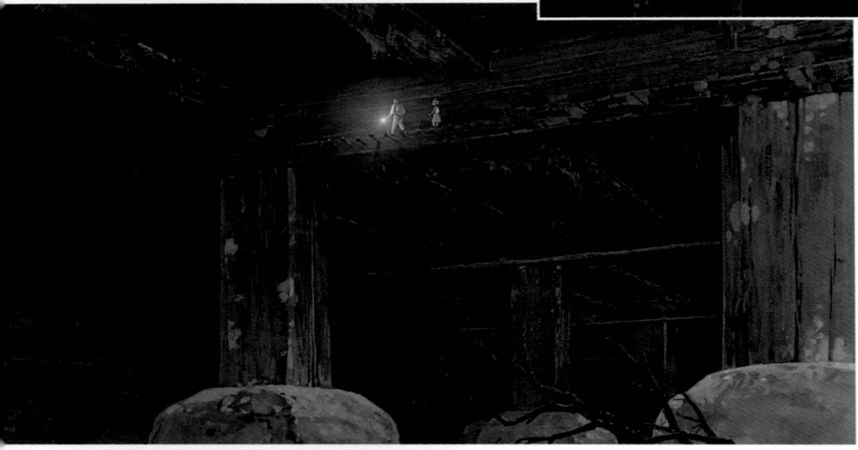

Pod and Arrietty left their home and walked across a row of nails sticking out of a floor beam. When they reached a pulley made from a spool, Pod used it to raise himself up high.

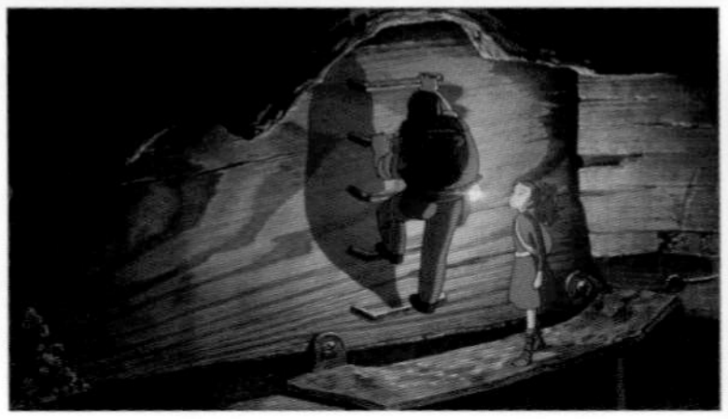

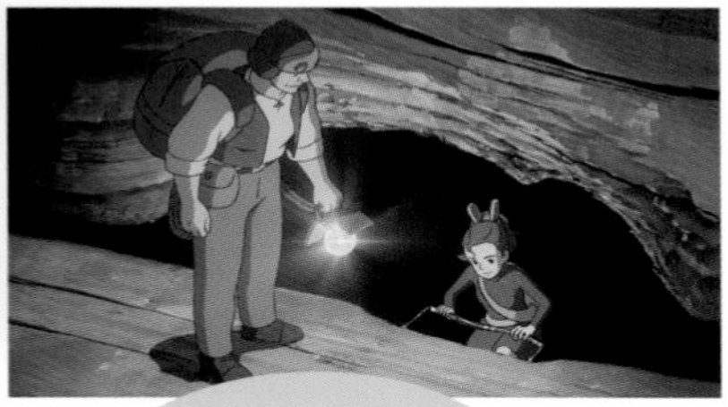

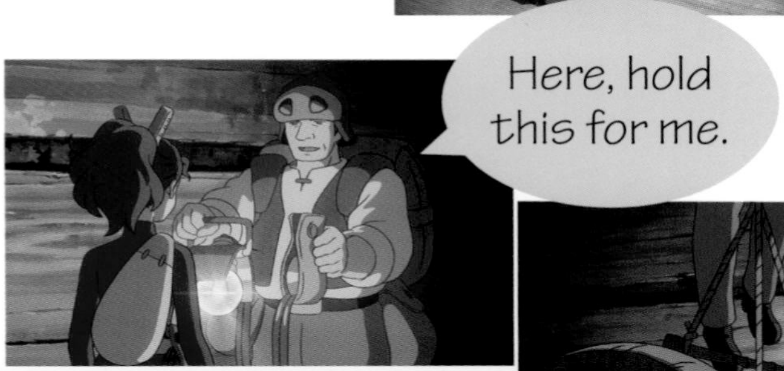
Here, hold this for me.

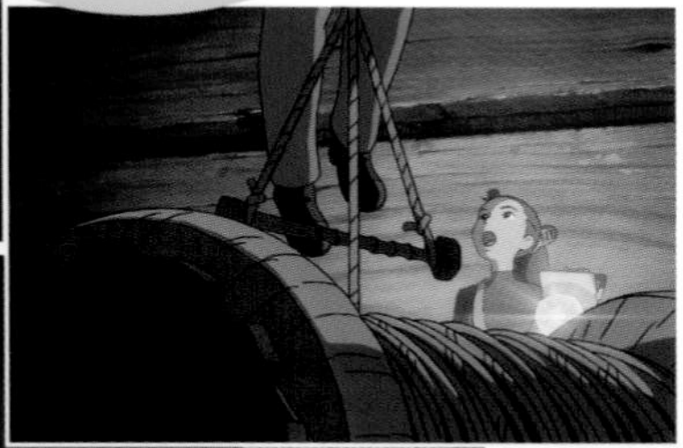

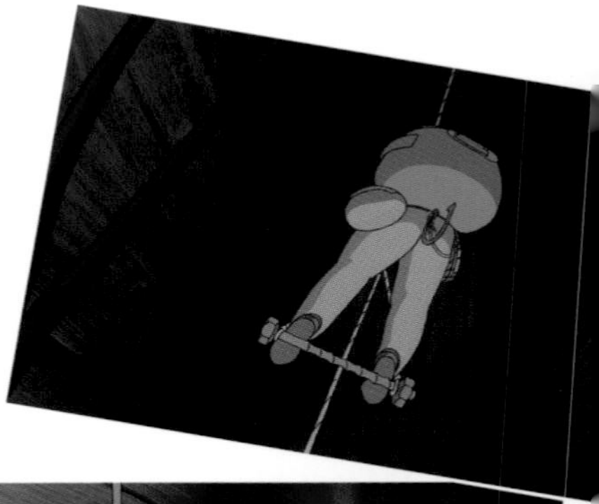

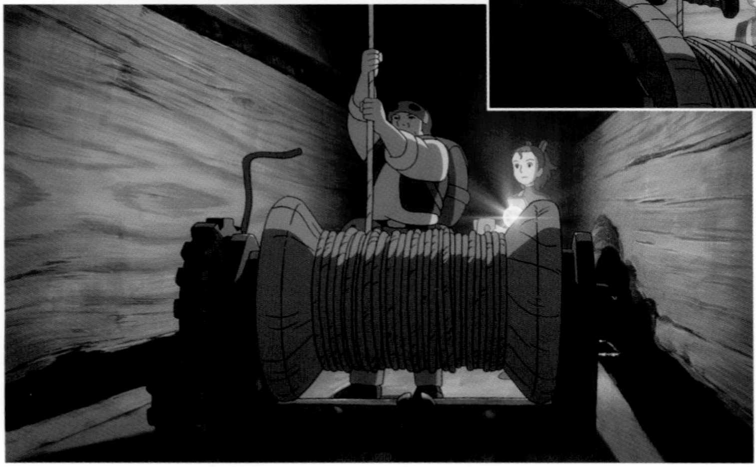

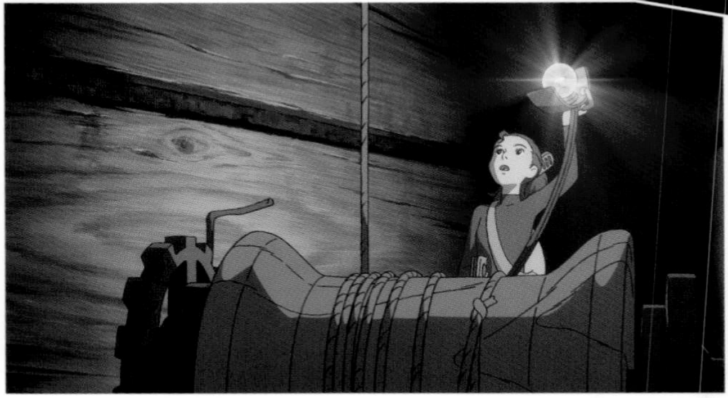

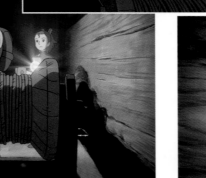

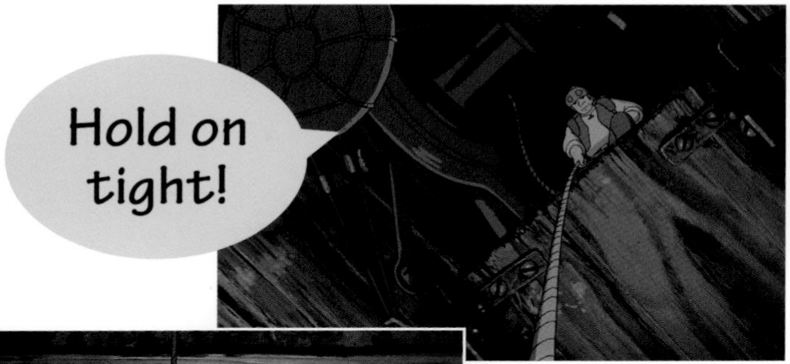
Hold on tight!

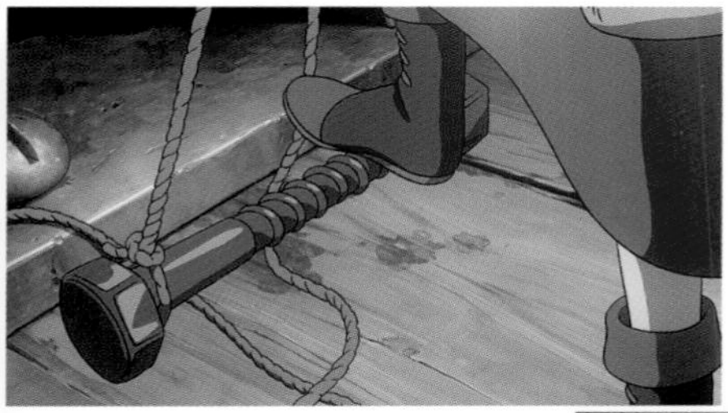

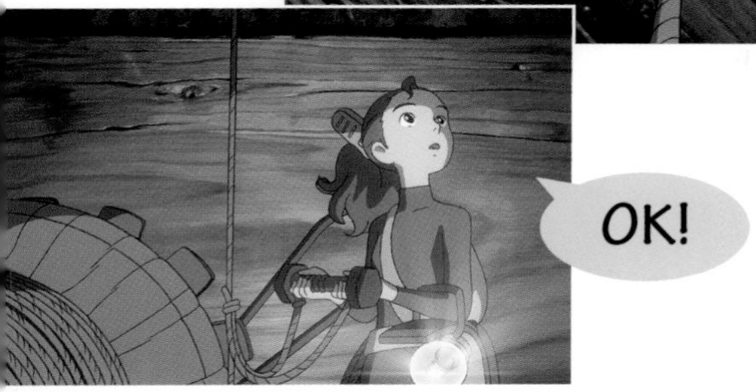
OK!

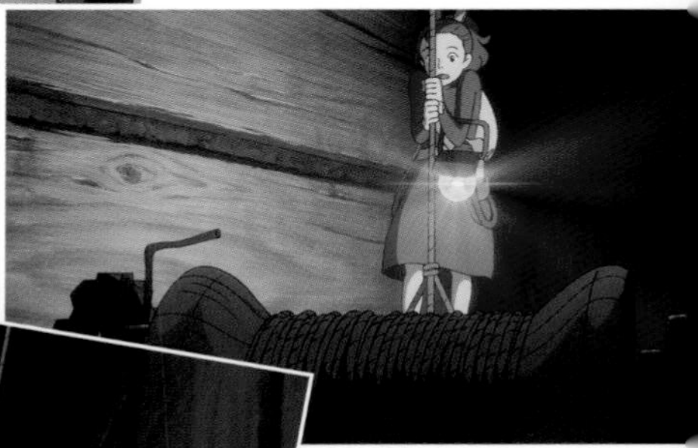

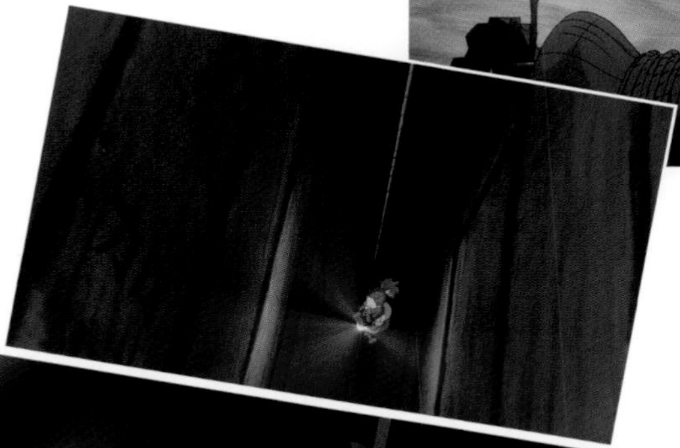

Now it was Arrietty's turn.

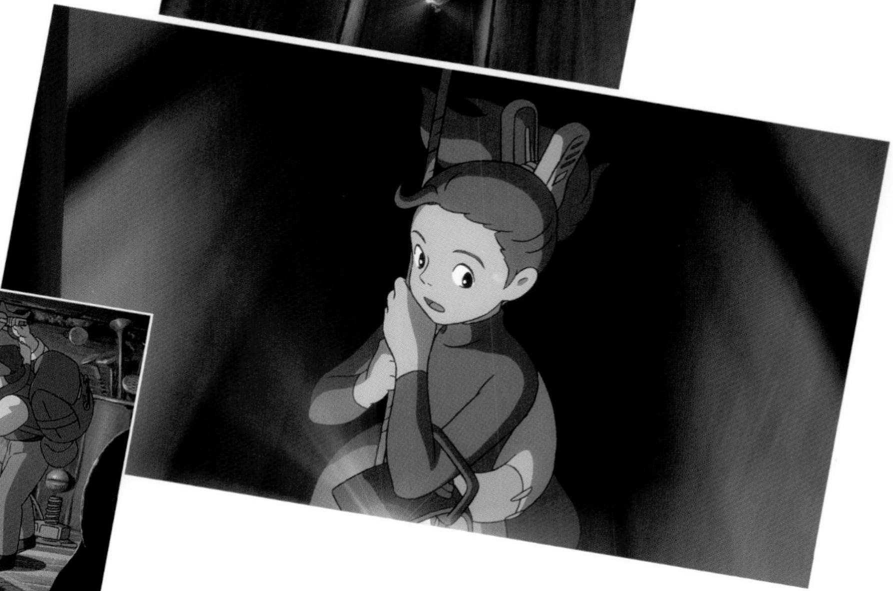

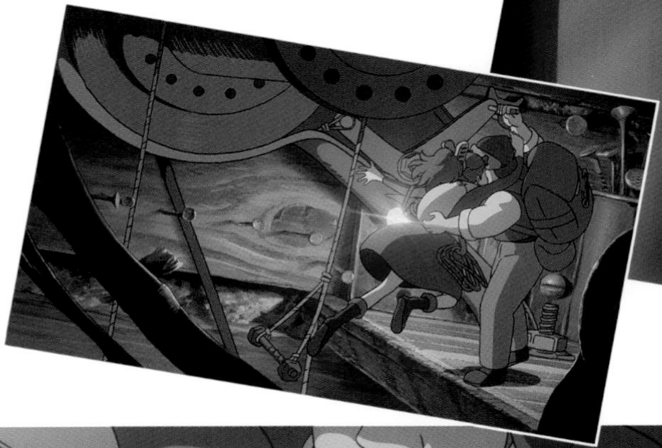

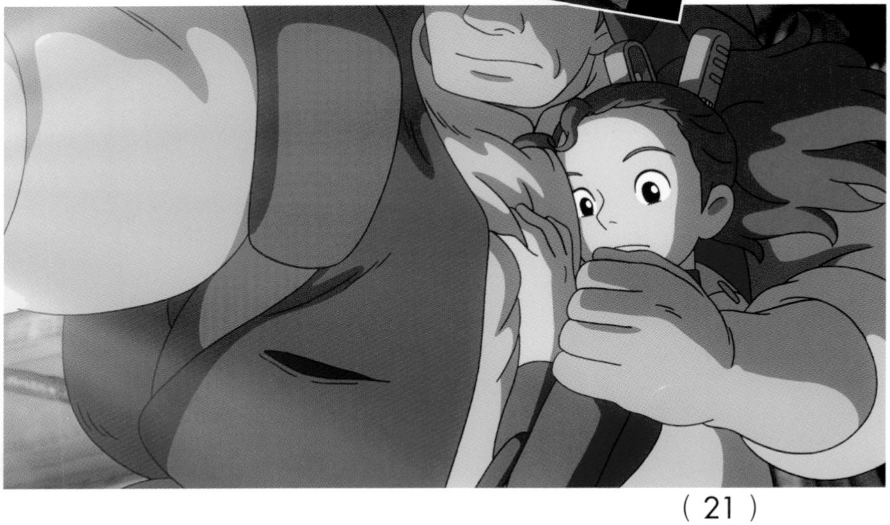

Arrietty rose up just as her father had, then leapt into his arms.

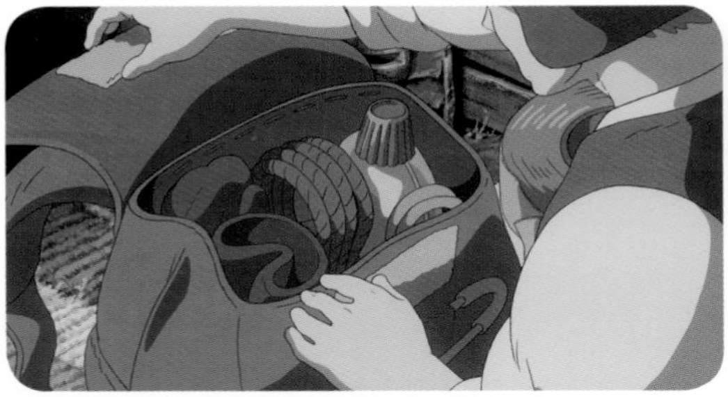
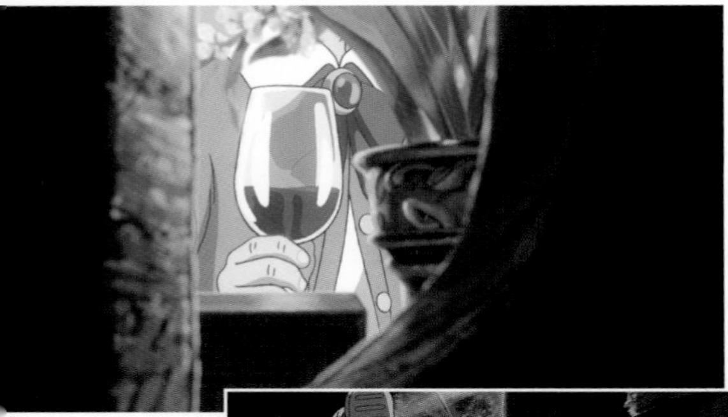
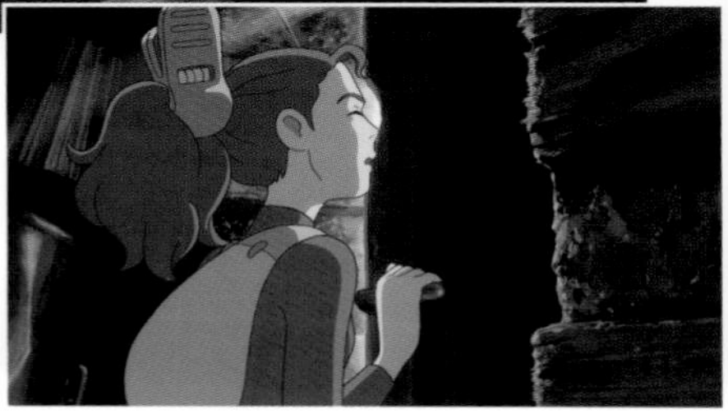
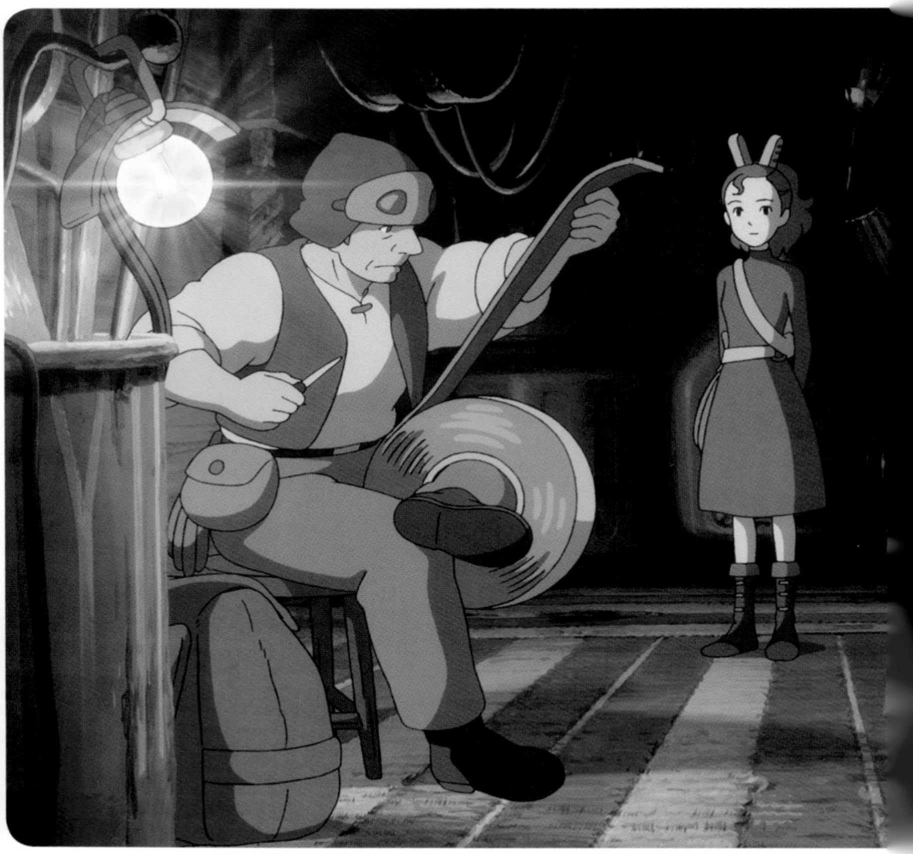

Now they were in the room where Pod kept all of his supplies. It was stocked with the tools he needed to go borrowing.

Pod took a knife from his bag and started to cut pieces of double-sided tape.

Arrietty watched her father work. Then she noticed the light shining in from a crack in the back wall.

She peeked through and saw a hand holding a large wine glass.

“Arrietty? Let’s go,” said Pod.

“Right,” Arrietty replied.

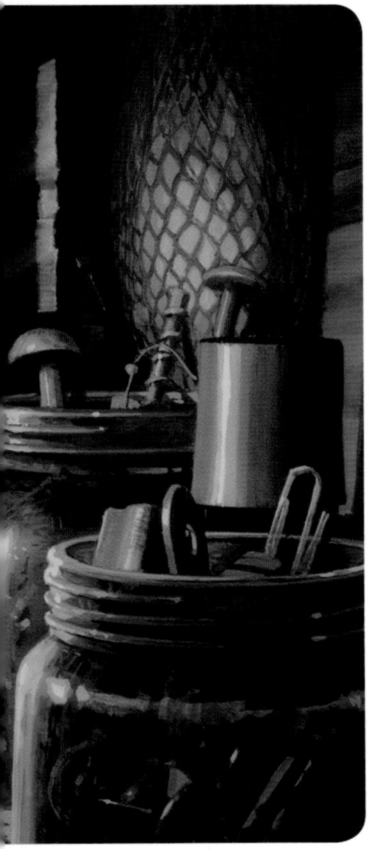

Pod turned the light off and opened the door.

It led to the inside of a china cabinet. Arrietty followed her father between big cups and plates.

At the cabinet door, Pod signaled to Arrietty to go through. She took a deep breath and stepped out nervously.

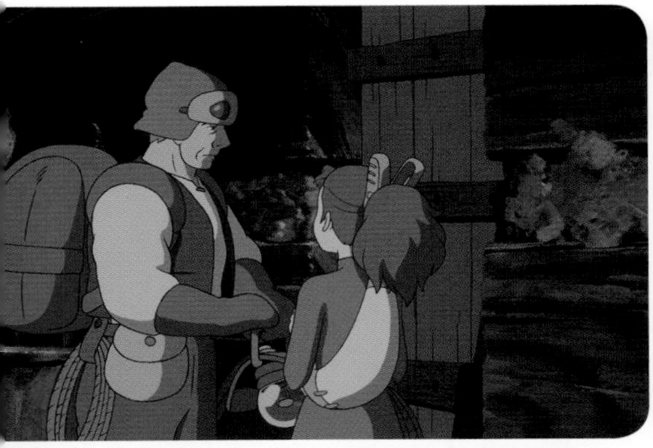

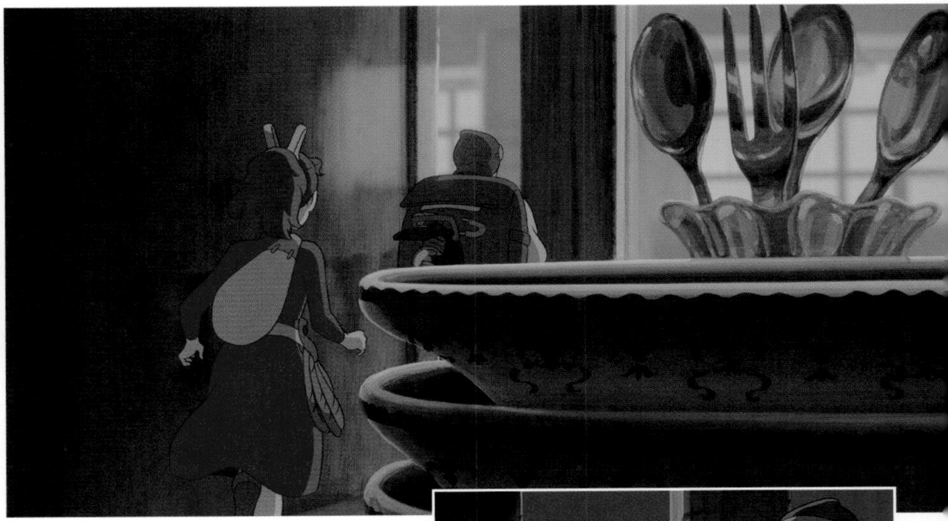

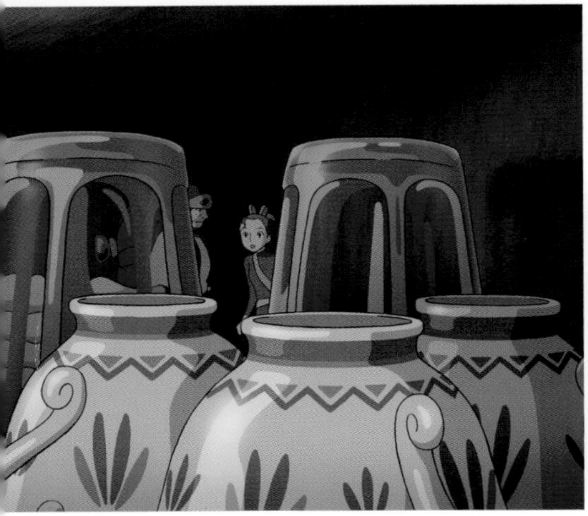

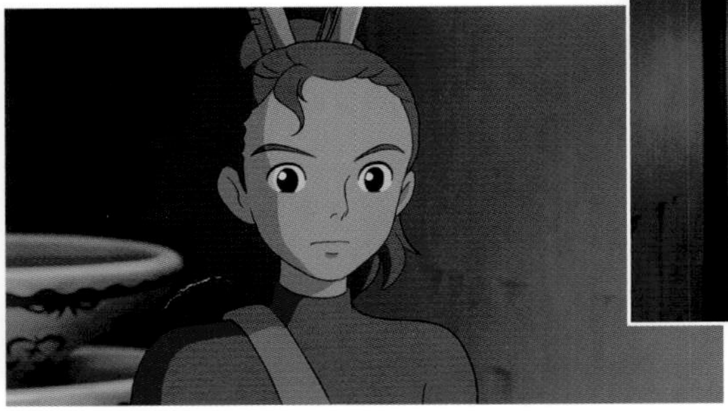

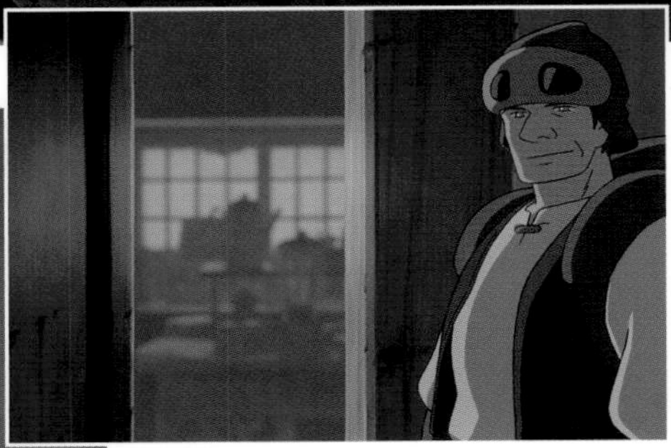

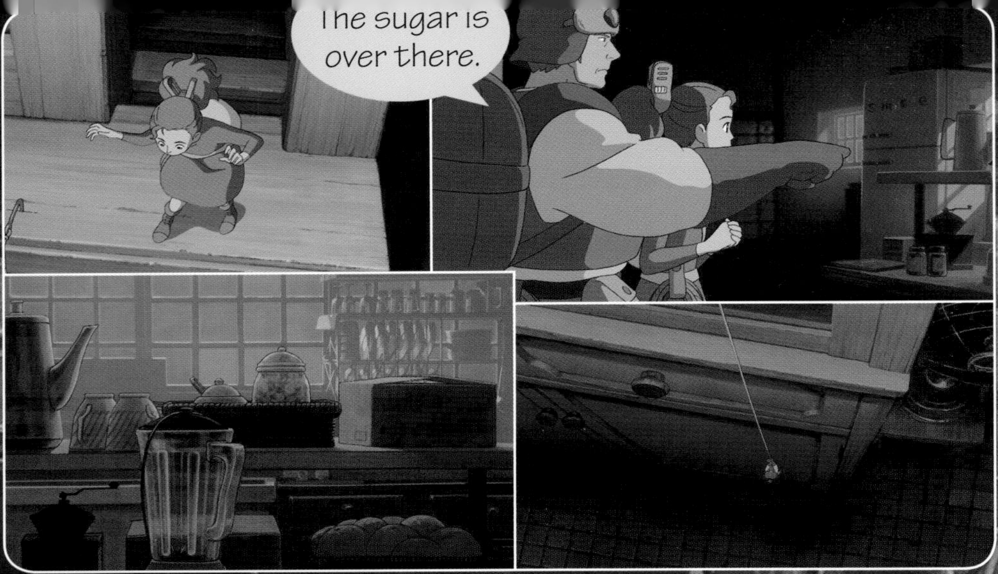
The sugar is
over there.

Arrietty stood still in wonder at her first sight of the huge kitchen. Everything in it was gigantic.

"It's so…big," she marveled.

"This is where beans store all their food," Pod explained. "When you get down there, wait for me."

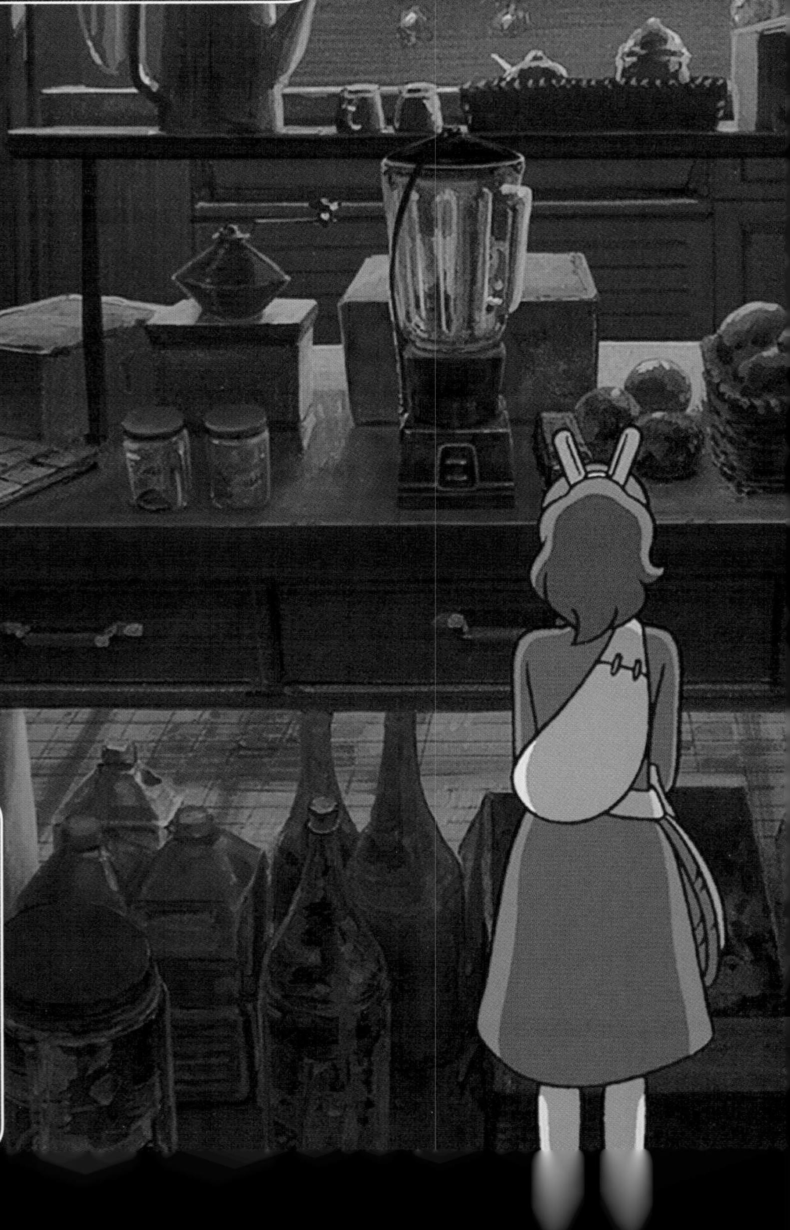

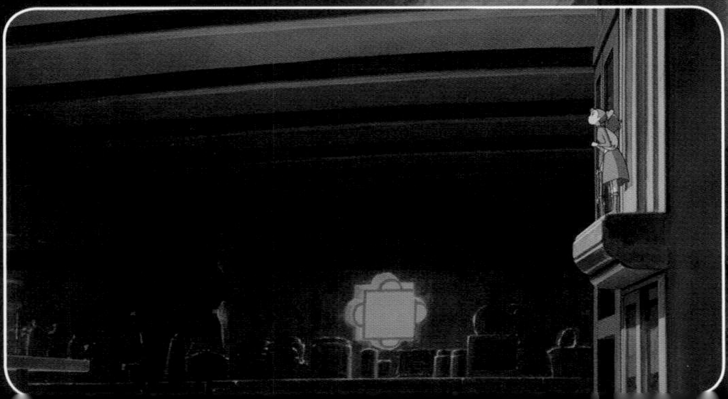

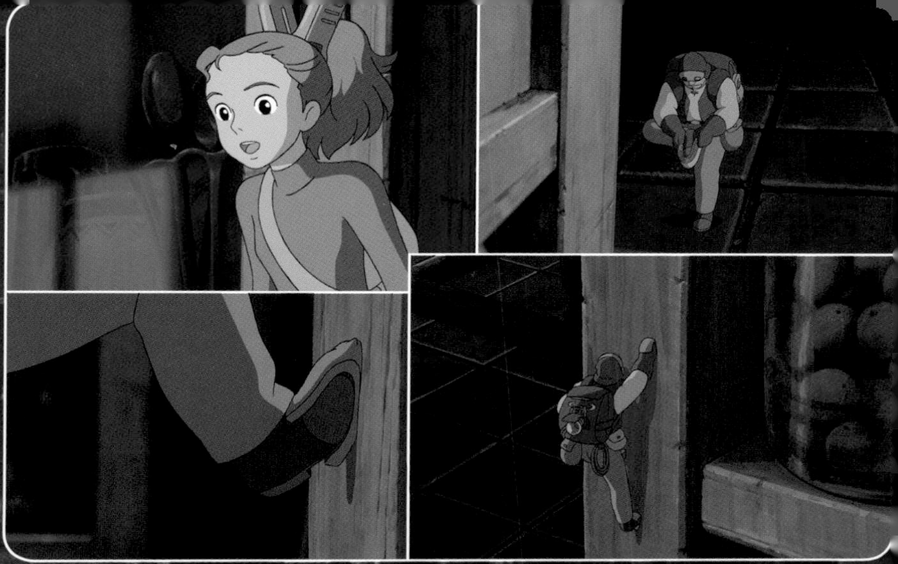

Pod attached his hook to the china cabinet and used a rope to rappel down to the floor. Then, putting double-sided tape onto his shoes and gloves, he climbed up a table leg to get to the sugar pot on top.

“Papa, you are amazing,” Arrietty whispered.

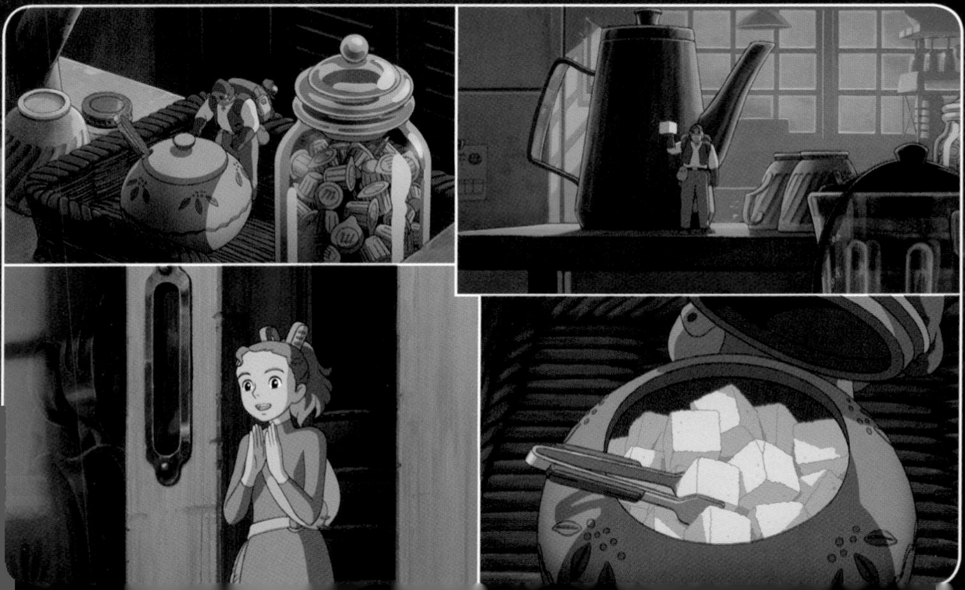

As Arrietty watched in admiration, Pod nimbly retrieved a cube of sugar and held it up for Arrietty to see.

Pod pointed down. *That's right!* Arrietty thought. *Papa told me to wait for him down there!*

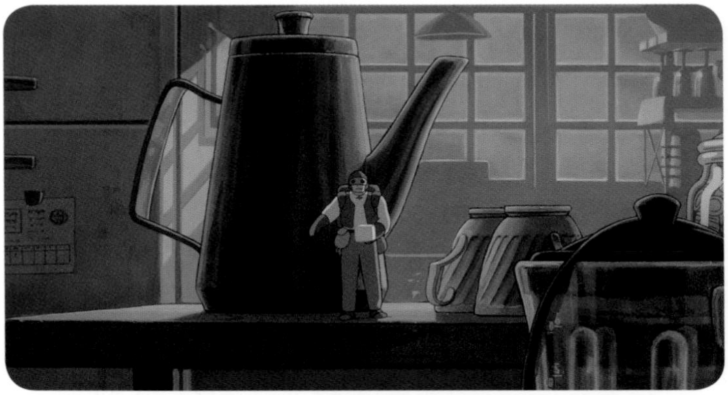

Arrietty hurriedly slid down the rope and ran to the base of the table.

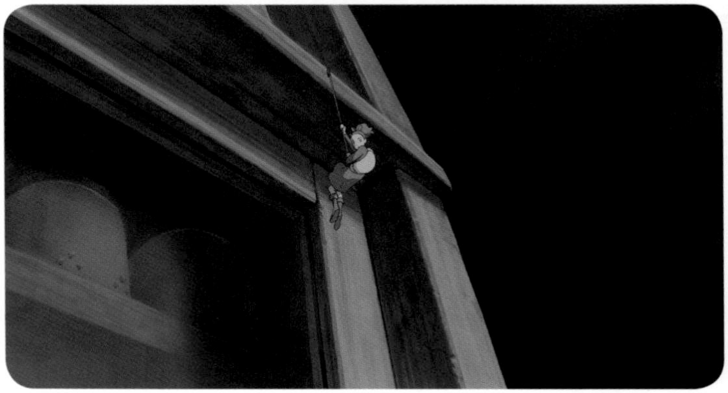

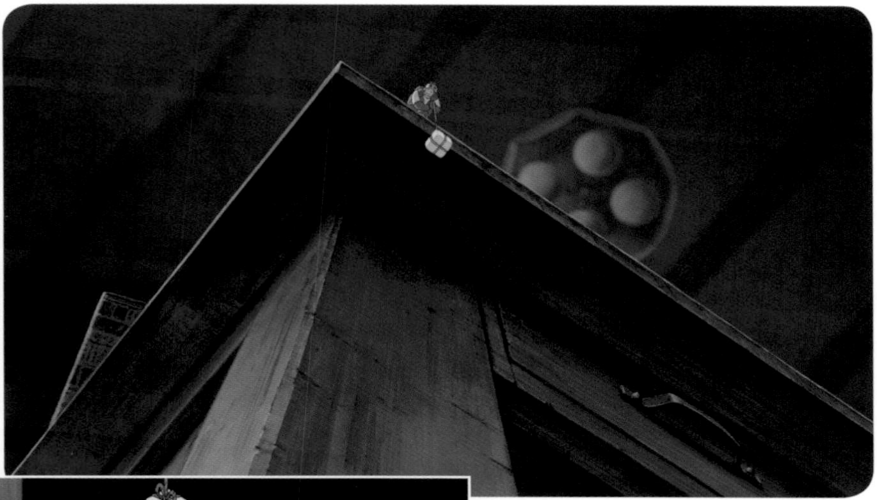

Pod lowered the sugar cube. Arrietty caught it and put it in her bag.

Next they needed tissues. Pod headed toward an electrical outlet.

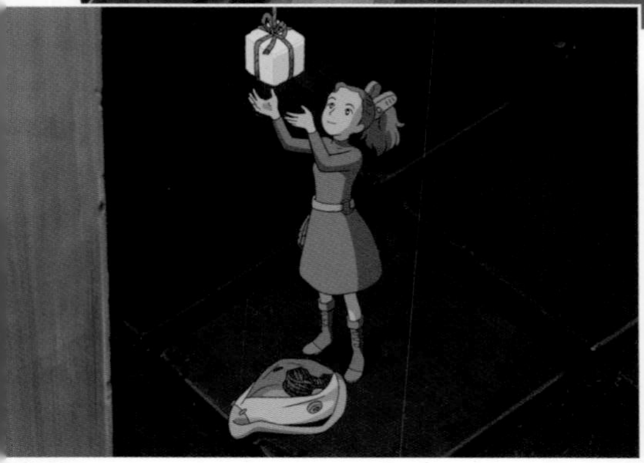

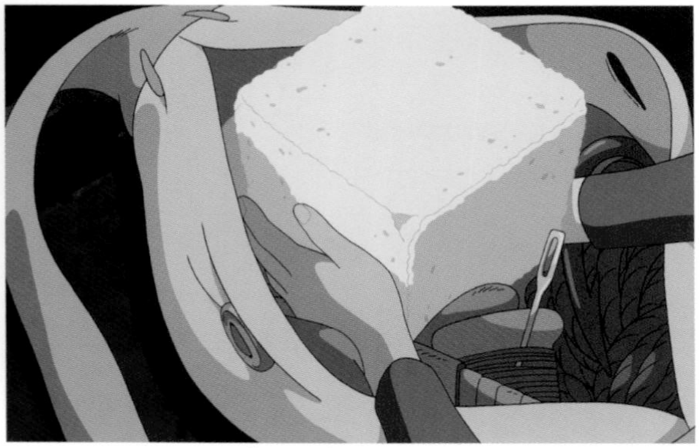

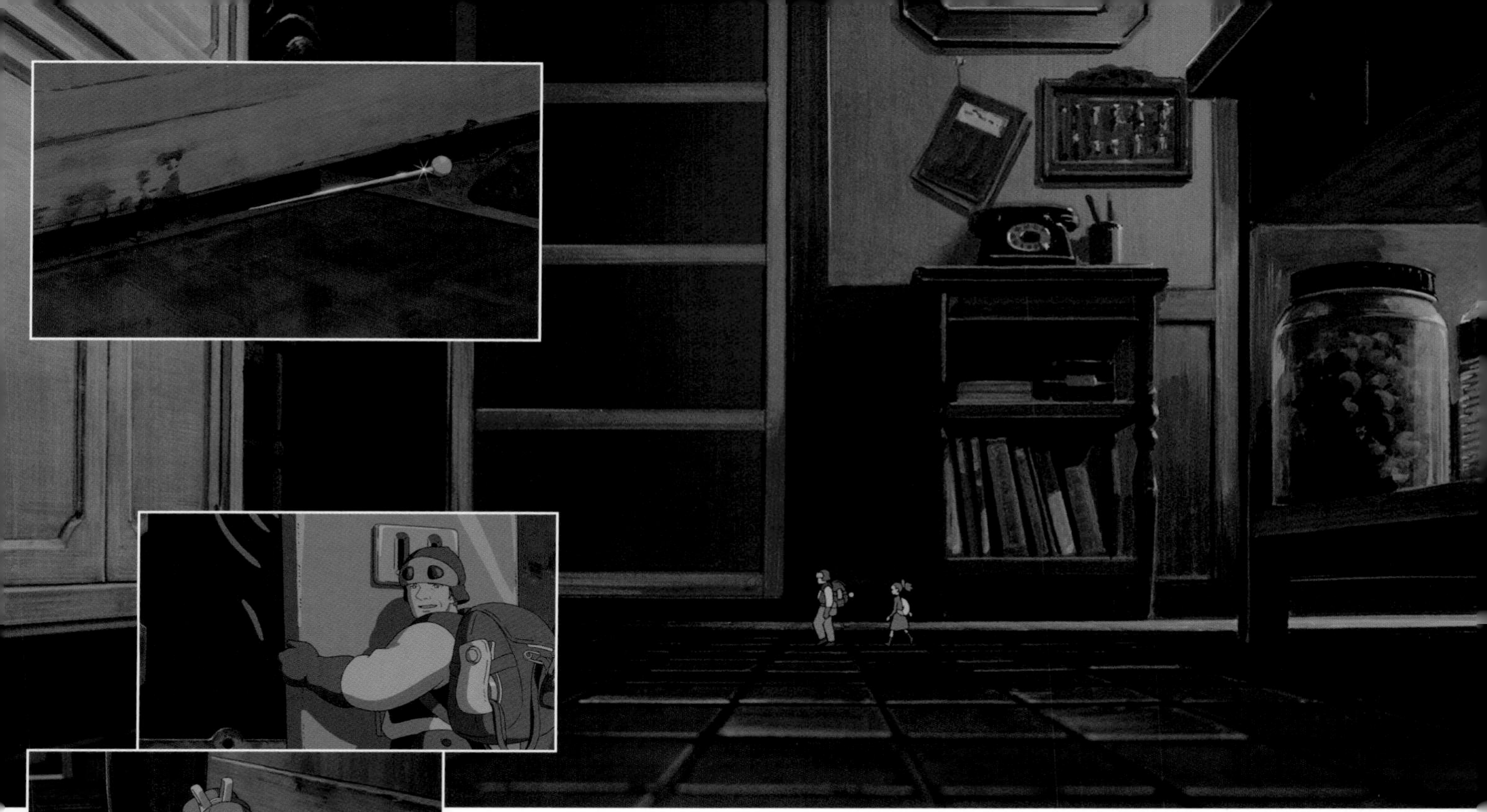

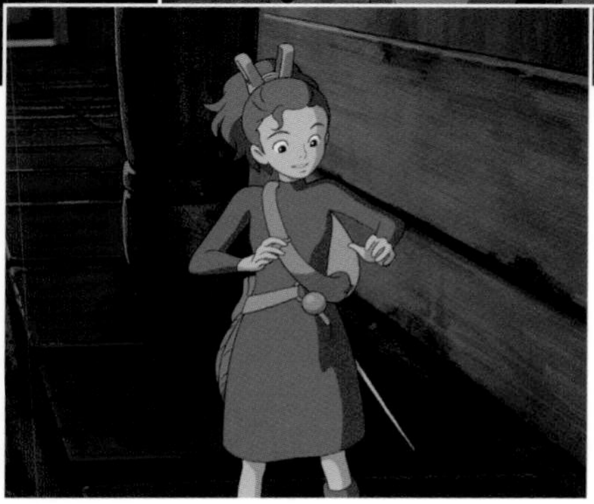

As Arrietty followed, she noticed something shiny on the ground.

What's that? she wondered.

"Papa, look what I found," Arrietty called.

"Looks like someone got their first borrowing," Pod said as he removed the outlet cover. "Careful with it – it's sharp."

"I will!" Arrietty glowed with joy and sheathed the pin on her dress like a sword.

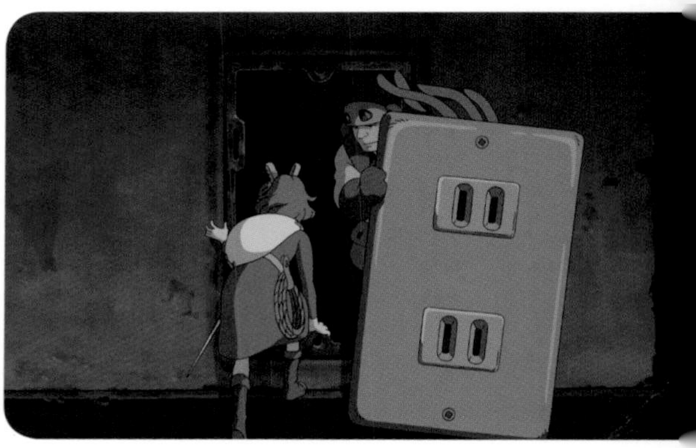

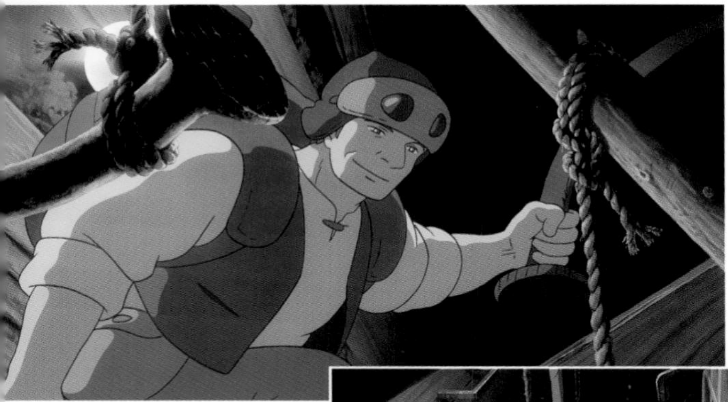

Beyond the outlet opening was a kind of ladder made from household objects.

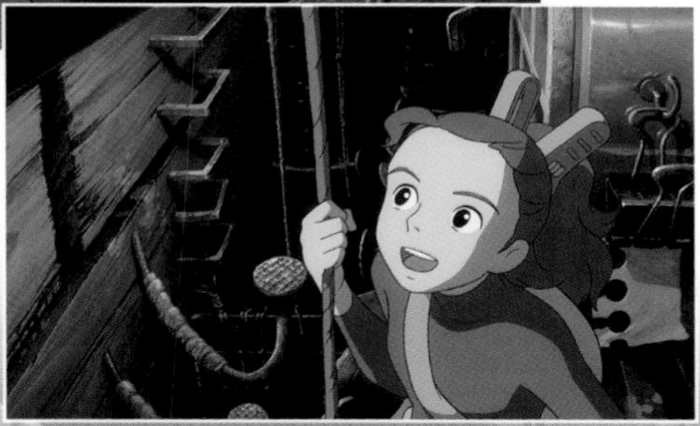

"Papa, borrowing is so much fun!" Arrietty said.

"Look down there," Pod warned.

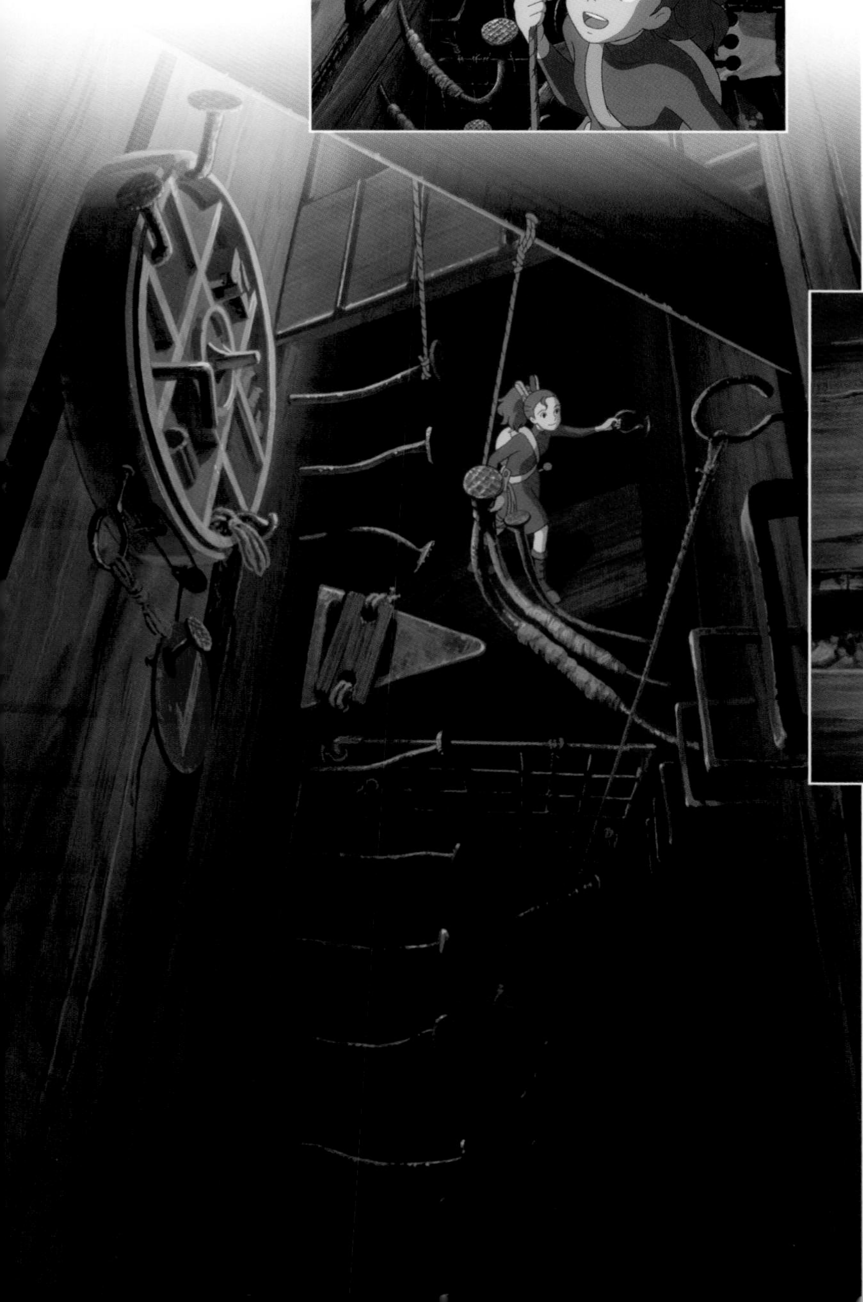

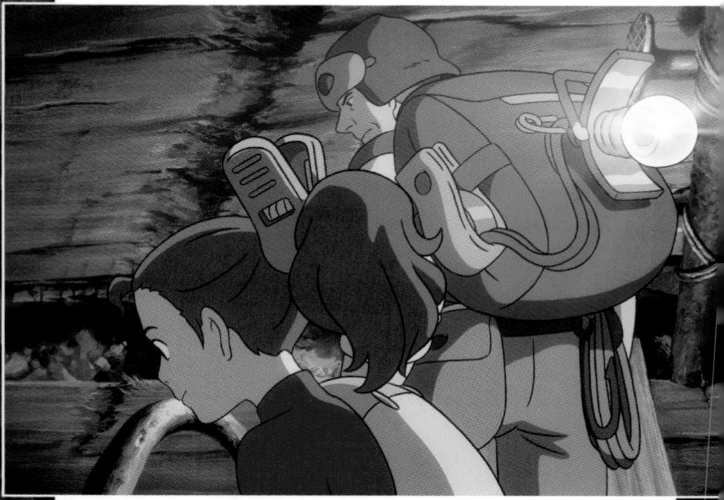

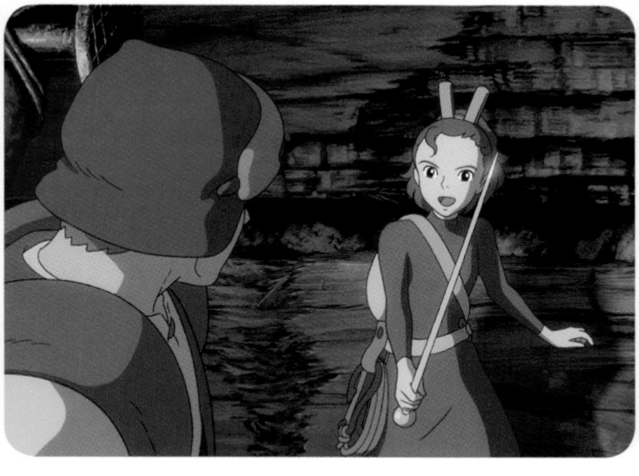

Arrietty saw two large creatures with glowing red eyes scurrying about.

"Filthy rats," Pod grumbled. "Stay away from those things."

"I'm not afraid," Arrietty said, drawing her pin-sword. "I will cut them down to size with my sword."

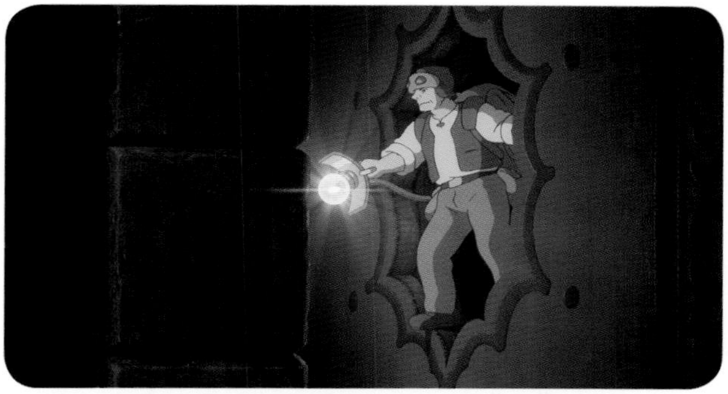

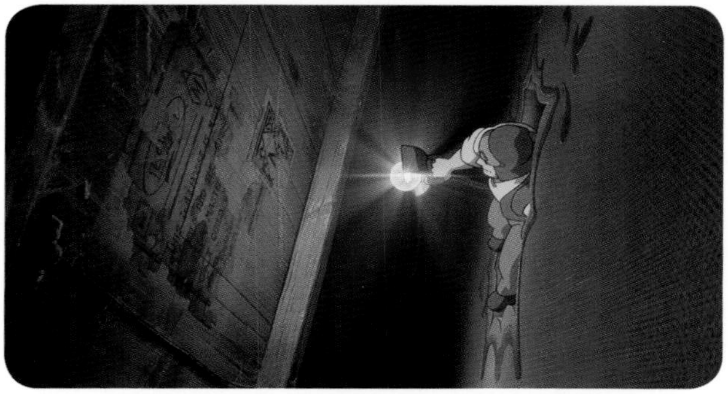

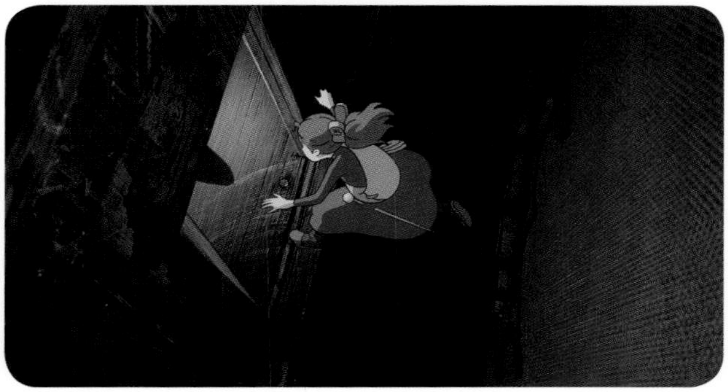

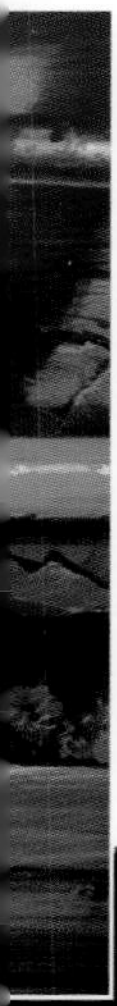

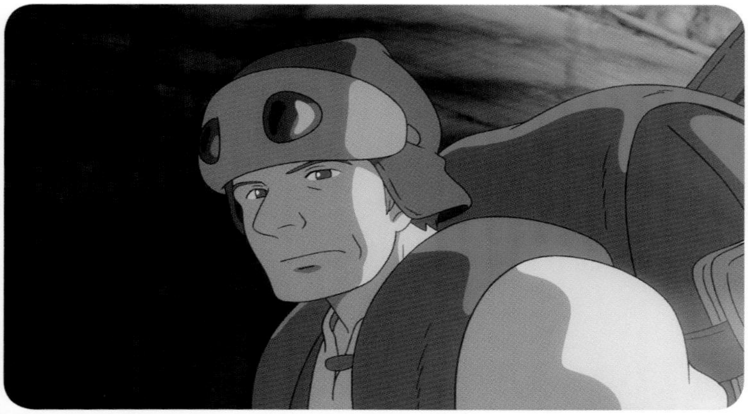

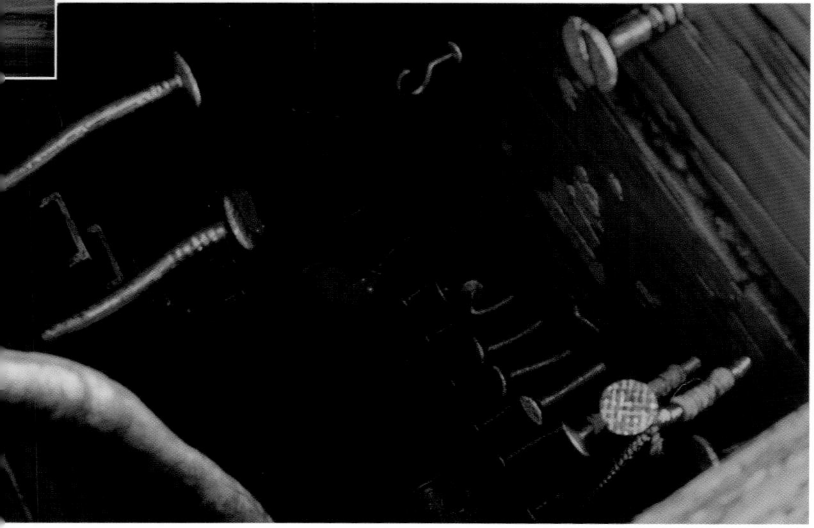

"Careful now," Pod said. "This could be dangerous." He opened the door in front of him and went through.

Arrietty followed Pod, then gasped. Suddenly she was in a dining room more gorgeous than any she could have imagined.

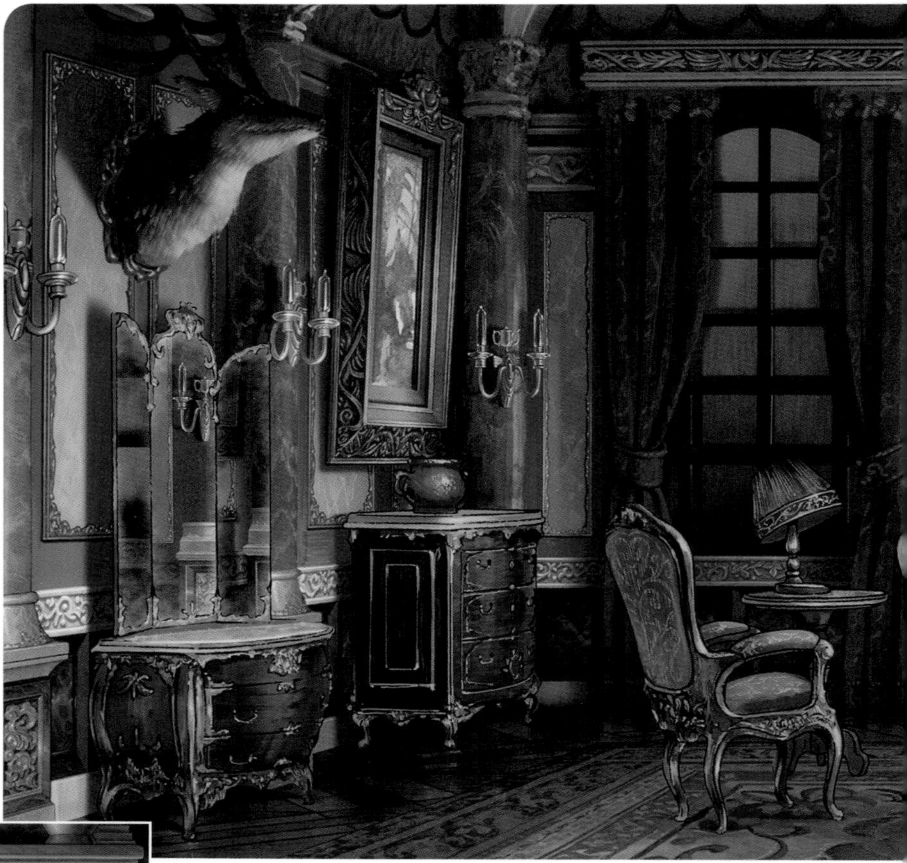

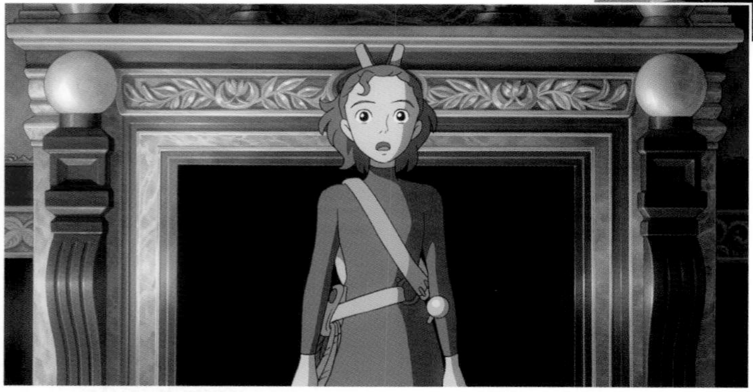

There were elegant furnishings, a chandelier, beautiful paintings and a tea set.

Arrietty looked around in wonder.

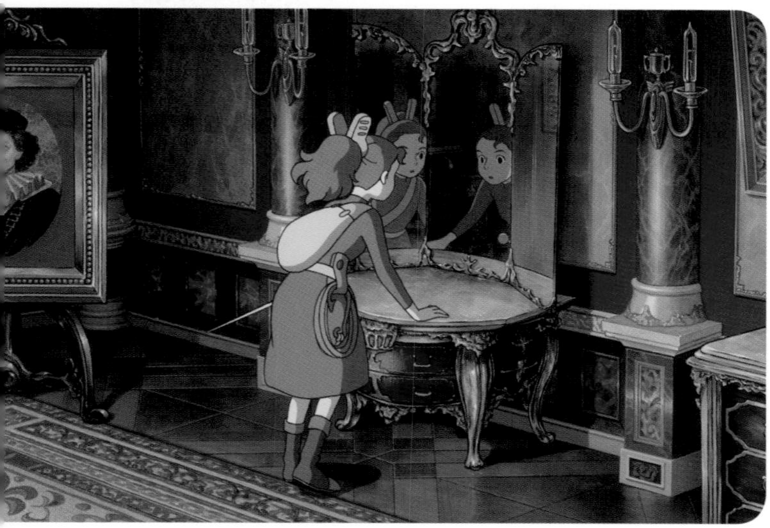

"What is this place?" she asked.

"I've heard human beans call it a *dollhouse*," Pod explained. "These things are not for borrowing."

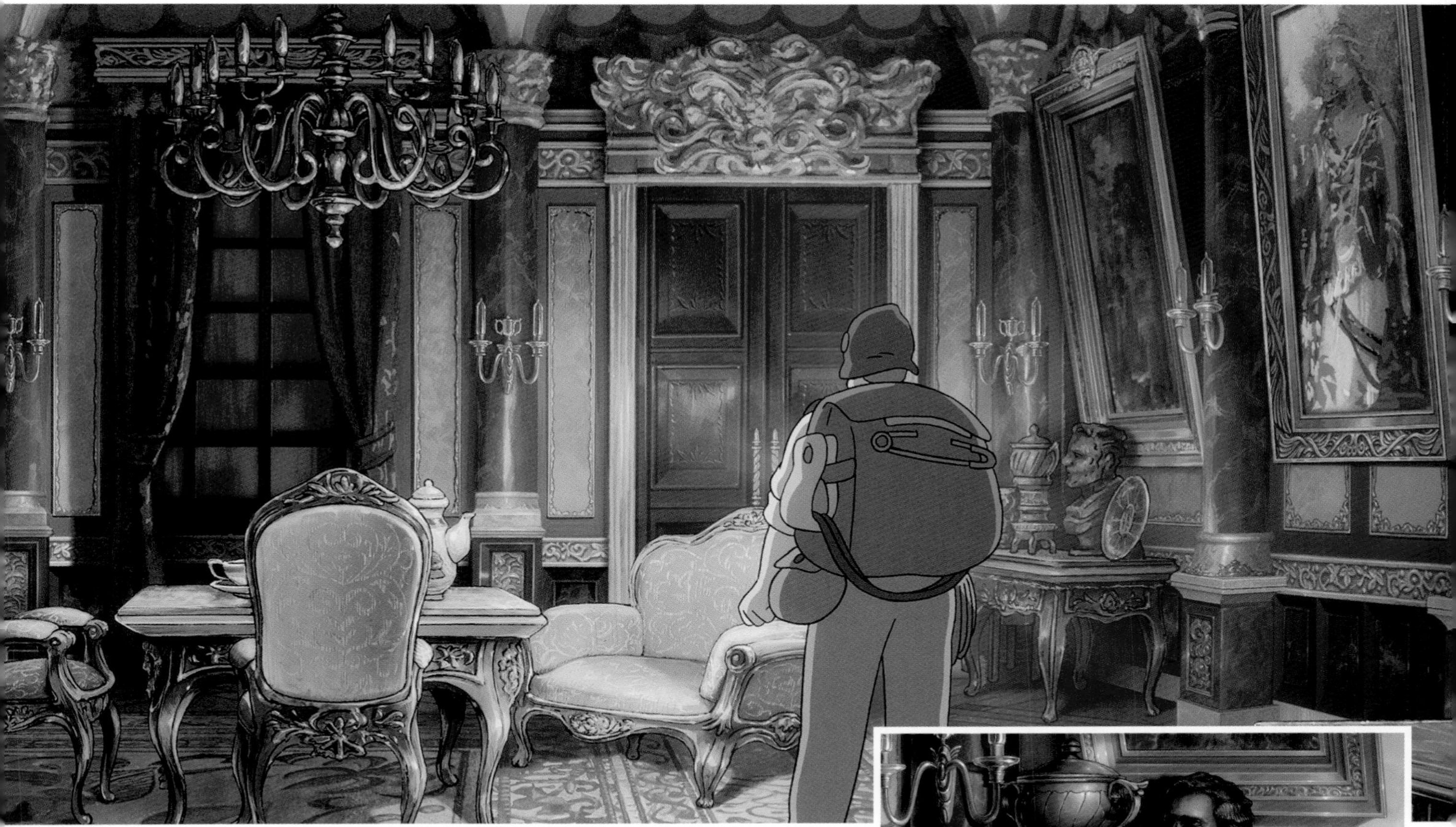

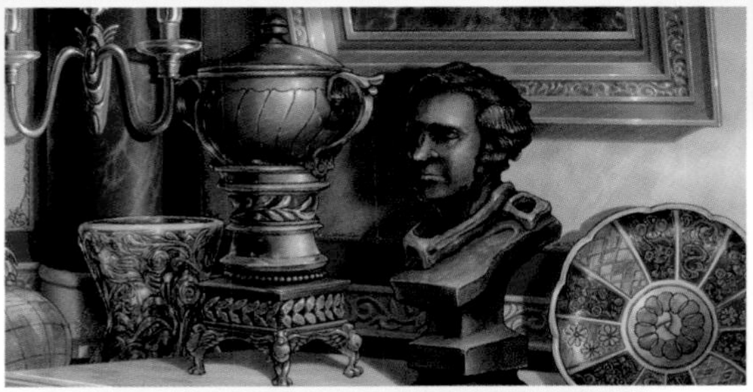

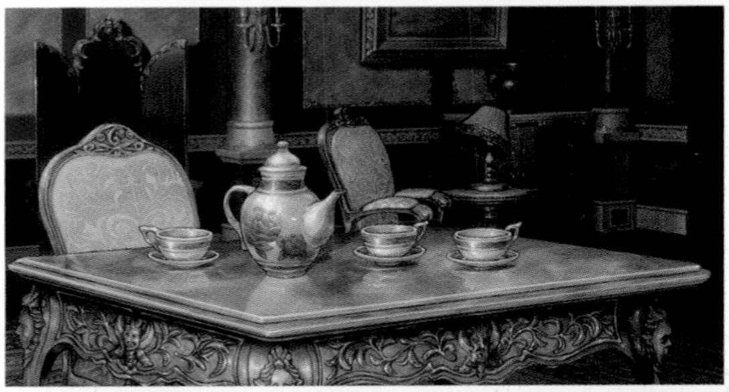

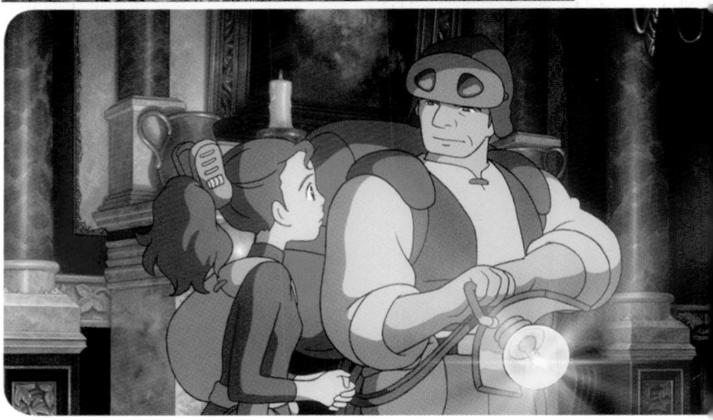

"But it's so perfect for us," Arrietty said. "Don't you think mother would absolutely love that dresser over there?"

"If anything went missing the beans would know right away," said Pod.

"Oh…" Arrietty replied.

Leaving the dining room, they walked out to the balcony. Before them they saw a large human room.

Arrietty gazed in awe at the enormous room. It was a strange sight.

In the dim light, she could see a table nearby with a carved wooden tissue box on top.

Arrietty and Pod left the dollhouse and crept carefully along the sideboard of the wall toward the table.

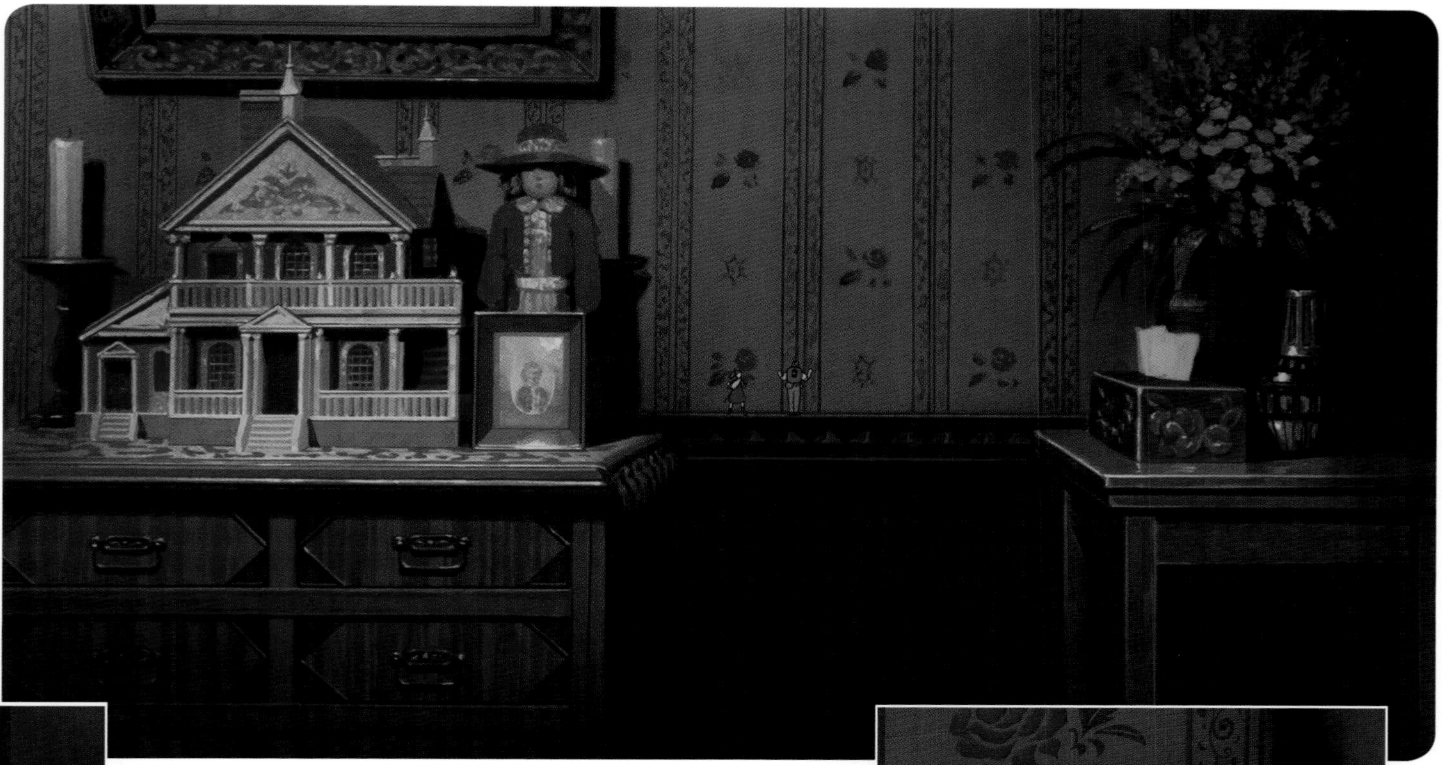

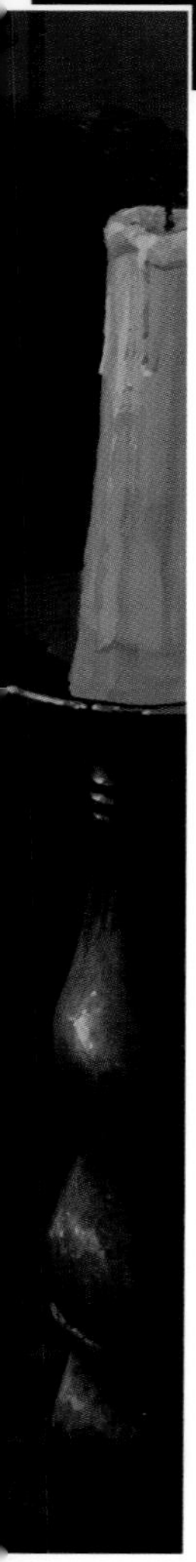

Pod climbed onto the tissue box and signaled to Arrietty to help him pull.

Arrietty ran over enthusiastically. She put her bag down and climbed onto the tissue box.

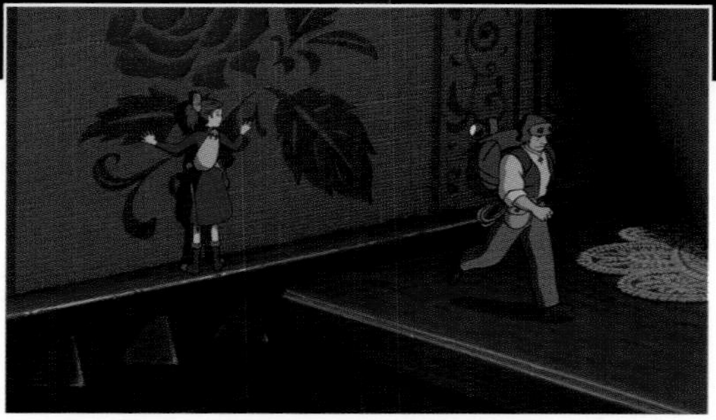

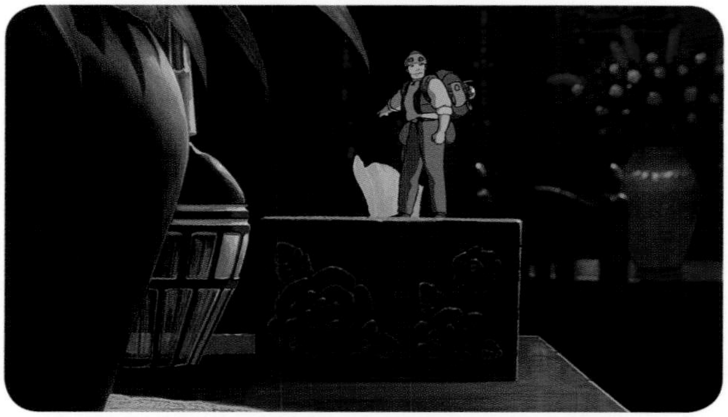

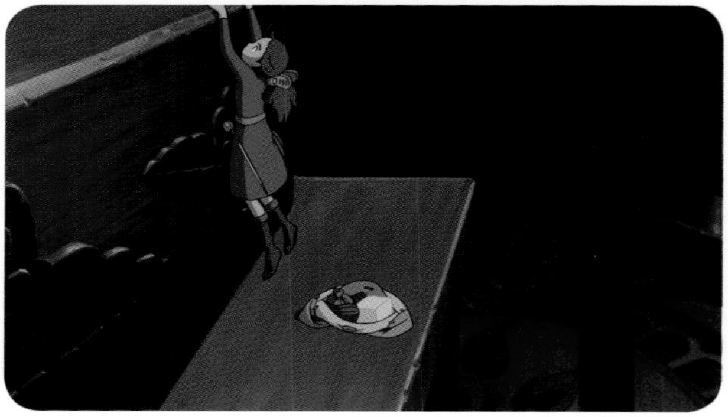

As Pod and Arrietty pulled on each end of the tissue, Arrietty glanced up. Her heart almost stopped.

A human boy!

He looked right at Arrietty with a weak gaze, and didn't seem surprised to see her.

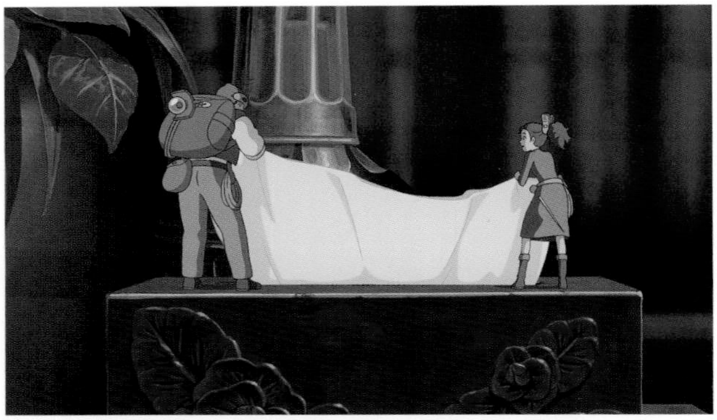

She sank to her knees and tried to cover herself with the tissue.

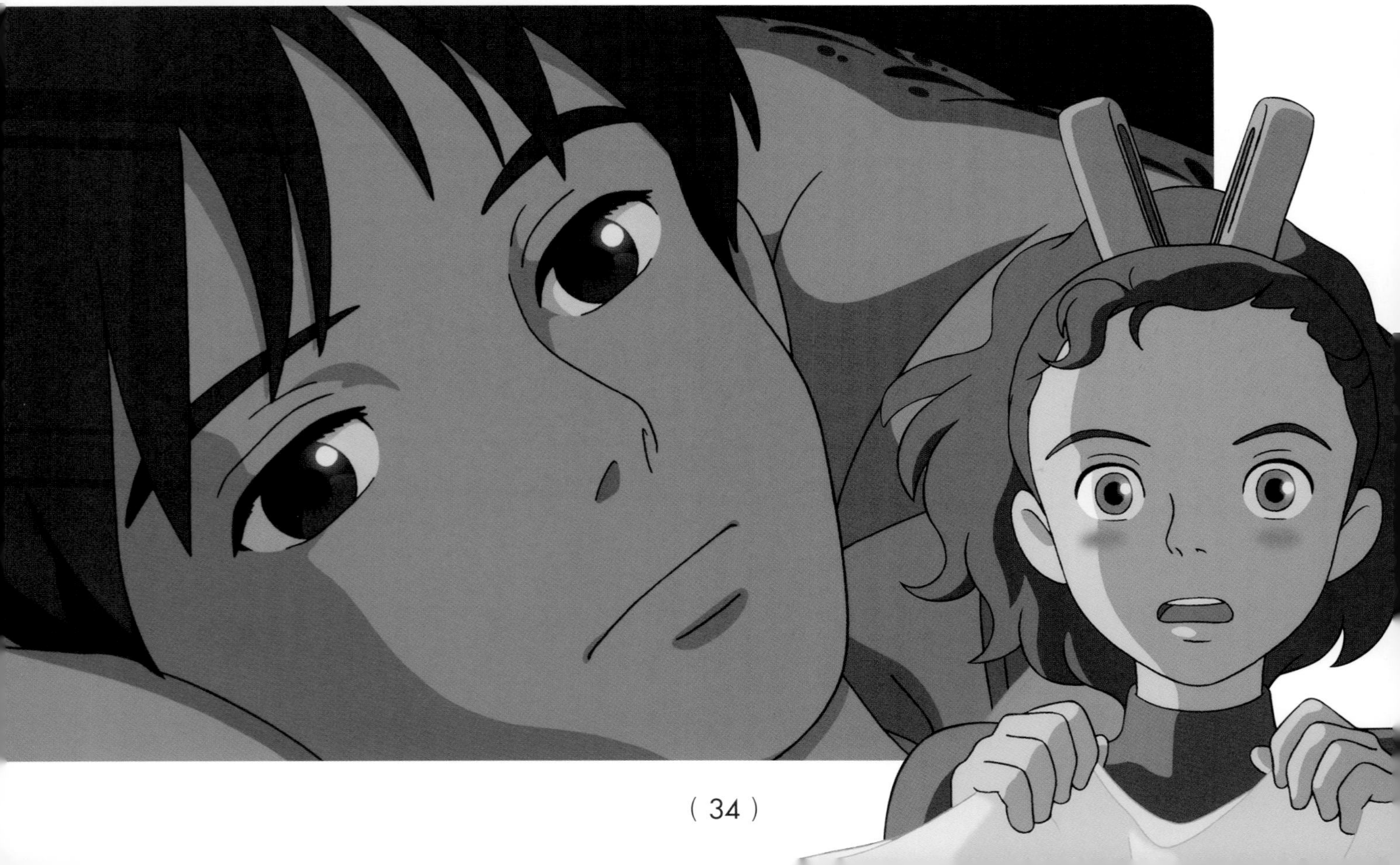

Pod guessed what happened and looked at Arrietty for confirmation. She gave a small nod and Pod noiselessly got off the tissue box.

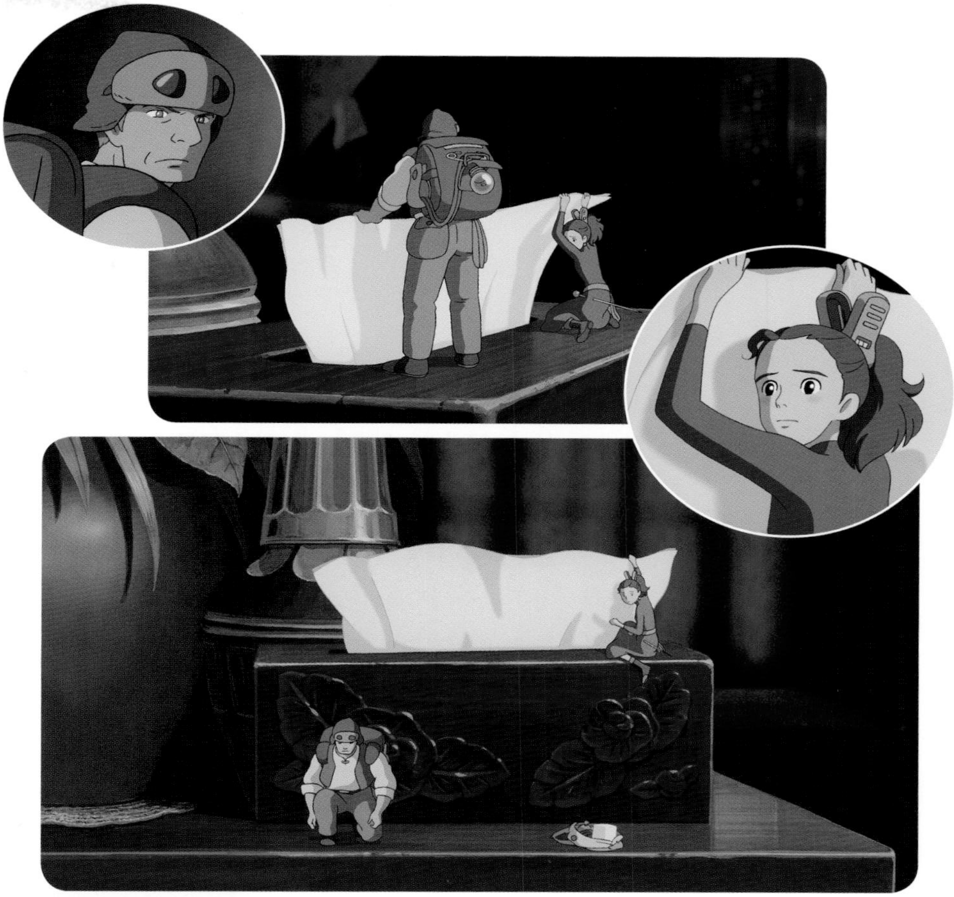

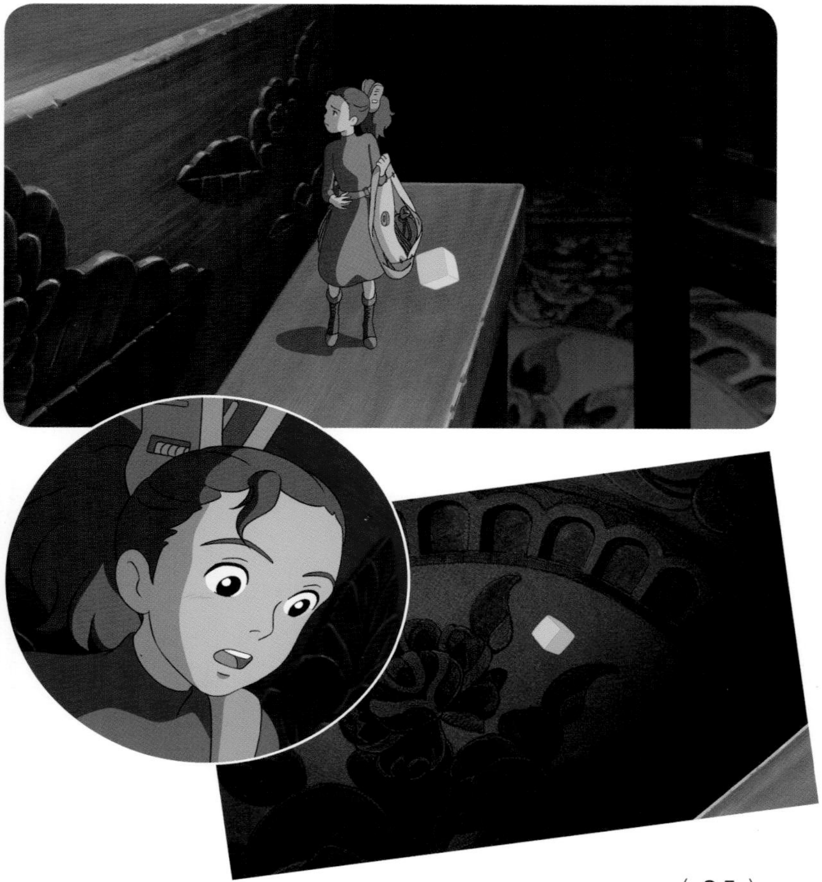

Arrietty lowered herself off the box too.

She quickly grabbed her bag, but the sugar cube fell out and tumbled to the floor.

"Don't be afraid," said the boy gently.

Not only did a human see her, but now the boy was being kind?

Arrietty fought back tears of frustration and embarrassment as she looked at the sugar cube on the floor.

There was nothing to be done. Arrietty buttoned her bag with trembling hands and followed Pod.

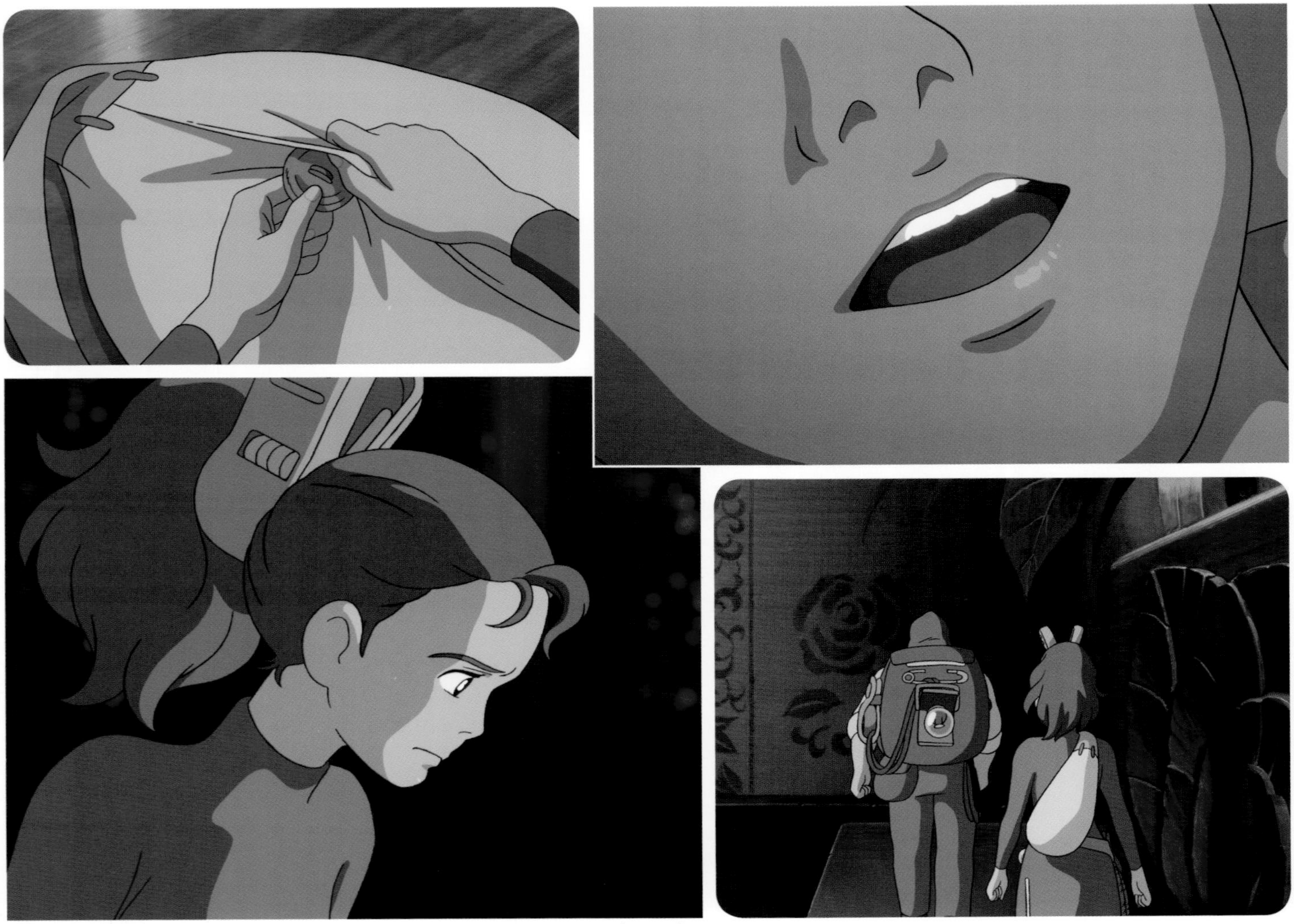

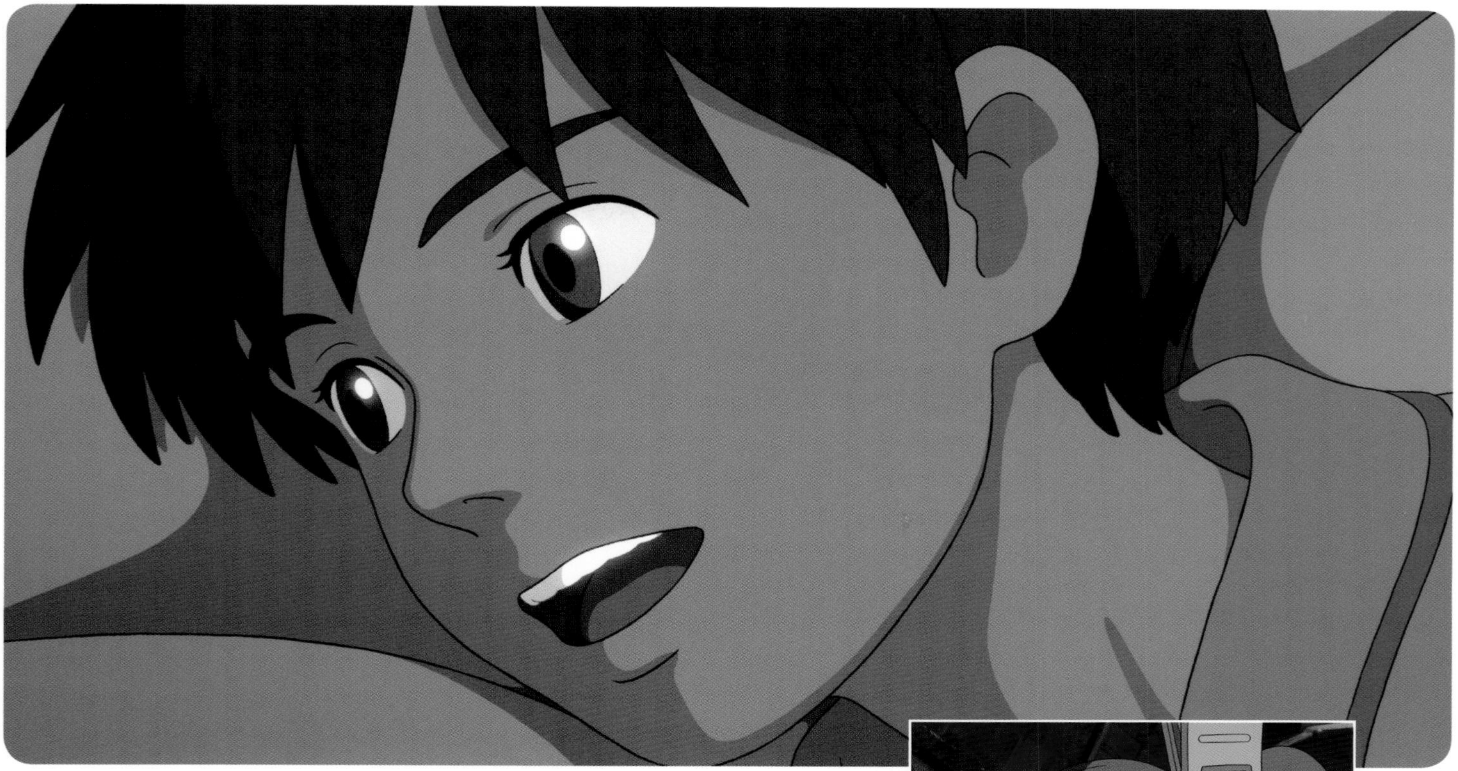

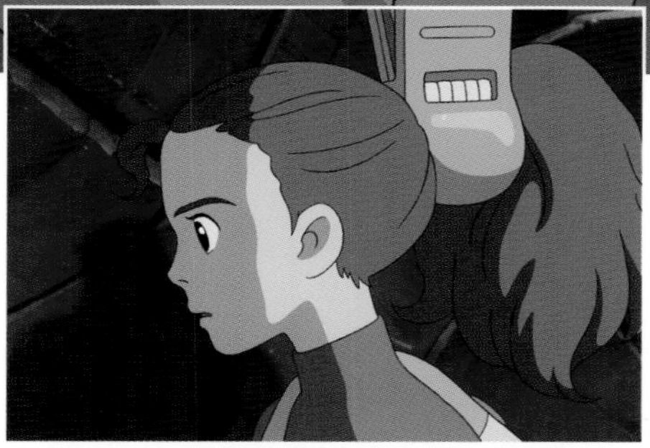

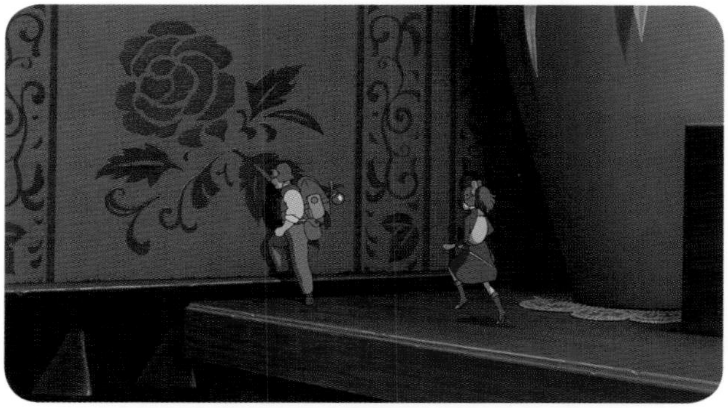

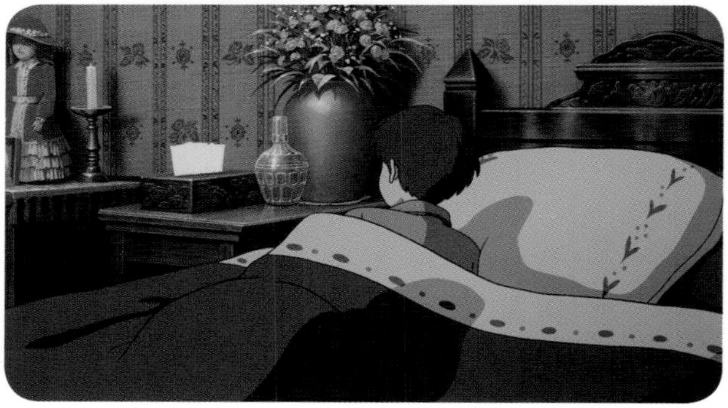

"I know it was you in the garden," the boy whispered. "I knew I saw you."

Arrietty heard this and stopped in her tracks.

"My mother used to tell me stories about the little people who lived under the floors," the boy continued. "Was she talking about you?"

Arrietty crept away, but she was still listening.

Arrietty was quiet as she descended the stairs.

"Papa, I'm sorry," she said, pausing. "The boy might have seen me out in the garden today."

"We all make mistakes, Arrietty," Pod said gently. "We'll just have to be extra careful now. Best not tell your mother about this… you know how she worries."

"Right."

Arrietty hung her head and looked very serious.

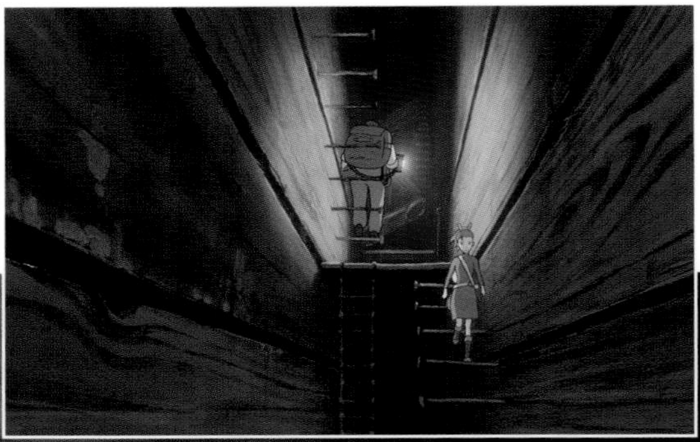

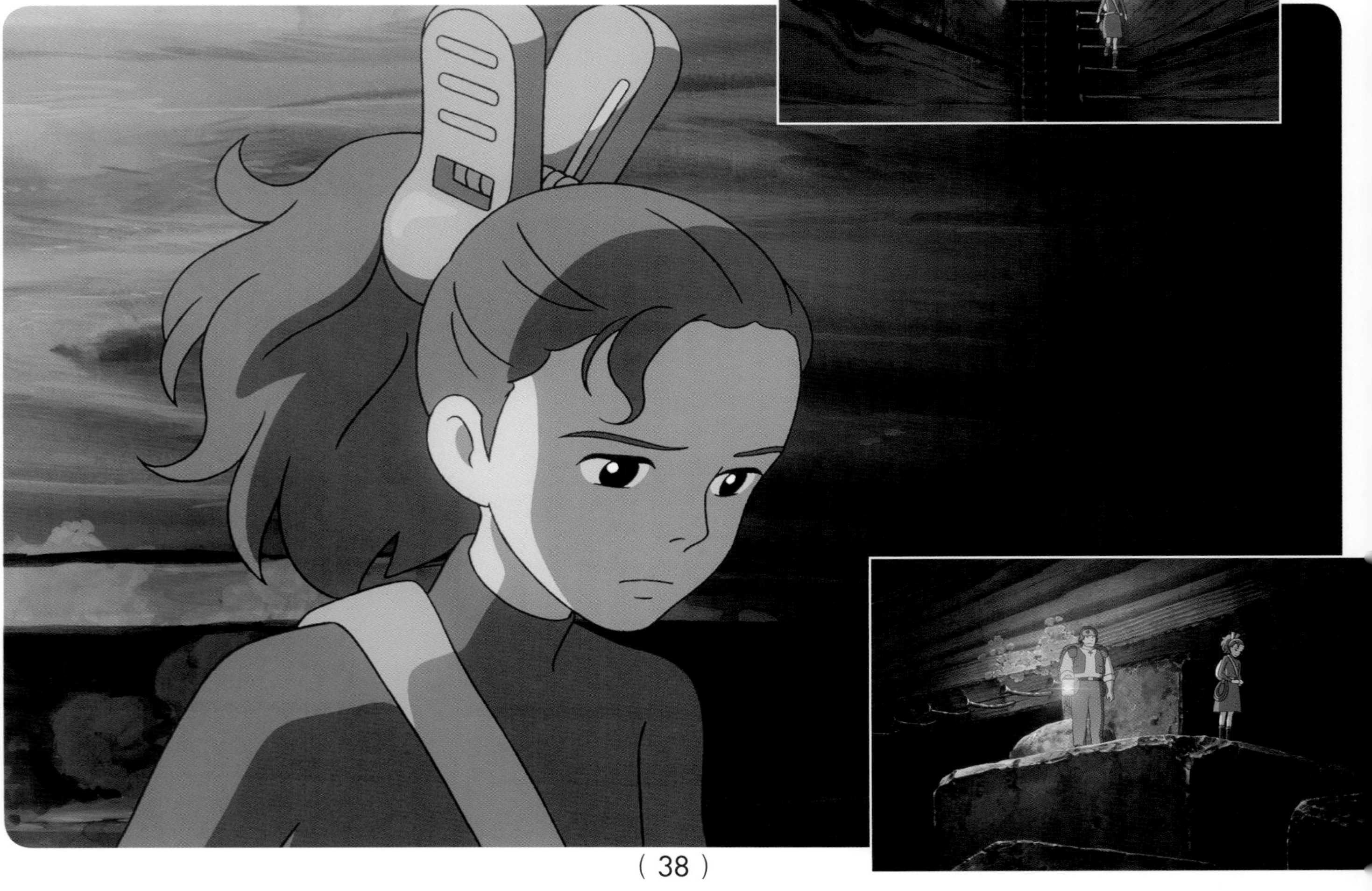

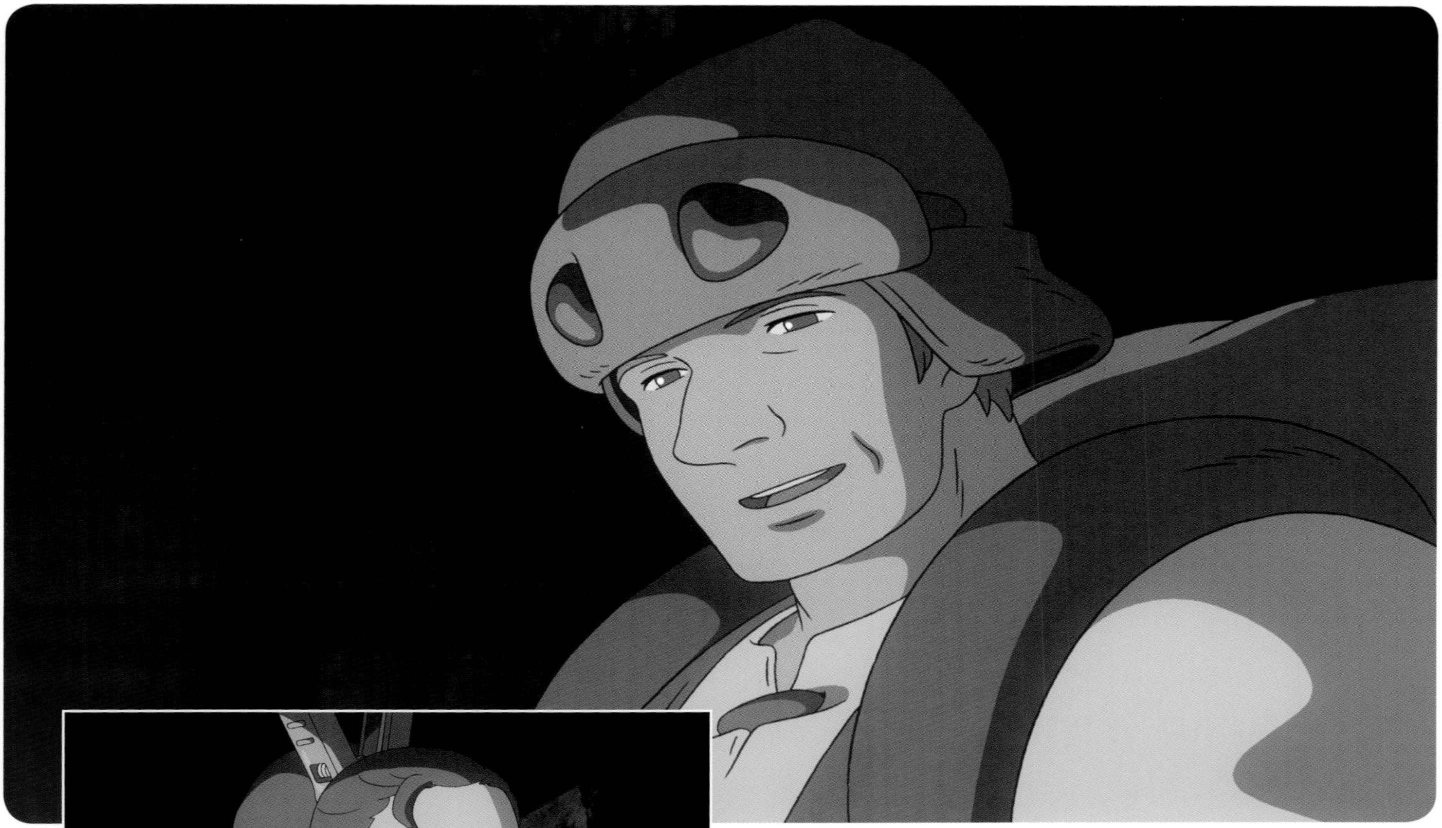

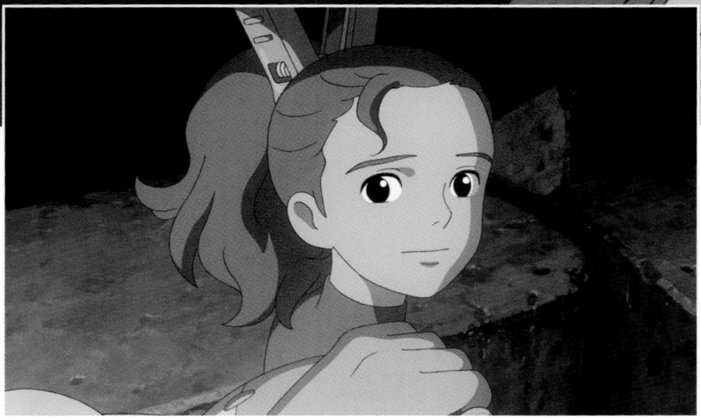

Pod tried to comfort her.

"I'm very proud of you, Arrietty," he said with a gentle smile. "A lesser Borrower would've panicked and run away."

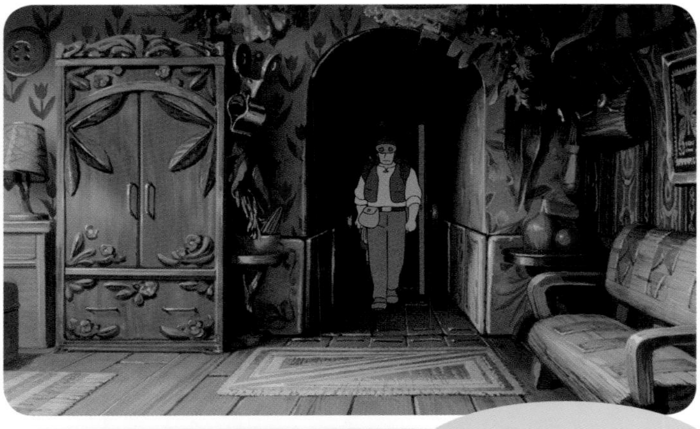

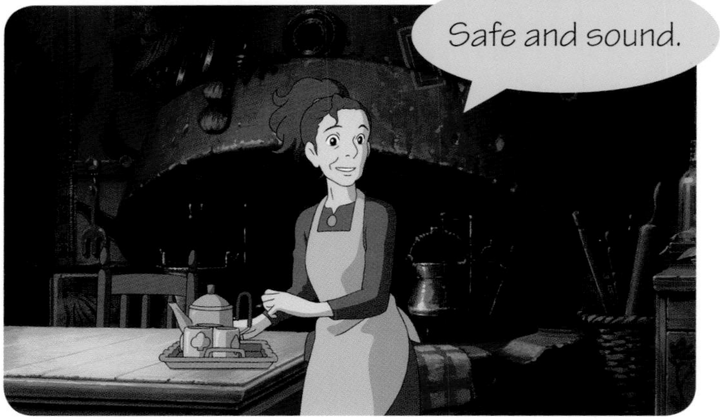
Safe and sound.

“Is everything okay?” asked Homily.

“Not quite the adventure we were expecting,” Pod replied. “The old light gave out halfway to the kitchen. We had to give up on the sugar.”

“That’s okay. I’m just happy you made it home.”

“It wasn’t a total loss. Arrietty, why don’t you show your mother your first borrowing?”

Arrietty unsheathed her pin-sword and handed it to her mother.

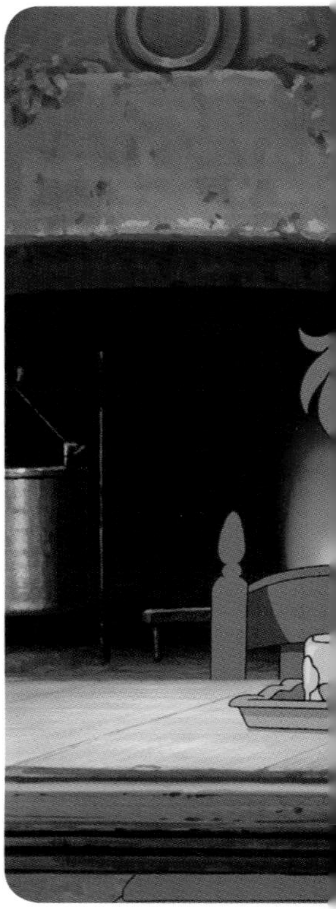

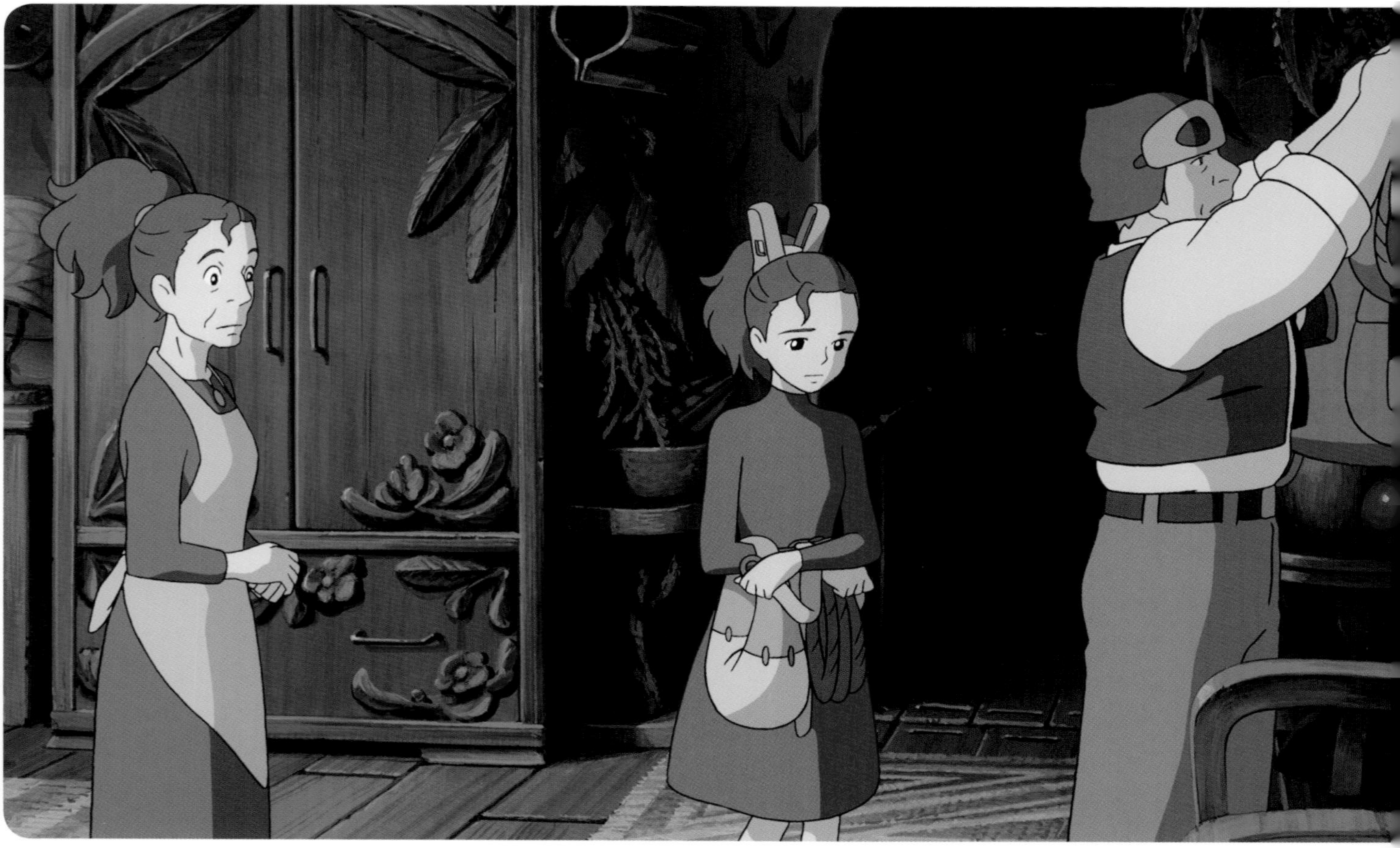

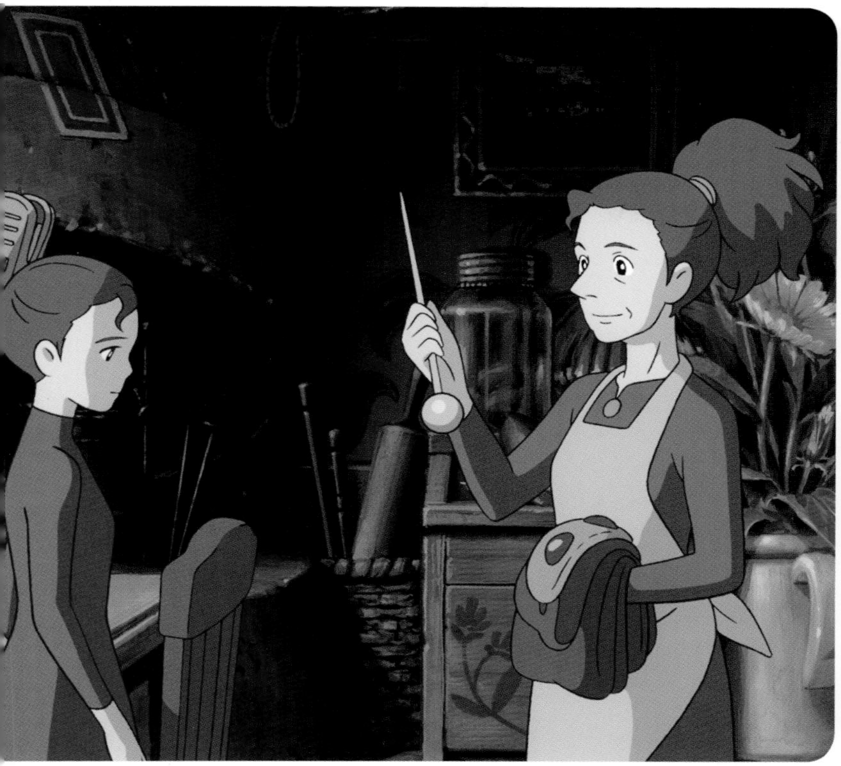

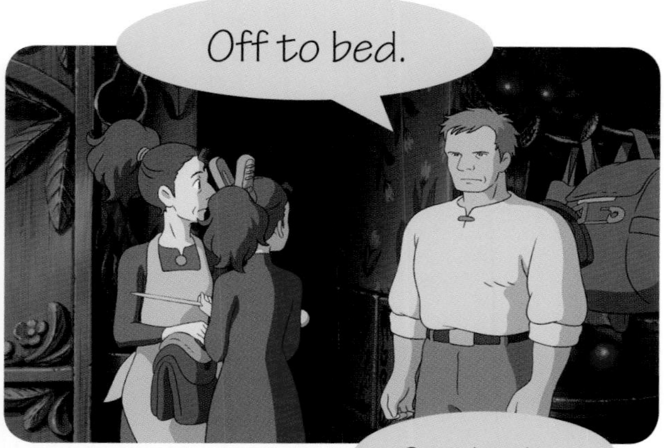
Off to bed.

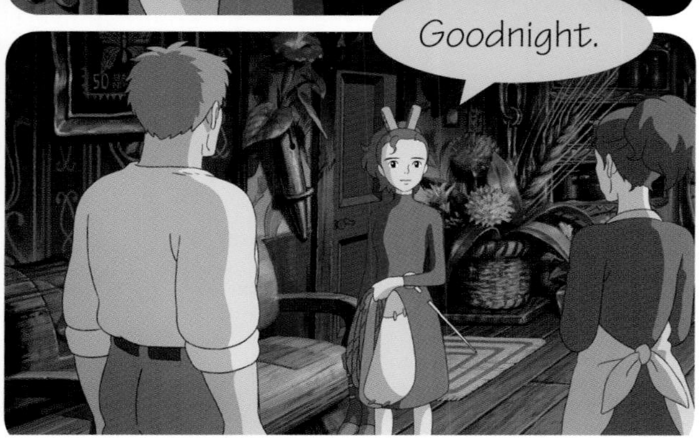
Goodnight.

"What a beautiful pin," said Homily with a smile.

That night it stormed. Arrietty lay in bed listening to the thunder and rain, unable to get to sleep.

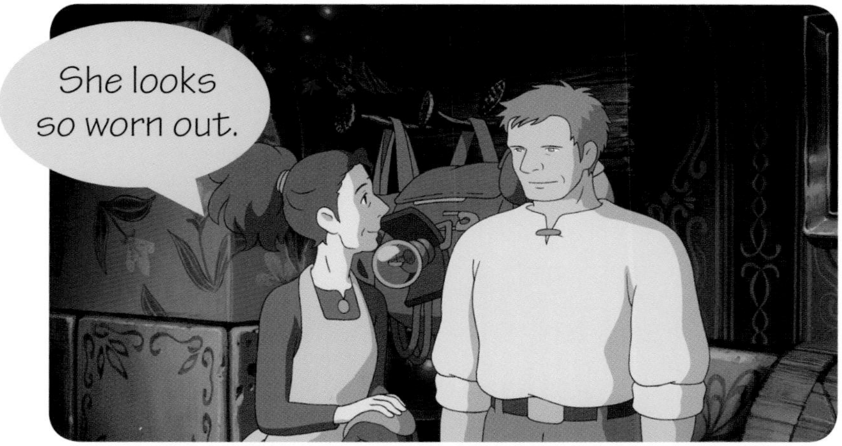
She looks so worn out.

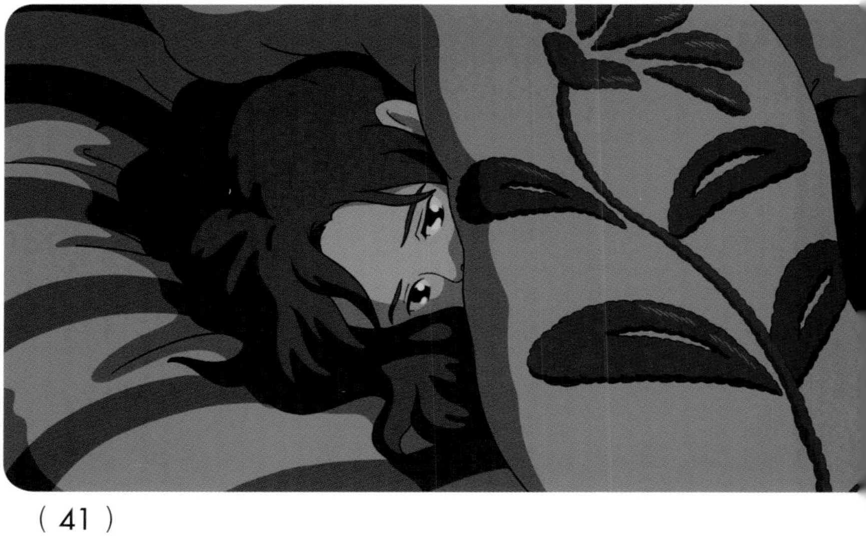

Shawn and Arrietty

The next day it was still
raining. Arrietty's mood hadn't improved either.

She was sitting in the dim light under the floorboards,
not paying much attention to anything, when someone
stopped and stood right in front of the grate!

A giant hand carefully placed
a sugar cube just outside.

It was the boy from last night!
He must have brought the
sugar cube Arrietty dropped!

Arrietty hopped through the grate. Using an ivy leaf as an umbrella, she followed the boy.

He sat on a chair on the patio, stroking the cat.

What is he thinking? Arrietty wondered.

She watched him intently.

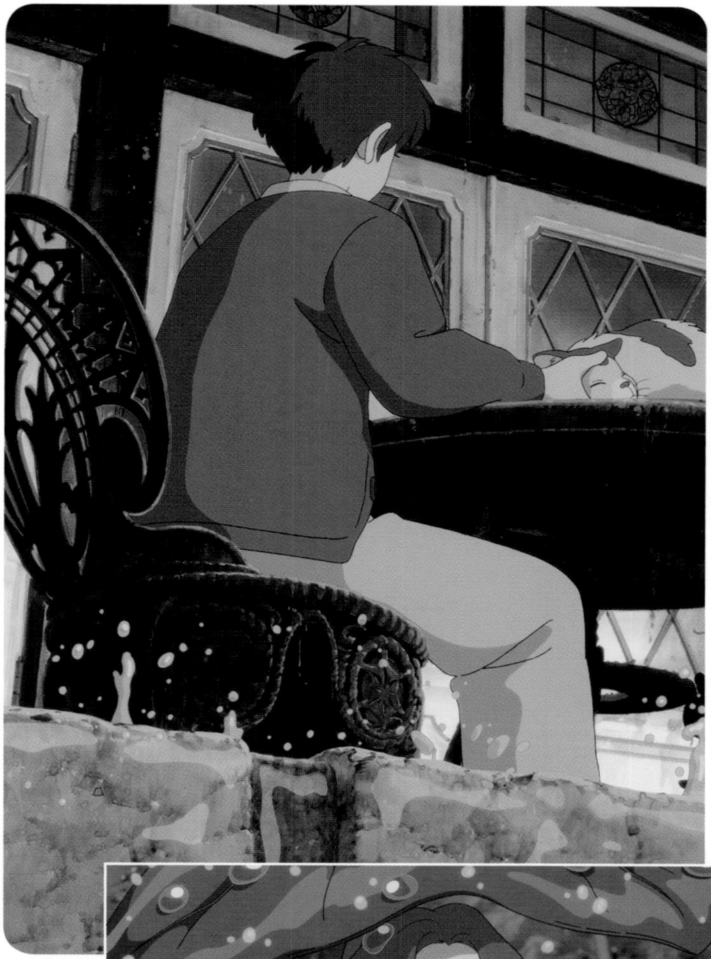

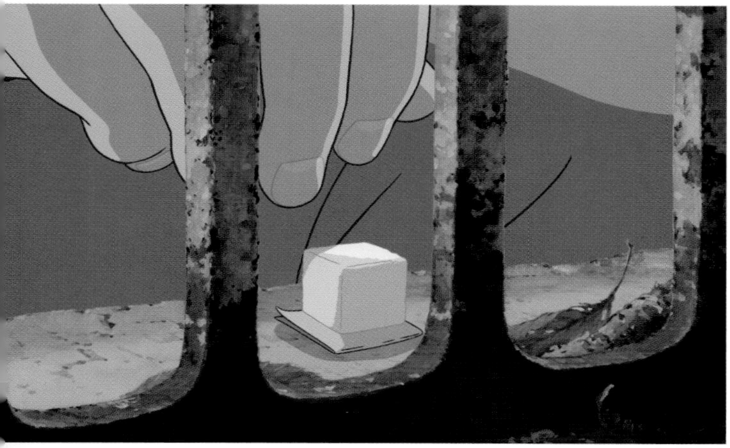

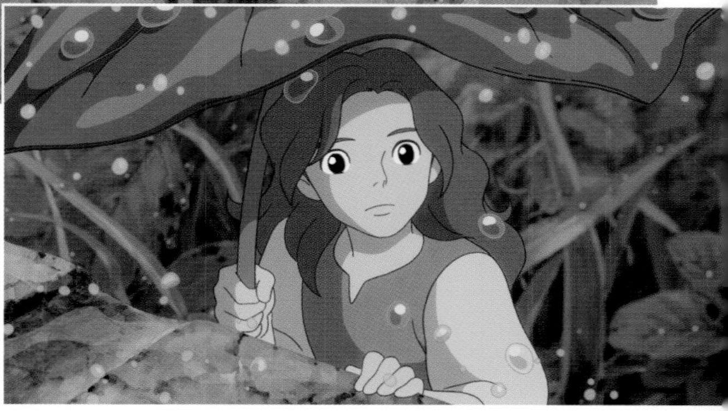

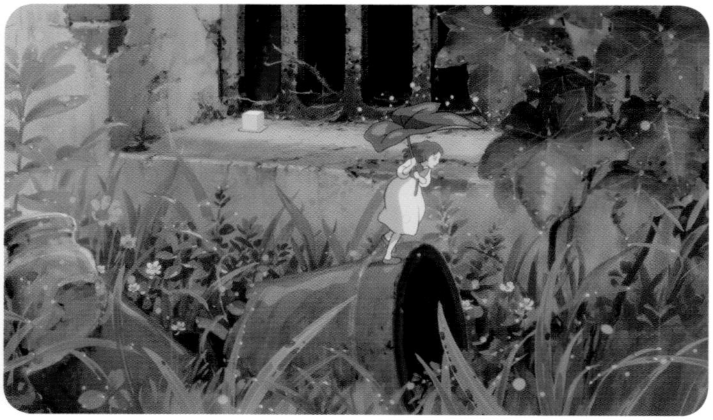

From inside the house, a woman called out, "Shawn! Come inside! You'll catch your death of cold."

The boy stood up and went inside.

Arrietty went back to the grate. She saw that the sugar cube was sitting on a small piece of folded paper.

When Arrietty lifted the sugar cube, the paper opened up a little. There was writing inside.

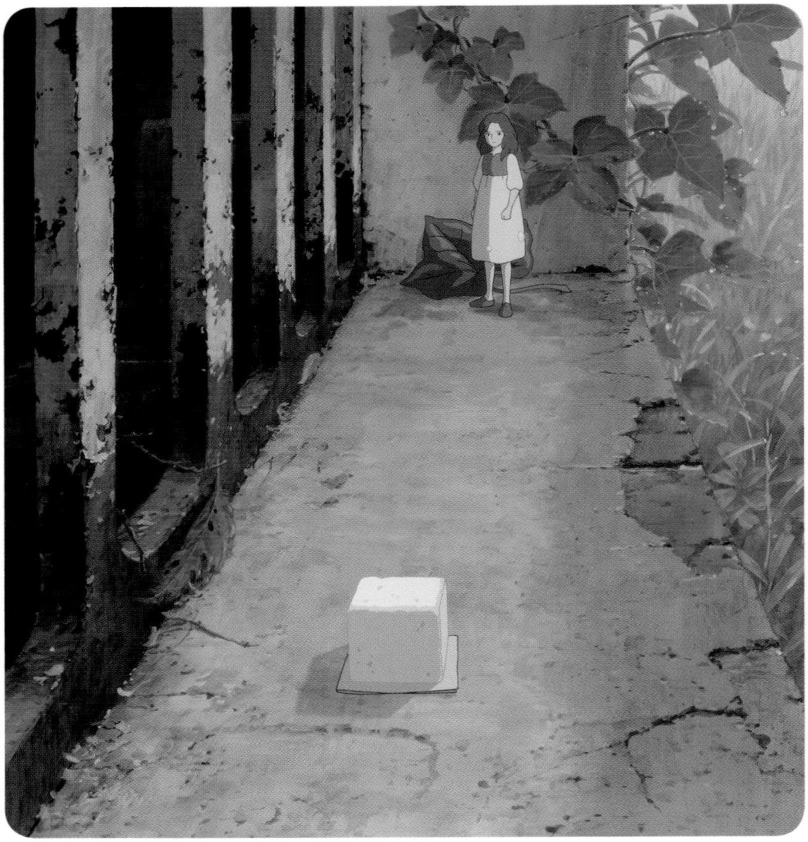

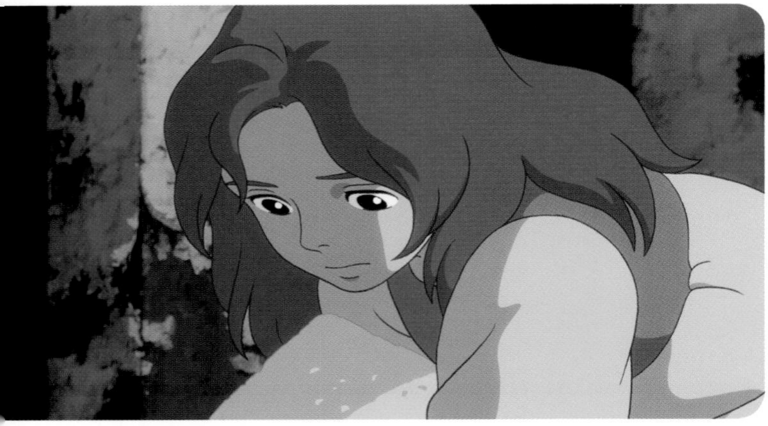

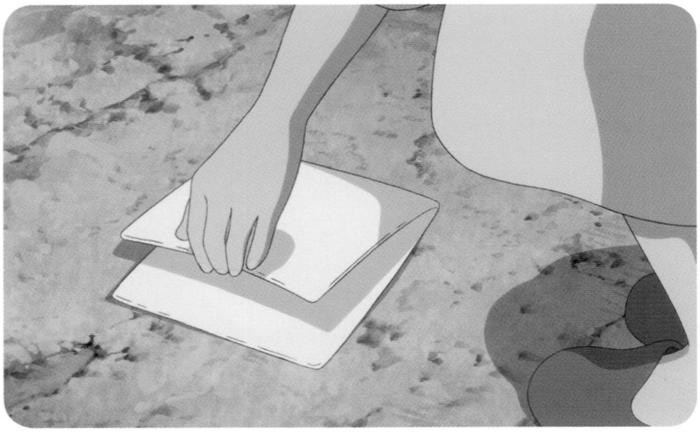

Arrietty started to open the note, but changed her mind and put the sugar cube back.

When she was back at home, Arrietty told Pod about the sugar and the paper.

"Do not touch it," Pod said sternly. "Understand?"

"Yes," Arrietty nodded.

Homily was very scared. “It’s a trap! I just know it!” she cried. “We’ll probably have to move now! Goodbye, old table. We had so many fun times together. Oh…”

“Let’s not say goodbye to anything just yet,” said Pod.

Arrietty listened silently to her parents’ discussion.

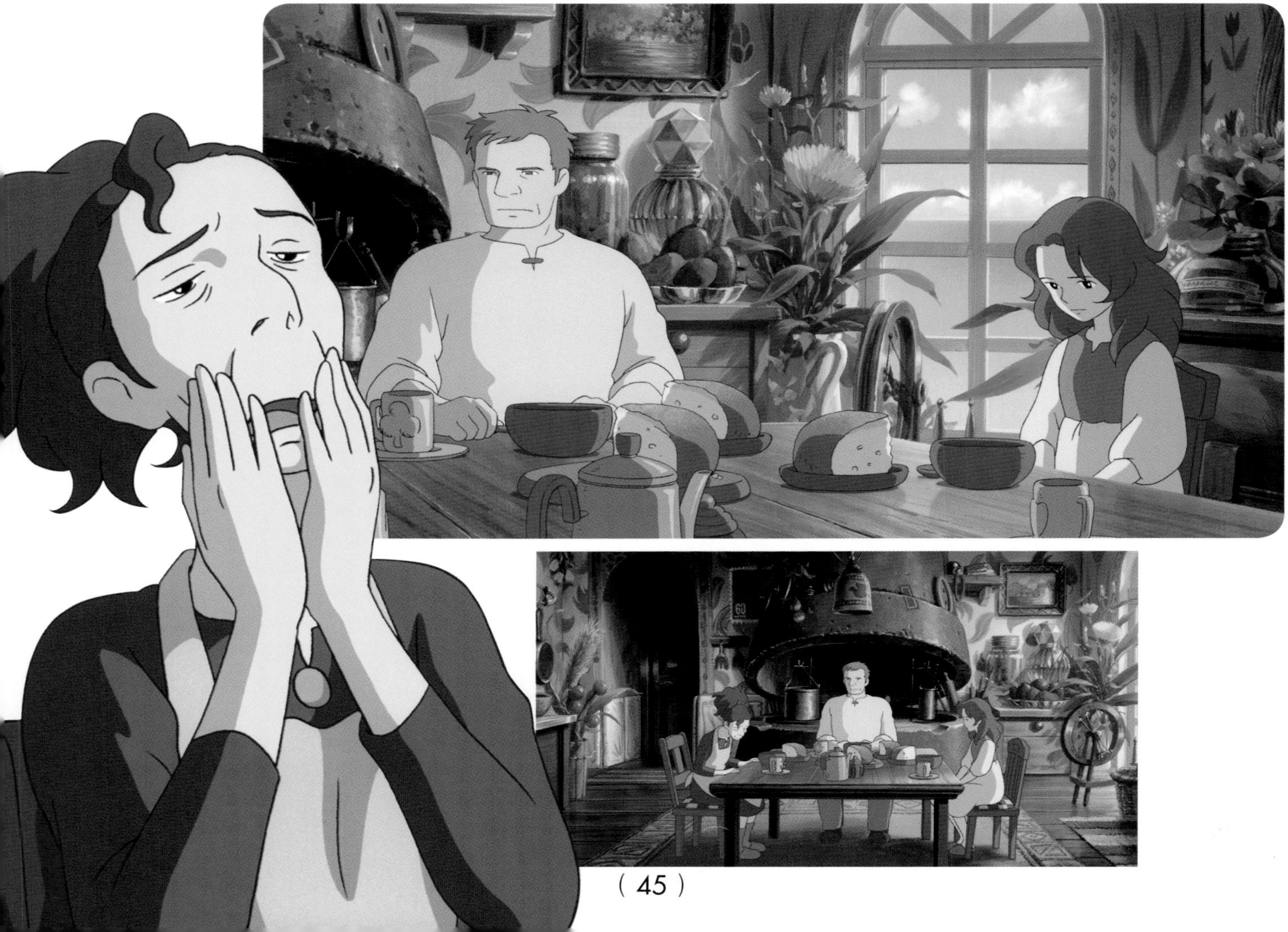

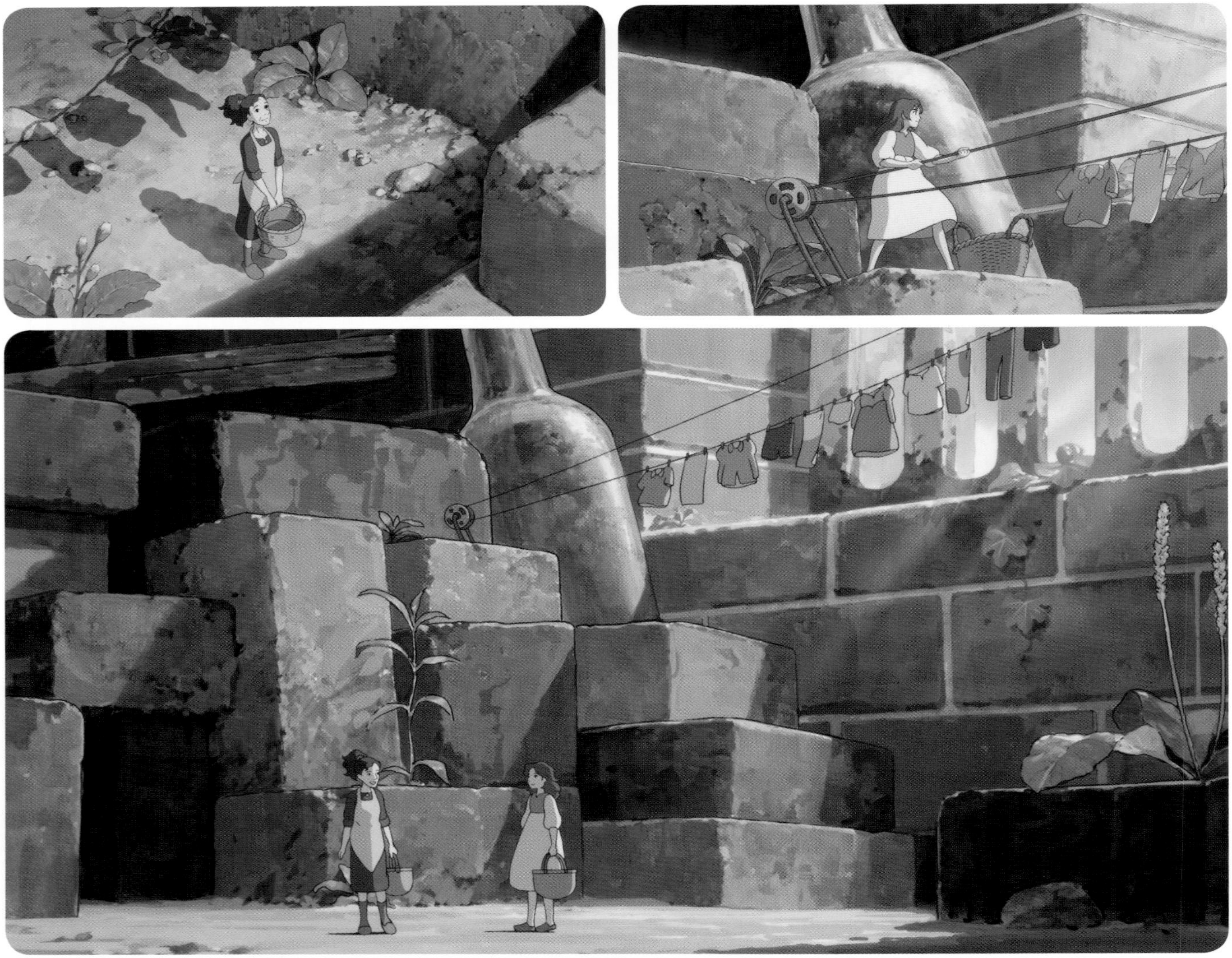

When the rain stopped, Arrietty helped Homily with the laundry.

“Thank you, Arrietty,” Homily said. “Smart girl, waiting until the sun came out.”

“Or maybe I have a smart mama who taught me well,” smiled Arrietty.

“If you’re okay here, I think I’ll go lie down a bit,” Homily said.

Homily went back inside. Arrietty looked up at the grate and wondered what had become of the sugar cube.

When she got to the grate, ants were swarming around the sugar cube. There was hardly anything left.

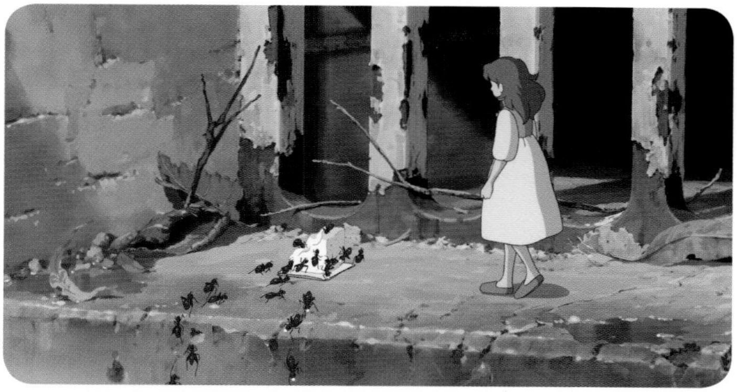

Papa went to all that trouble to borrow the sugar, but we lost it because of me, Arrietty thought.

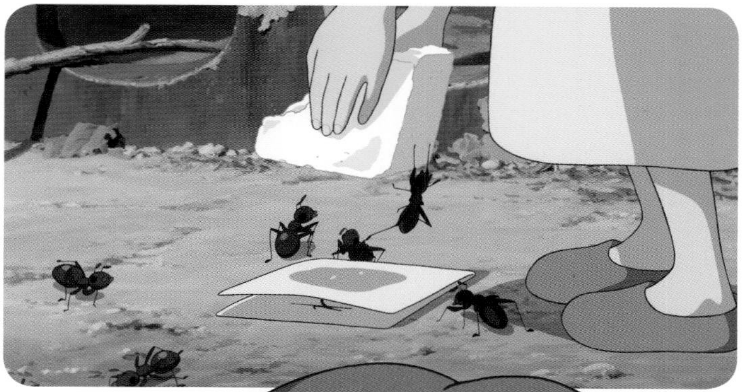

Arrietty shooed the ants away, picked up what was left of the the sugar cube and opened the note.

"You forgot something," it read.

I can't accept this. Arrietty thought. *I must return it. That will be my reply.*

Arrietty looked determined.

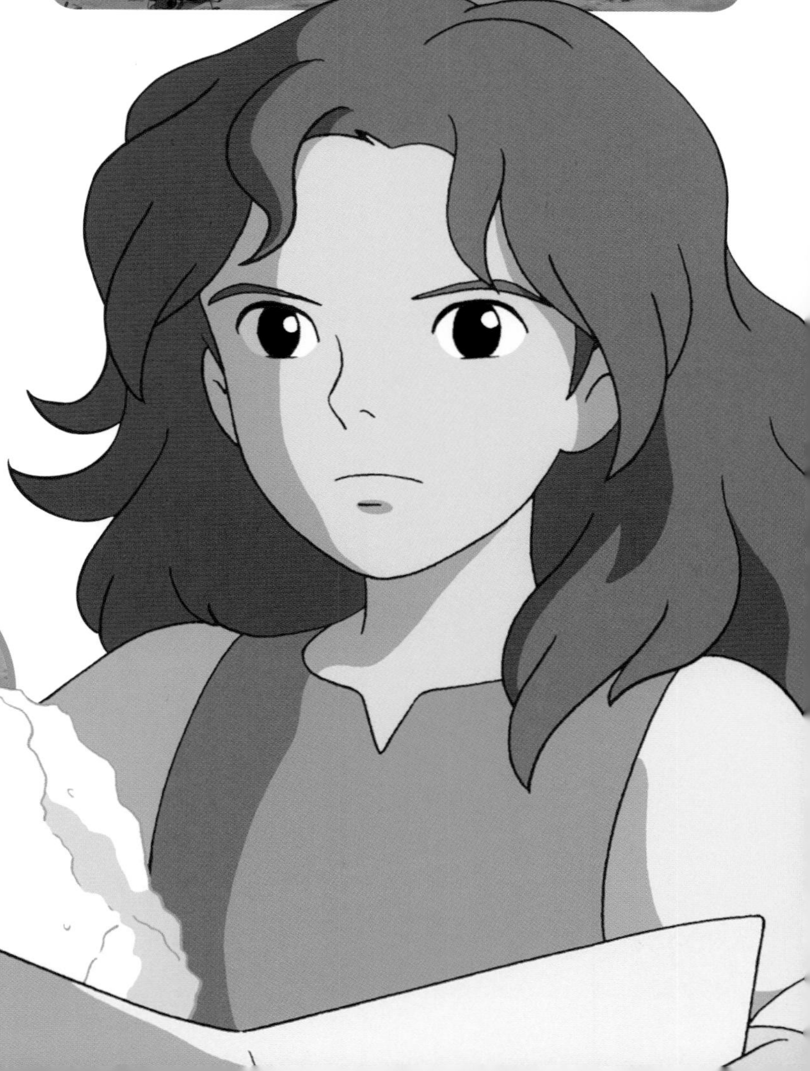

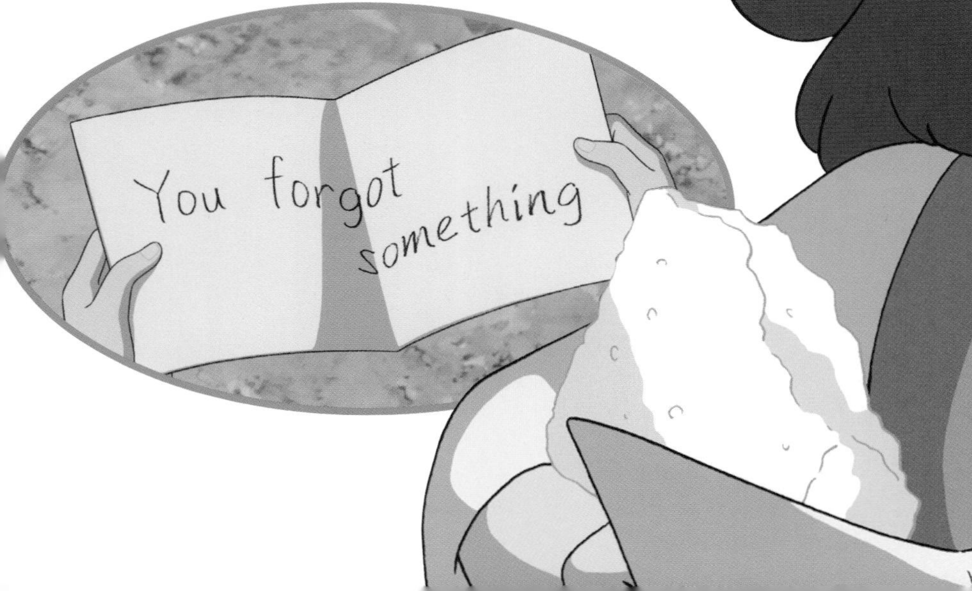
You forgot something

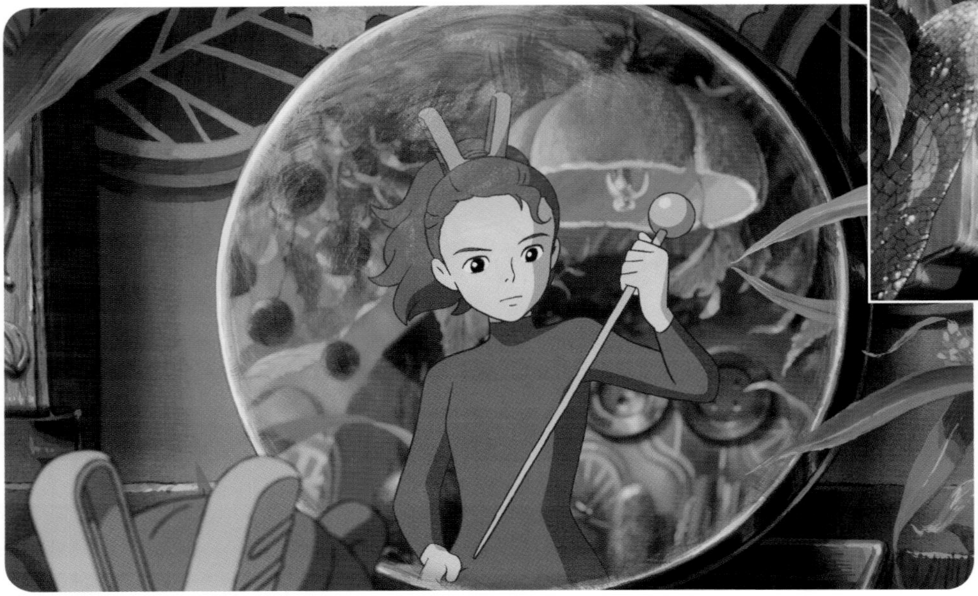

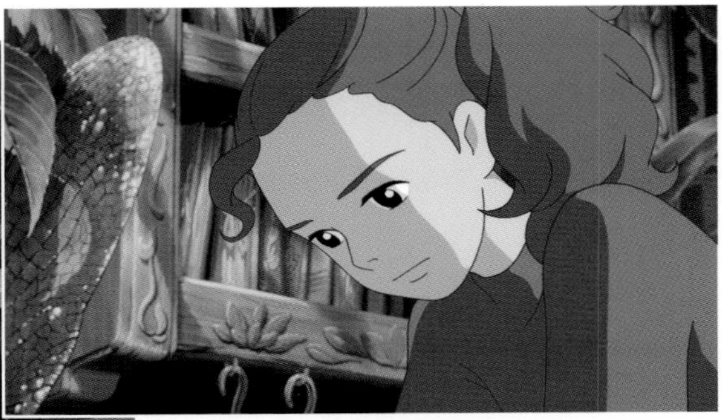

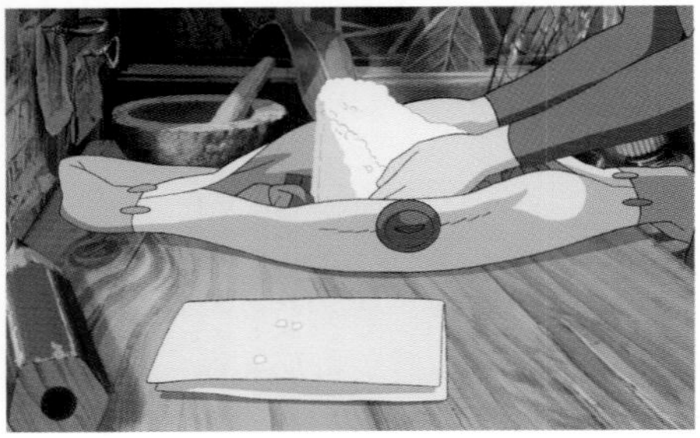

She put on her borrowing dress, fastened her hair, and prepared for her mission.

She sheathed her pin-sword at her side, placed the sugar cube in her bag, and quietly peeked in on her parents.

Homily was napping in her bedroom. Pod was busy in his workshop. Next to his worktable, a little furnace glowed red.

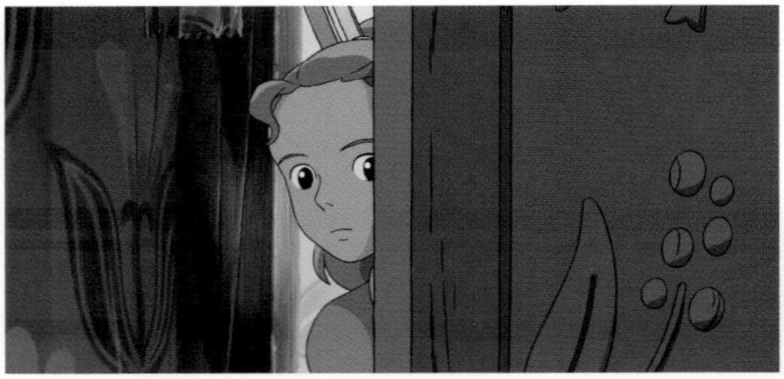

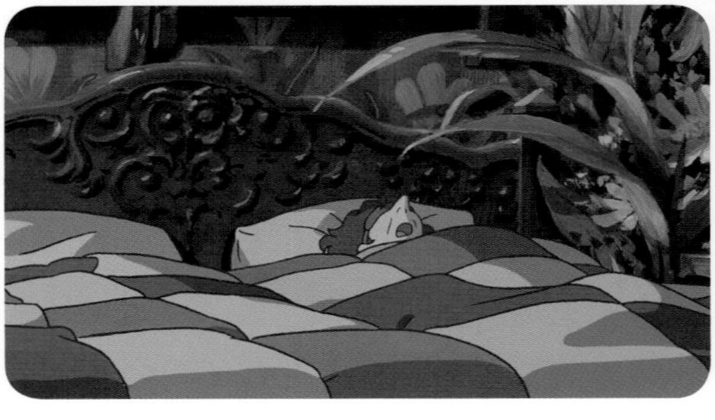

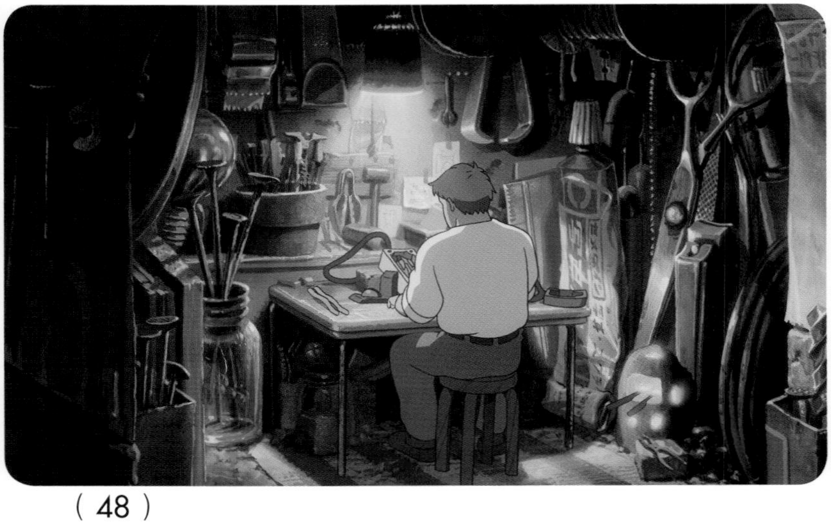

Arrietty slipped quietly out of her home and looked up at the roof.

Quickly, she climbed up the vines. Droplets of rainwater still clung to the ivy.

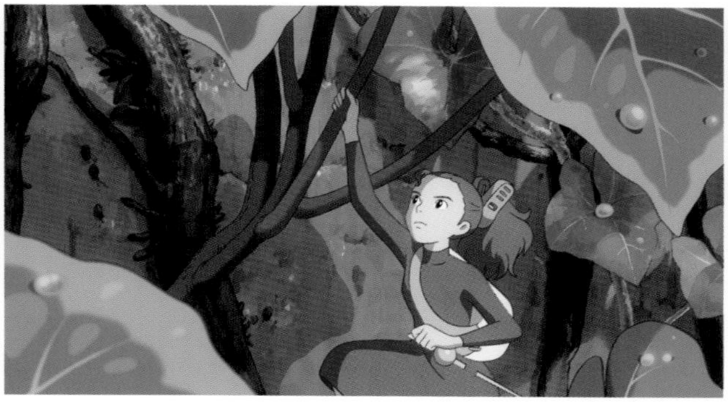

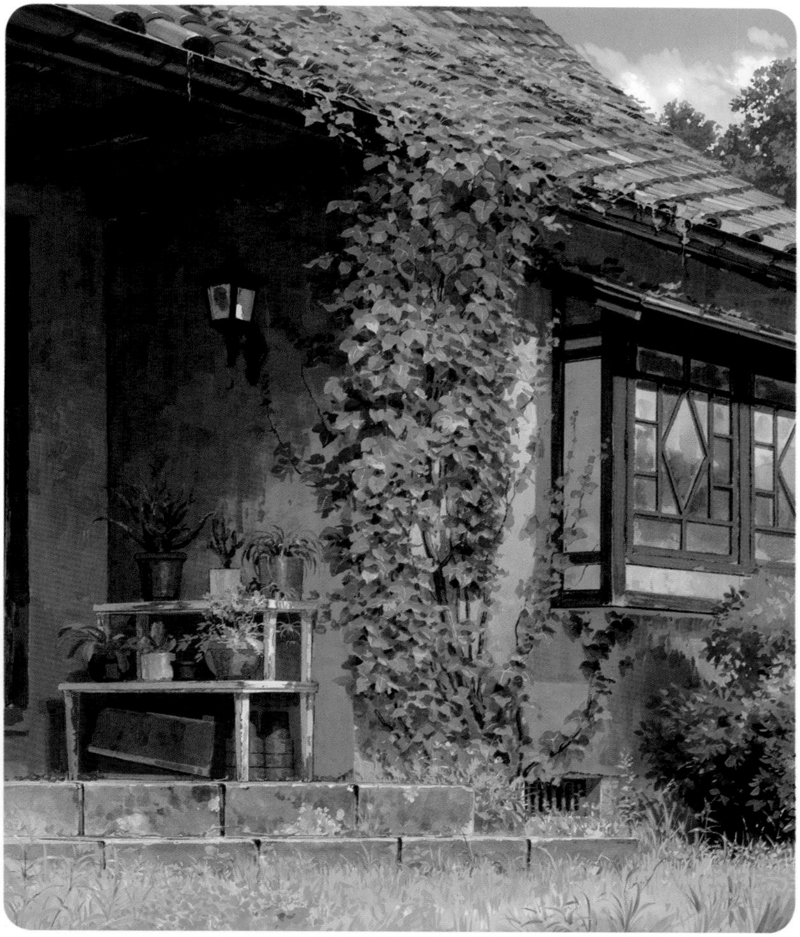

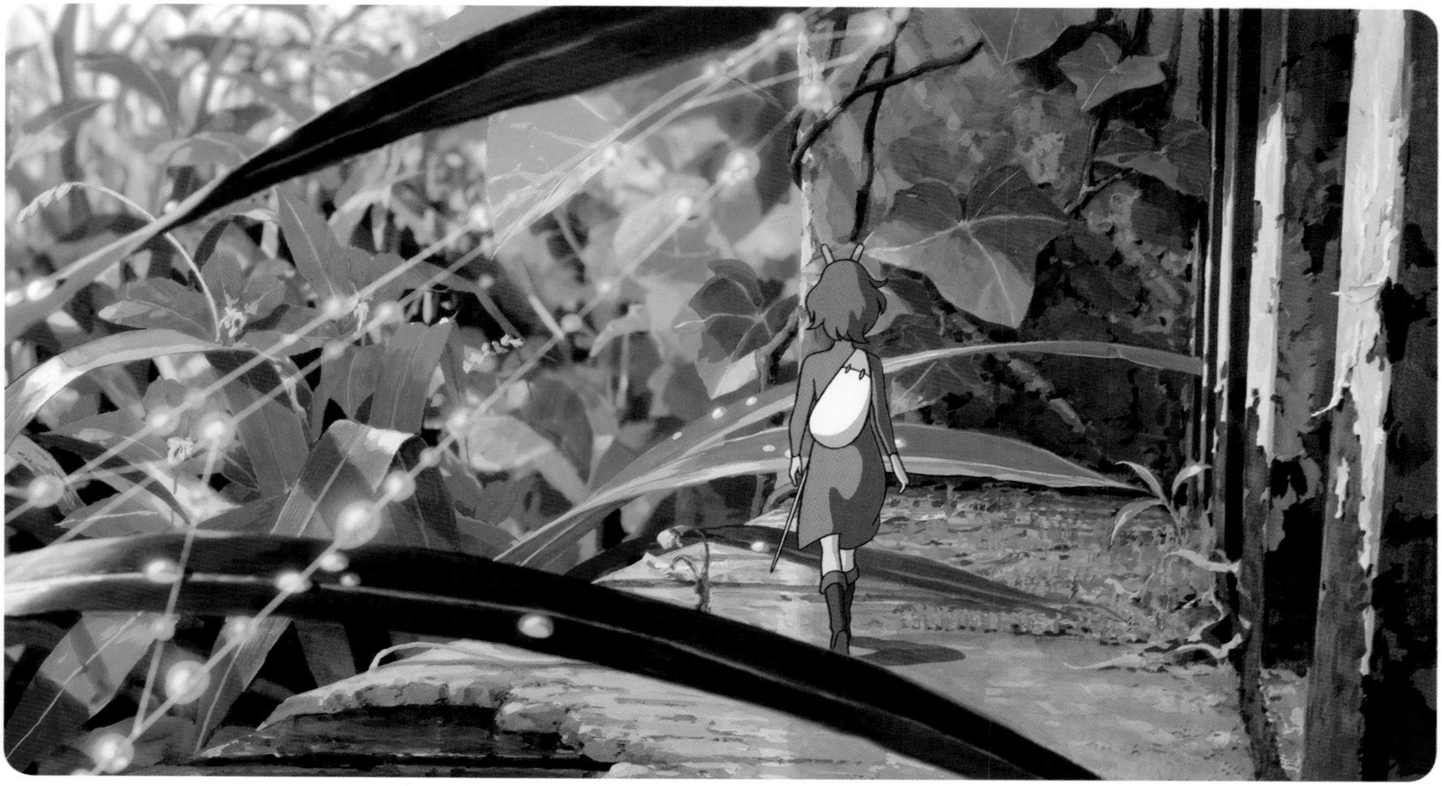

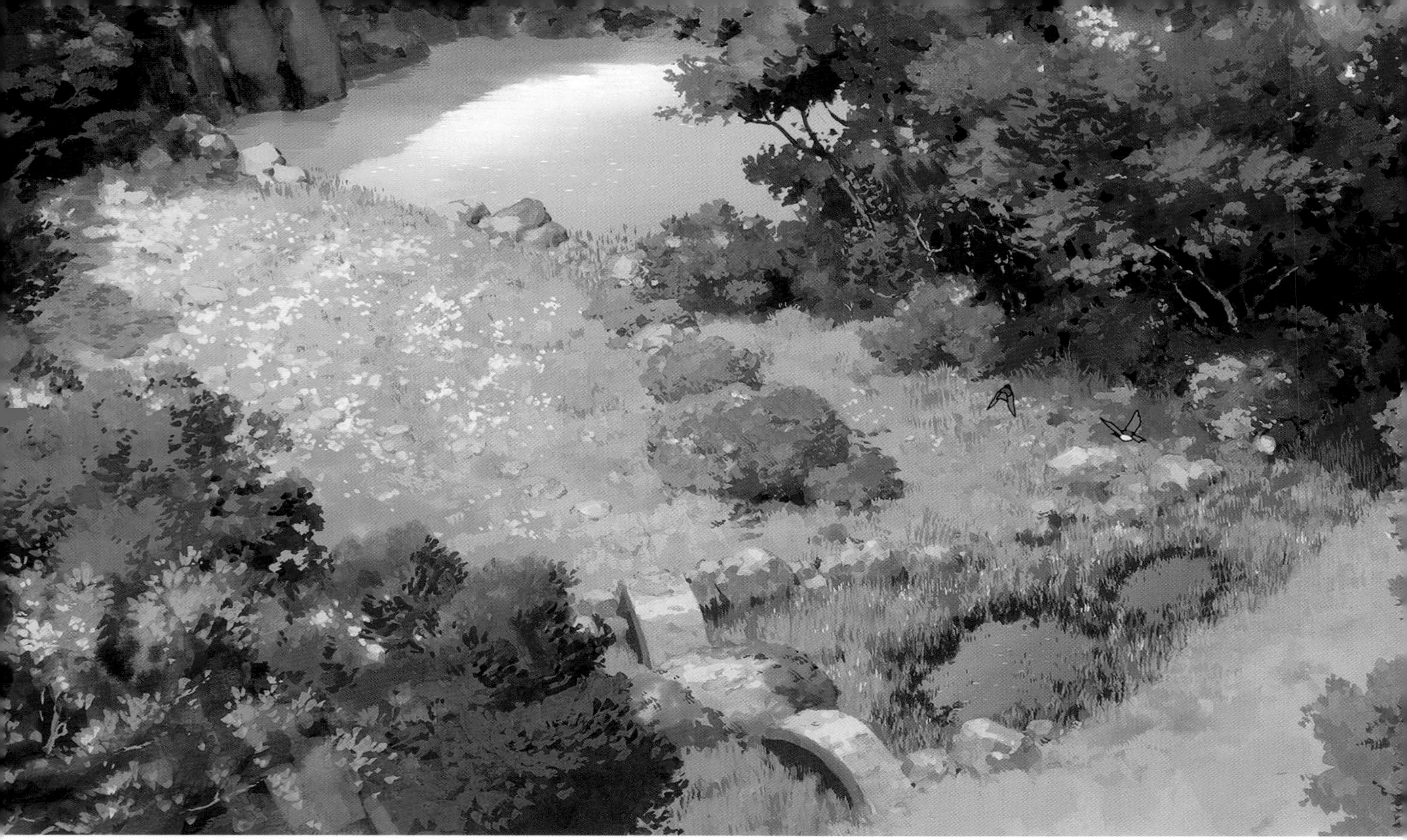

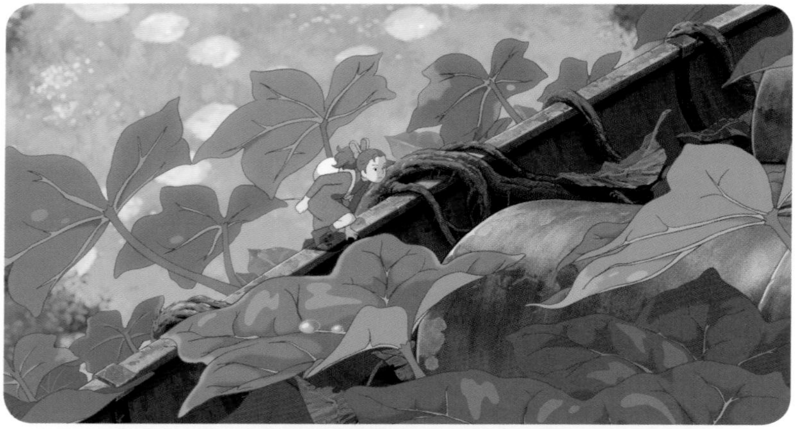

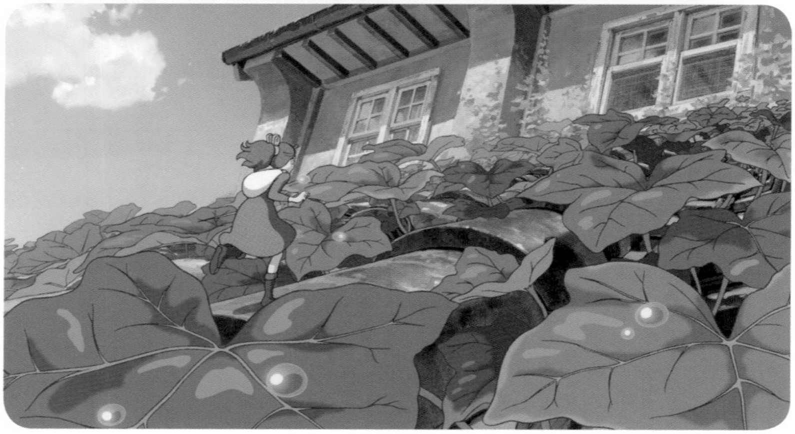

When she finally got
to the top of the roof,
Arrietty looked down at
the rain-soaked garden.
The cool breeze felt nice
on her clammy skin,
and the wet grass and
trees glittered in the sun.

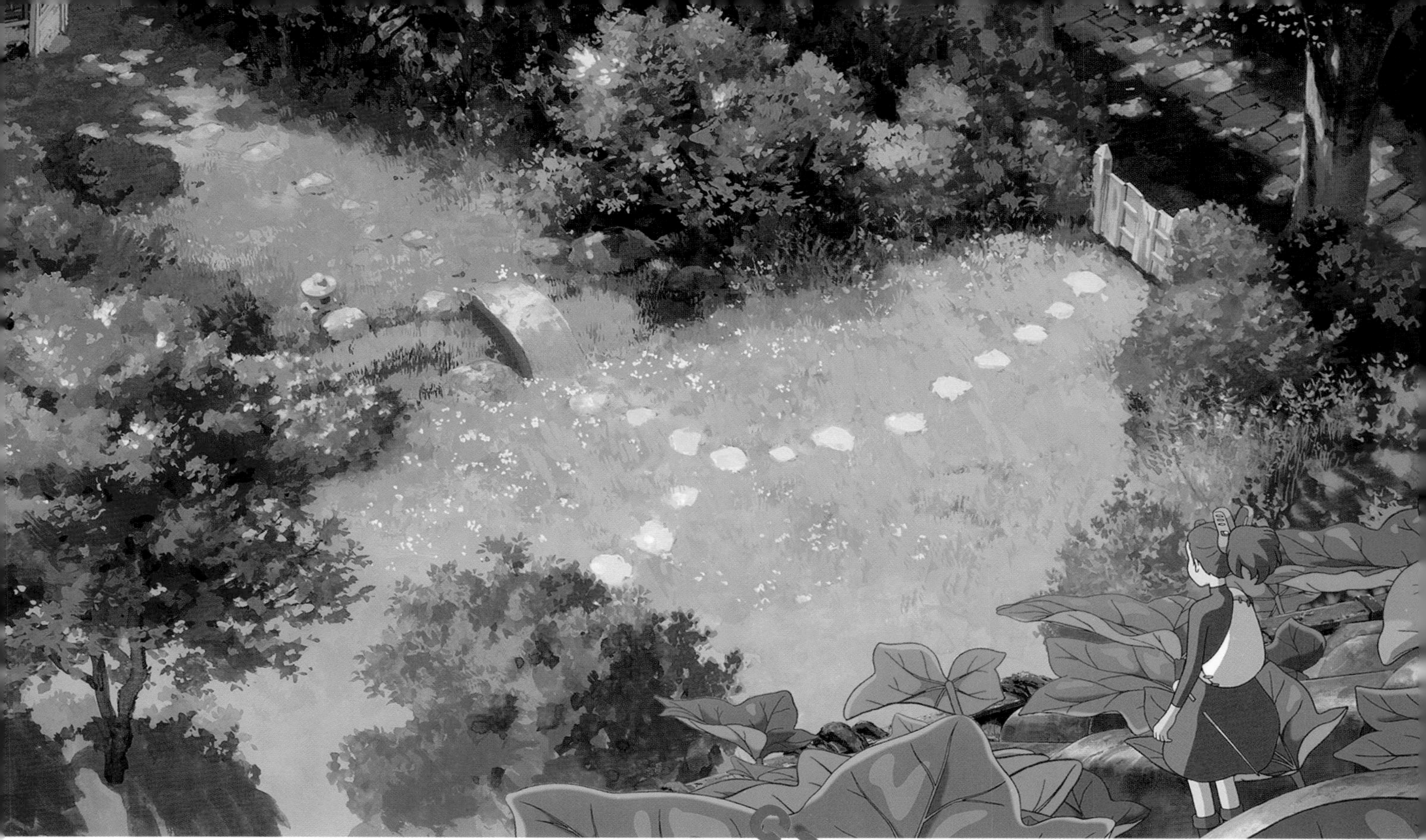

Caw, caw!

Arrietty looked up and saw a crow on a branch of a tree.

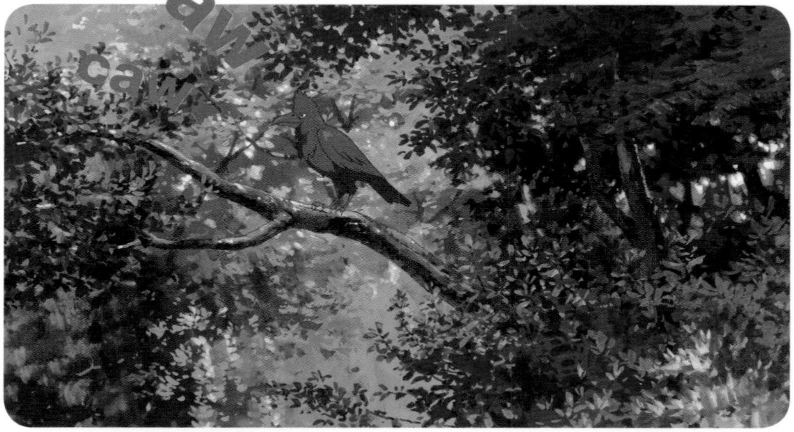
caw
caw

I have to hurry, she thought.

She climbed up onto the roof.

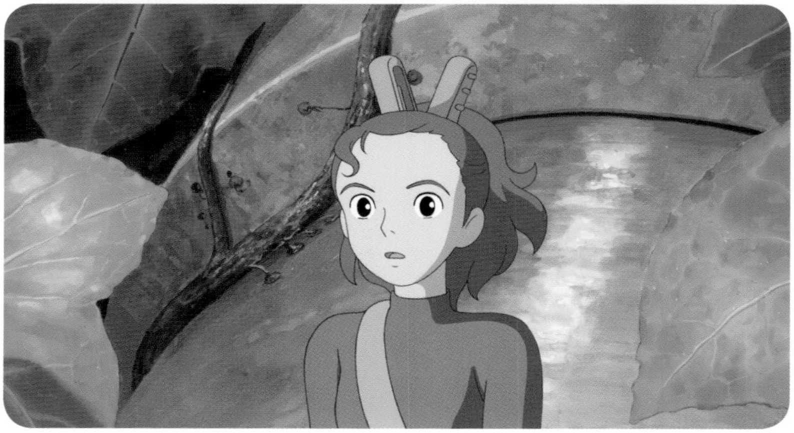

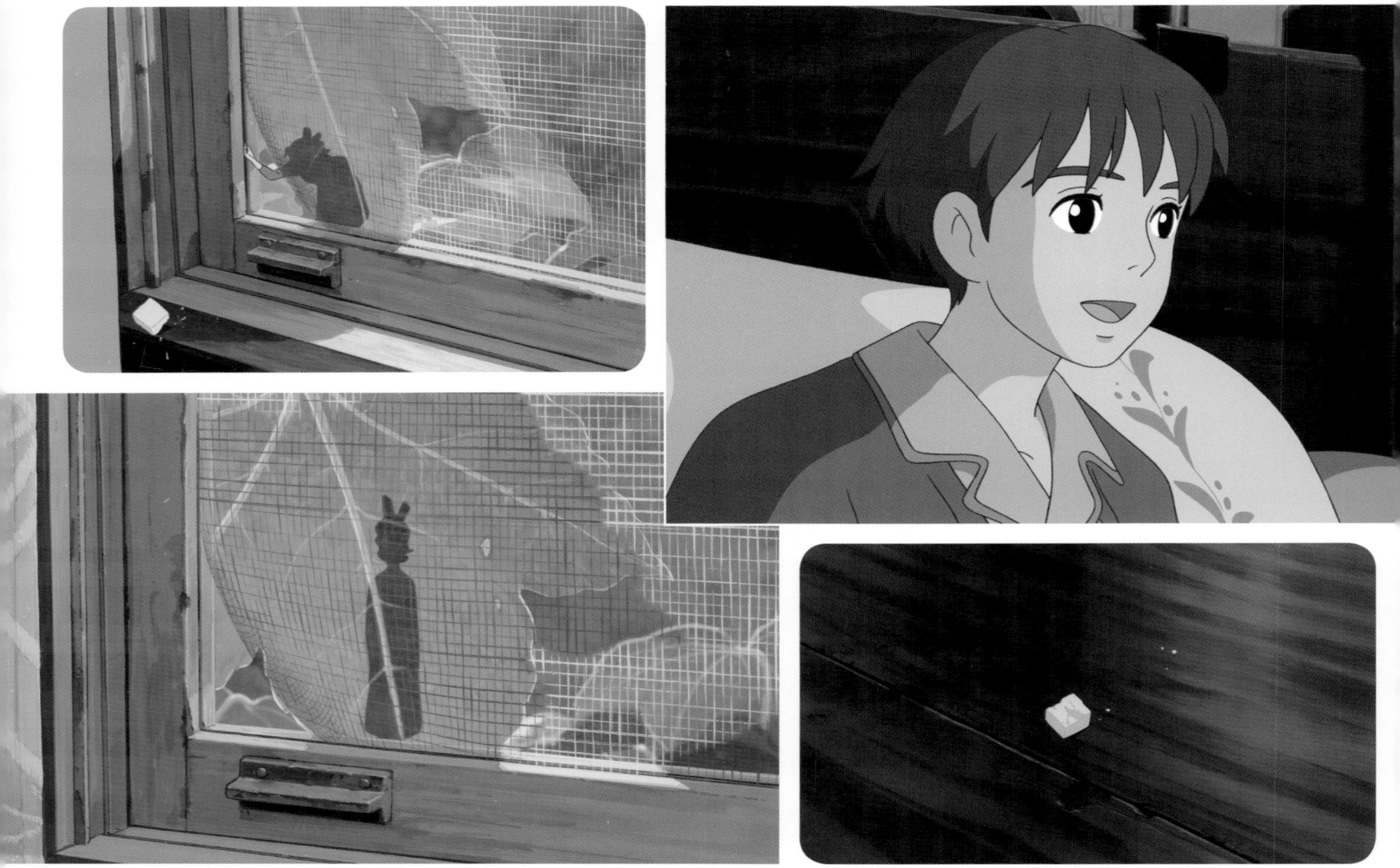

When she reached the boy's window, she tossed the sugar cube through the corner of the screen.

The boy noticed right away and leaned forward eagerly.

"Is that you from last night?" he called.

Arrietty turned to leave.

"No, wait. Don't go."

From beyond the screen Arrietty said, "Please leave us alone. We don't need your help."

“Can’t I please just talk to you?” the boy pleaded.

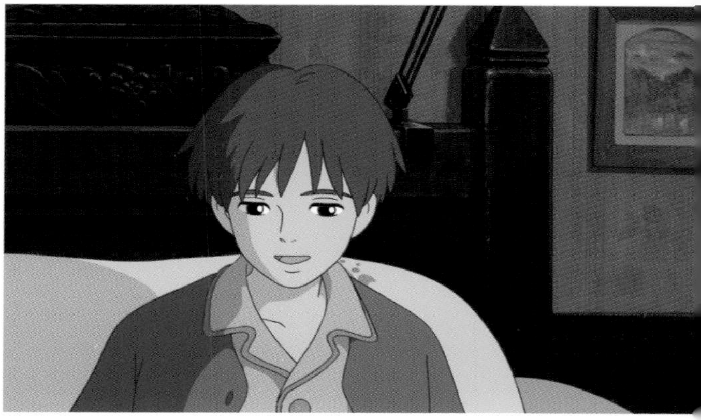

“No. Human beans are dangerous,” Arrietty replied. “Whenever we’re seen, we have to move. My parents said so.”

“So you have a family? That must be nice.”

“Don’t you have a family?”

“I have one—but they’re very busy,” the boy replied. “They sent me here so someone could take care of me.”

“I’m sorry to hear that,” Arrietty said.

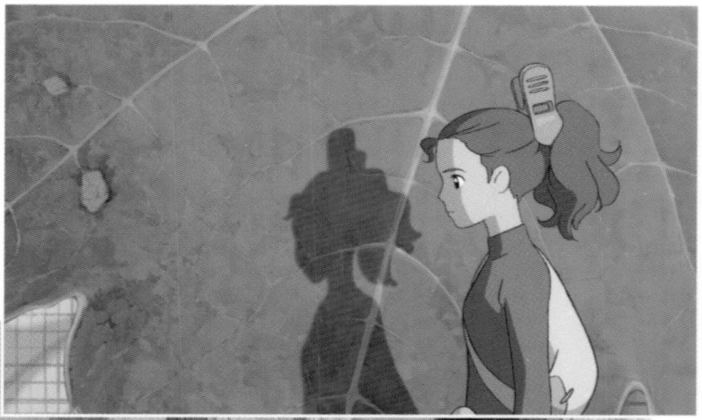

“Anyway, my name is Shawn. What’s your name?”

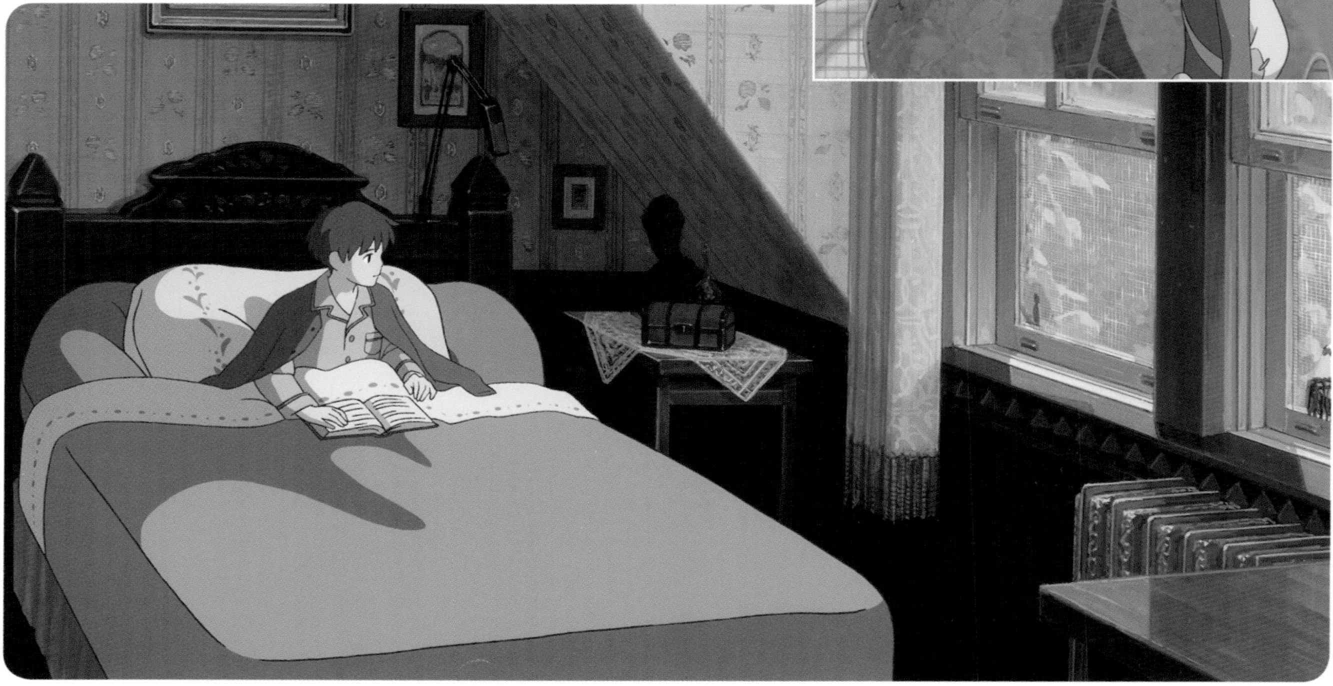

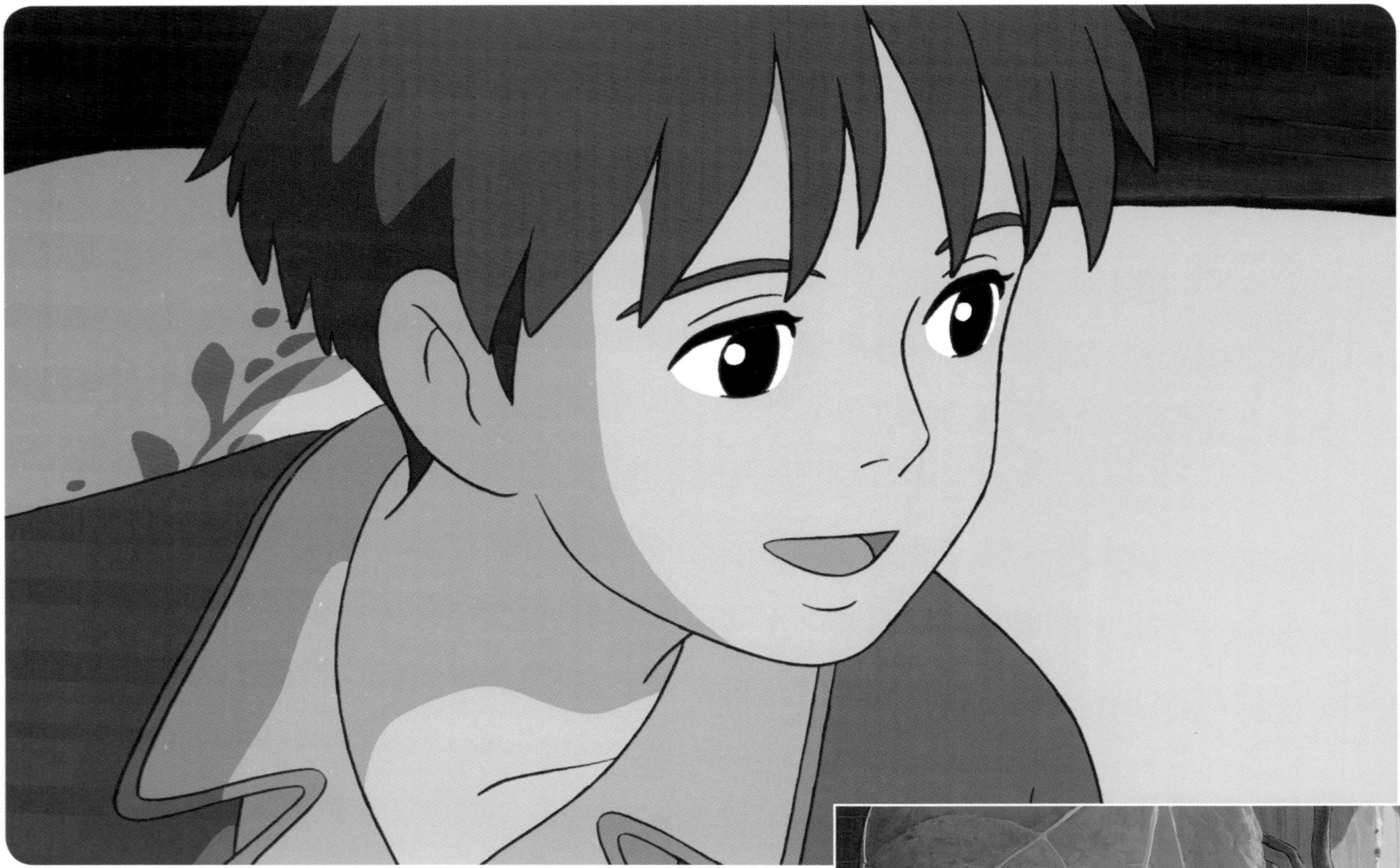

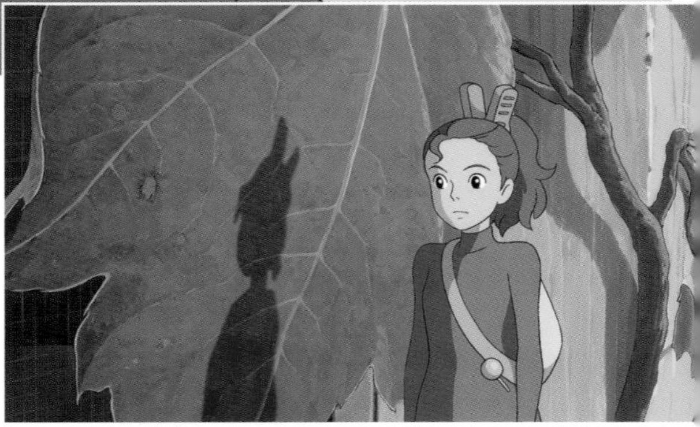

Arrietty stiffened and did not answer.

My name?

Shawn asked again,
"What do they call you?"

"Not that it's any of your business," Arrietty found herself saying, "but it's Arrietty."

"Arrietty… Arrietty… that's a beautiful name."

A beautiful name? Nobody had ever told her that before.

Arrietty did not know what to say, so she just stood there looking down.

“Could you at least come out so I can see you?” Shawn asked.

Arrietty was surprised. She shook her head no.

“I won’t hurt you, I promise.”

Arrietty hesitated but Shawn’s sincerity drew her in. She stepped forward.

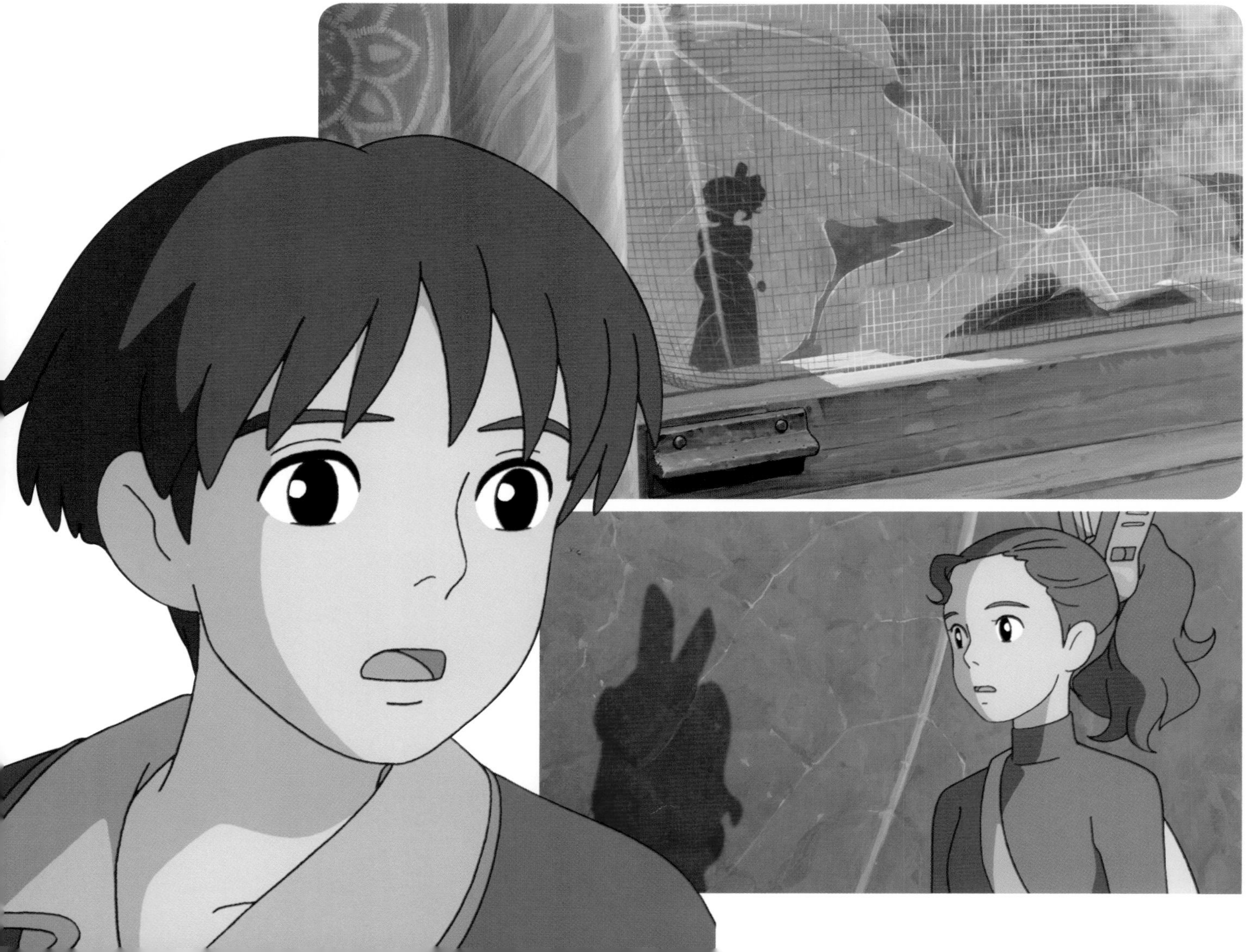

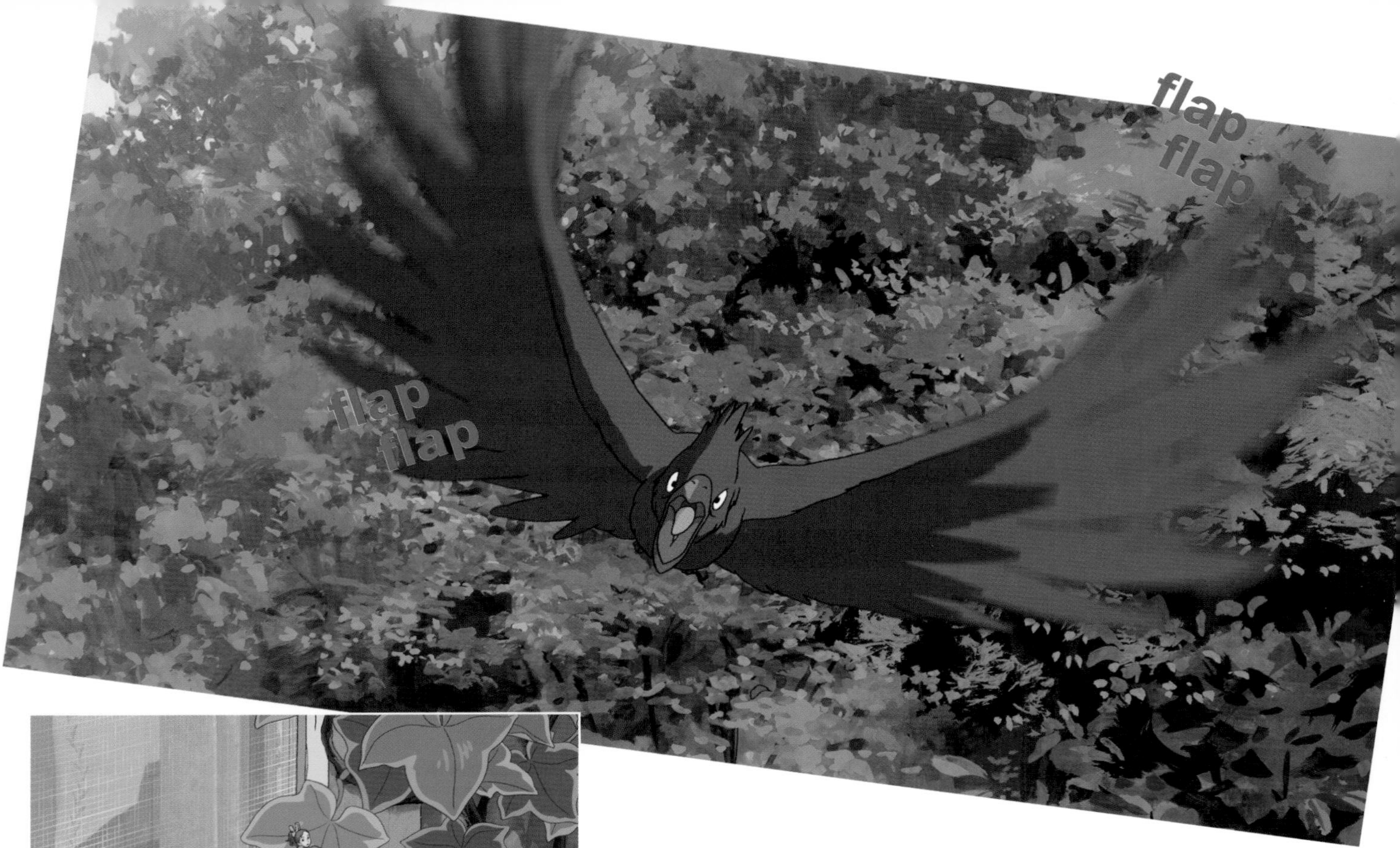
flap
flap
flap
flap

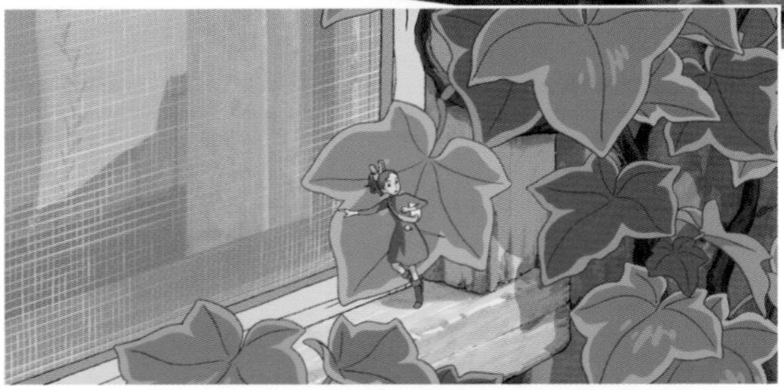

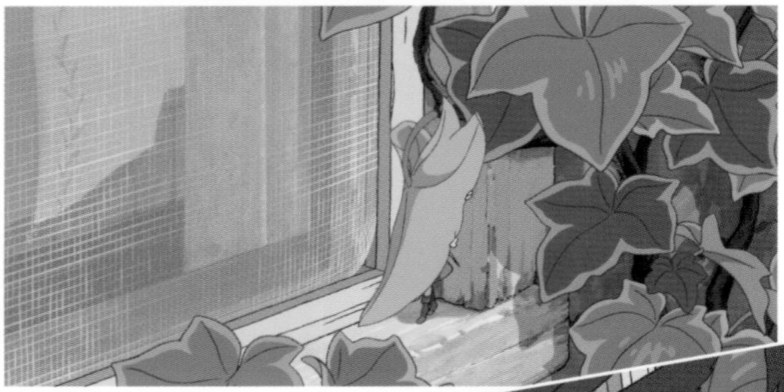

Suddenly the crow came flying toward her!

Arrietty shielded herself with an ivy leaf and the crow flew headfirst into the screen.

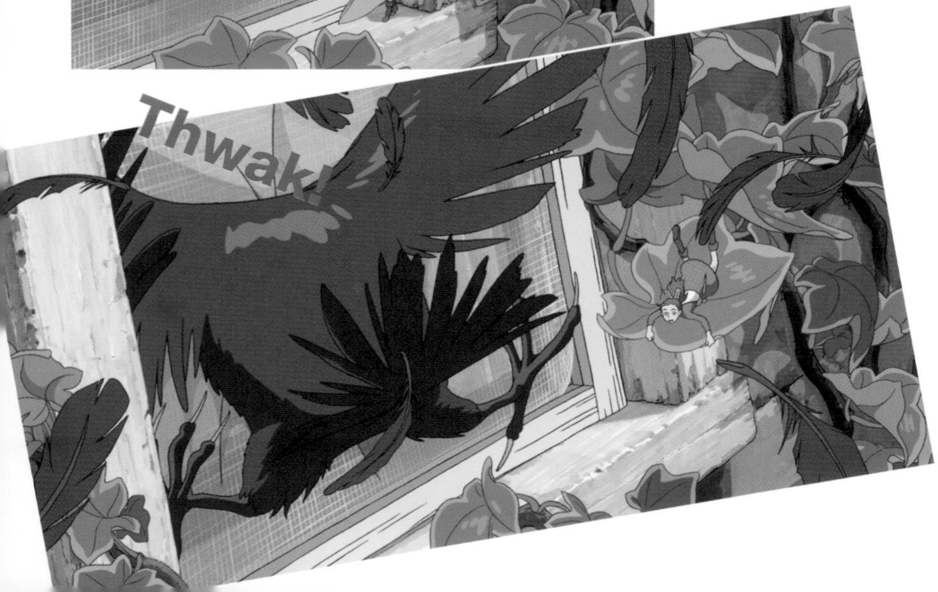
Thwak!

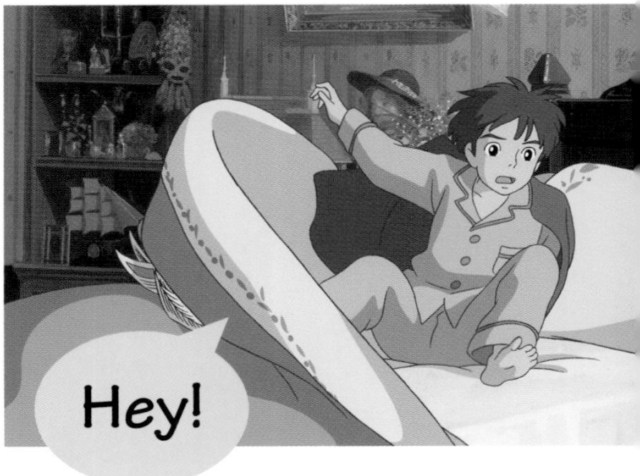
Hey!

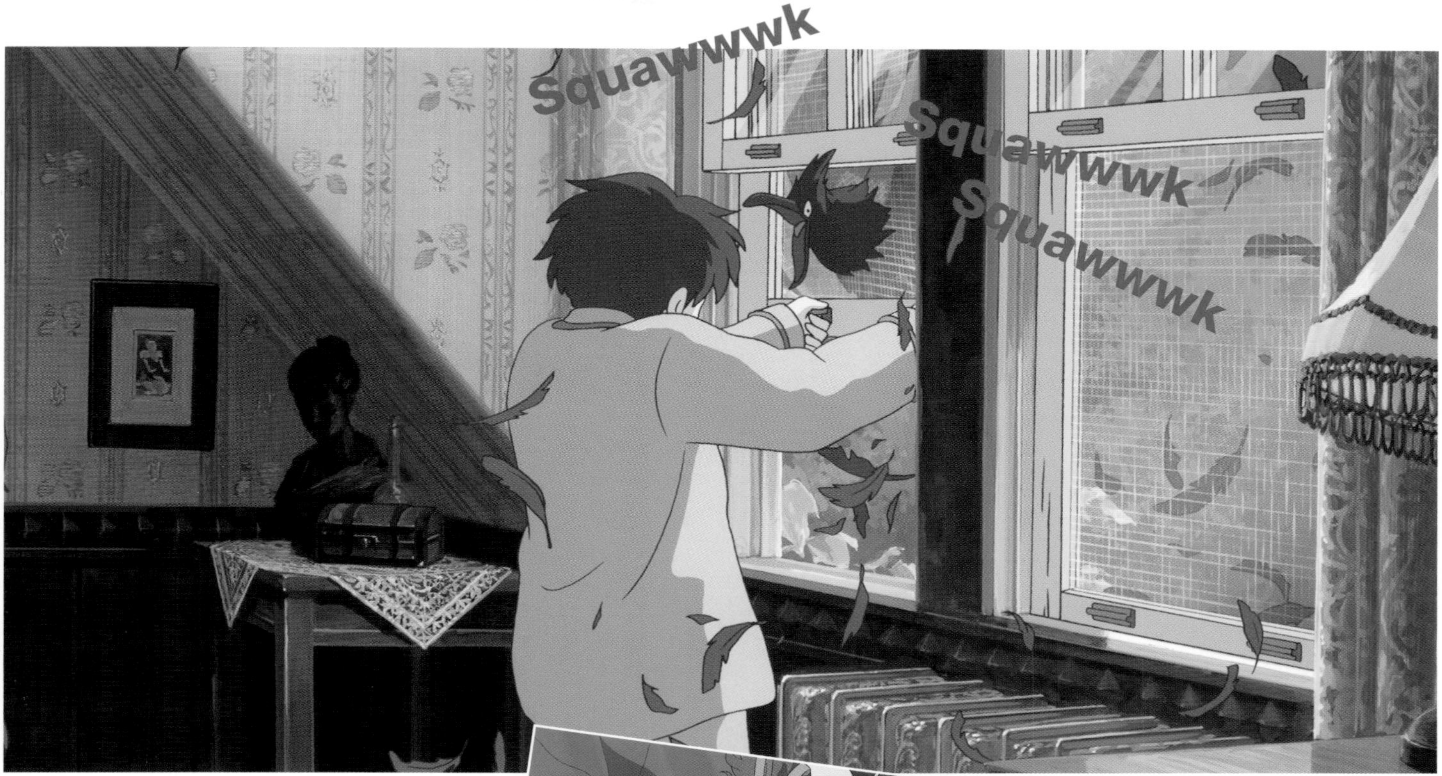
Squawwwk
Squawwwk
Squawwwk

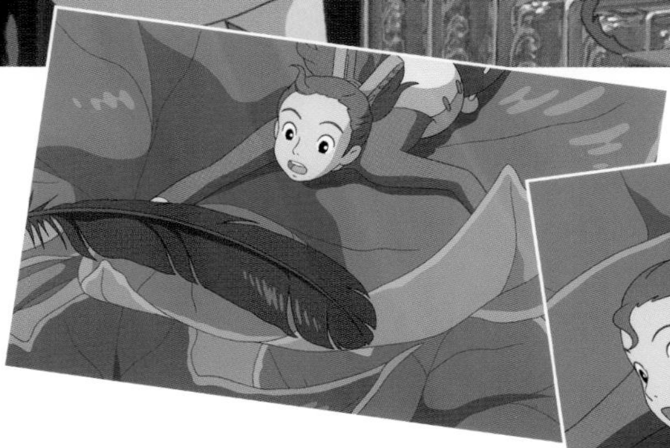

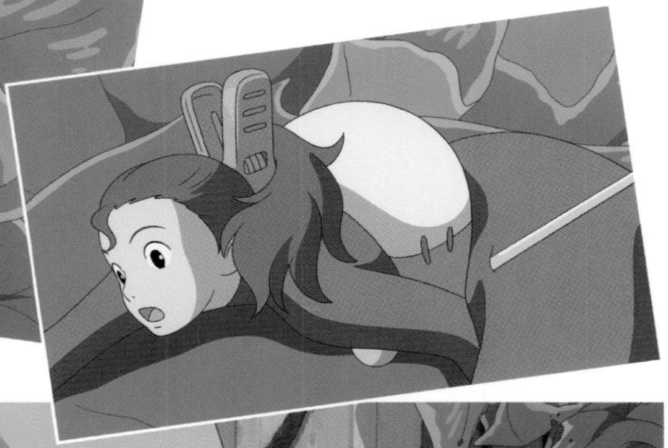

Flap flap, flap flap!

The crow squawked and struggled wildly to free its head. Arrietty could barely hold on to the ledge.

Shawn leapt off his bed, raised the screen, and grabbed Arrietty, leaf and all.

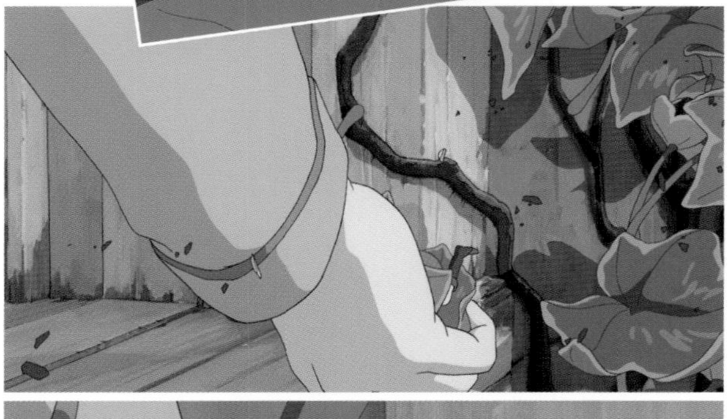

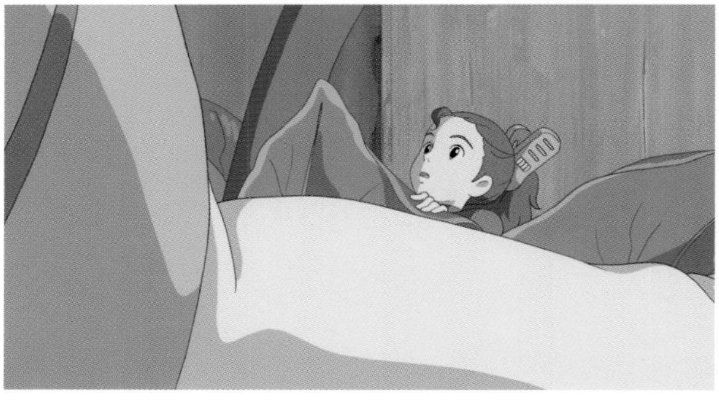

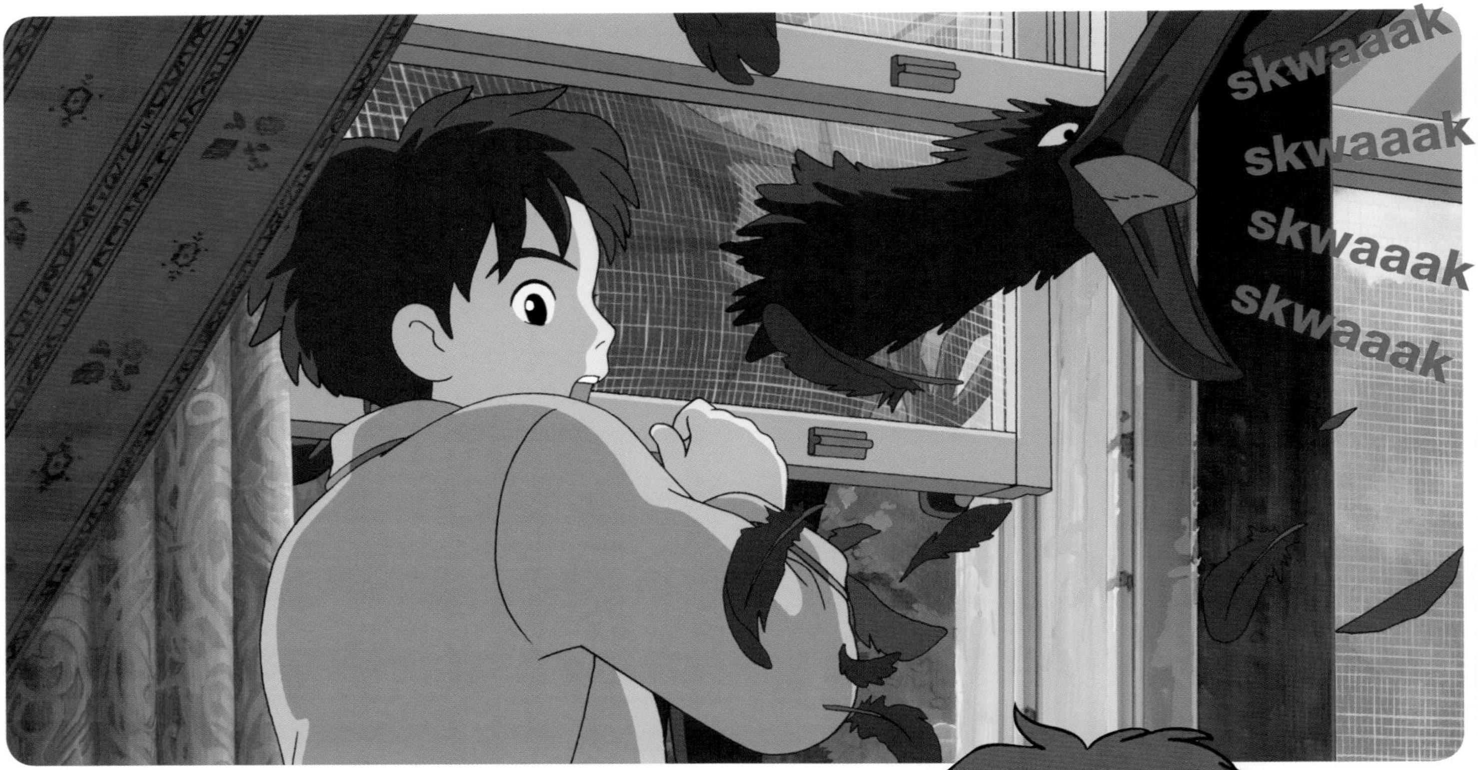
skwaaak
skwaaak
skwaaak
skwaaak

"What in the world?" Hara cried. She had come running when she heard the commotion. "Aack! A crow!" she screamed in surprise.

Shawn quickly tore the leaf wrapped around Arrietty off the vine.

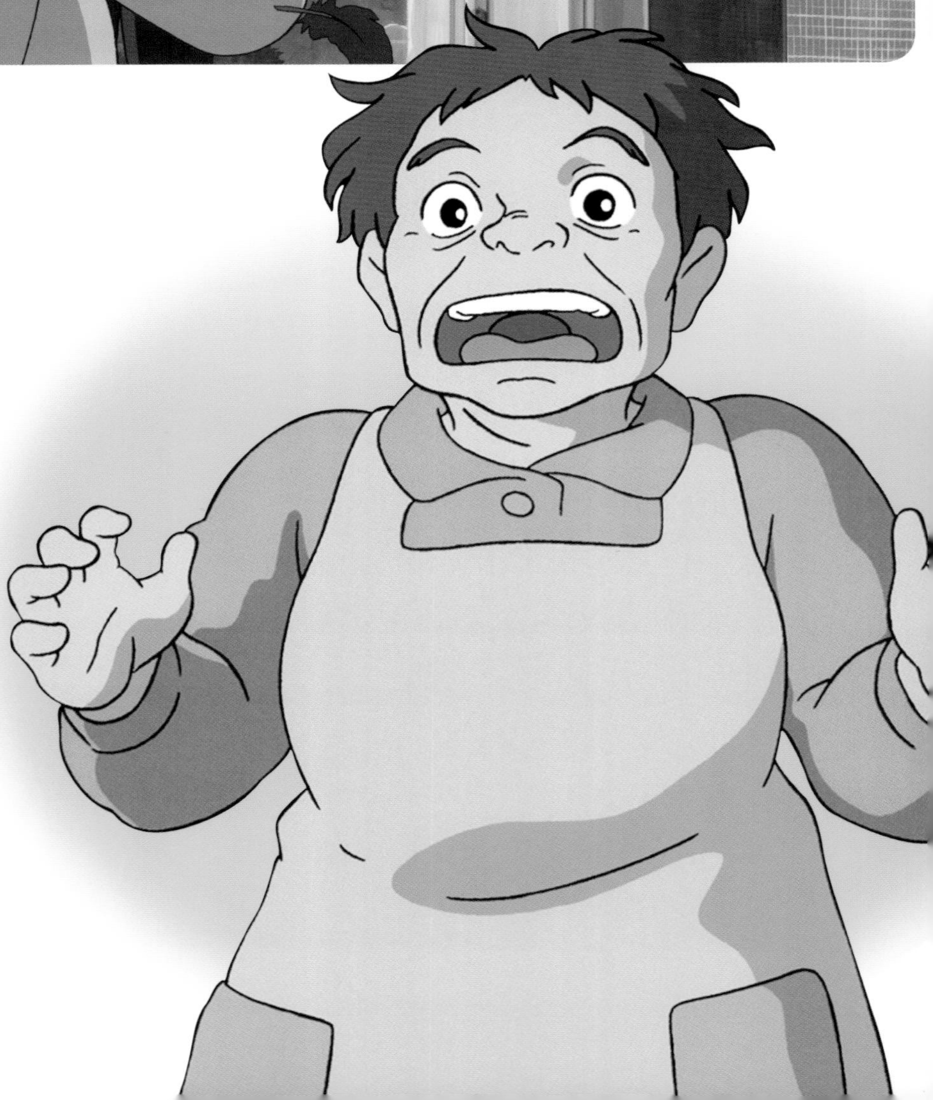

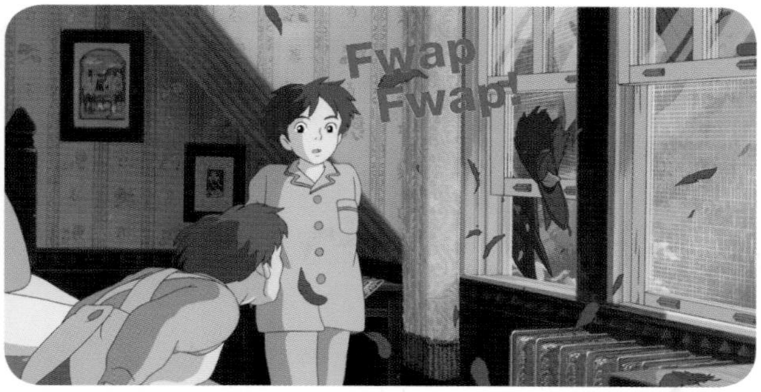
Fwap
Fwap!

As Hara ran to the window, Shawn hid Arrietty behind his back.

Whap! Whap!

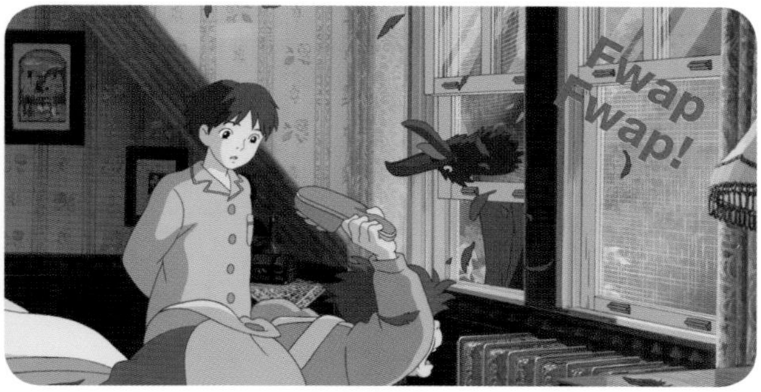
Fwap
Fwap!

Hara hit the crow as hard as she could with her slipper.

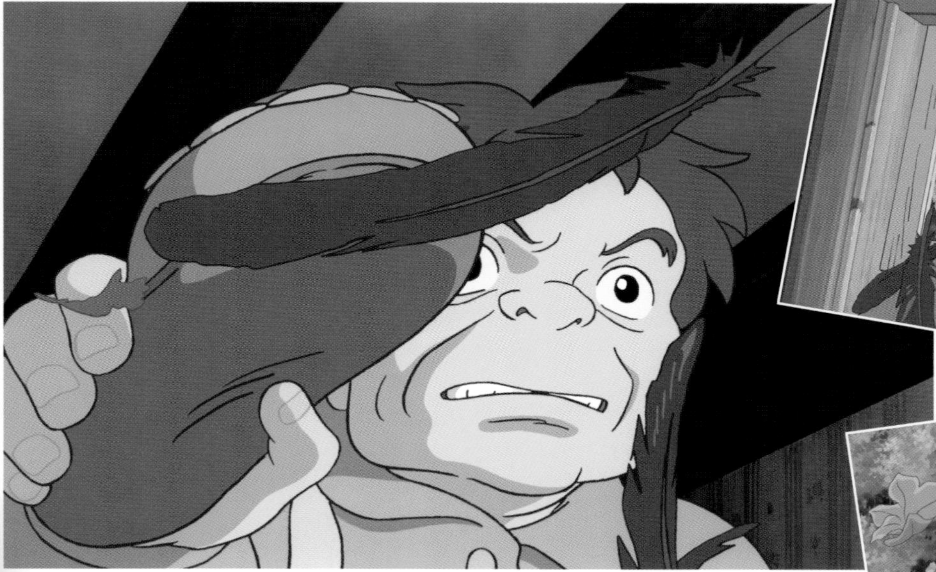

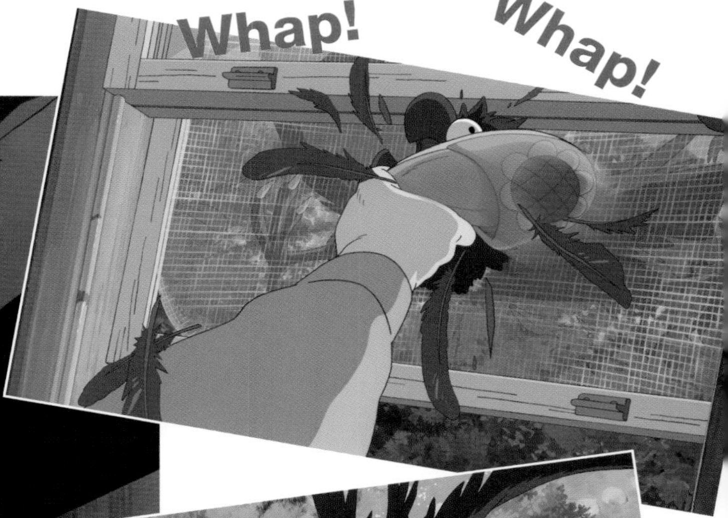
Whap!
Whap!

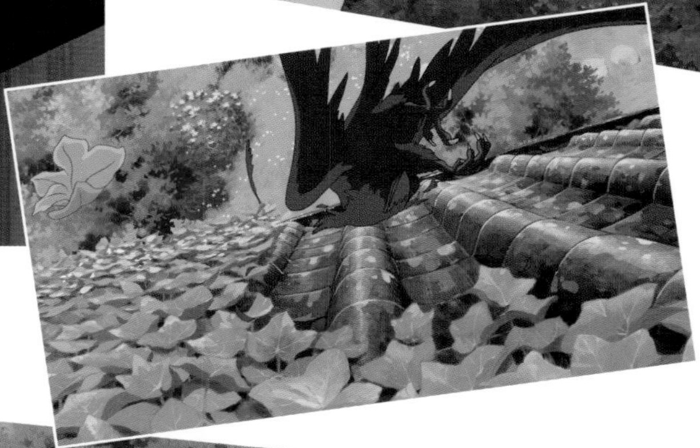

Whap, whap, whap!

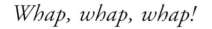

Finally the crow broke free of the screen, tumbled down the roof, and flew away.

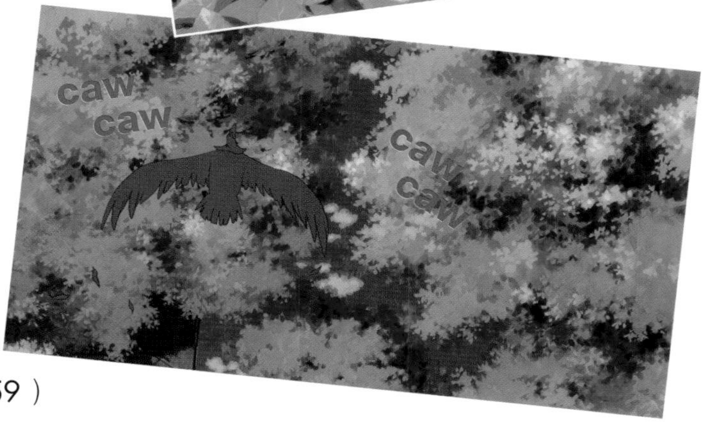
caw
caw
caw
caw

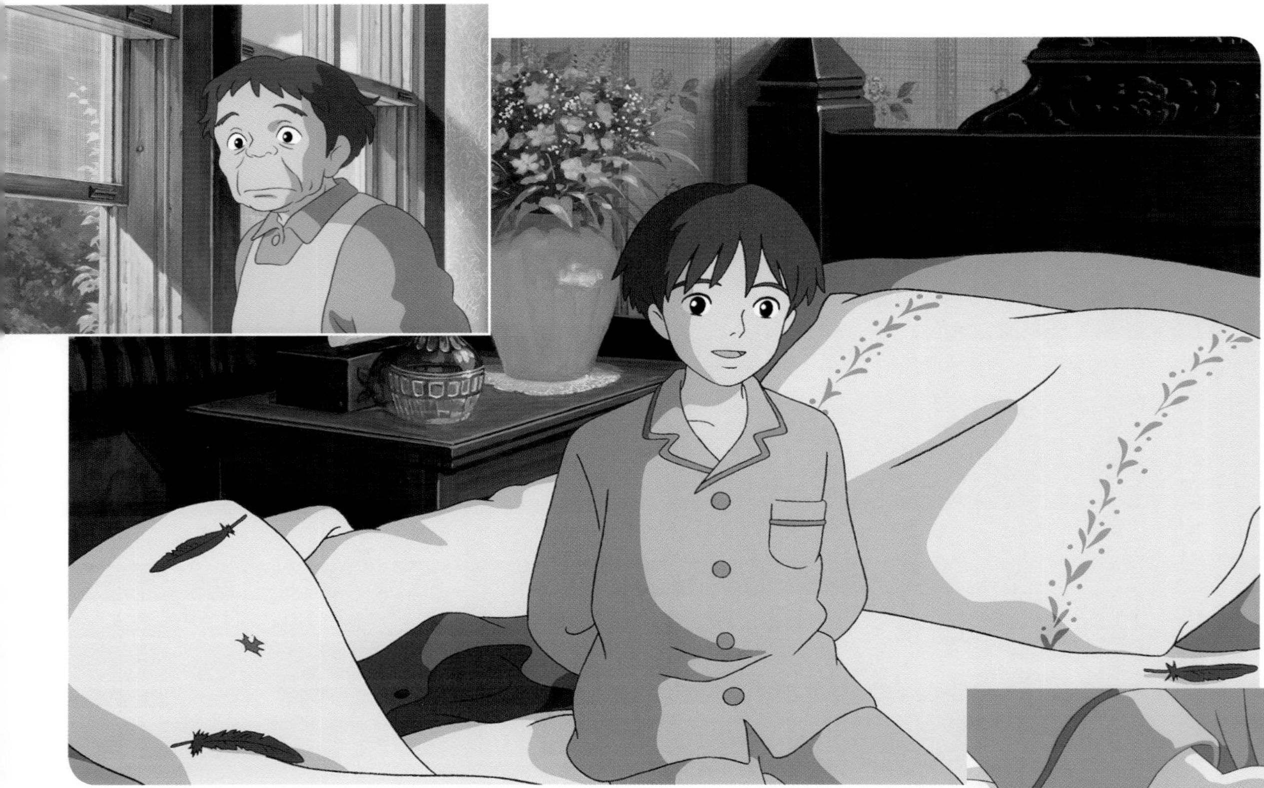
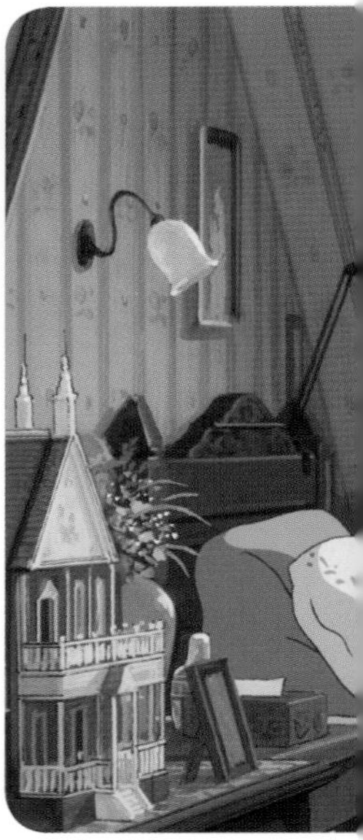
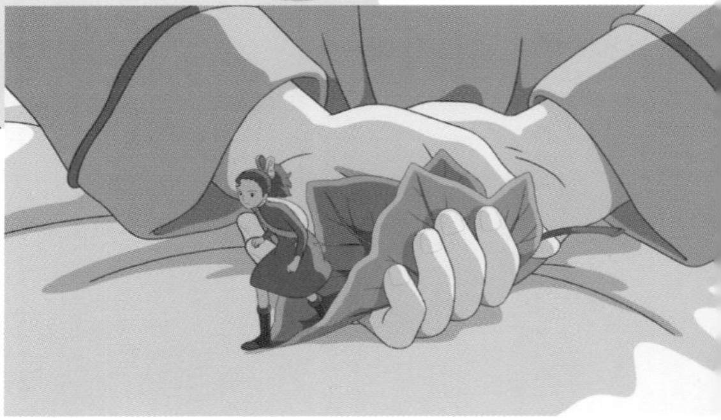

"What got into that bird?" Hara wondered. "Don't think I've ever seen one behave like that."

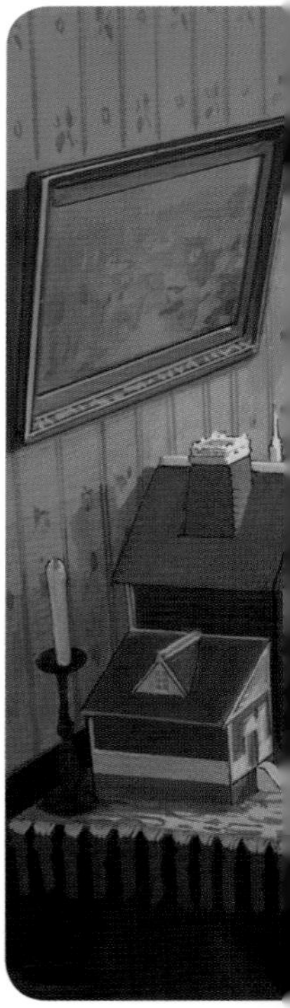

"Maybe it's nesting season or something," Shawn said as he sat on his bed, trying to act casual.

"Look at the holes in this screen," Hara muttered.

"Oh my goodness, are you all right?" she said, turning back to Shawn. "Should I get your medicine?"

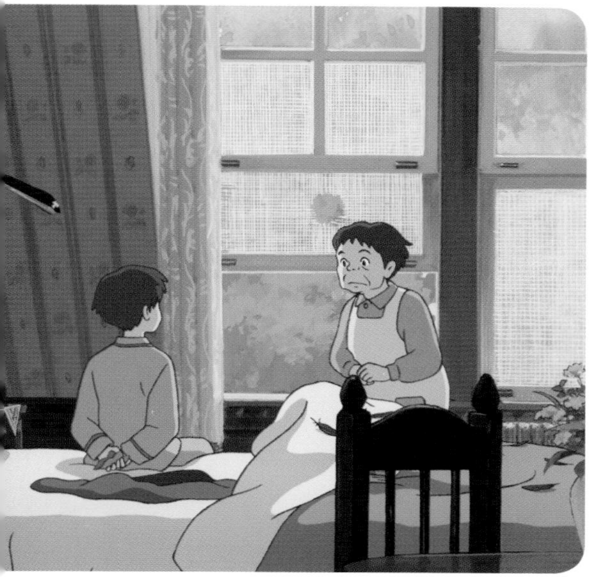

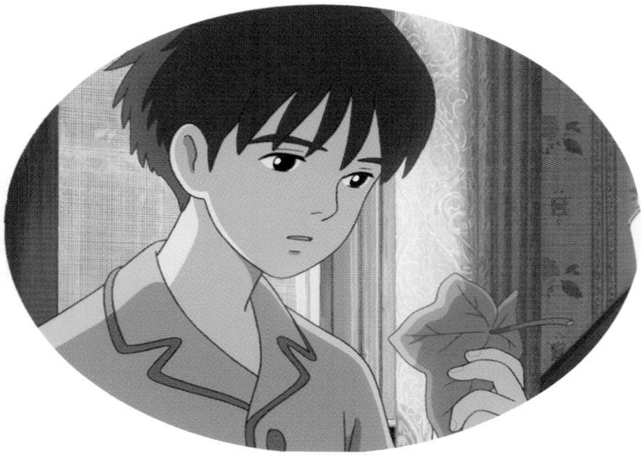

"No, that's okay, Ms. Hara," Shawn replied. "I'm actually feeling pretty good."

"Nesting season?" Hara grumbled. "Hmph."

"Well, Shawn. You have a nice long rest, now." Hara continued eyeing Shawn suspiciously. Then she left the room.

Relieved, Shawn looked into his hand. Arrietty was gone. Only the leaf remained.

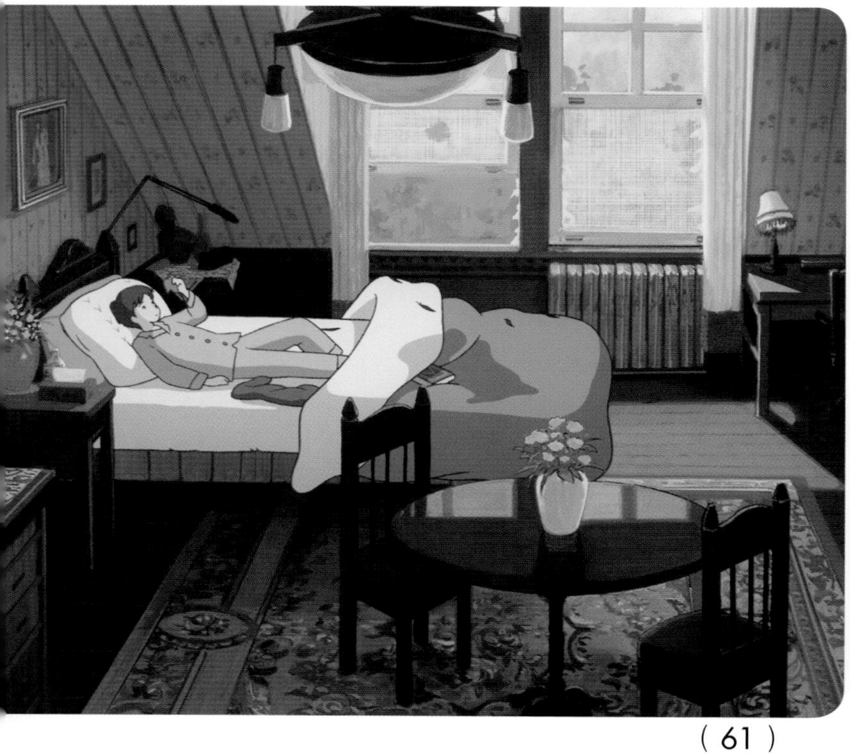

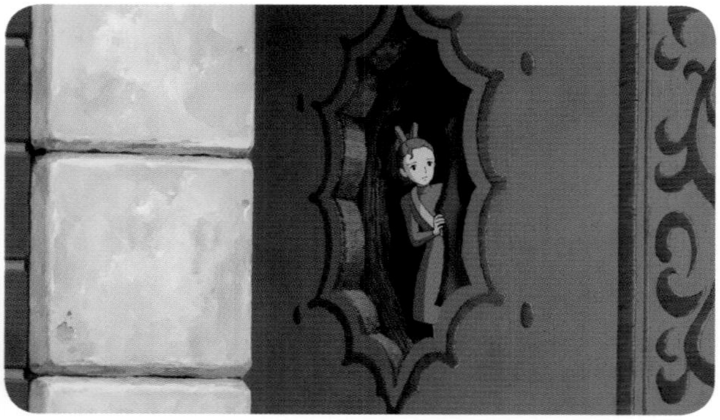

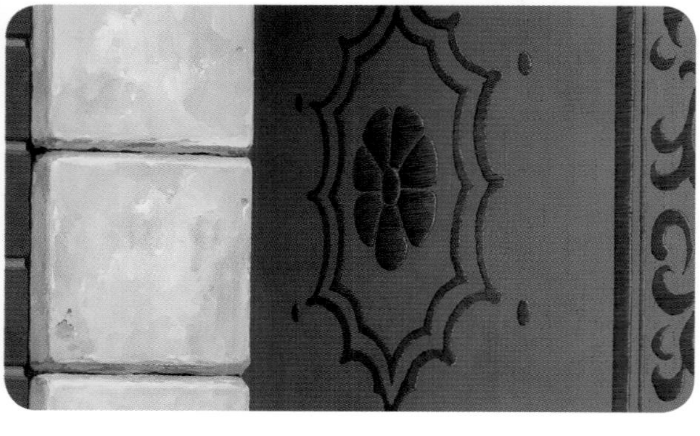

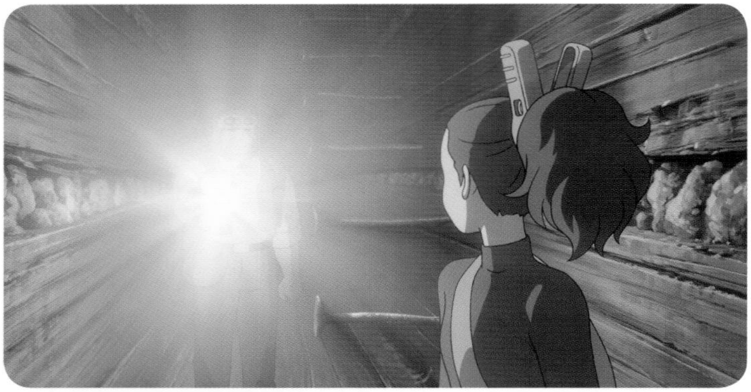

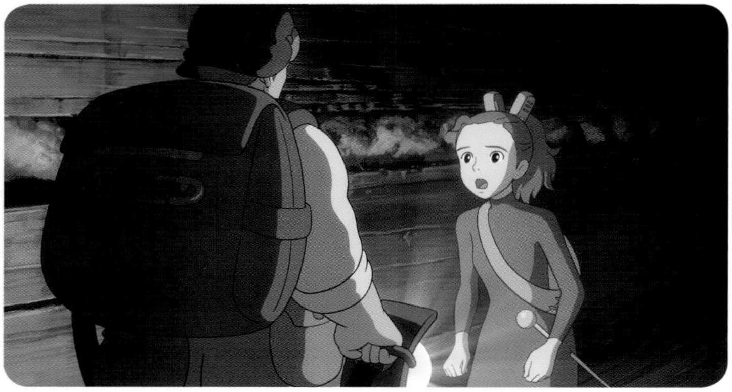

Arrietty crept through a hole in the wall and trudged down the dark stairs just as she had done the night before. Suddenly a light shone behind her.

It was Pod.

“I understand you visited the young bean,” he said.

“I’m sorry.” Arrietty said. “I went to ask him to leave us alone. But I really don’t think he intends to hurt us!”

“Many Borrowers have lost their lives thinking the same thing.

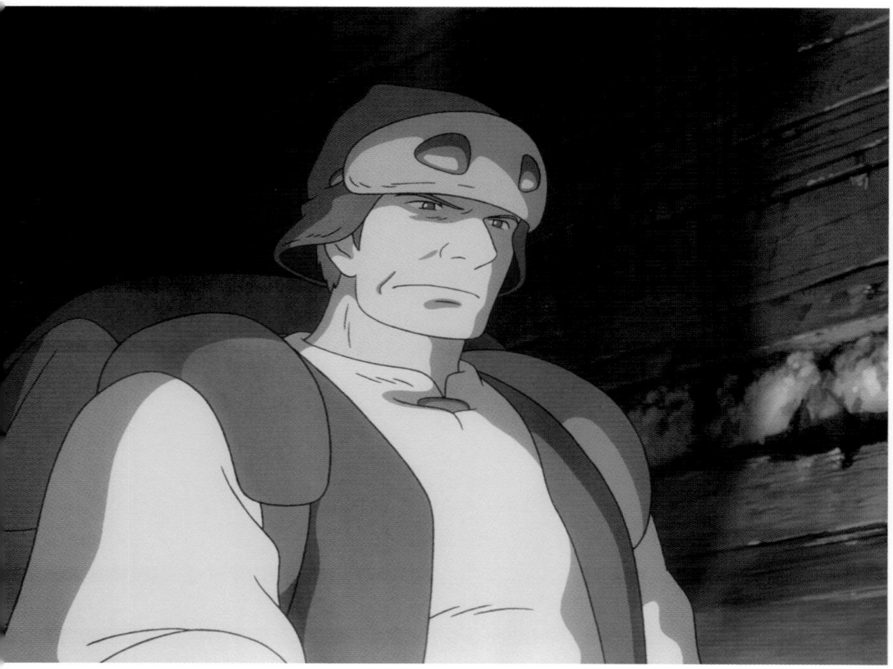

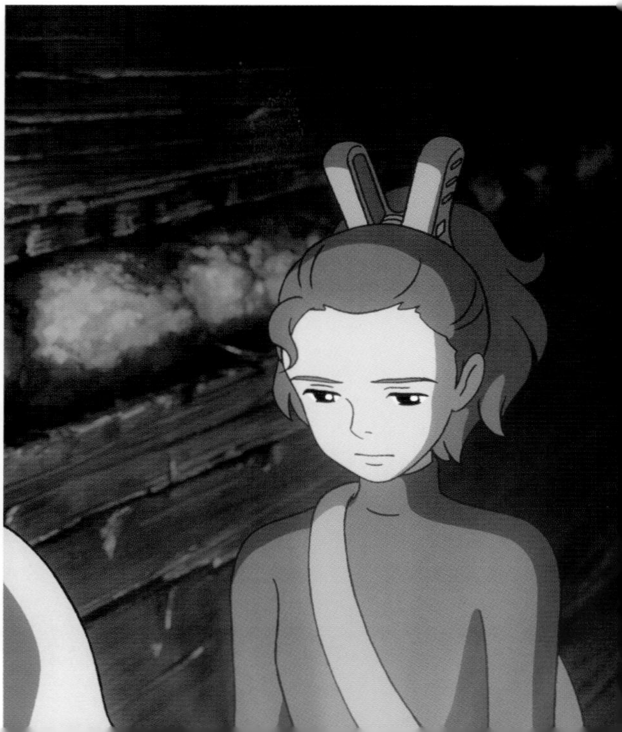

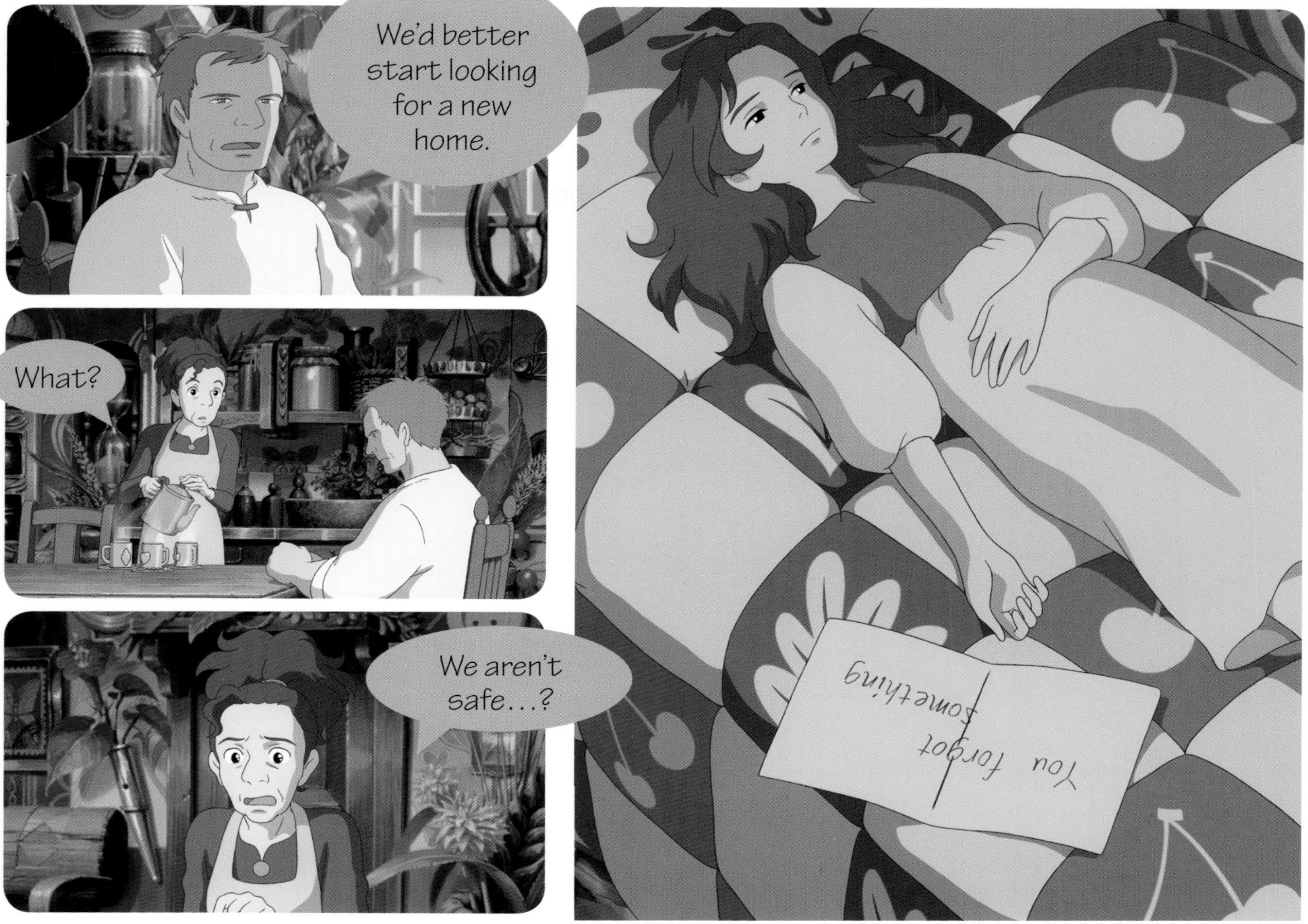
We'd better start looking for a new home.
What?
We aren't safe...?
You forgot something

"This must never happen again, Arrietty! Do you understand me?!" said Pod sternly.

"Yes, Papa," Arrietty said, hanging her head.

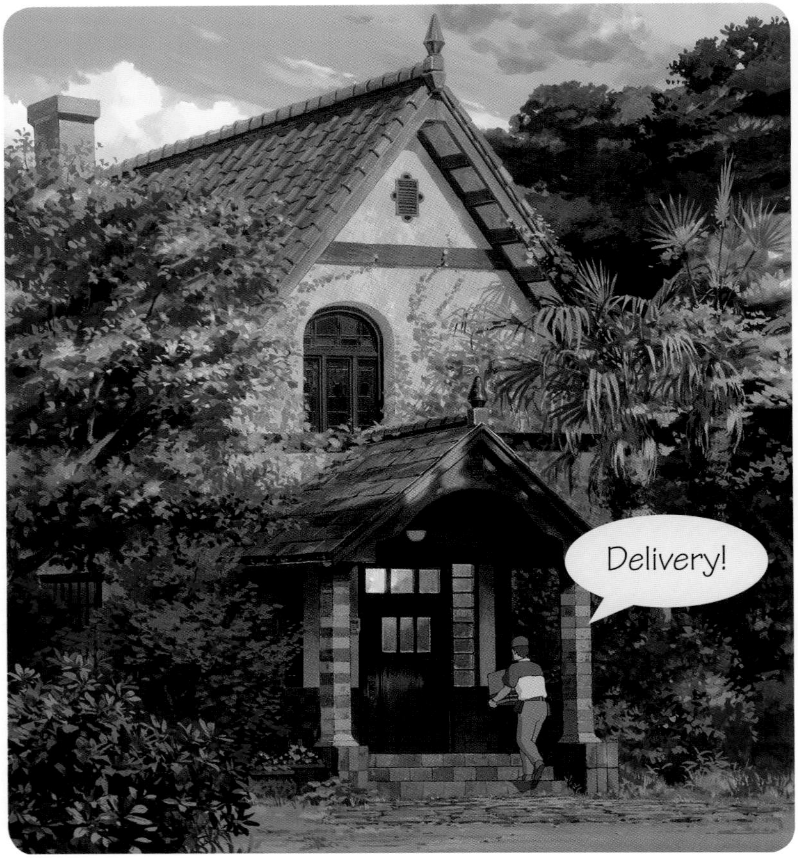
Delivery!

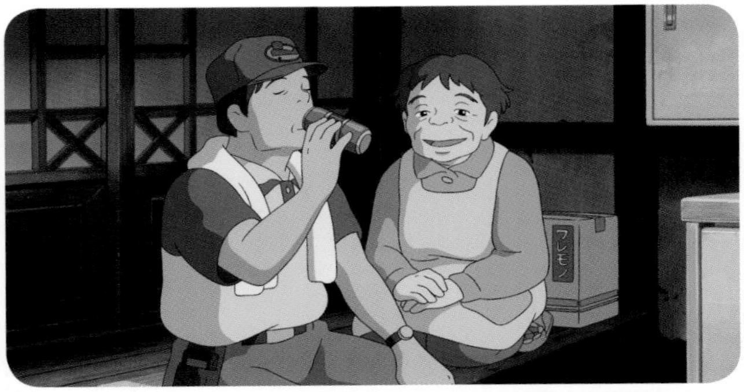

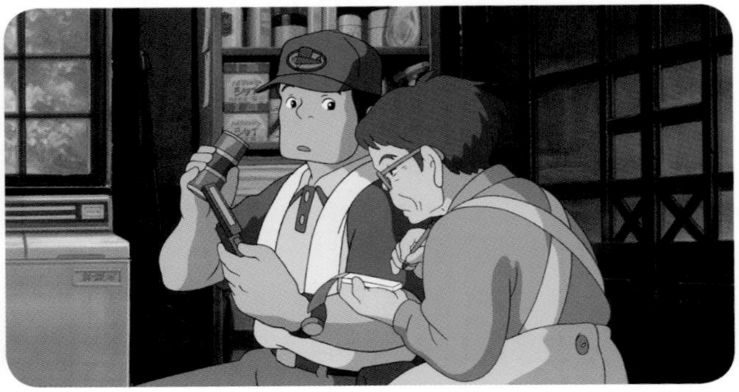

The Dollhouse

In the evening a young delivery man came with a package. “Do you happen to know of any good pest control companies?” Hara asked him.

The deliveryman looked something up on his cell phone.

“Here’s one… Squeaky Klean Pest Extermination. You got yourself a mouse problem?”

Hara put on her glasses and wrote down the number. “Maybe it’s mice,” she whispered. “Maybe it’s little tiny people.”

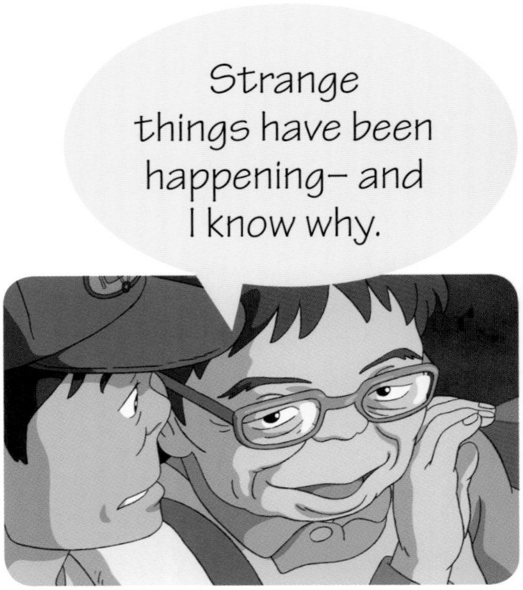
Strange things have been happening– and I know why.

That evening at dinner, Jessica was very concerned about Shawn.

"Why on earth would a crow try to fly into your room?" she wondered. "Were you frightened? That's the last thing your poor heart needs," Jessica sighed.

"Well, let's not relive the excitement. Shawn came here for a little peace and quiet before his operation.

"Though why his mother chose now to take a business trip is just beyond me. Why couldn't she be here when her son needs her so?"

"Aunt Jessica, I was noticing that miniature house in my room," said Shawn, changing the subject. "The detail is amazing!"

Jessica smiled. "Oh, you mean the dollhouse? That beautiful little house belonged to your mother. She left it here when she moved away."

"It was Mother's?!" Shawn cried.

"Your grandfather had it specially made," Jessica replied. "He was hoping it would be a lovely home for the little people."

"What?"

"That's right," Jessica said. "The little people who live in the walls.

"My father was quite obsessed with them. People laughed, of course, and called him mad, but your mother—SHE believed him.

"They worked on that house together for hours—and he told her they would come, but of course they never did."

"Can we look inside it?" Shawn leaned forward with sparkling eyes.

Jessica nodded. "You know, I haven't looked inside for quite a long time."

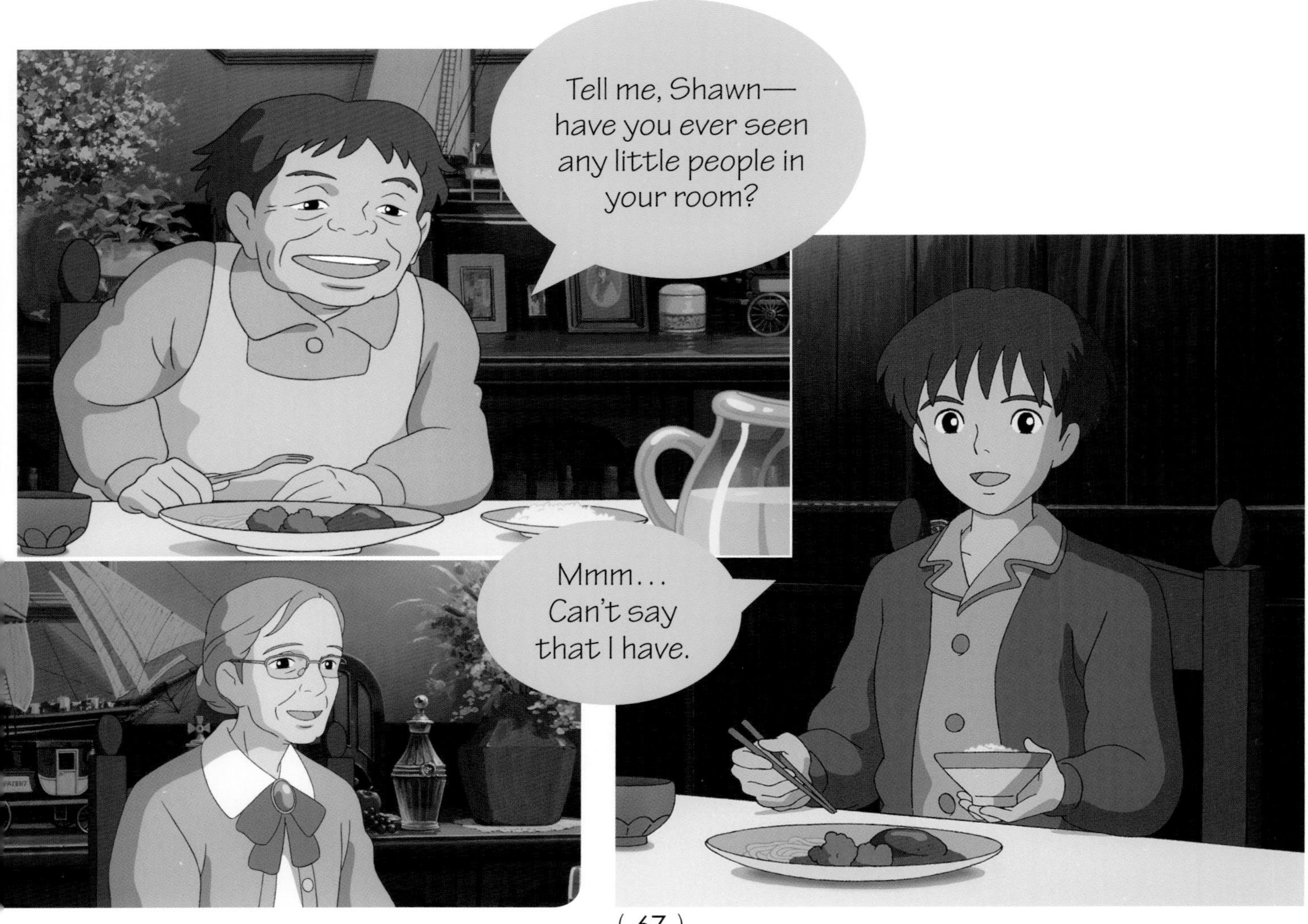
Tell me, Shawn—have you ever seen any little people in your room?
Mmm... Can't say that I have.

Jessica led Shawn and Hara to Shawn's room and opened up the dollhouse.

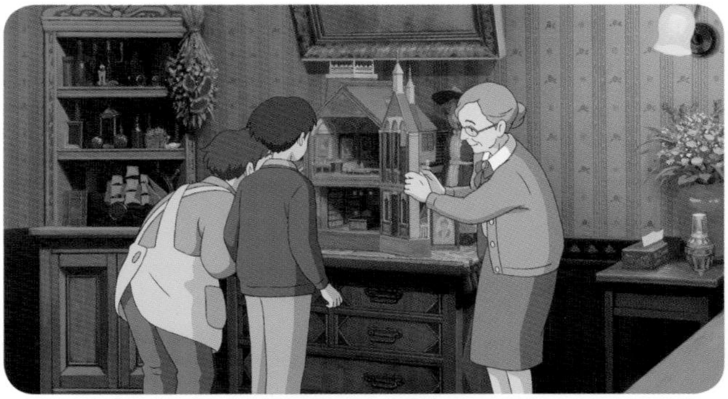

With the room light turned off, the dollhouse's tiny lights glowed.

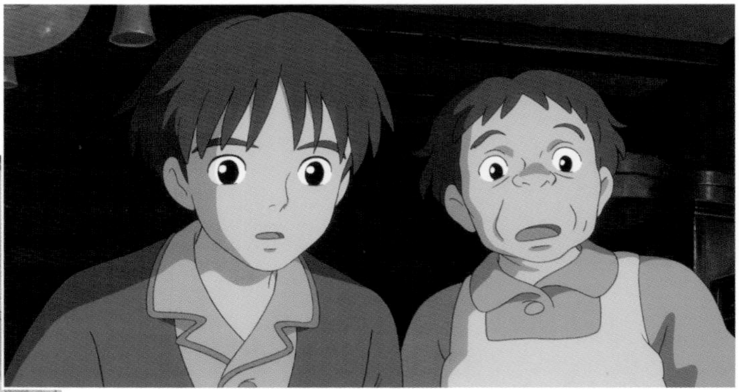

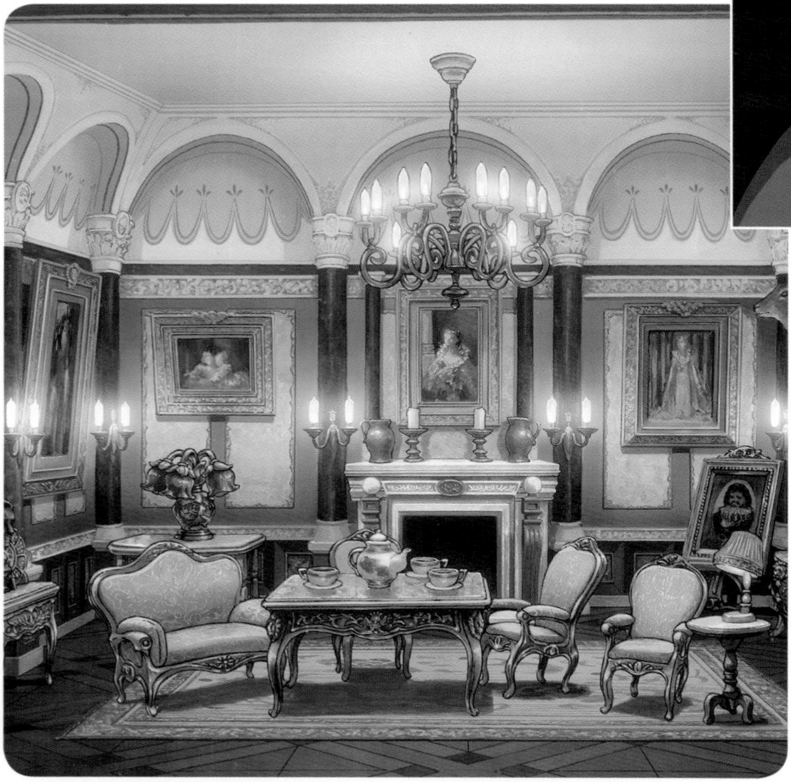

"This is the living room," Jessica said. "Your grandfather had all of this hand-made by a furniture maker in England.

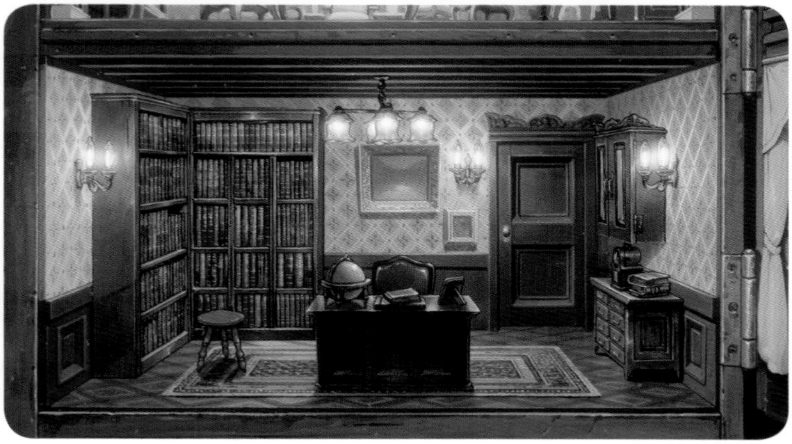

"Look at the attention to detail. They really were preparing it for someone to live in. Look in that room right there."

Jessica pointed to a kitchen full of beautiful cooking equipment.

"Everything in it is a miniature of the real thing. That oven actually works!" she said.

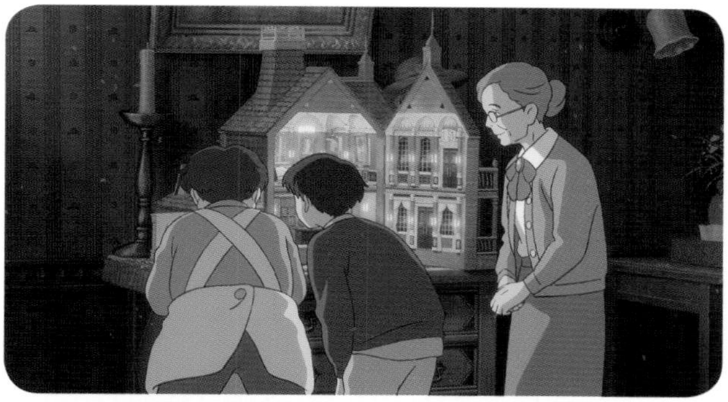

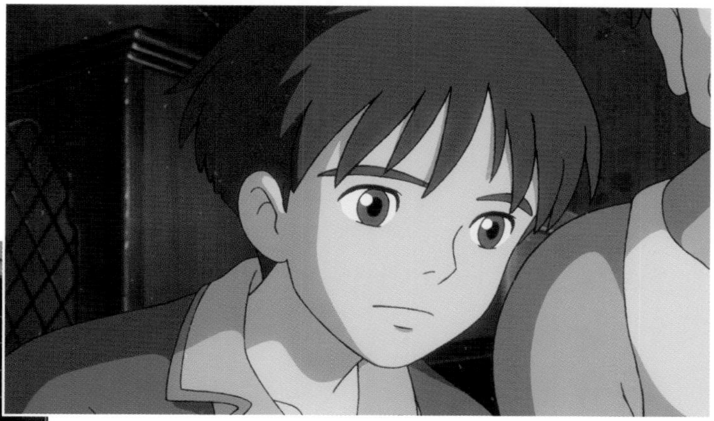

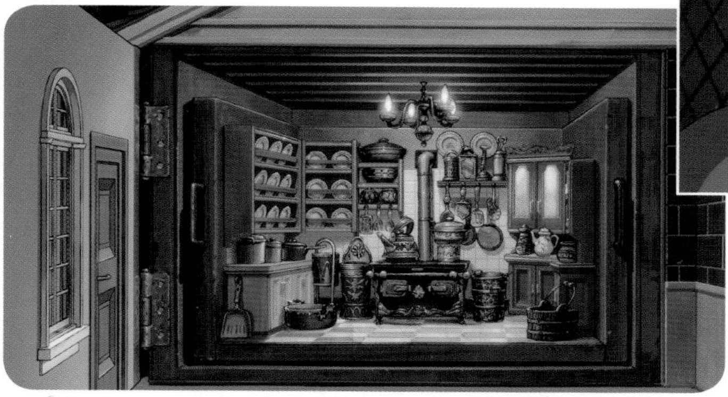

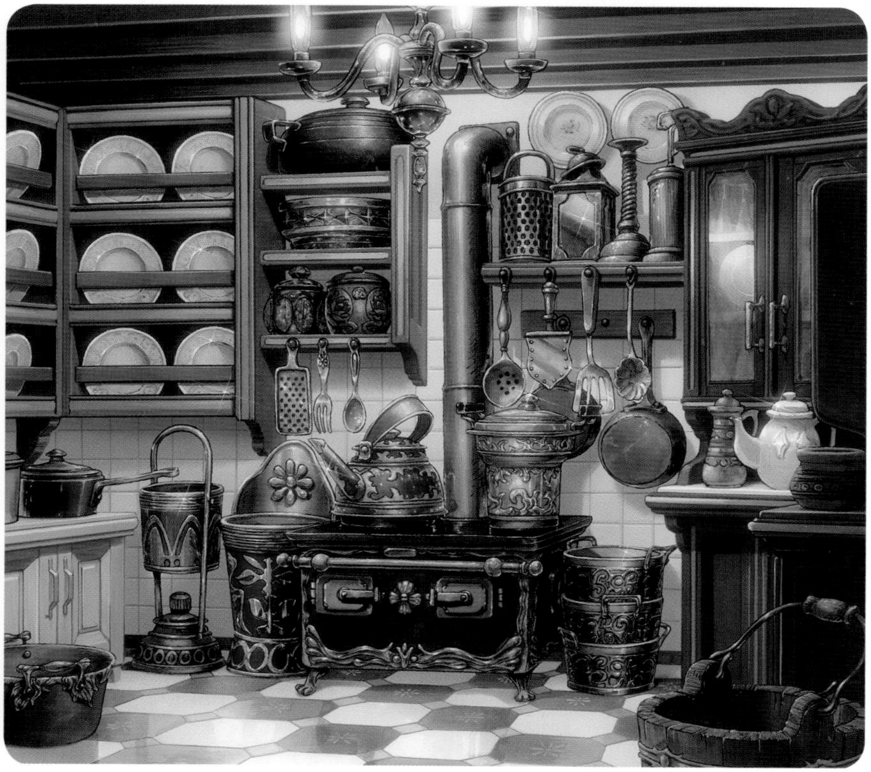

"What a pity the little people never came," Jessica sighed. "This dollhouse really would've made a lovely home."

Shawn listened to his aunt, his gaze fixed on the sparkling kitchen.

The next day, Shawn lay a poppy and a note by Arrietty's grate. Then he went to the garden and lay down.

Gentle rays of sun broke through the clouds and shone down on him.

Half hidden on the patio, Hara quietly watched.

From time to time Shawn sat up and looked around, as if waiting for something.

When it began to rain,
Shawn went back inside.

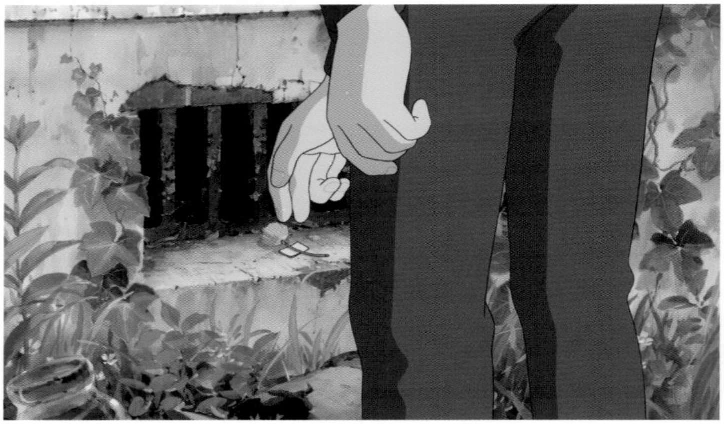

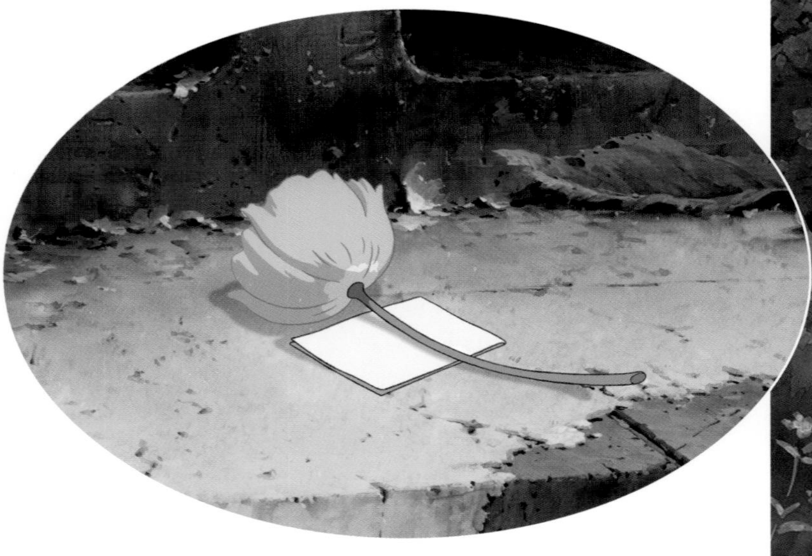

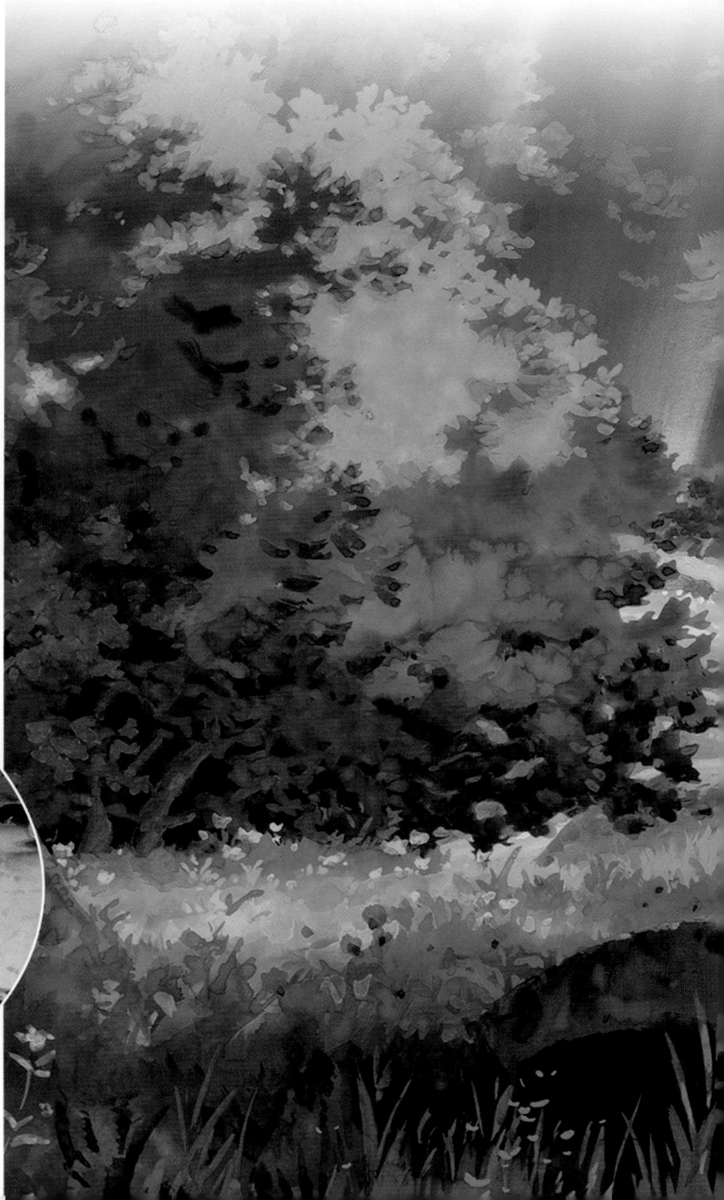

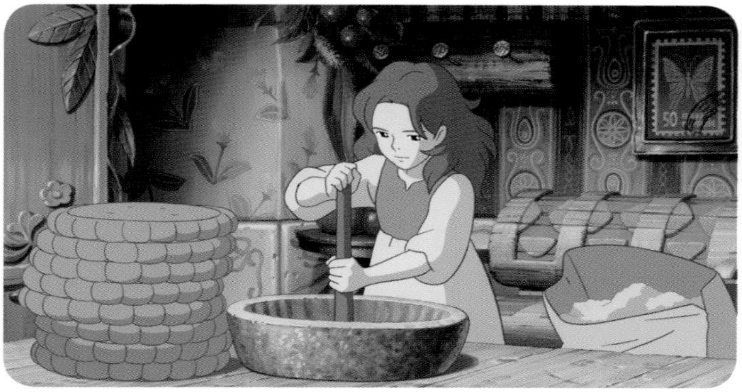
50
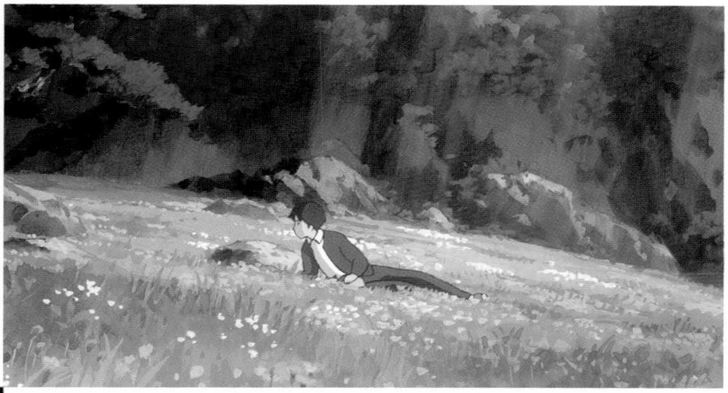
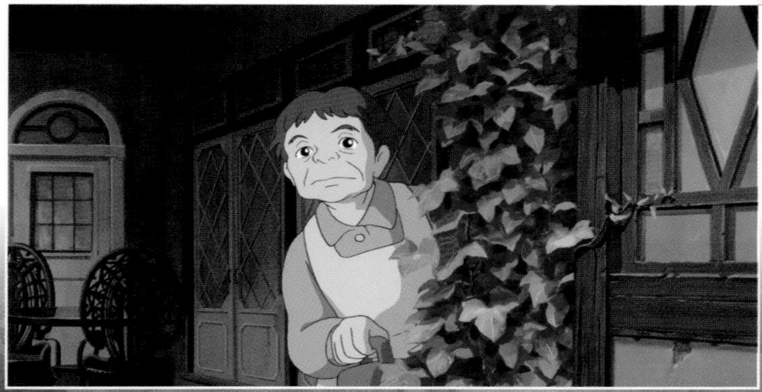
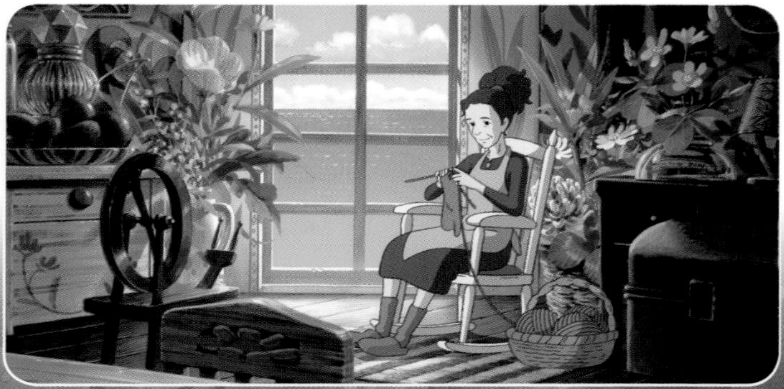
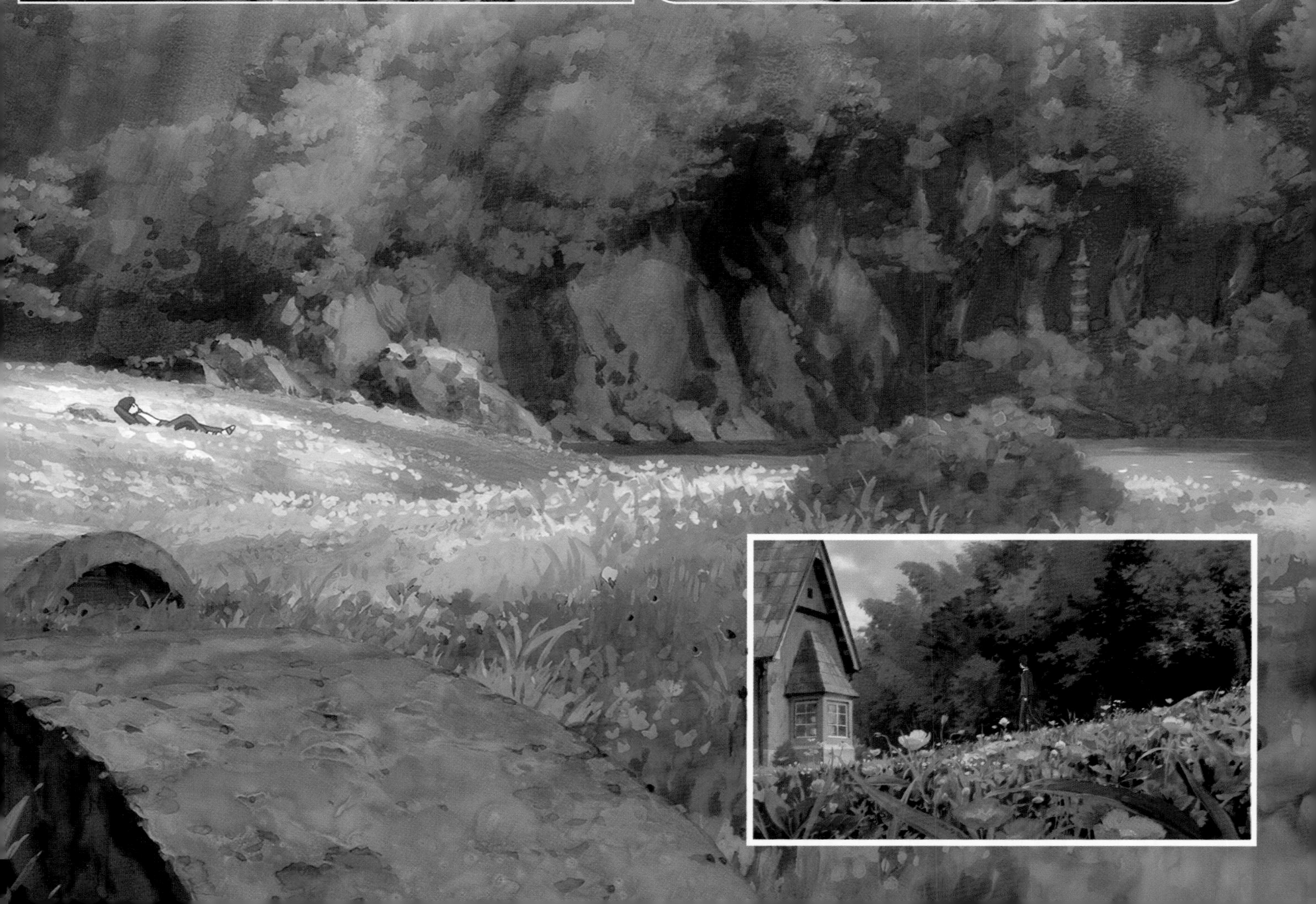

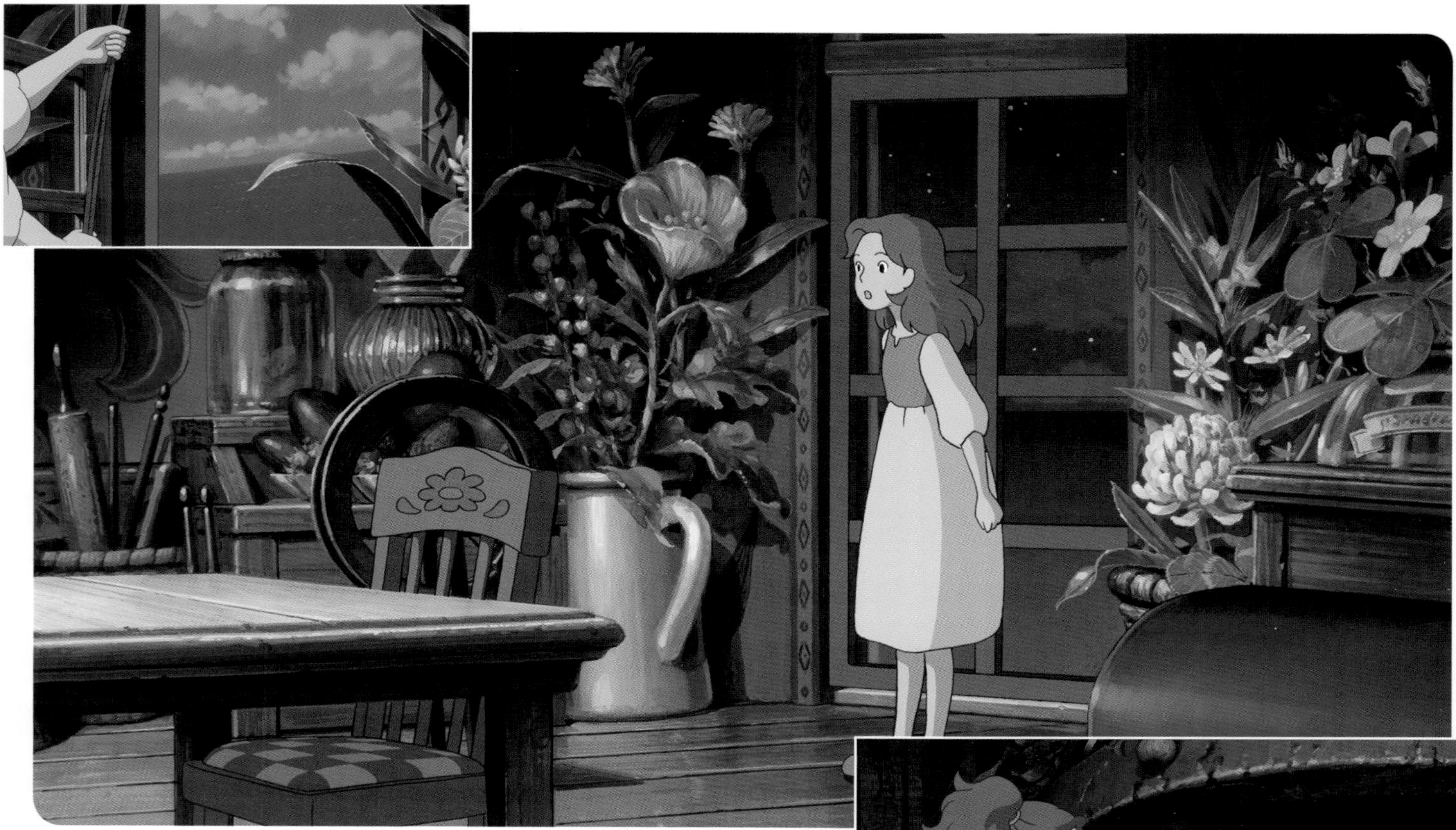
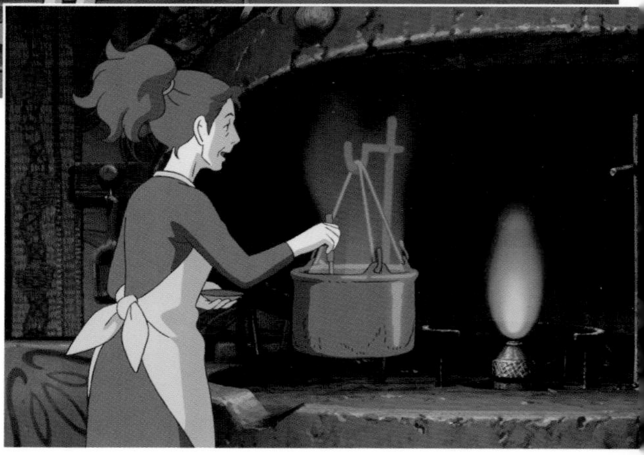

At sunset, Arrietty changed the window photo from a picture of an ocean and blue skies to one of an ocean at night.

"You know mother, we've had these same pictures for years. Wouldn't you like new ones?" she asked.

"I like those pictures," Homily replied as she prepared dinner.

"I've always dreamed of seeing the real ocean someday," Arrietty sighed. "Besides, there's no point in changing the picture now.

"Wonder what's taking Papa so long."

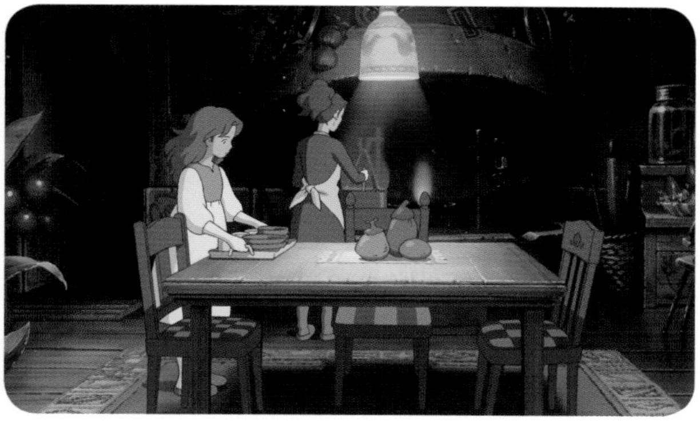

“Why is my first thought always that he got eaten by the cat?” Homily said.

Just then, they heard a noise by the back door.

“He’s home!” Arrietty cried. She ran to the back door, then stopped in her tracks.

Pod was limping along, leaning on the shoulder of another little person—a young man Arrietty had never seen before.

“I slipped and twisted my leg,” Pod explained. “I’m lucky Spiller here found me.”

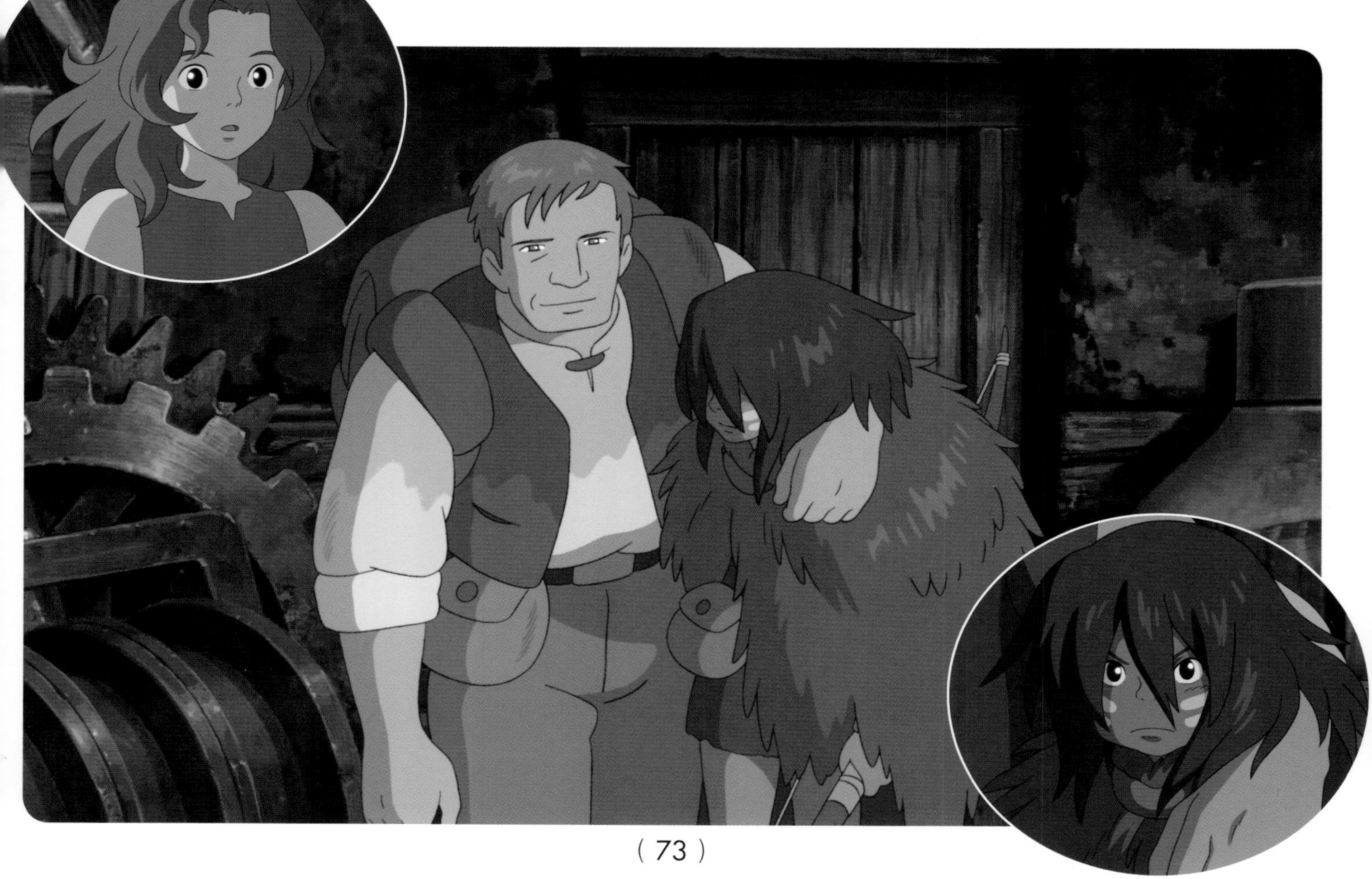

“I'll get some cold water,” Arrietty said.

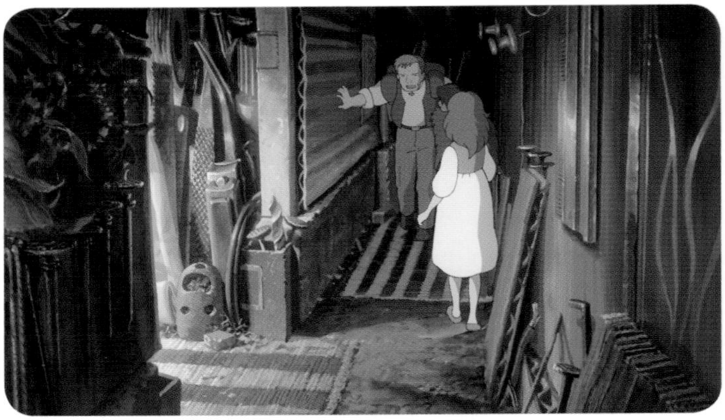

As she filled a pail, her surprise turned to joy.

I wonder if he has news about any of the other Borrowers?

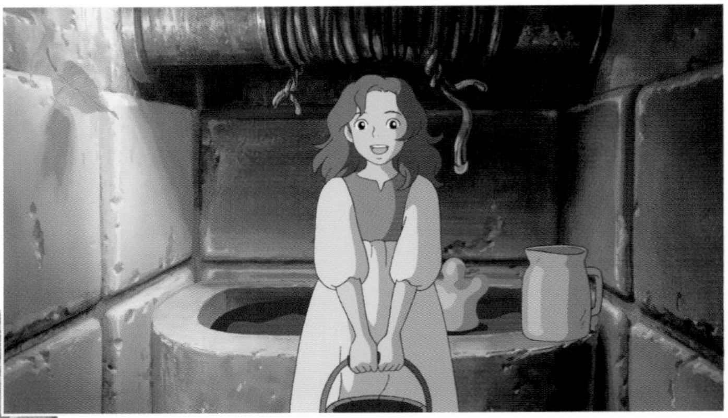

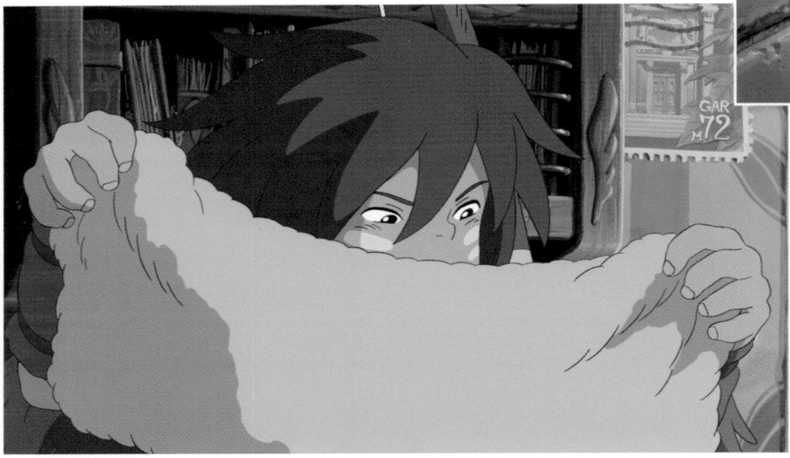
GAR
M72

“Here’s a towel,” Homily said to Spiller. “Dry yourself off.”

Spiller took the towel. He examined it and sniffed it as if it were an unfamiliar object. “I leave now,” he said.

“At least stay and have some tea,” urged Homily.

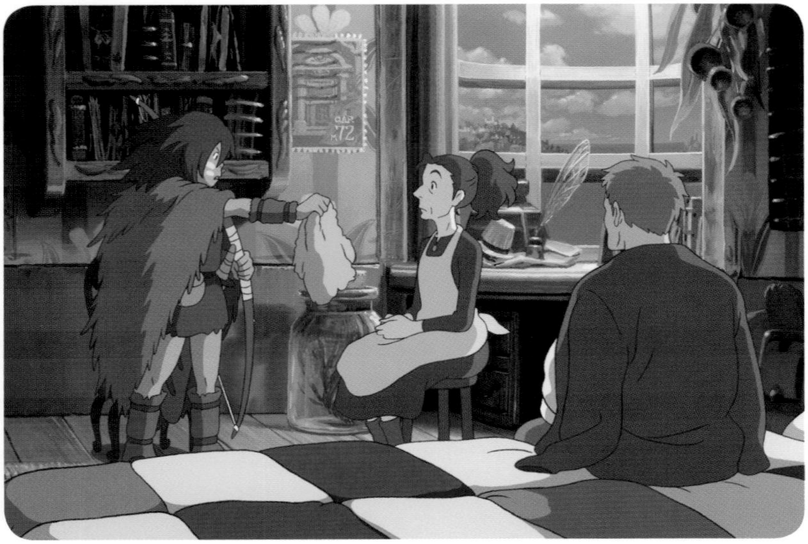

Spiller only shook his head.

Just then Arrietty returned with the water.

Spiller stared wide-eyed. He stood stock still, following Arrietty's movement with his eyes.

"Won't you please stay, Spiller?" Arrietty asked. "I've never met another Borrower before."

Spiller nodded, his eyes glued to Arrietty's smiling face.

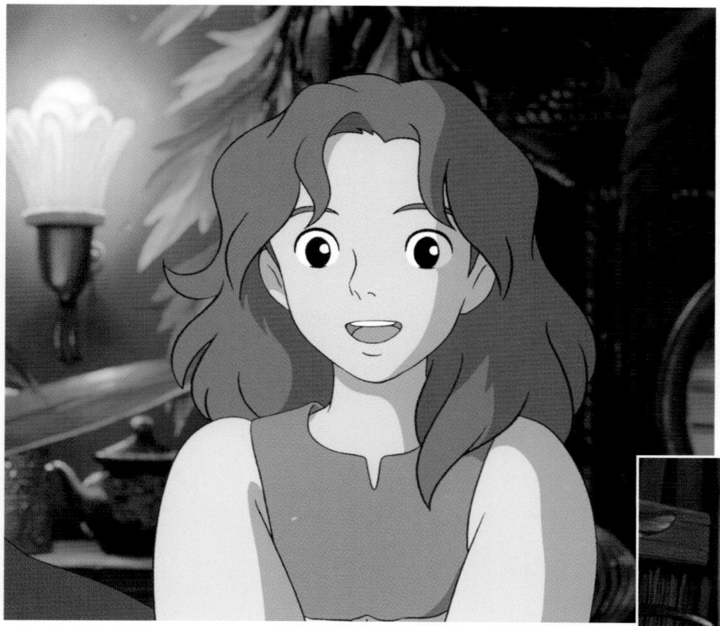

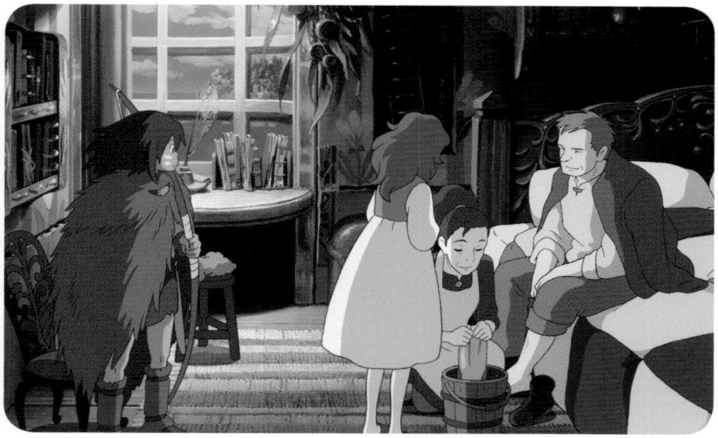

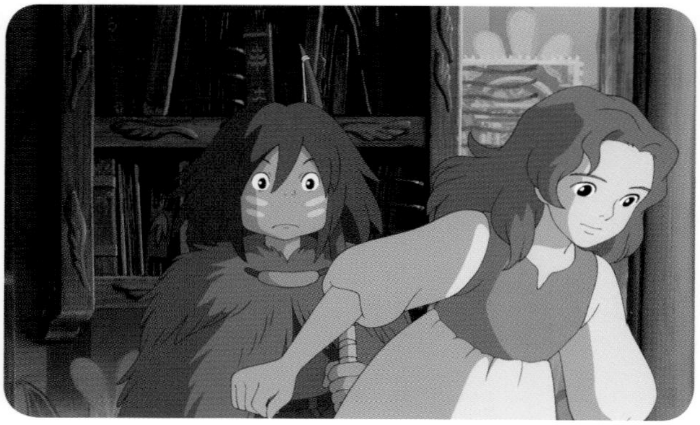

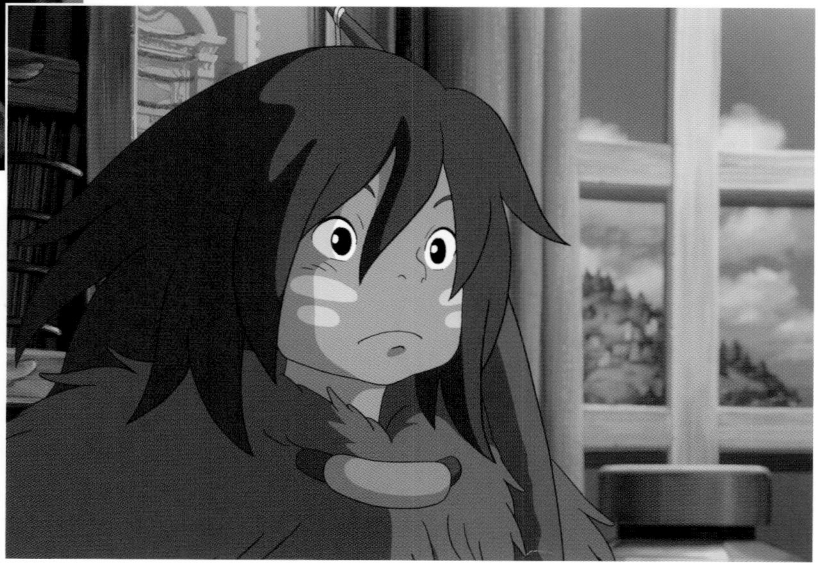

"We can't thank you enough for your help. Tell us, have you seen other Borrowers?" asked Homily as she prepared the tea. "We're all alone here and were starting to believe we're the only ones left."

Spiller bent his fingers in an odd way. "This many," he said.

"Oh! Cousin Lupy could still be alive!"
Homily exclaimed happily.

Pod nodded.

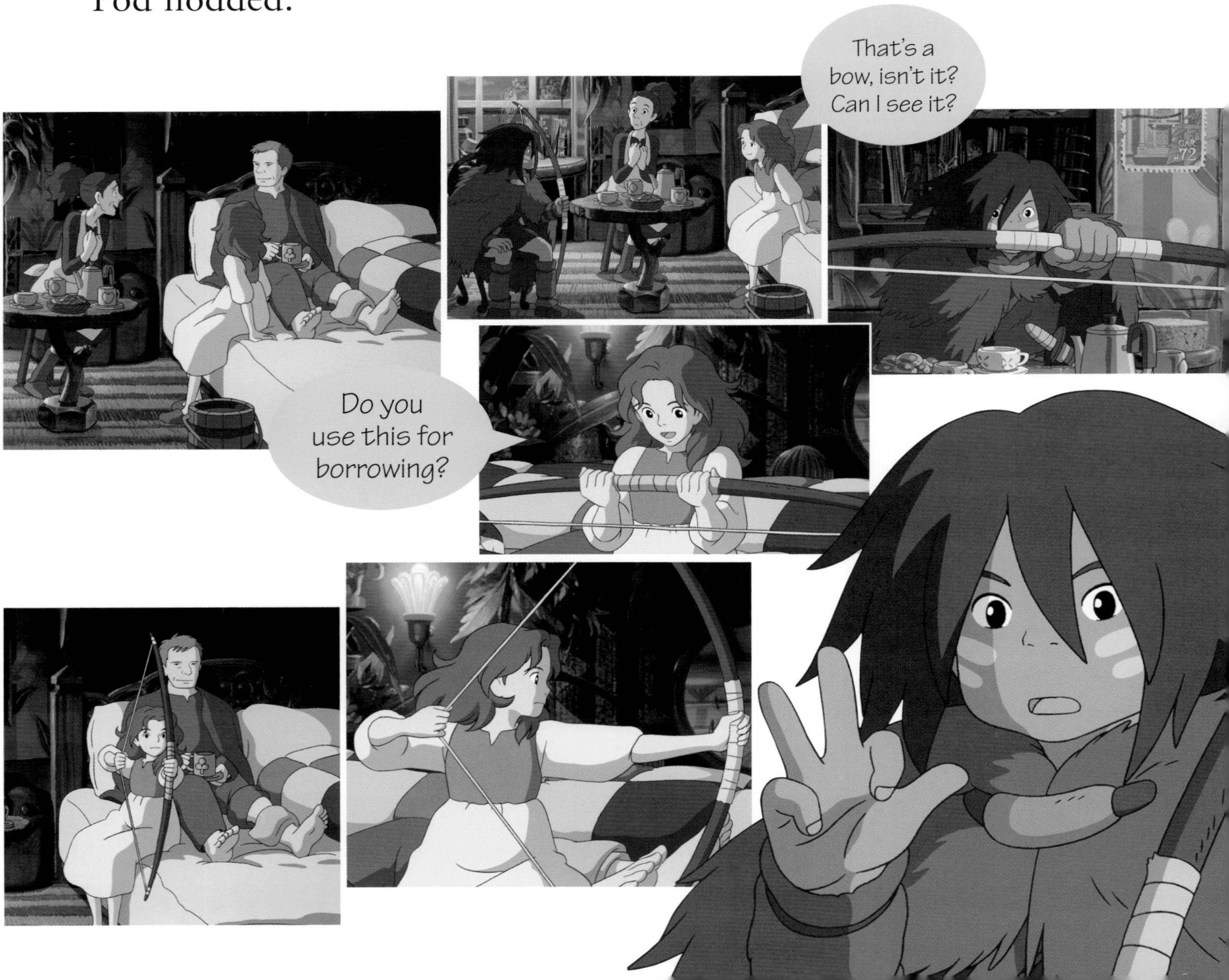
That's a bow, isn't it? Can I see it?
Do you use this for borrowing?

"Okay. Go now," Spiller said.

"Oh…but… couldn't you stay a bit longer?" Homily asked. "I'll cook dinner."

Spiller pulled out a cricket leg.

"Already got this."

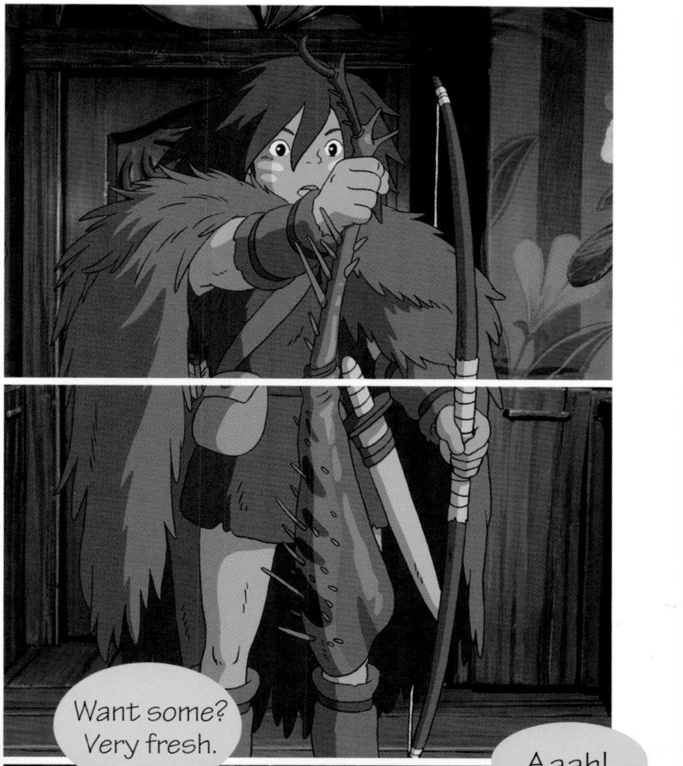
Want some? Very fresh.

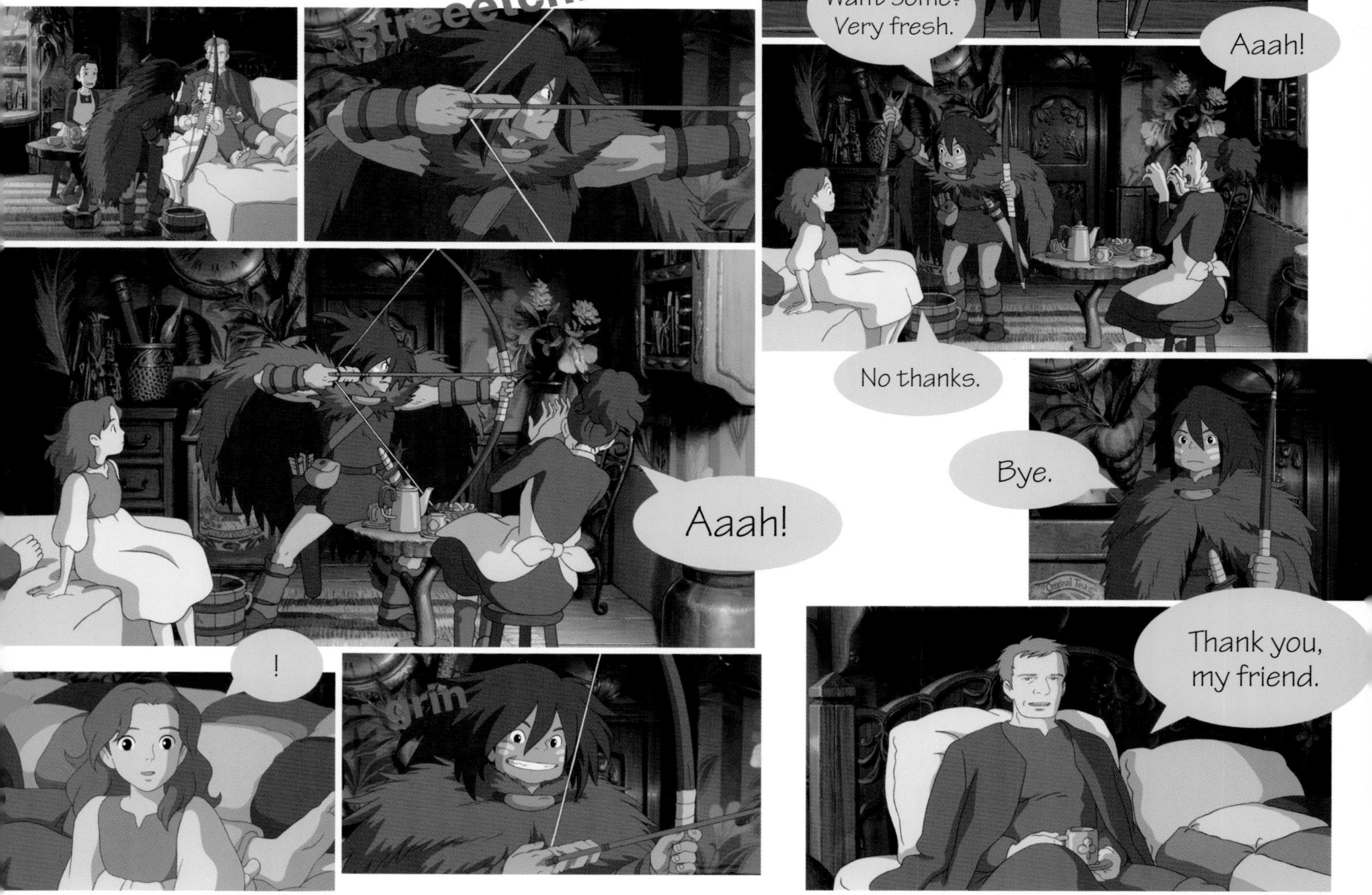
Aaah!
No thanks.
streeetch…
Aaah!
!
grin
Bye.
Thank you, my friend.

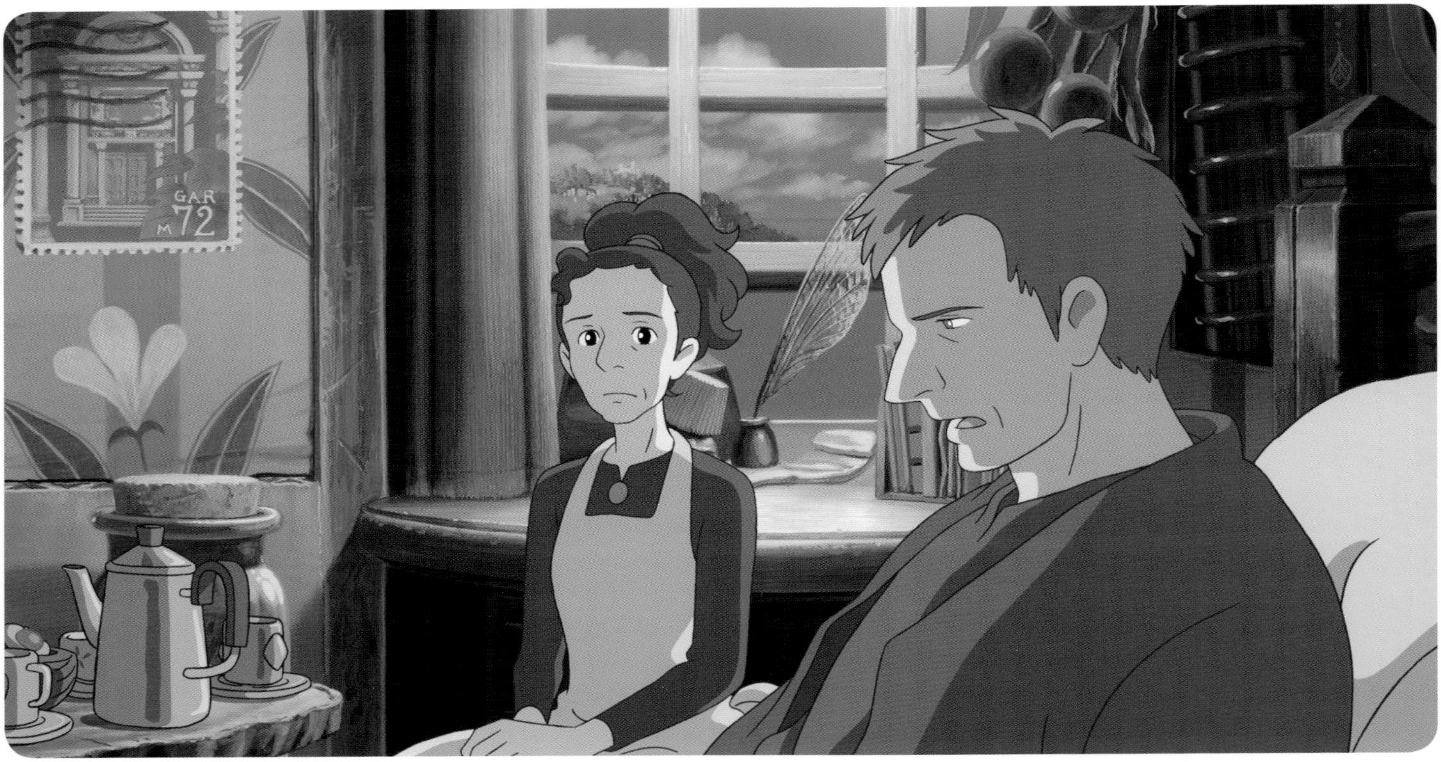

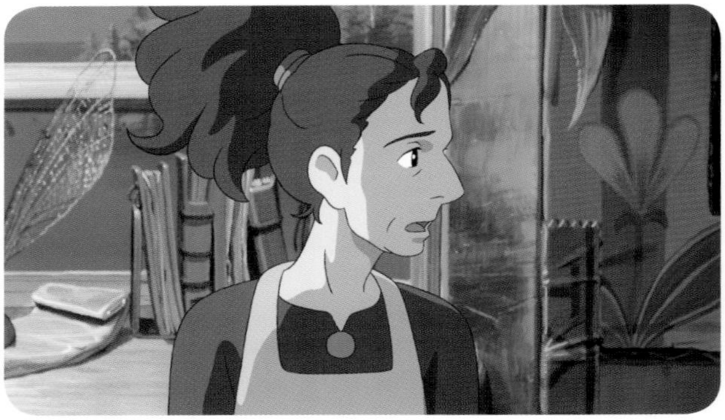

“I’ll see him out,” said Arrietty, following Spiller from the room.

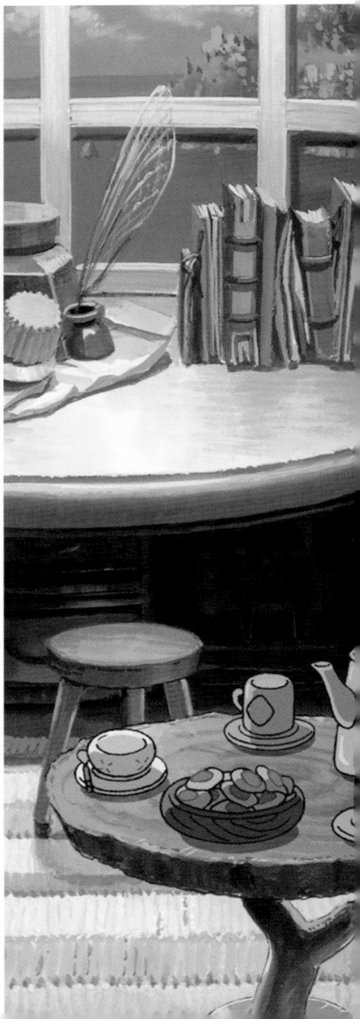

When Homily and Pod were alone, Homily asked, “What were you doing out in that storm?”

“I was looking for a safe route for our journey,” Pod replied. “And now I know which route not to take.”

“Oh Pod,” Homily sighed.

"Spiller knows of more Borrowers a few days' journey away," Pod said. "He's offered to take us."

"That's great," Homily said. "I'm sure we'll find a new place in no time."

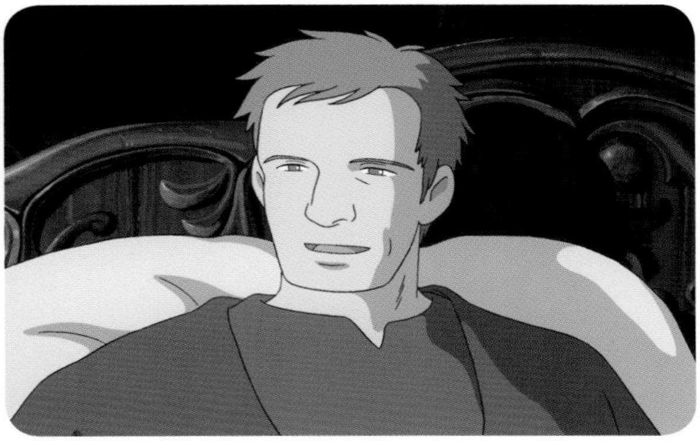

She placed a wet towel on Pod's ankle and sat down on the bed. "And I'm sure it will be almost as nice as this."

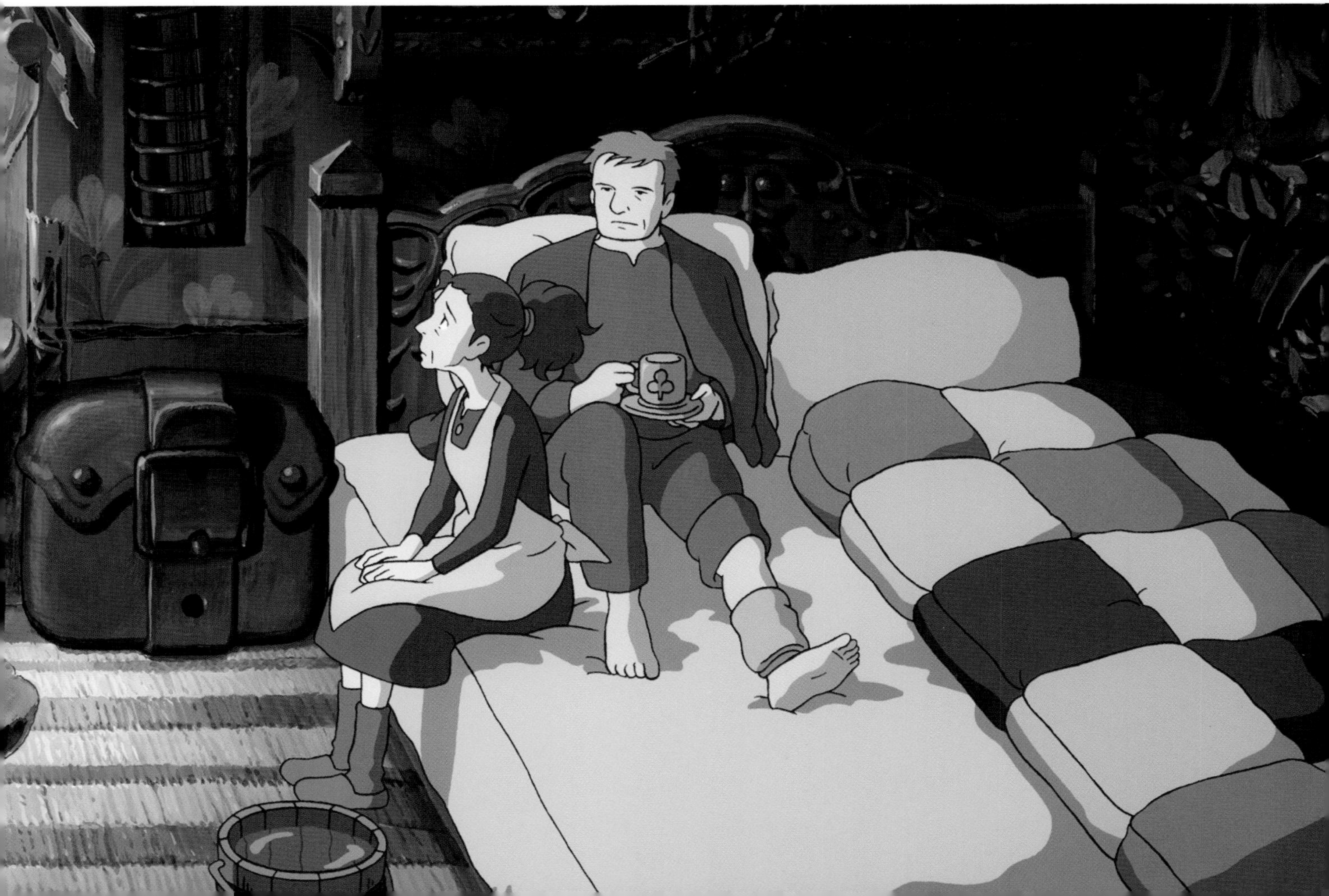

Moonlight shone in through the grate.

"I'm really glad I met you, Spiller," Arrietty said. "That I met anyone."

"Maybe next time you could bring your family with you?"

"No family. Only Spiller."

"Oh… Well, we can be your family," Arrietty suggested. "And when you come back you can stay for a family dinner."

Spiller nodded.

Spiller climbed quickly up
a vine, spread open his fur
cloak, and flew toward the
forest like a flying squirrel.

The next day, Aunt Jessica left. From his bedroom window, Shawn heard her car as it rumbled away.

Vroooom...

He went downstairs and looked into the kitchen.

"Hara?"

Nobody answered.

Realizing he was alone, Shawn made a decision.

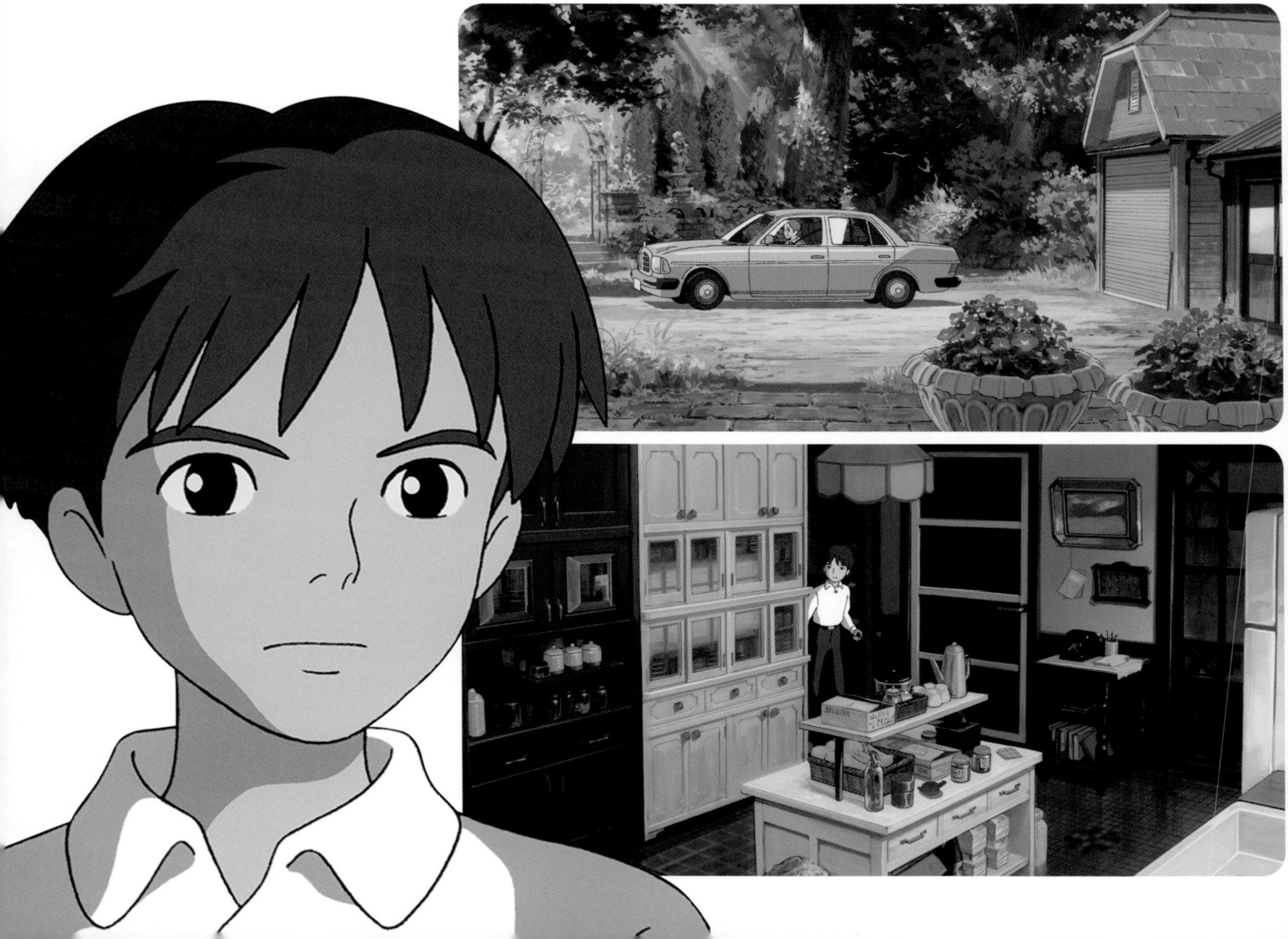

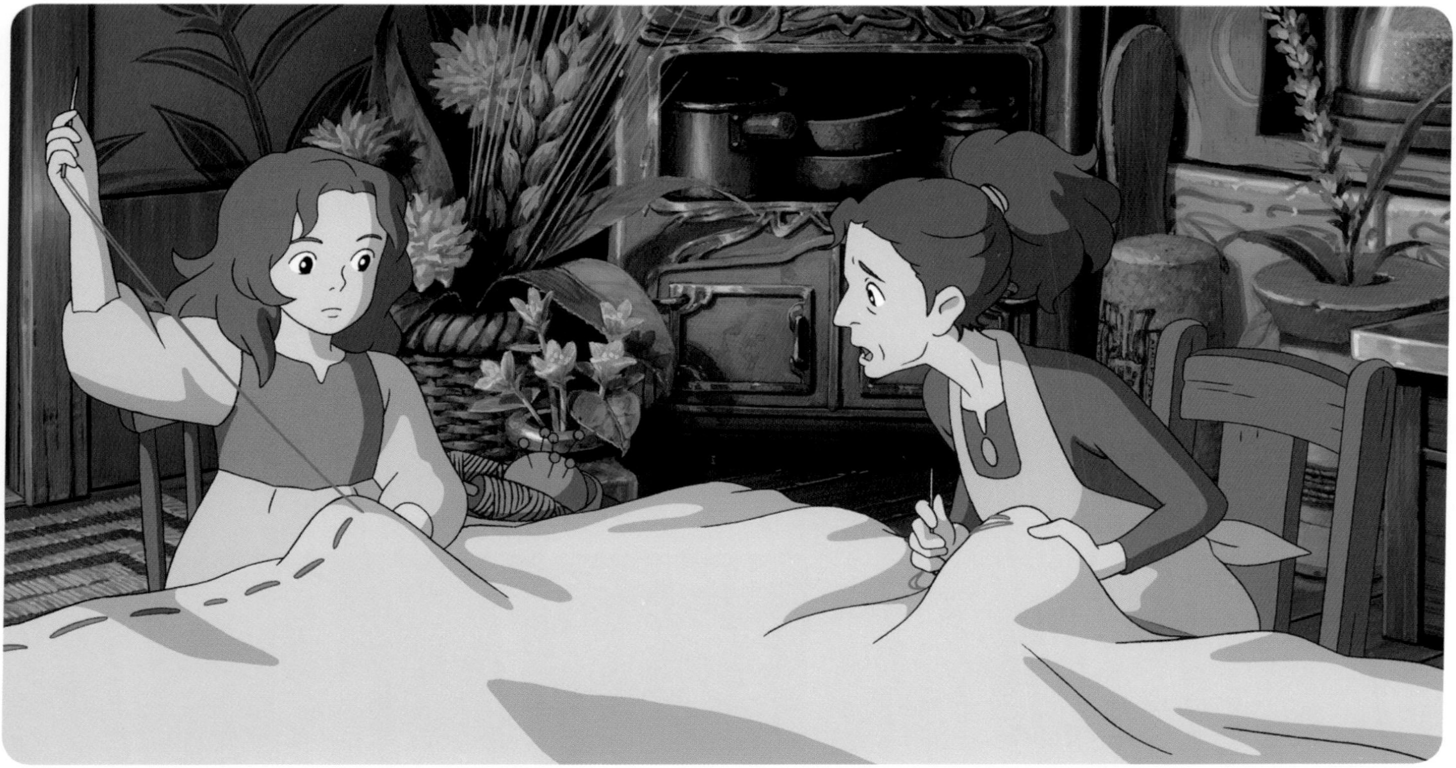

At just about the same time, Arrietty was helping Homily sew a large bag.

"Arrietty, your stitches need to be closer together," Homily said. "You'll have to start over."

"Why do we need such a big bag anyway?" Arrietty complained. "Are we putting the whole house in here?"

Homily kept on sewing.

"I'm going to go check on Papa," Arrietty said.

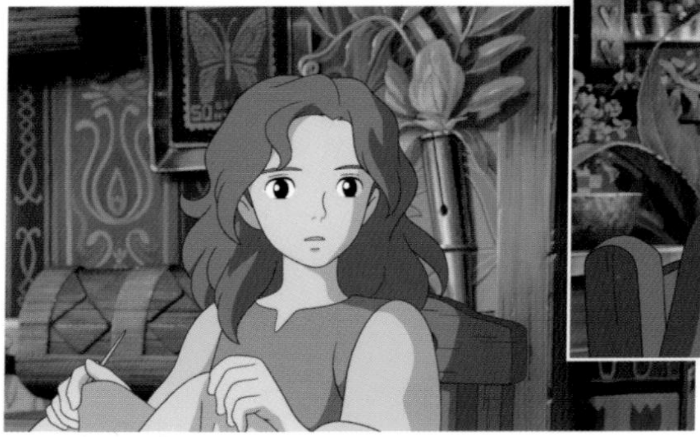

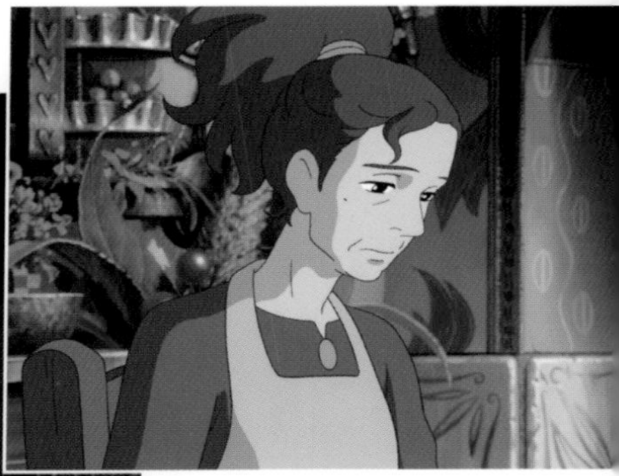

Arrietty found Papa on his bed, weaving a basket.

"How's your leg?" she asked.

"Well…better than that cricket's," Pod replied.

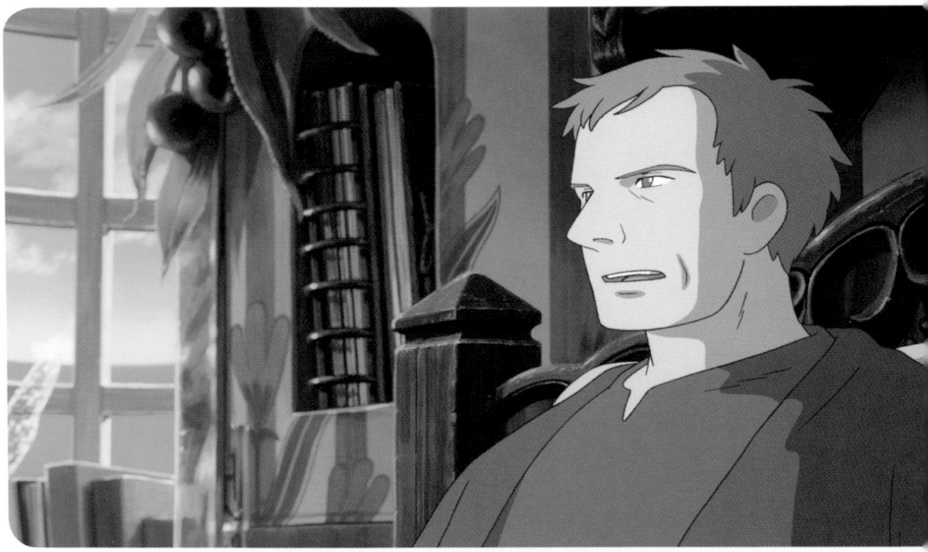

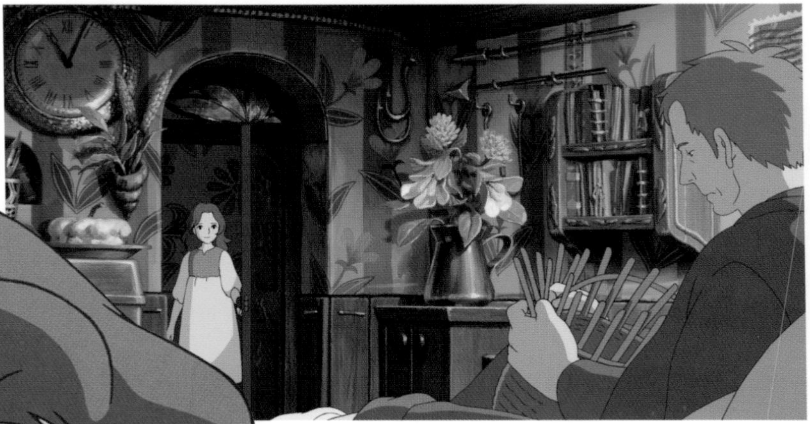

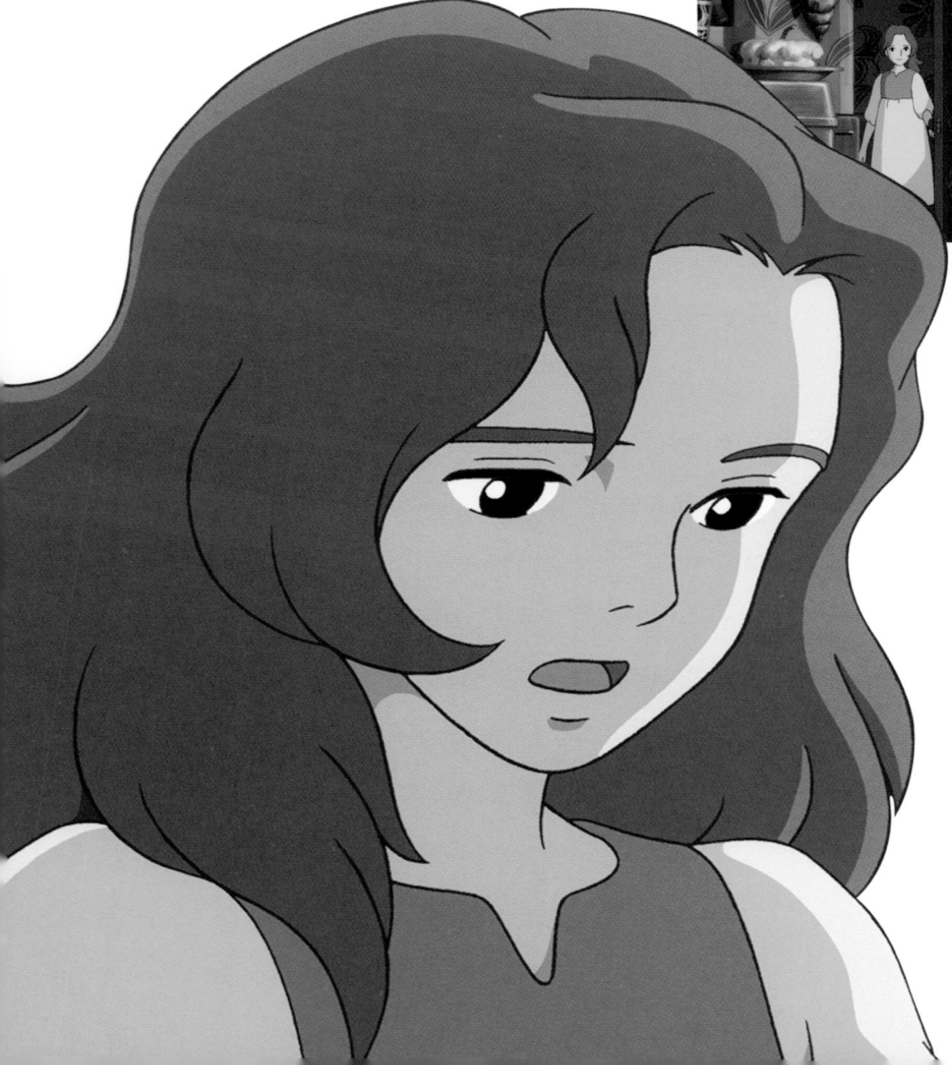

"Papa? Why do we have to move?" Arrietty asked.

"Once a Borrower has been seen, the beans' curiosity can't be stopped," Pod explained.

"But isn't it possible that not every human bean is dangerous?"

"Arrietty... Before you were born, two other families lived in this house."

"They were seen by humans. One family went missing. The other one moved away. And so, we have to do whatever it takes to survive."

Creeeeeeeeak....

Suddenly the house shook violently!

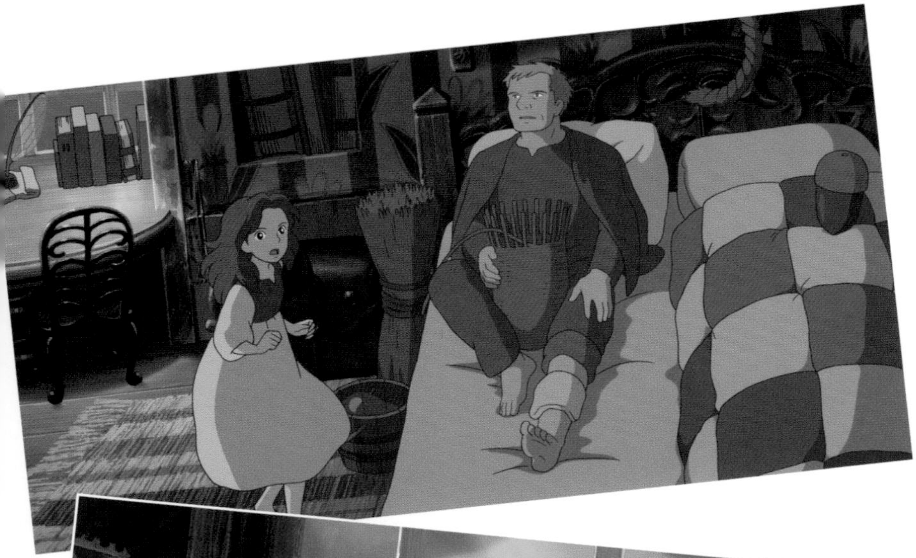

Craashh!

A picture by the window fell down. Arrietty could see bricks and clouds of dust.

What happened?

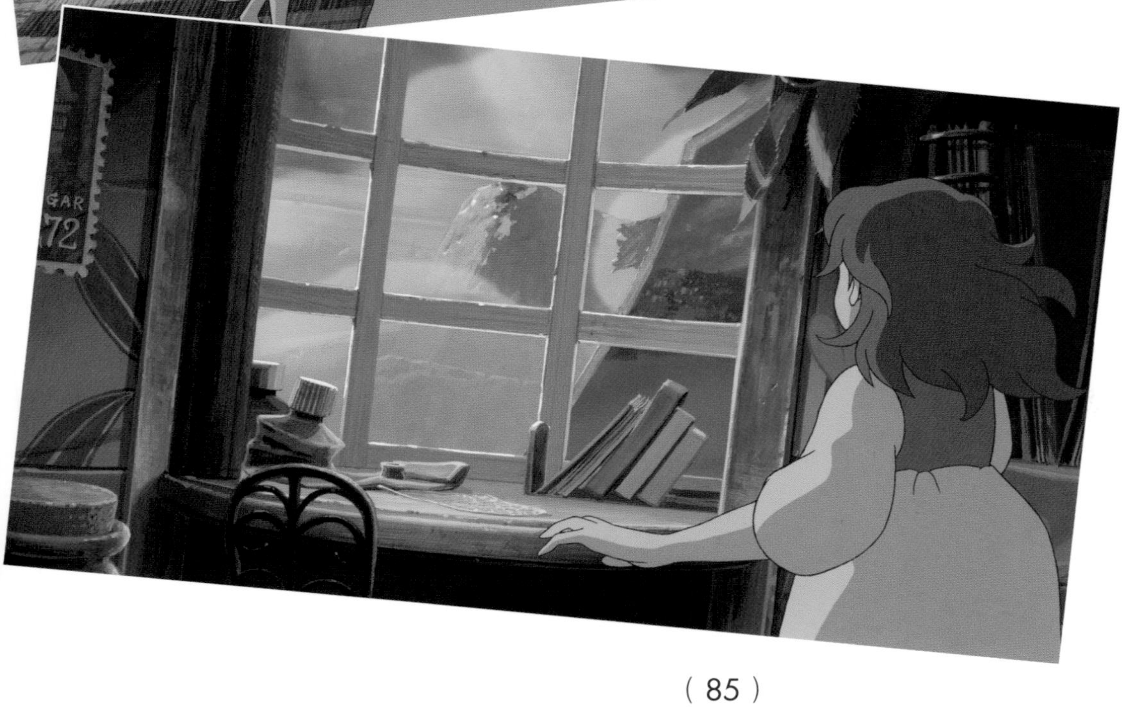

Arrietty and Pod tried to get to the room where Homily had been, but the door wouldn't open.

Inside the room, Homily crawled cautiously out from under a table.

"What is it…? An earthquake?" she wondered.

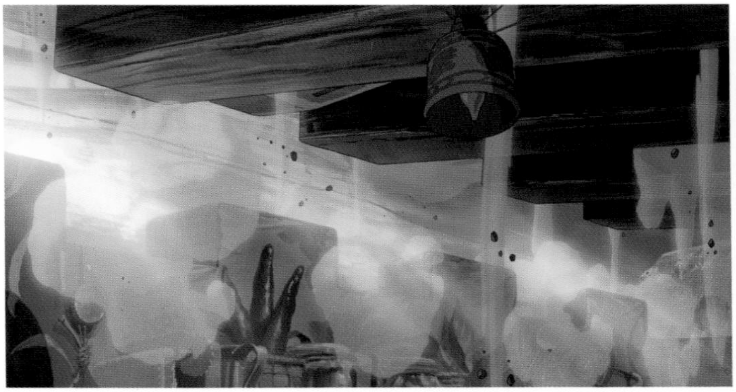

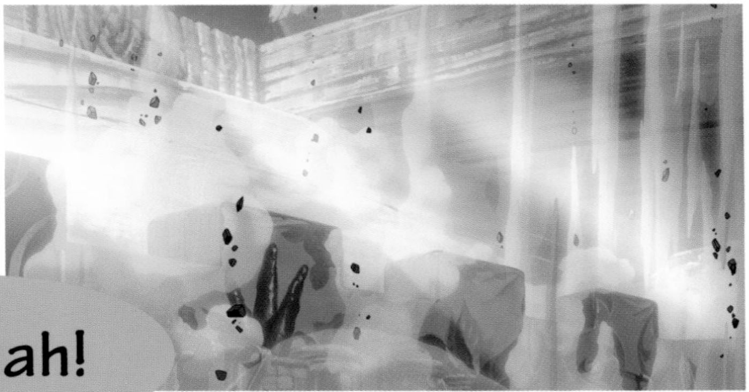

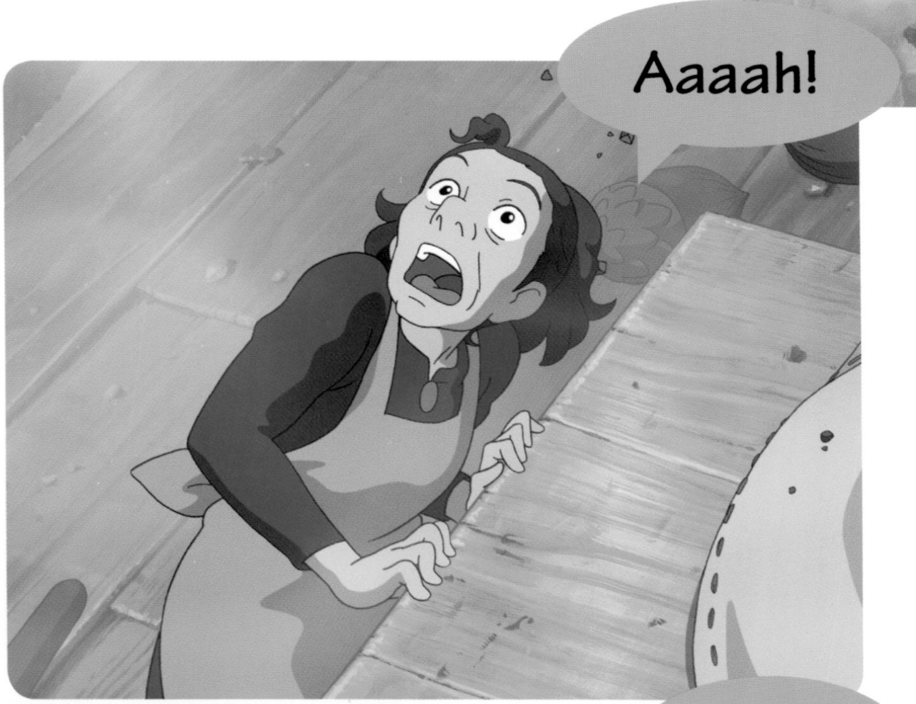
Aaaah!

Creeeeak, Bang, Crash!

The house thundered and shook violently again.

Before Homily's eyes, the kitchen ceiling was ripped out! A blinding light shone in.

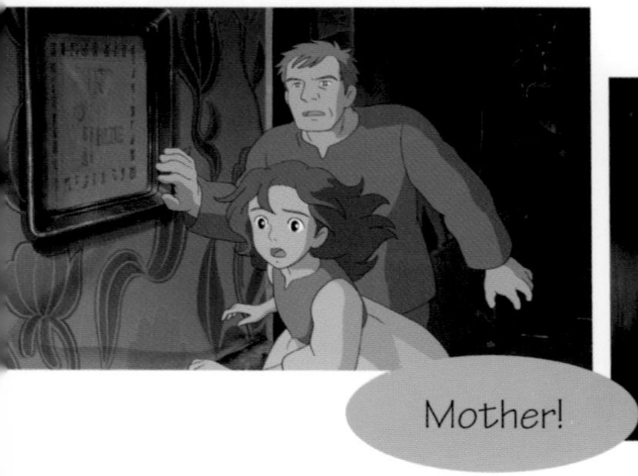
Mother!

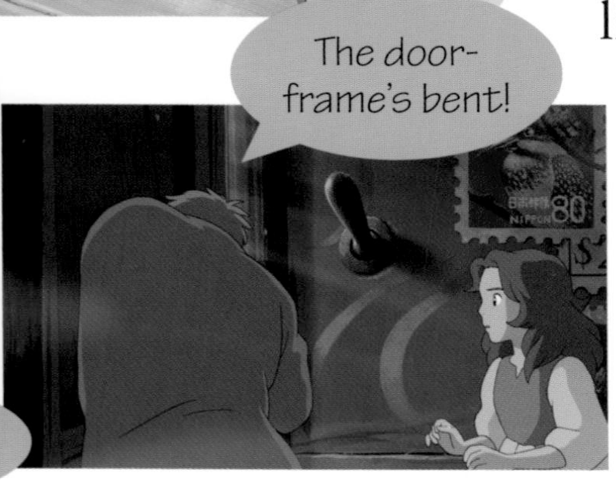
The door-frame's bent!

Giant hands emerged from the light and…

Rumble rumble!

… ripped away the kitchen wall!

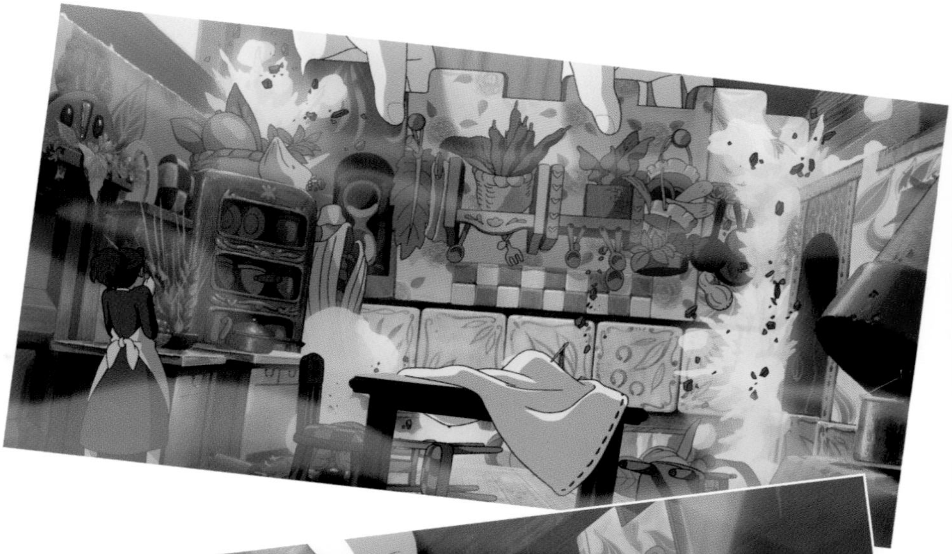

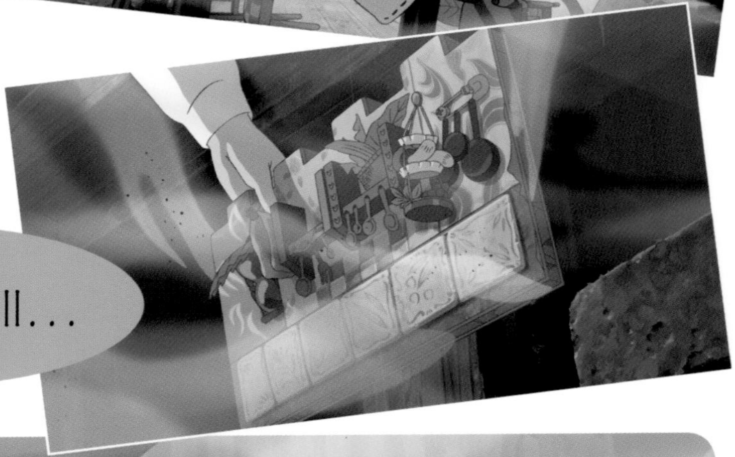

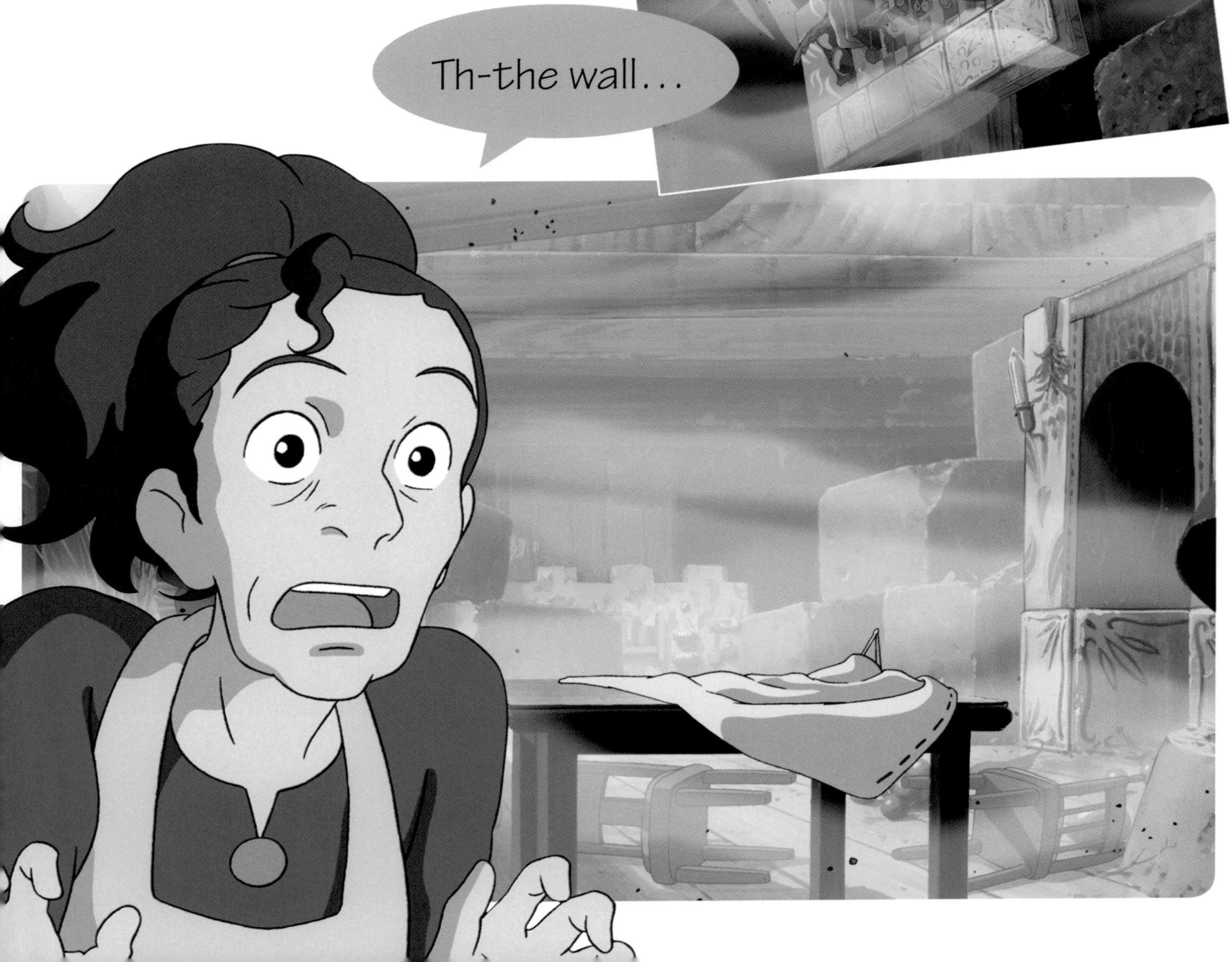
Th-the wall…

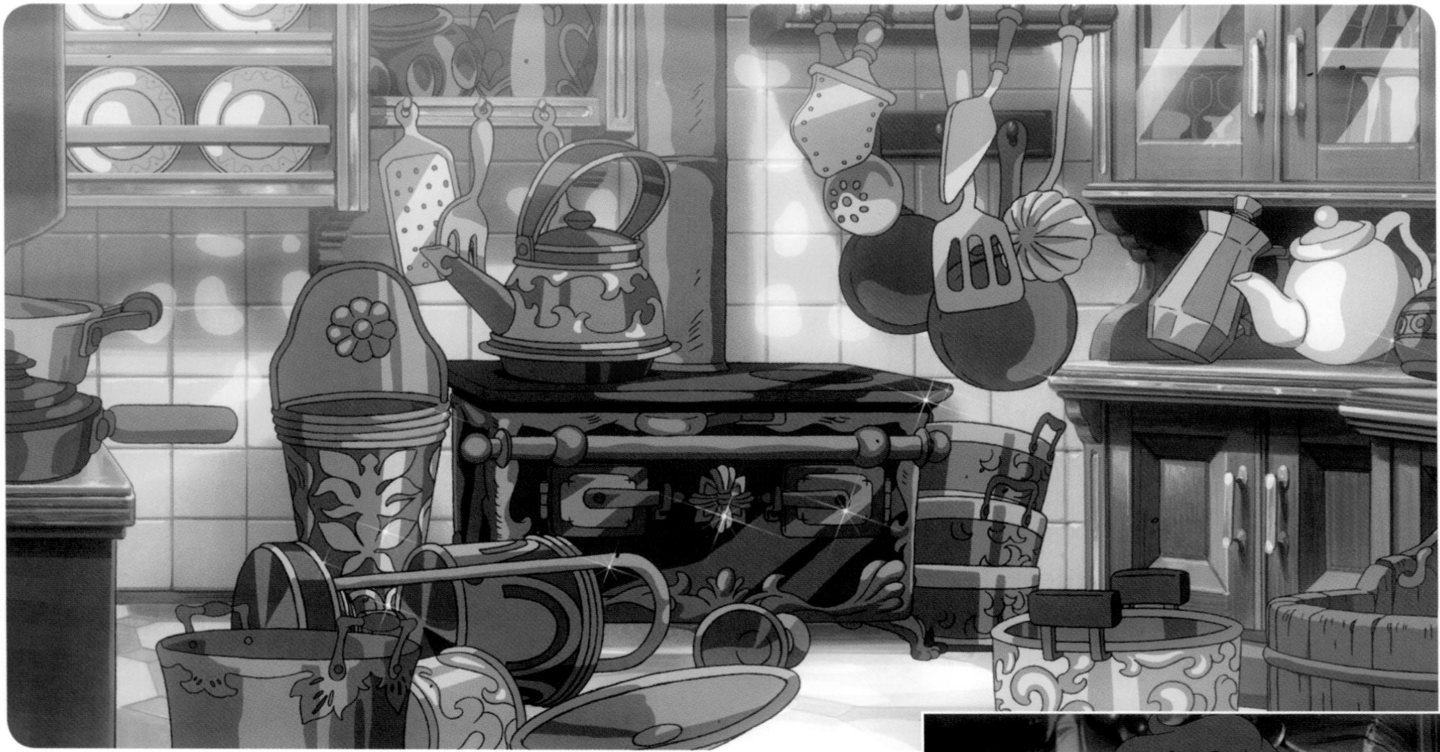

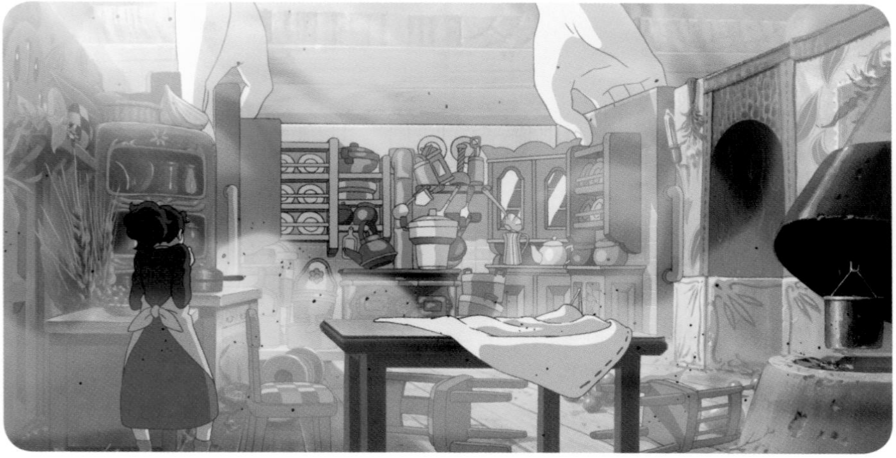

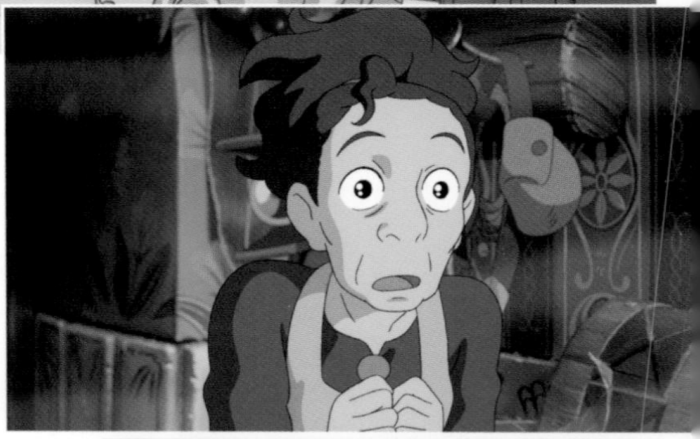

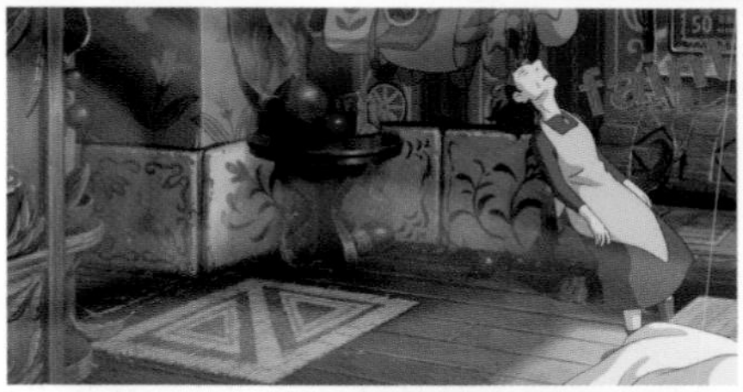

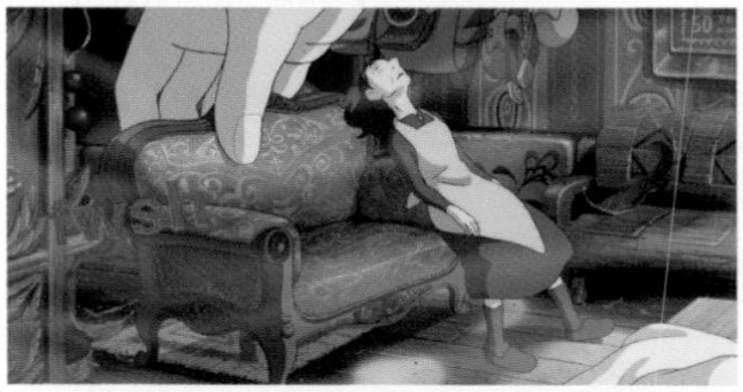

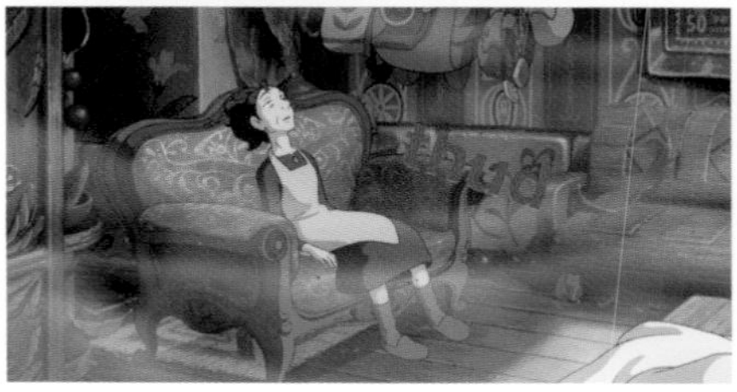

Then the giant hands returned, put the dollhouse kitchen where the old wall had been, and replaced the ceiling.

Pots and pans and cooking utensils sparkled. Homily was stunned speechless.

Pod rushed into the living room.

He and Arrietty gaped at the sparkling new kitchen.

"Pod... Remember how I always said I wanted a new kitchen?" Homily asked in a daze.

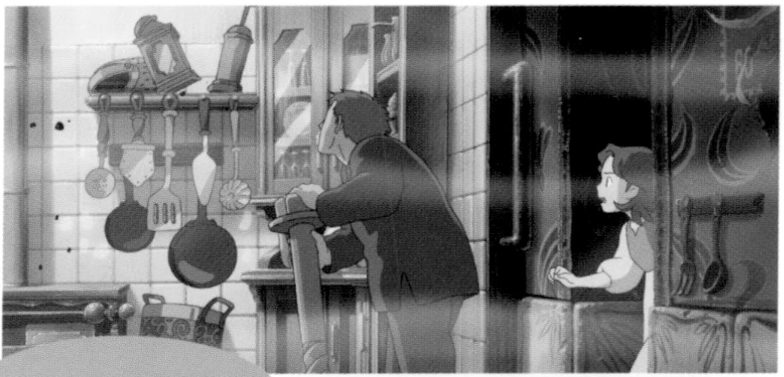

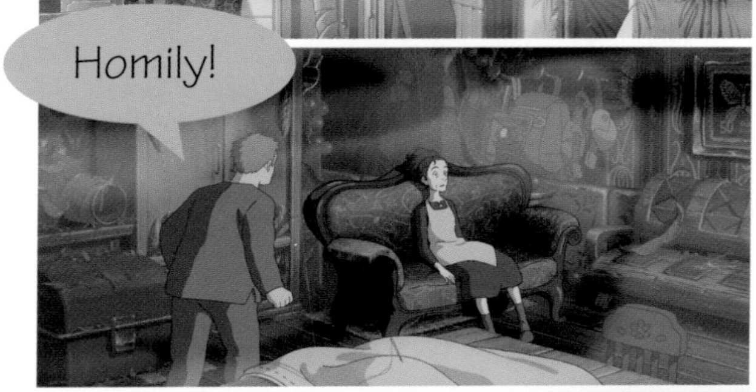
Homily!

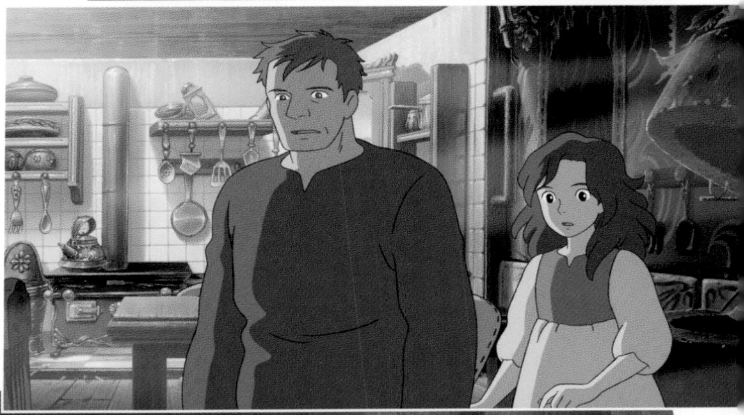

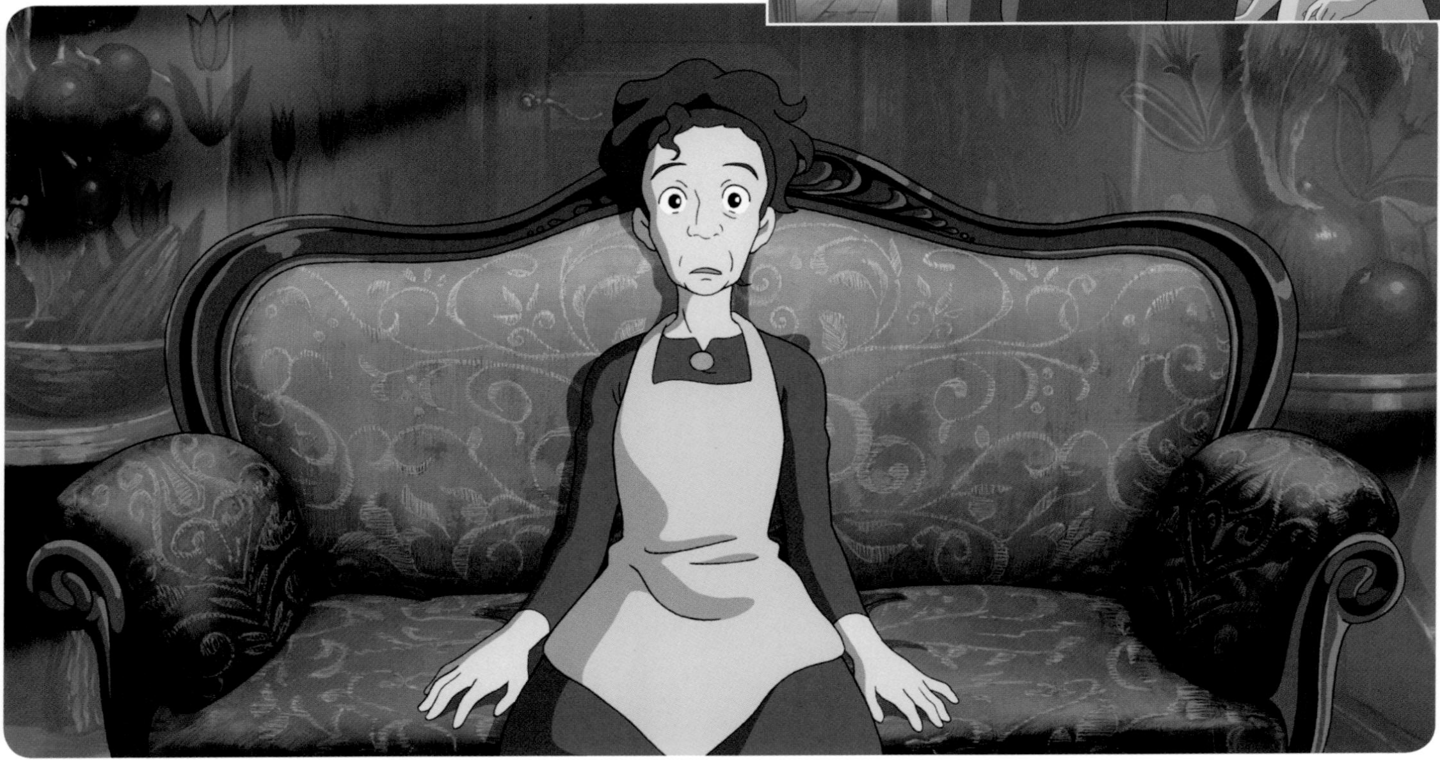

Shawn looked at the tiny house under the closet floor. From beneath the board that served as the roof, he could see a little of the dollhouse kitchen. He gently shut the lid in the floor. Just then…

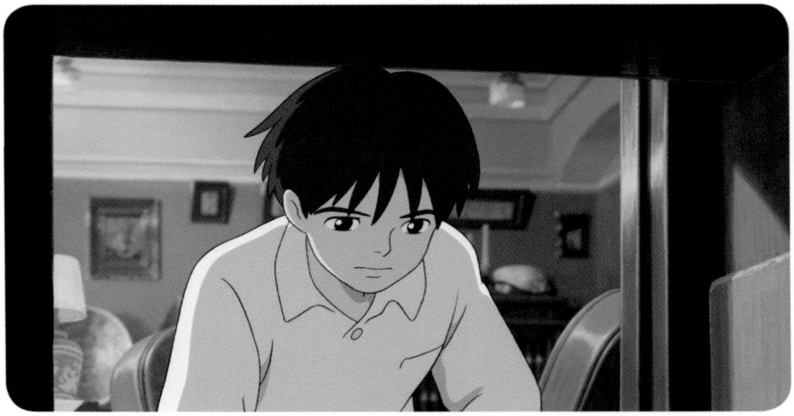

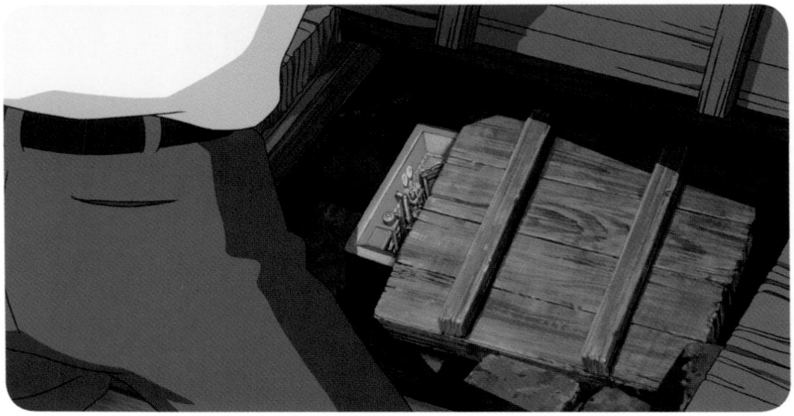

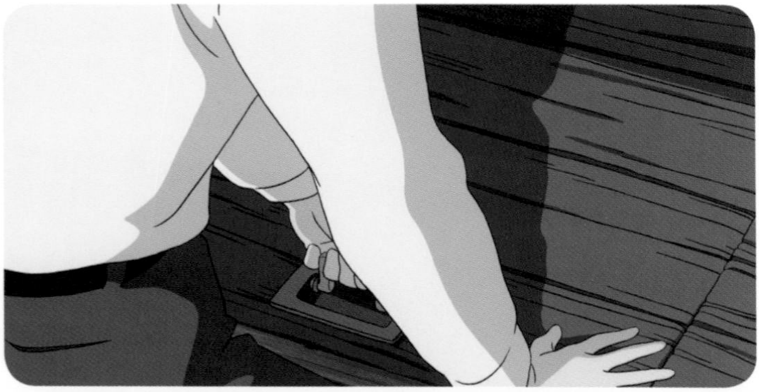

Rattle, slam!

Shawn heard the front door opening. Somebody was home!

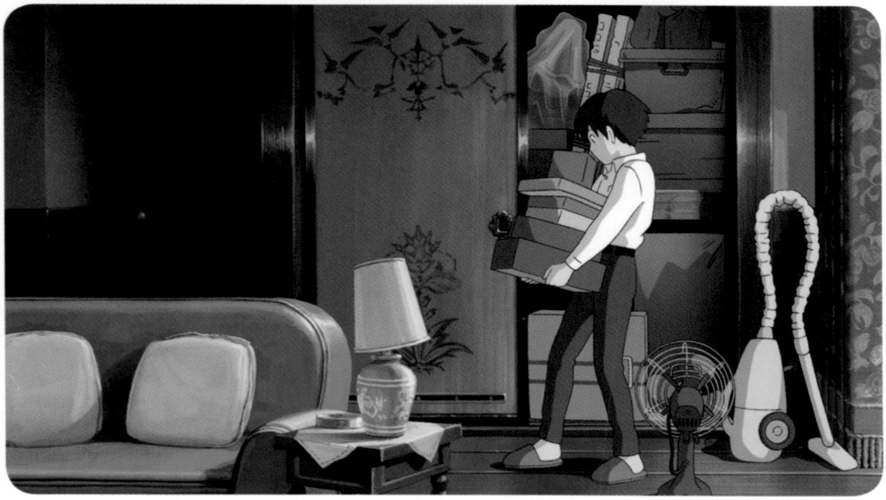

Shawn hurried to put everything in the closet back the way it was.

Hara was back from shopping. As she watched Shawn go back upstairs, she noticed something small on the stairs.

Putting on her glasses, she took a good look. It was a pot from the dollhouse kitchen!

“Hmph…” Hara’s eyes gleamed.

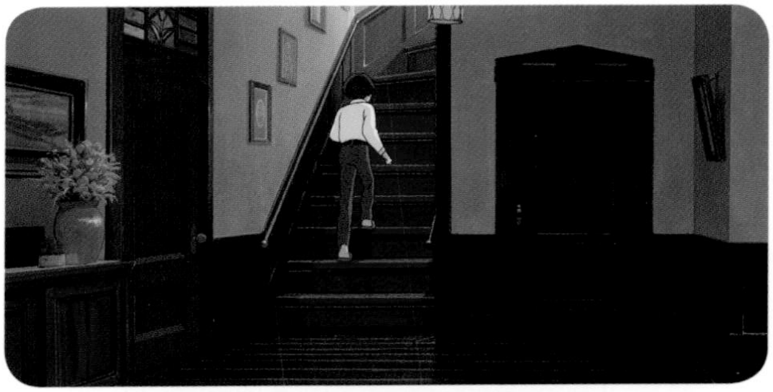

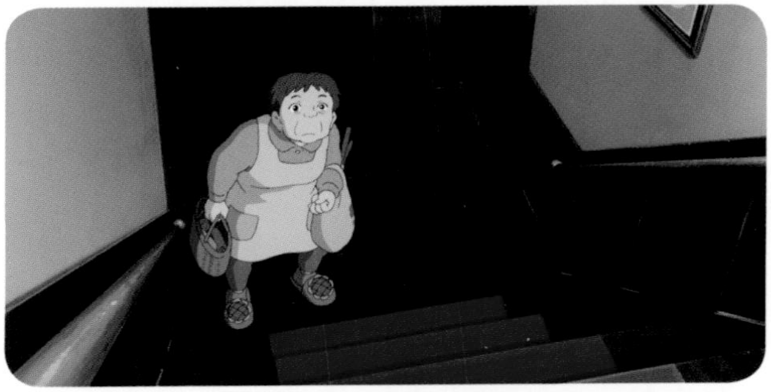

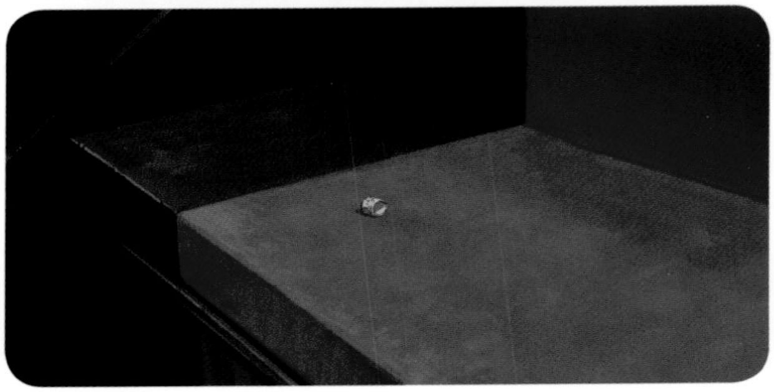

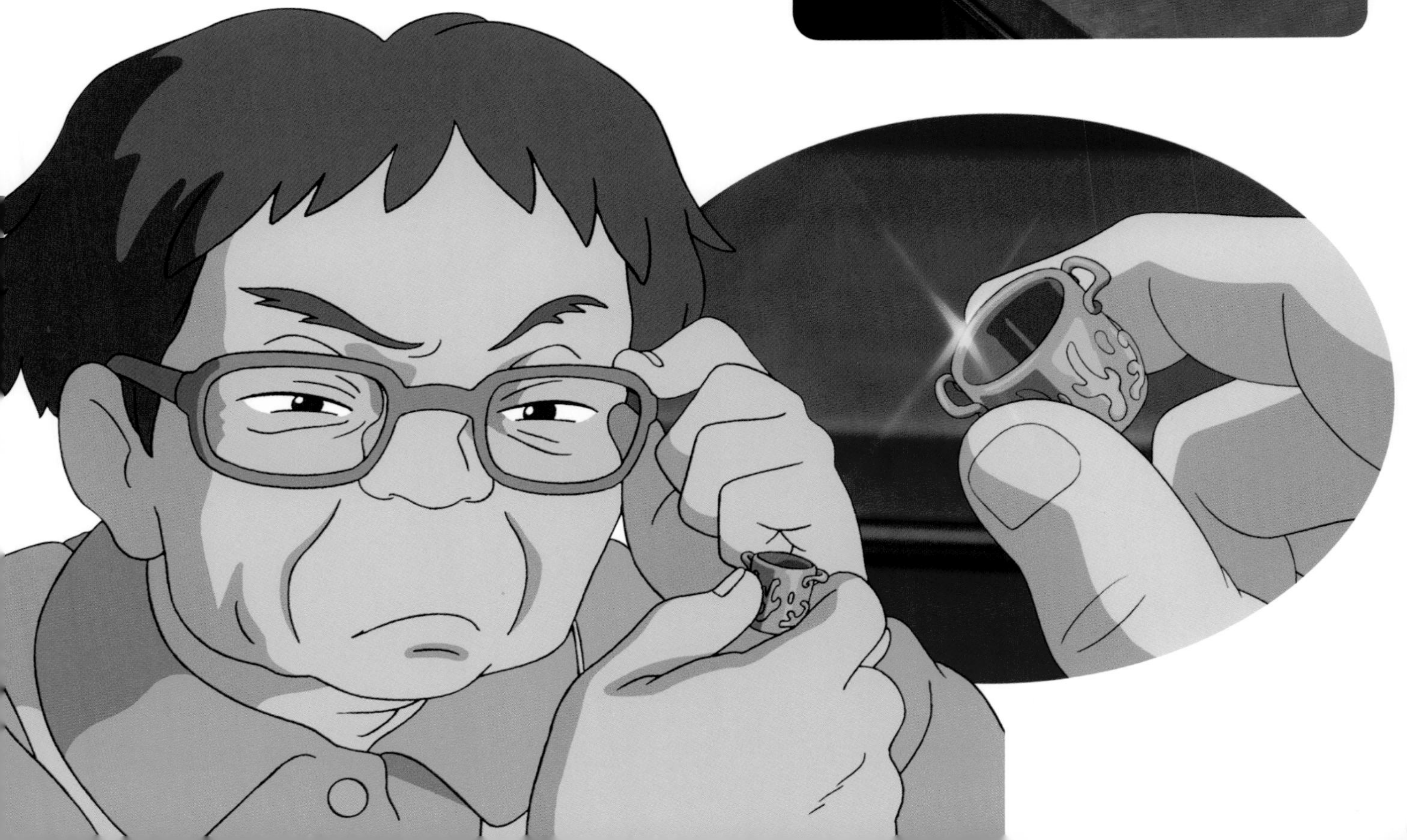

Homily is Kidnapped

Pod decided they needed to move out right away. Homily packed this and that into the big bag she and Arrietty had sewn.

"We can't possibly carry all of this. And Homily, don't take anything from the dollhouse," warned Pod.

"I'm going to make sure that it's safe out there," he continued. "Arrietty, you stay with your mother."

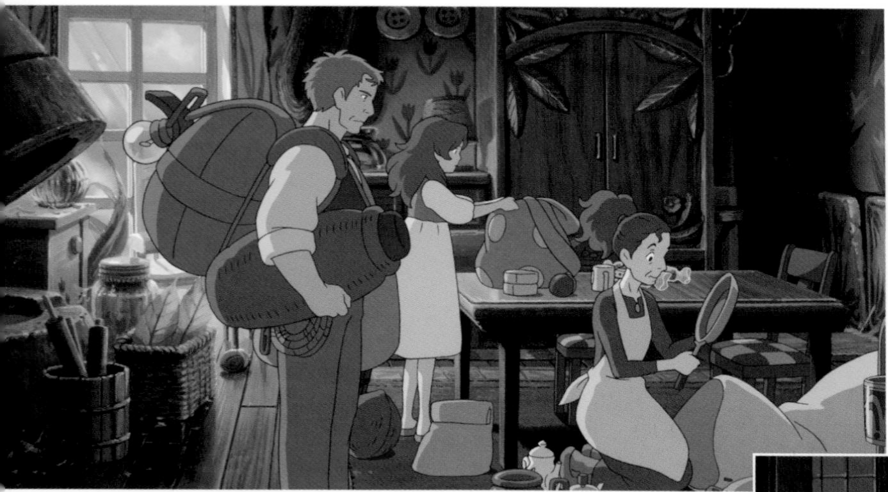

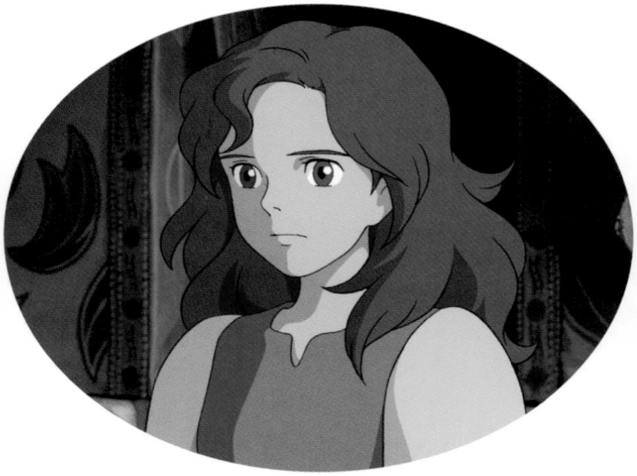

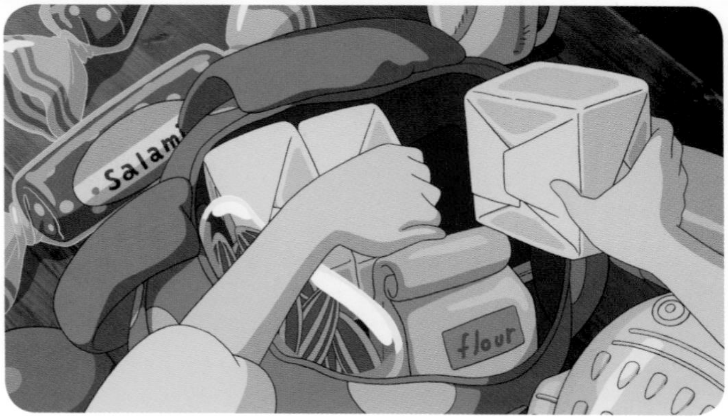
Salami
flour

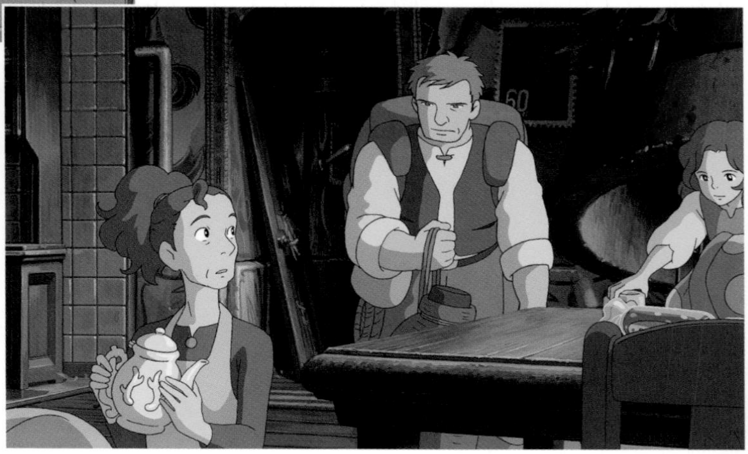

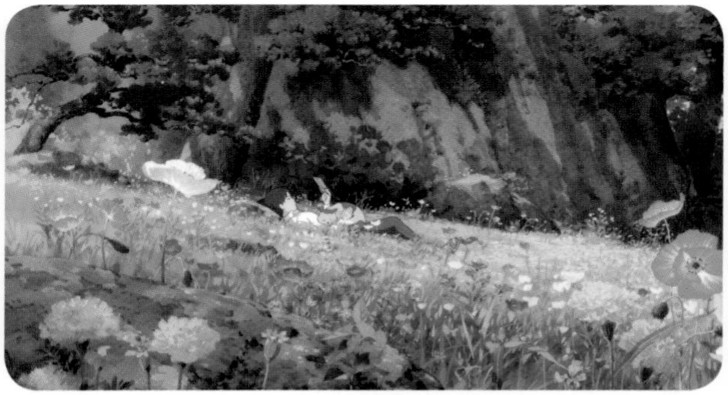
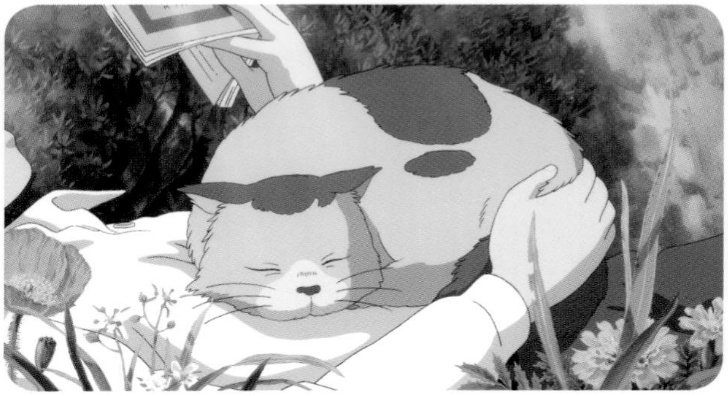
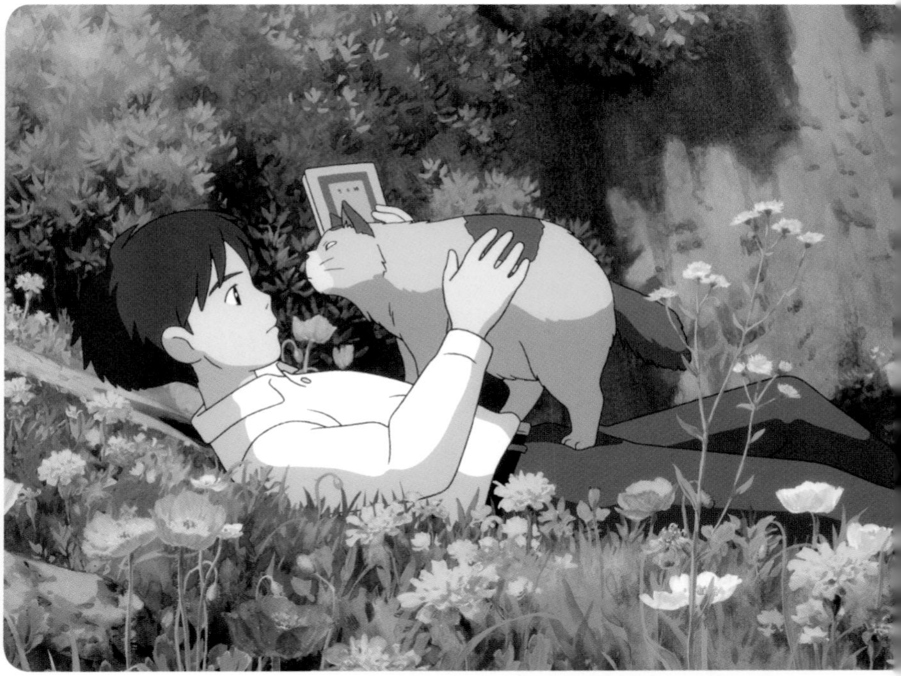

Shawn lay in the field of flowers reading a book. Nina the cat slept comfortably on his stomach. Suddenly Nina stood up, as if sensing something.

Shawn lowered his book and said quietly, "So you finally came."

Arrietty stood behind his head and put down the poppy and his note.

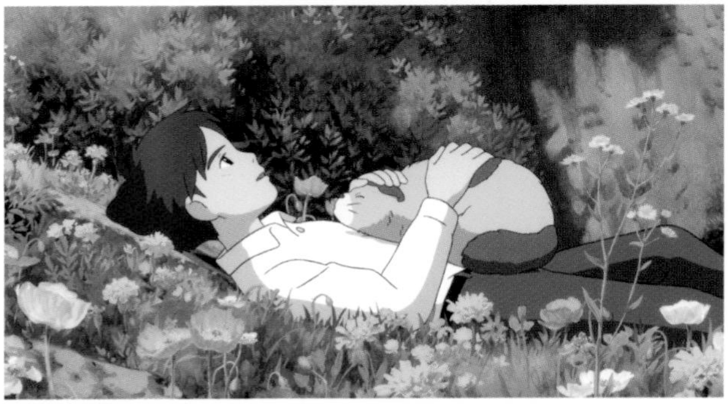
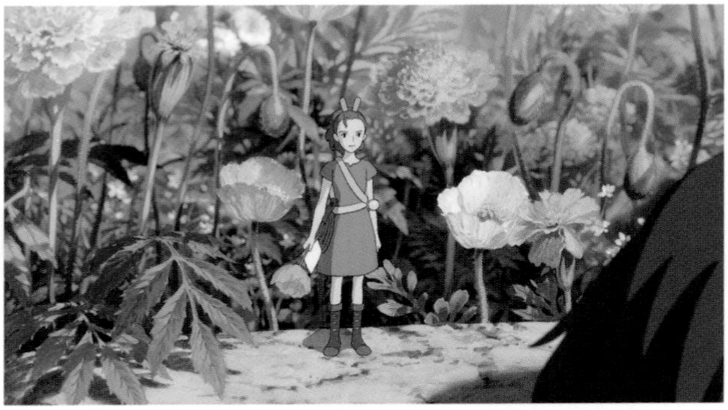
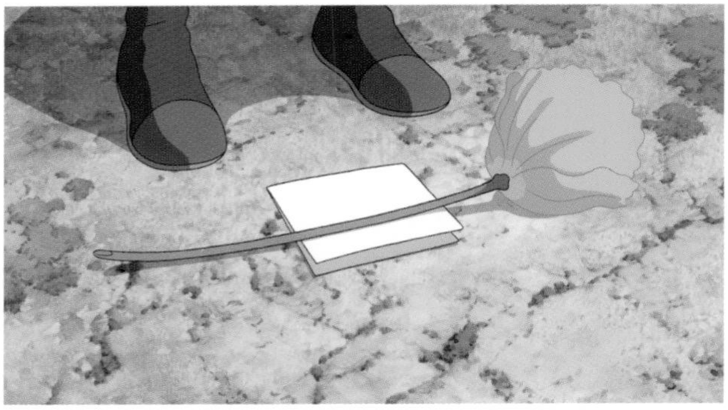

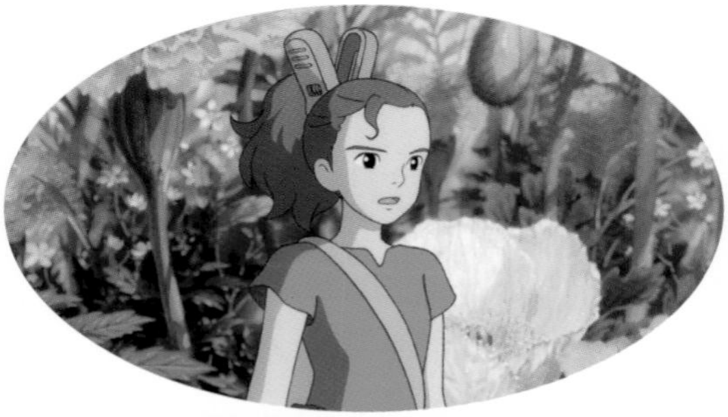

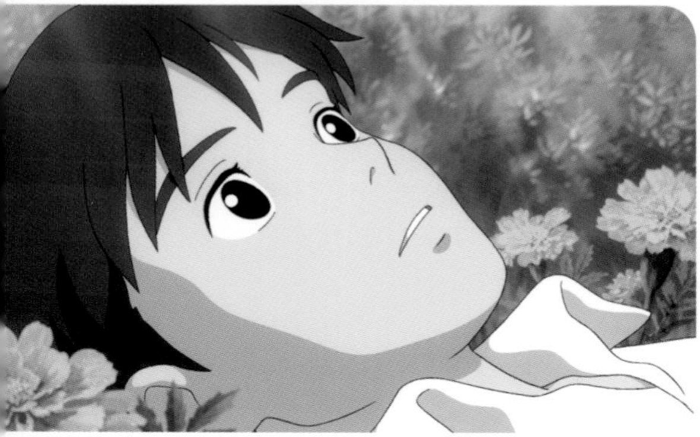

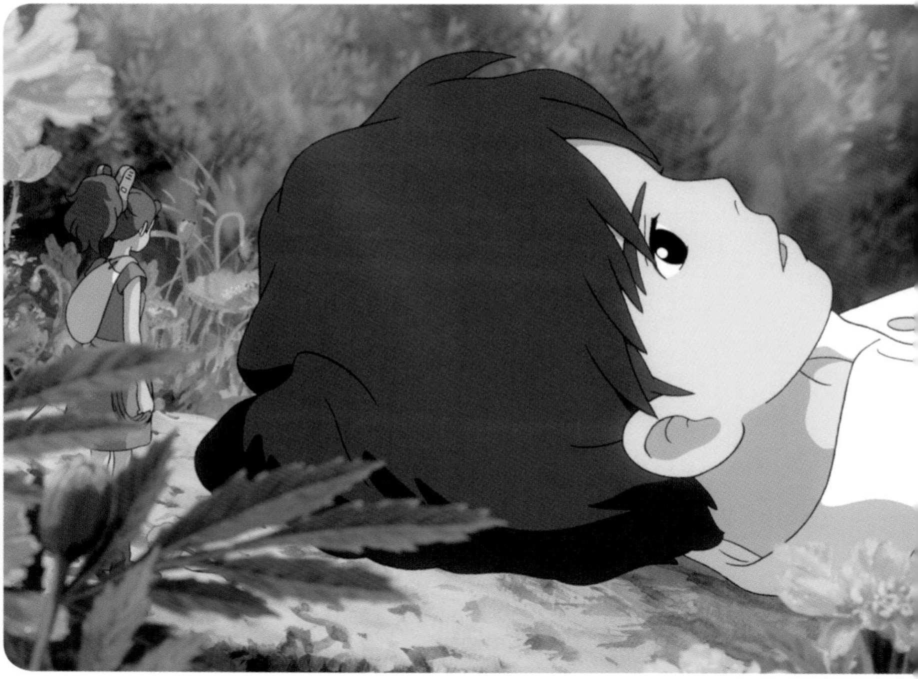

"Do you like your new kitchen?" asked Shawn.

"Well our house looks like a train wreck," Arrietty answered angrily. "But it doesn't matter because I came to tell you goodbye."

Shawn was surprised by Arrietty's response, but he didn't let it show. "May I turn around?" he asked calmly.

Arrietty looked down and was silent. Shawn slowly sat up.

Arrietty lifted her face and looked straight at Shawn. He gazed at her in wonder.

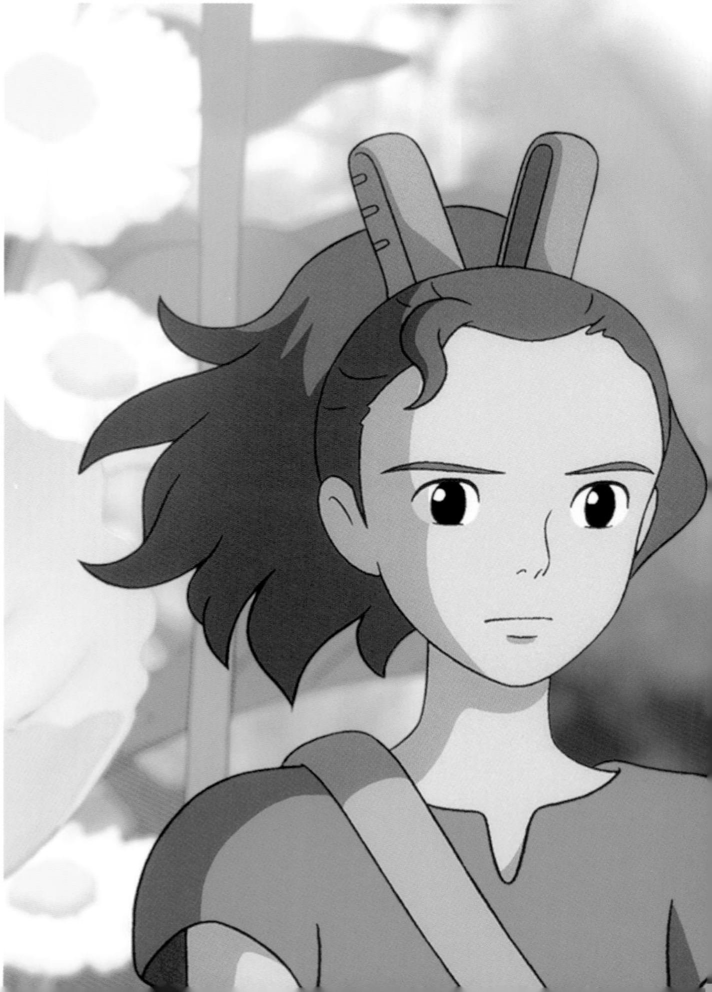

"You're beautiful…" he said.

Arrietty was touched, but her expression did not soften.

"My Papa said we have to move now," Arrietty said. "You've seen us and… Borrowers aren't supposed to be seen."

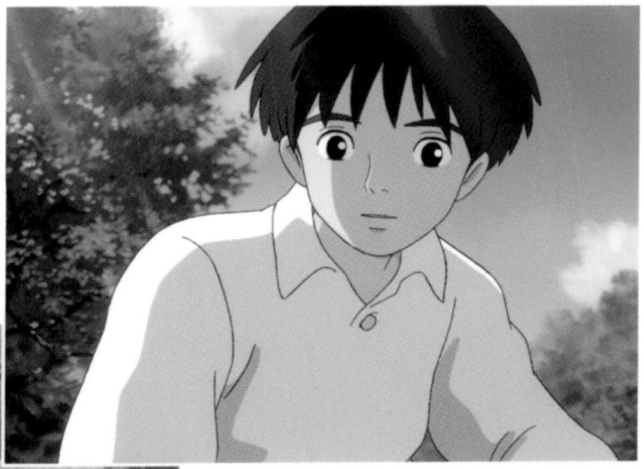

"What are Borrowers?" Shawn asked.

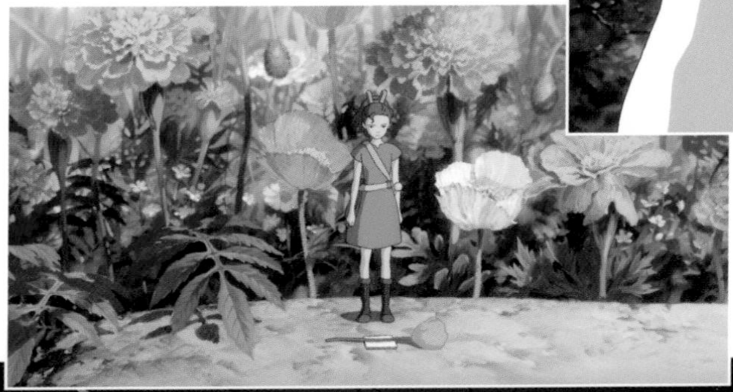

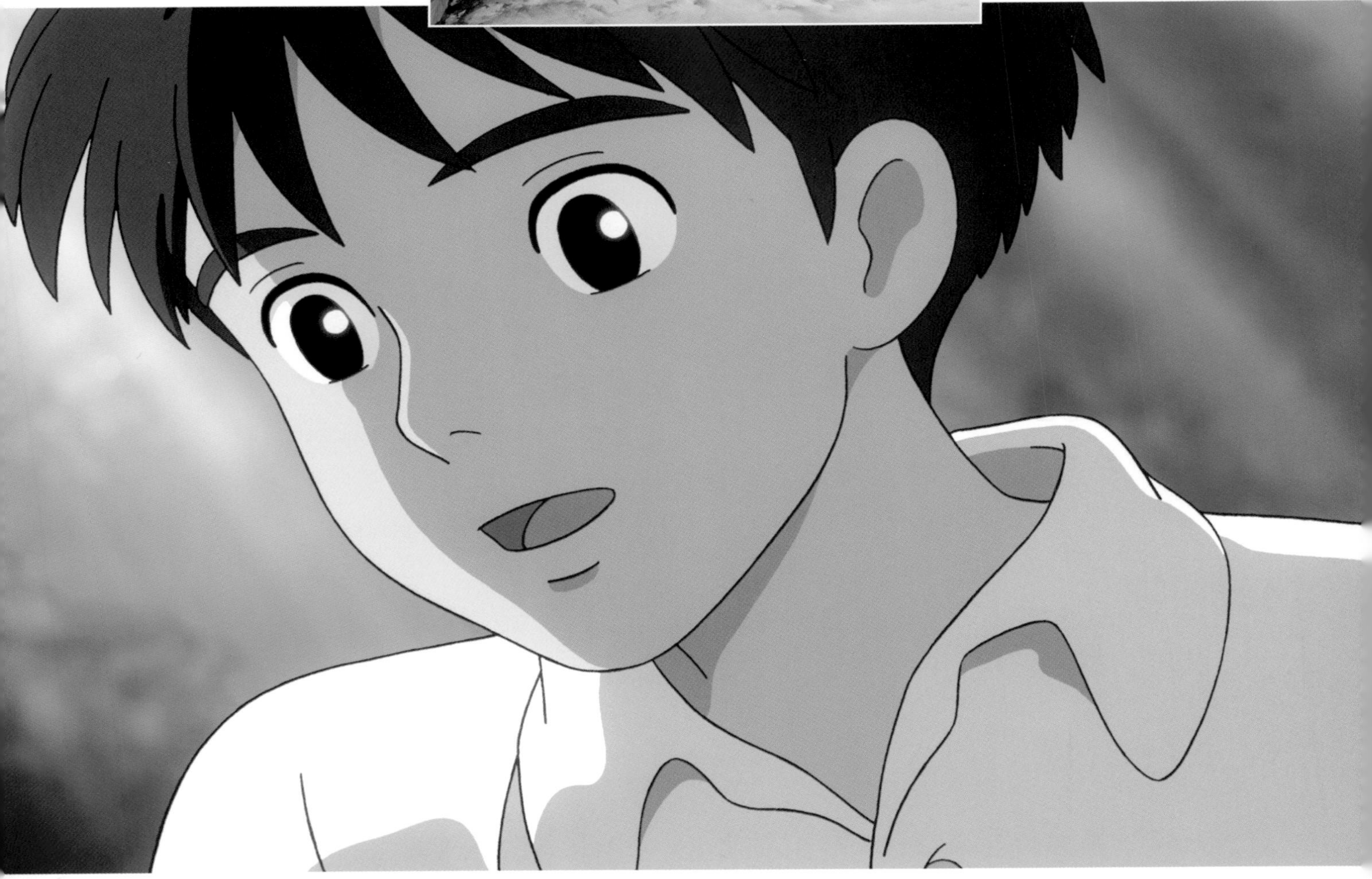

"My mother, father and I are all Borrowers. We borrow things that beans won't miss. Just little things—soap and cookies and sugar. All things that we need to survive. Even my great-grandfather was a Borrower."

"So in my aunt's house, how many other Borrowers are living with you?"

"Just my father and my mother and me."

"What about in other houses?"

"I'm sure there are some," Arrietty replied. "But I've only met one other so far."

"Oh… you must be afraid you're the only ones of your kind who are left."

"What do you mean?" Arrietty asked.

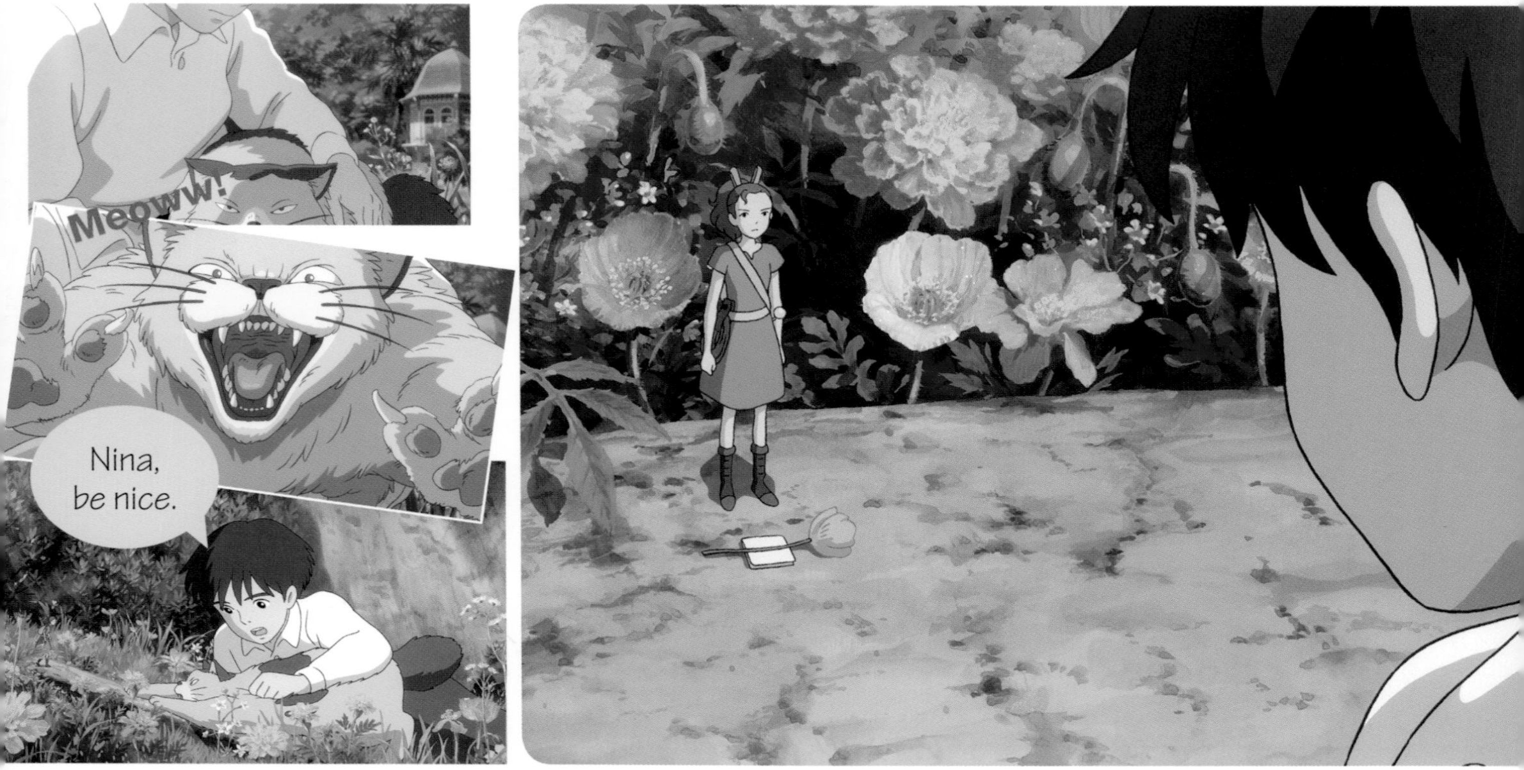
Meoww!
Nina, be nice.

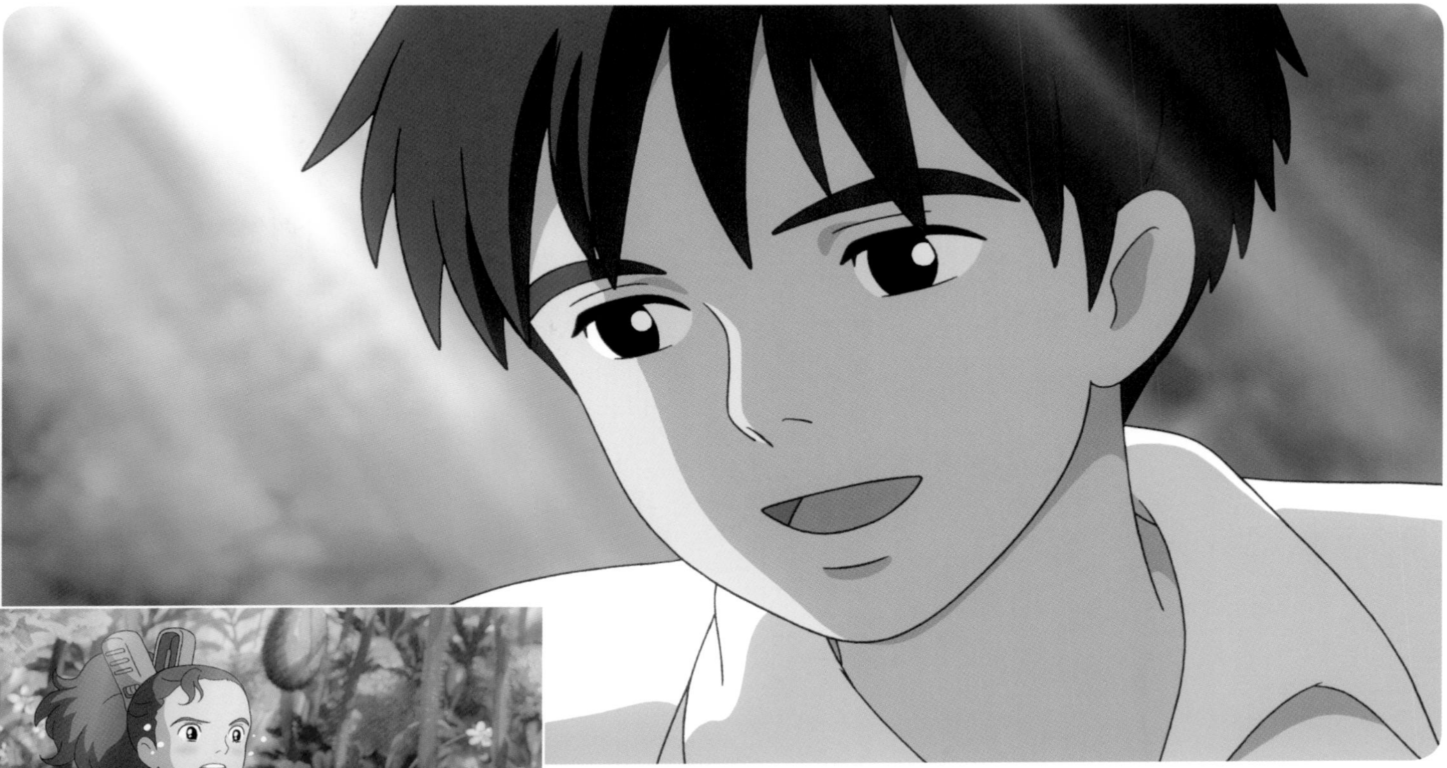

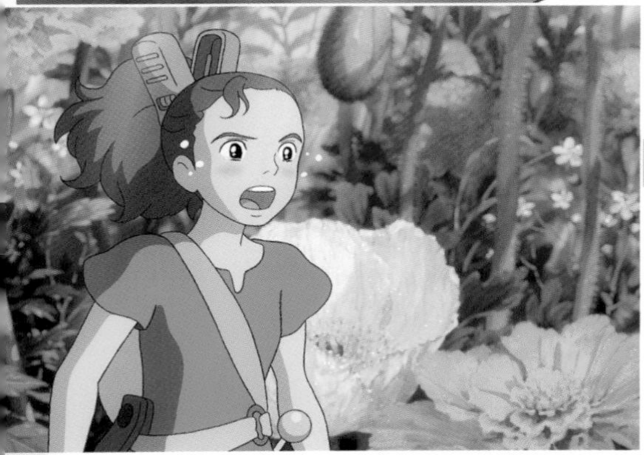

“Every year there are fewer and fewer of you. Aren’t you scared that soon you’ll all be—gone?”

“What a horrible thing to say!” Arrietty shouted. Tears of anger and sadness filled her eyes.

“But you know none of us can live forever, right?” Shawn said. “We all have to die sometime.”

“I guess so…”

“Believe me, I know what I’m talking about,” Shawn said. “Sometimes things happen that are just beyond your control. There’s really nothing you can do about them. Sometimes, you just have to accept the hand of fate.”

"No you don't!" Arrietty cried, glaring at Shawn.

"Sometimes you have to stand up and fight for the things that are worth fighting for. You have to survive. That's what my Papa says.

"And so we're leaving, even though it's dangerous," Arrietty continued. "We are going to survive. We are Borrowers and we'll make do—we always have. As long as we have each other to live for, we'll keep on living!"

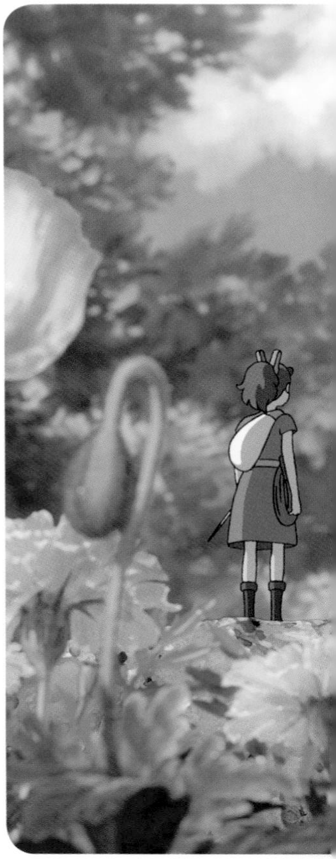

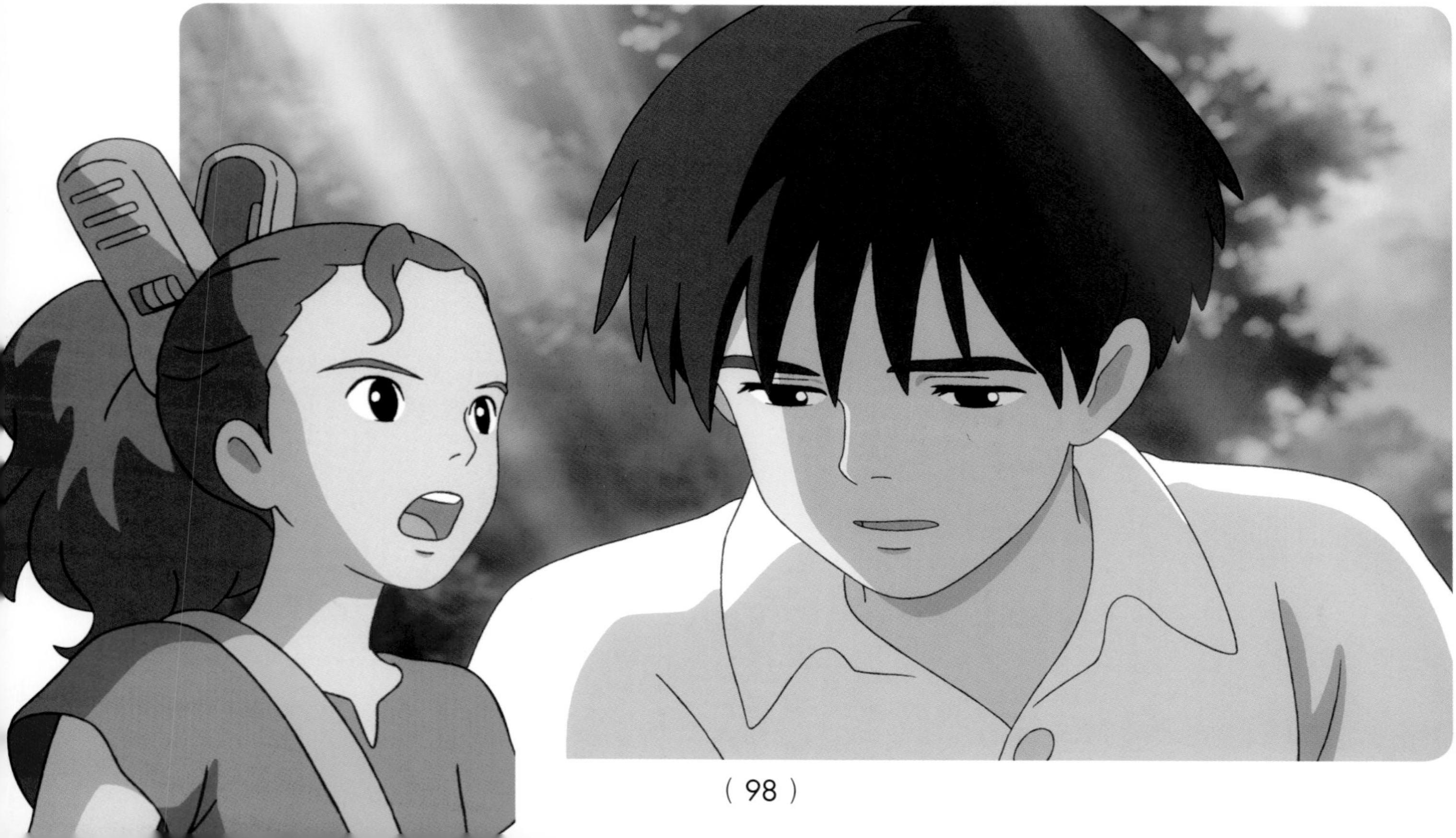

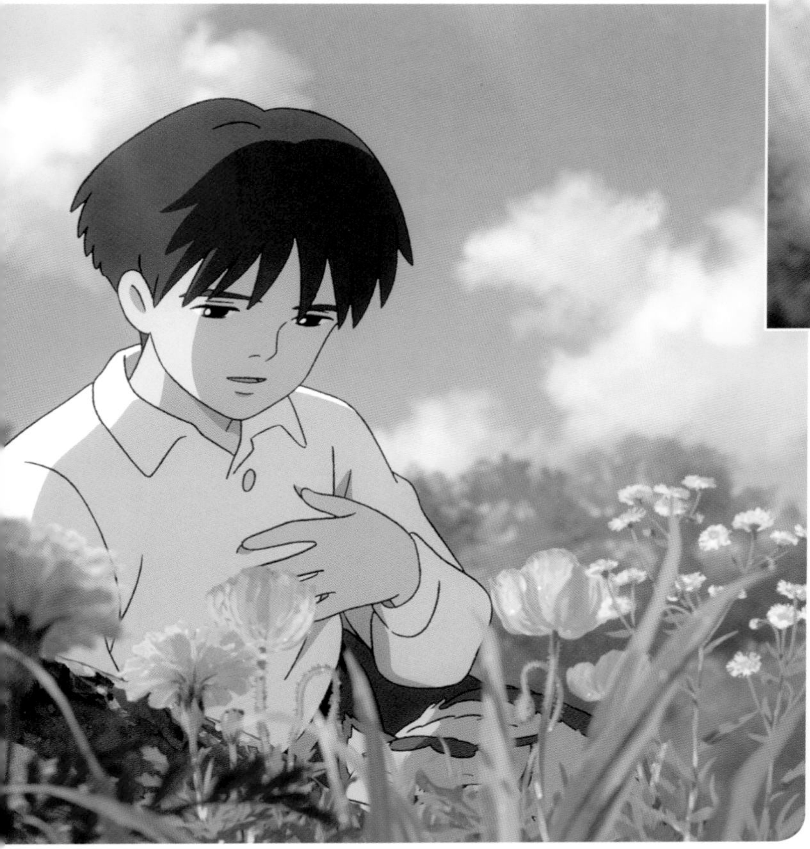

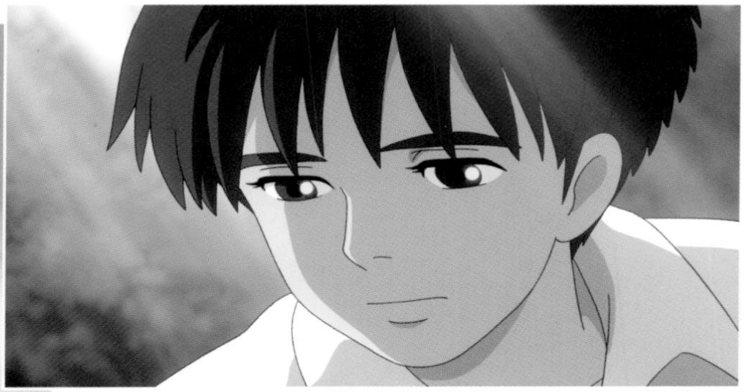

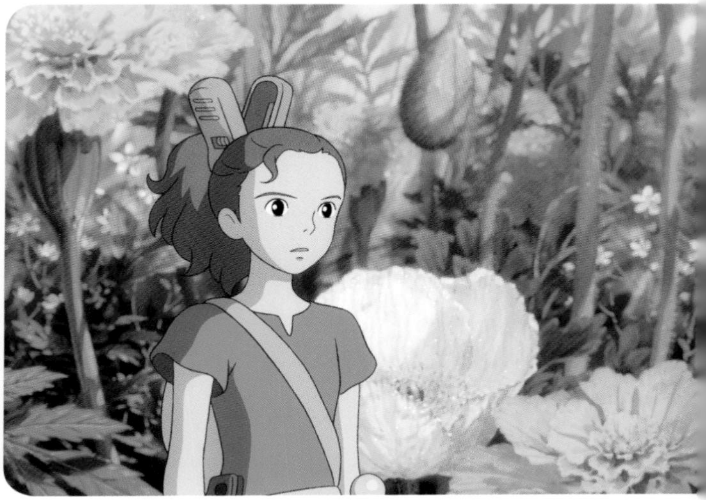

"I'm sorry. I didn't mean to upset you," Shawn said quietly. "Actually…I'm the one who's going to die."

"What?"

"There's something wrong *here*," said Shawn, putting his hand over his heart. "They're going to operate next week, but—it probably won't help.

"I've always been sick and someone always has to look after me… And when I saw you, I just wanted to look after *you*. But I guess I've ruined things. I'm sorry."

"And I'm sorry to hear about your heart," said Arrietty. Her anger was gone.

Hara was spying on Shawn again. She saw nobody near him, yet he looked like he was talking to someone.

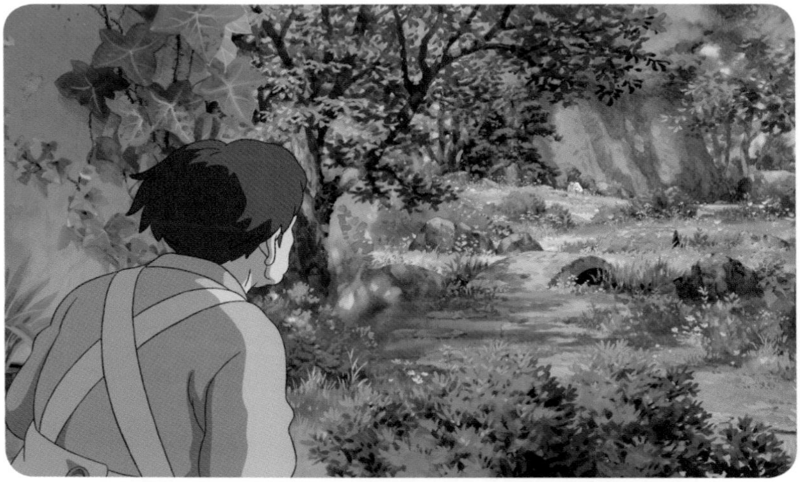

She went back inside the house.

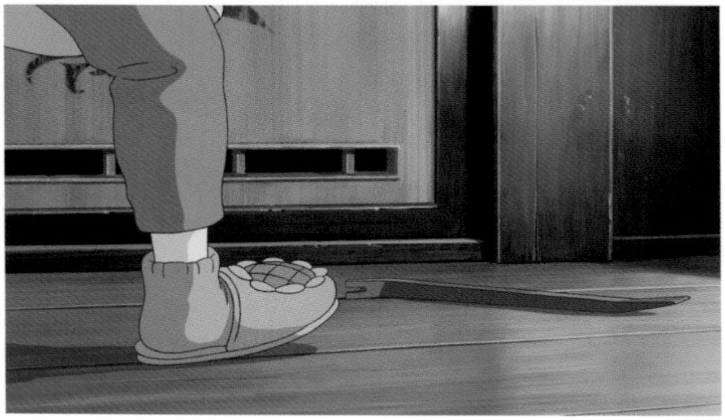

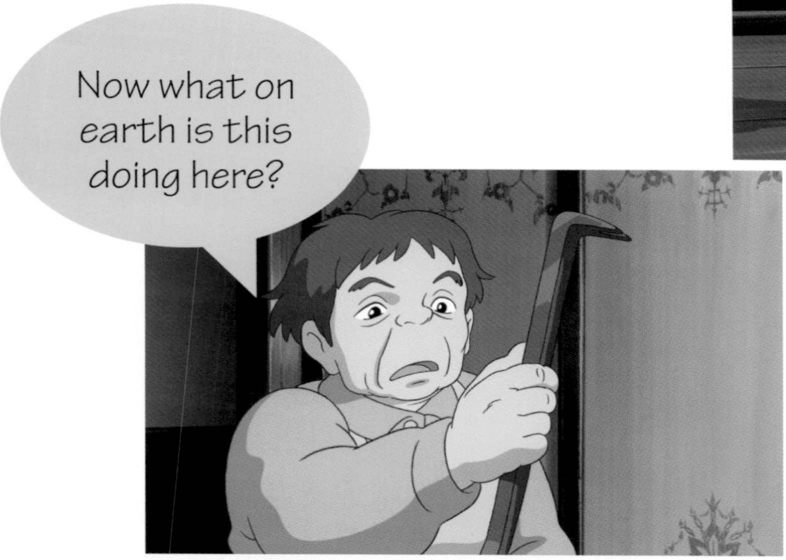
Now what on earth is this doing here?

On the floor in front of the living room closet, Hara found the crowbar Shawn had used to pry the ceiling off of Arrietty's home.

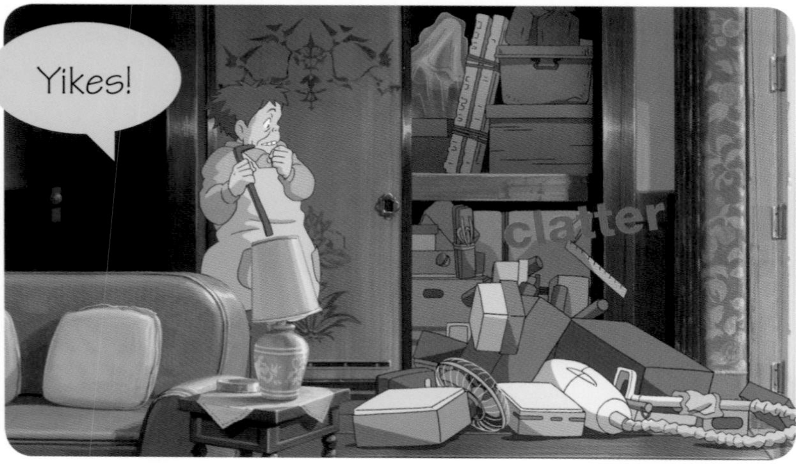
Yikes!
clatter

She opened the closet door. All the things Shawn had shoved inside came tumbling out.

Suddenly Hara noticed a door in the closet floor. She grabbed the handle and lifted it.

There was the kitchen from the dollhouse!

Hara lifted the door all the way up and peered inside.

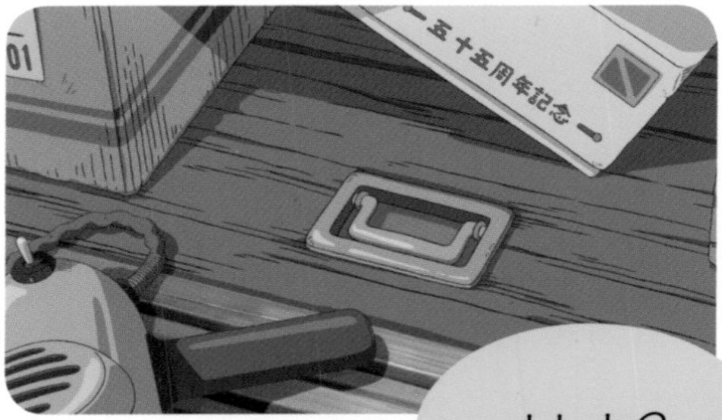

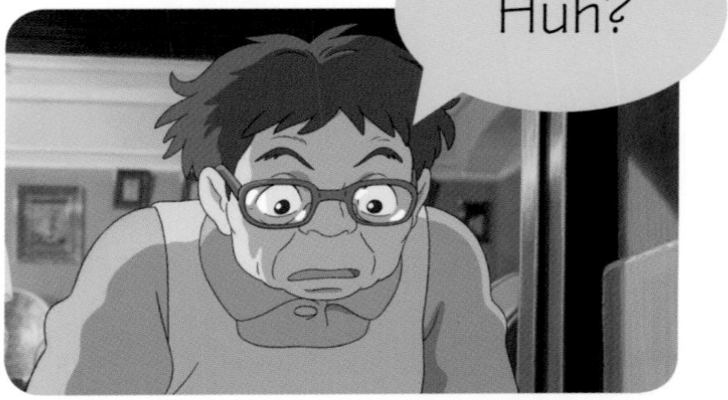
Huh?

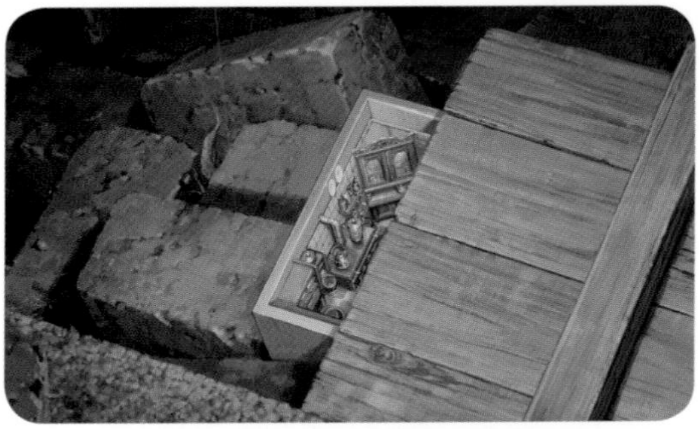

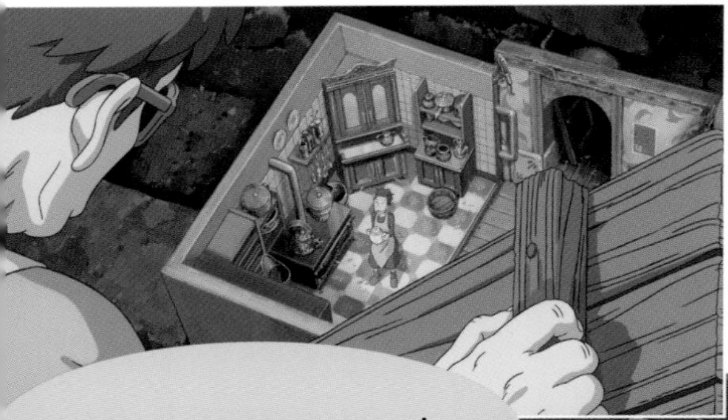

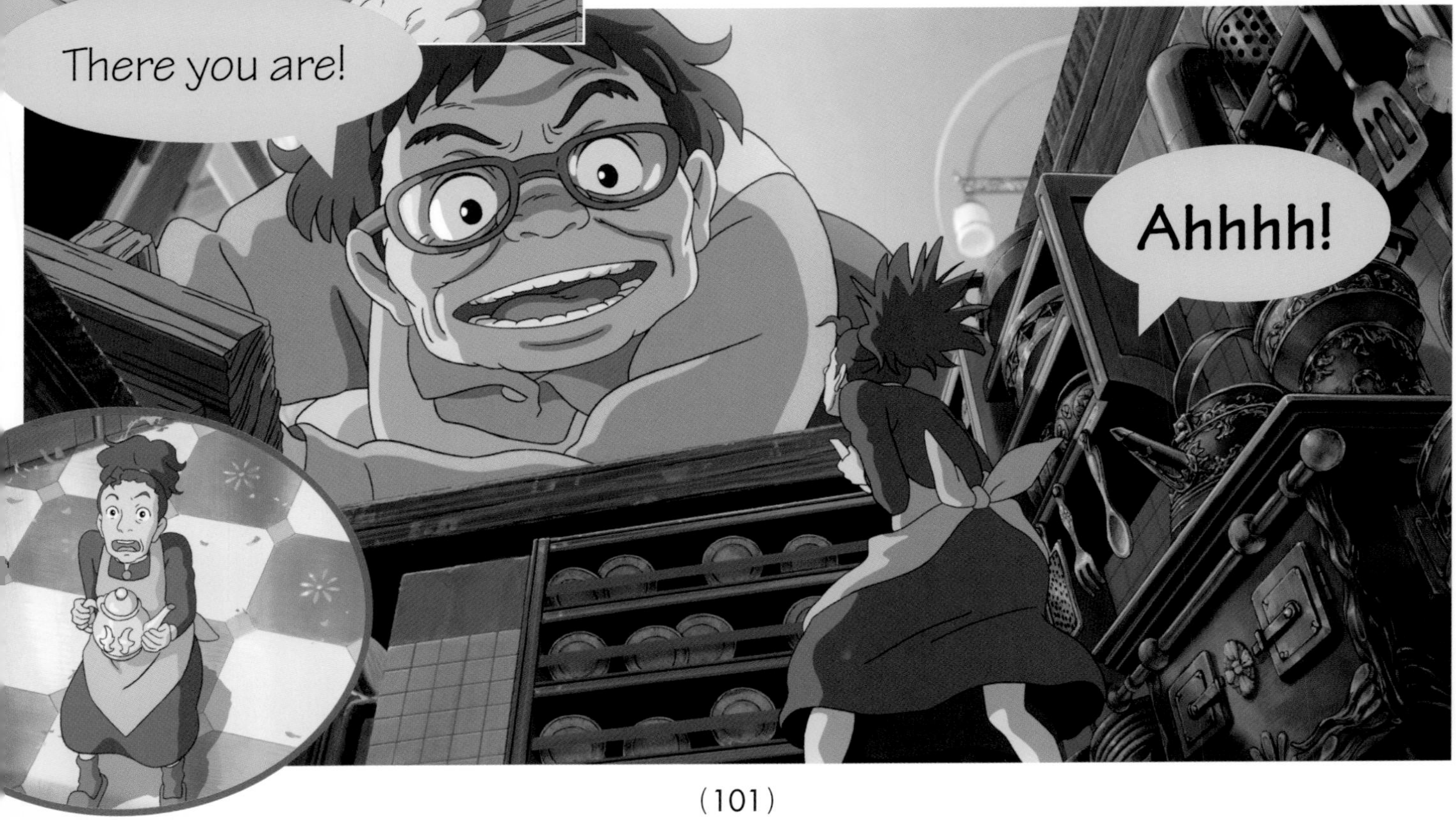
There you are!
Ahhhh!

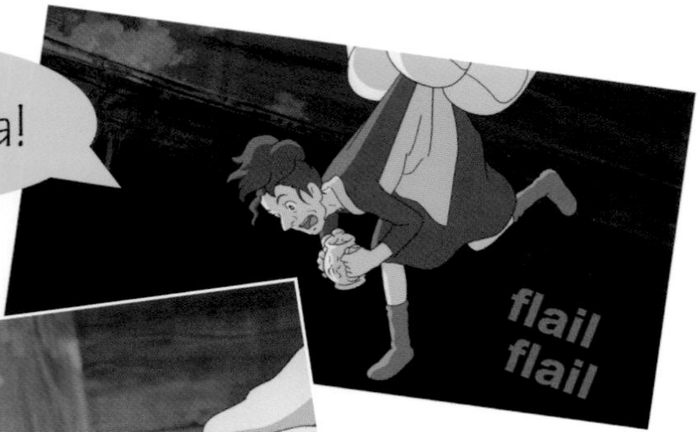
Whaaaa!
flail
flail

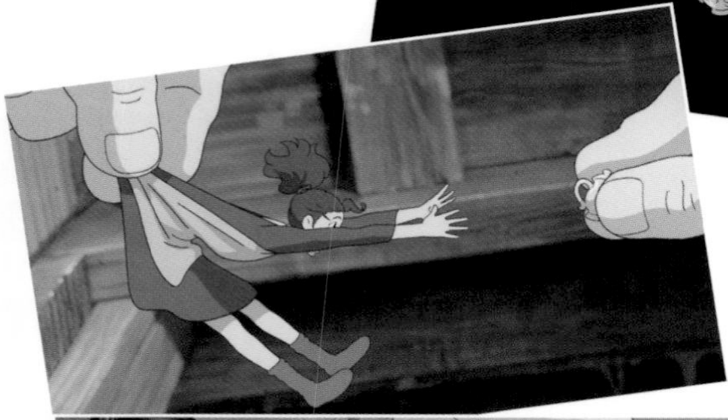

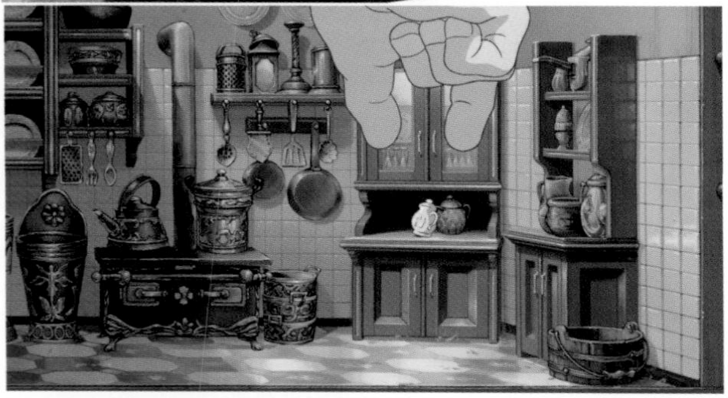

Hara picked Homily up and took her teapot away. She tried to put the teapot back on a shelf but it fell to the floor.

Hara put Homily in the pocket of her apron, replaced the door, and put everything back in the closet.

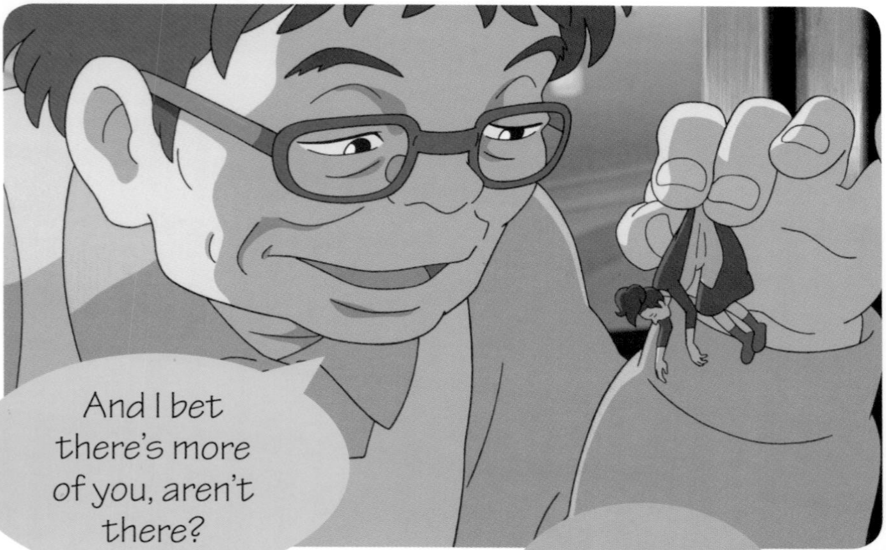
And I bet there's more of you, aren't there?

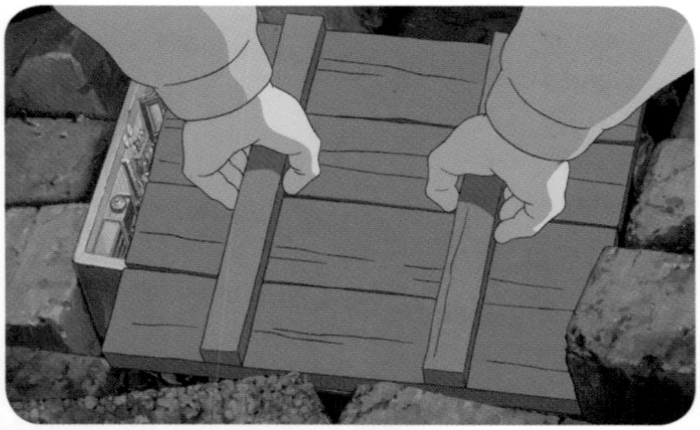

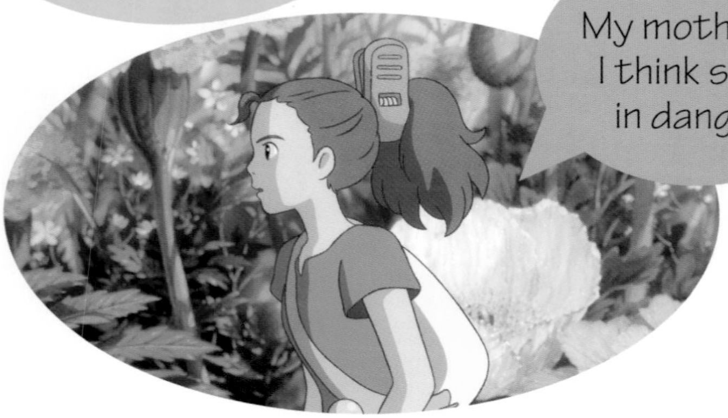
My mother... I think she's in danger!

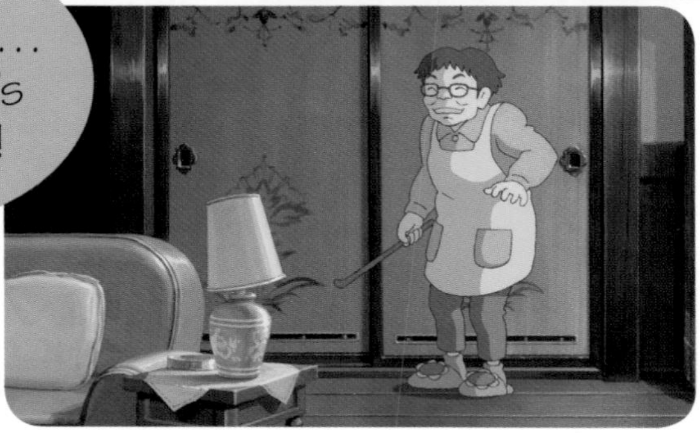

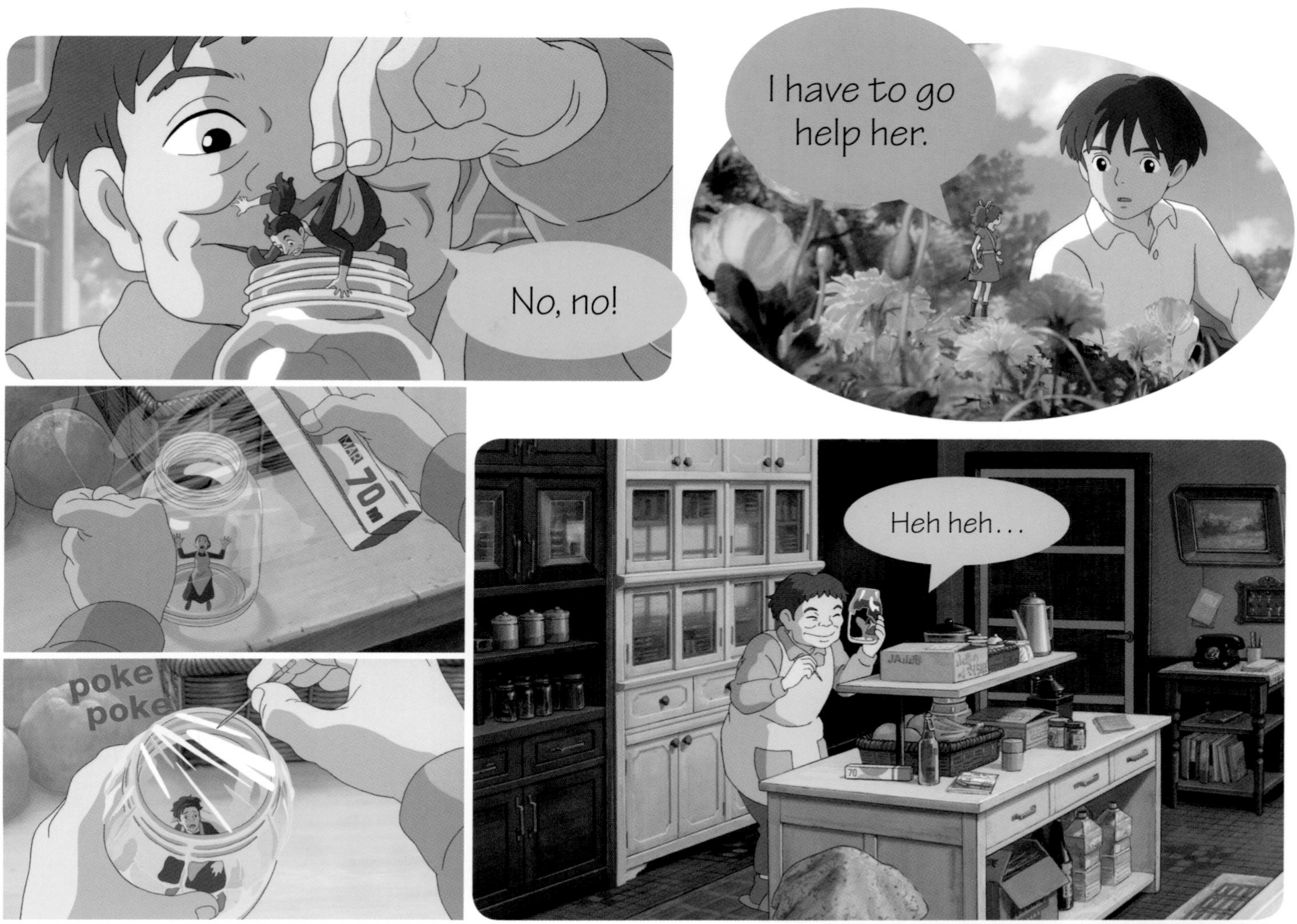
No, no!
I have to go help her.
poke
poke
Heh heh...

Then she went into the kitchen and put Homily in an empty jar. She wrapped the top of the jar in plastic and poked it with holes so Homily could breathe.

Hara was very pleased with herself. She hid Homily on a pantry shelf among the food.

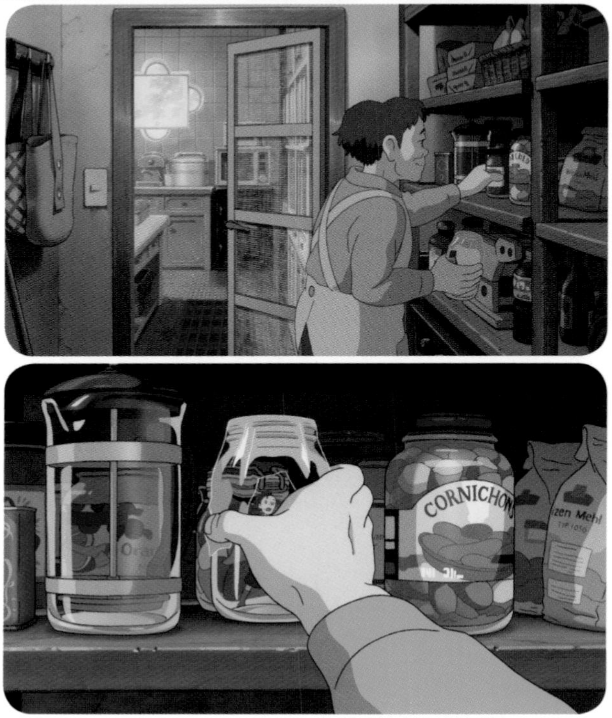

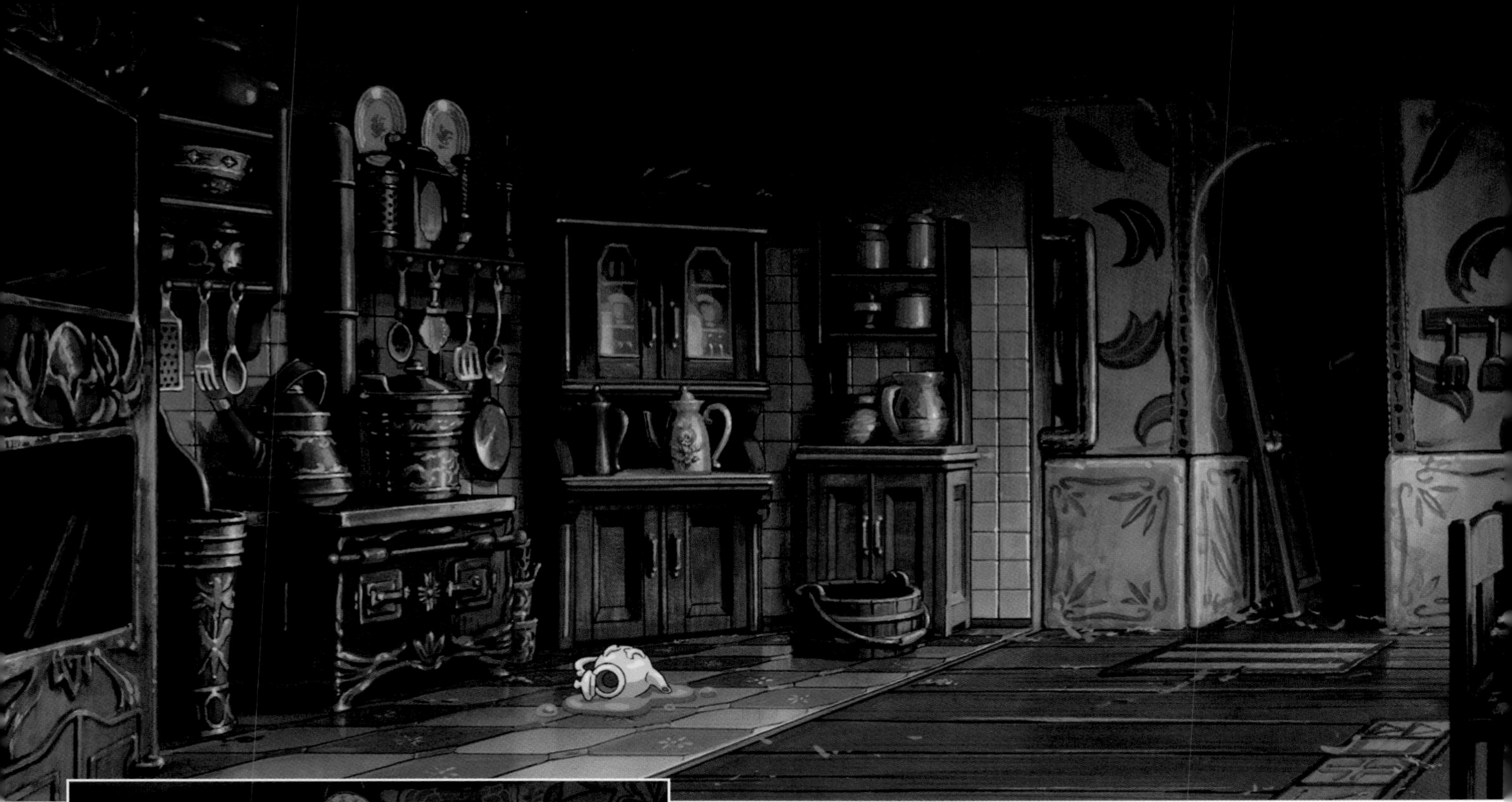

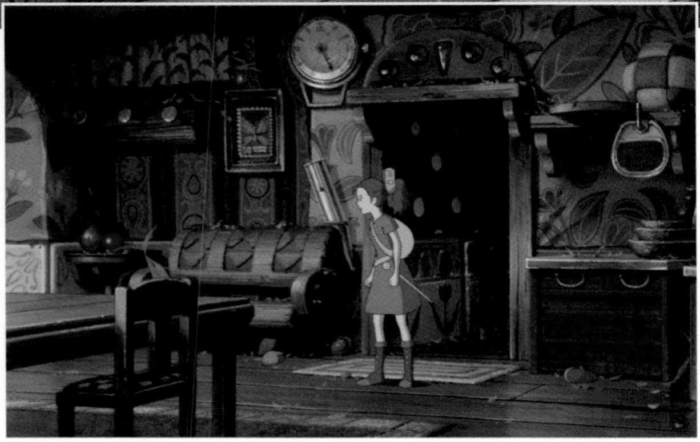

When Arrietty got home, her mother was nowhere to be found. The teapot had fallen on the floor and the tea had spilled.

Arrietty picked up the teapot and looked at the ceiling. It was not on straight.

"Something terrible has happened," she said.

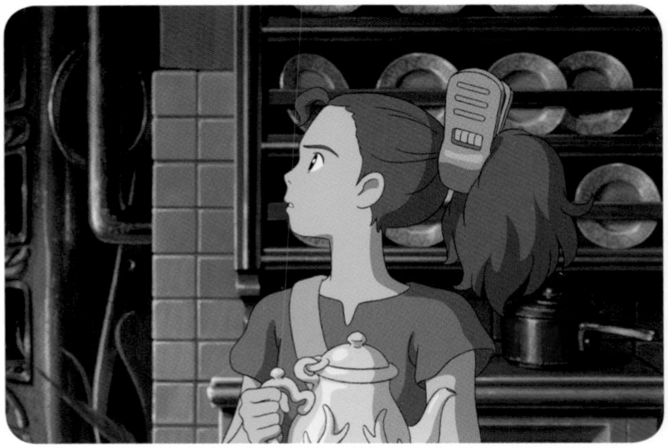

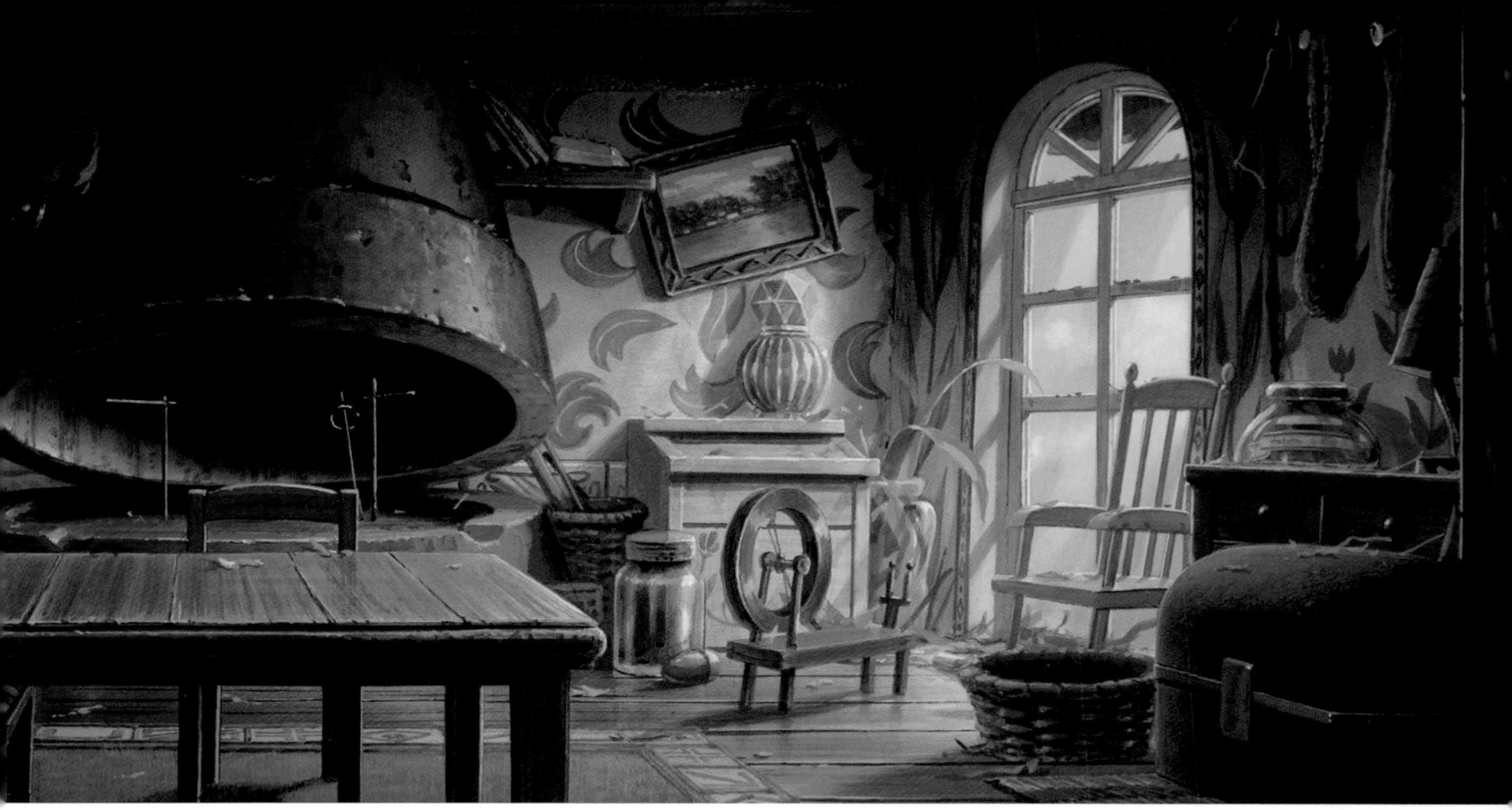

Arrietty hurried back out to the yard, but Shawn was no longer there.

She started climbing up the vine to Shawn's room.

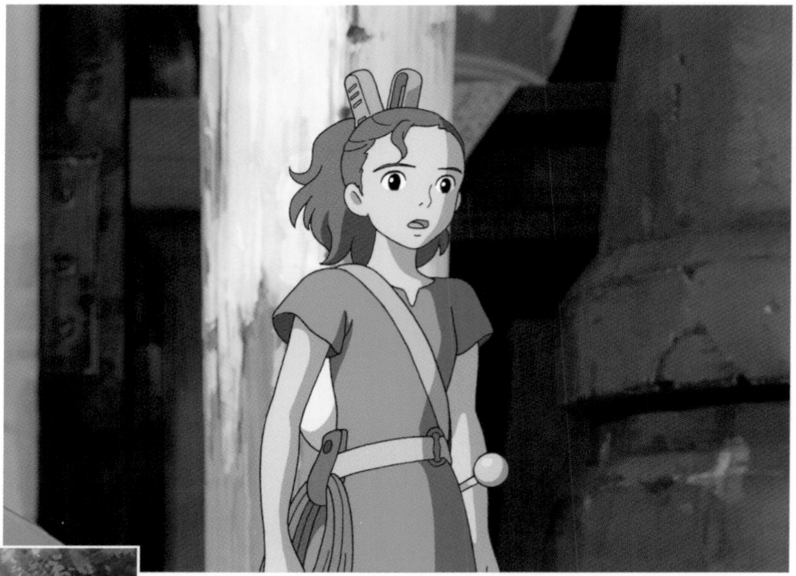

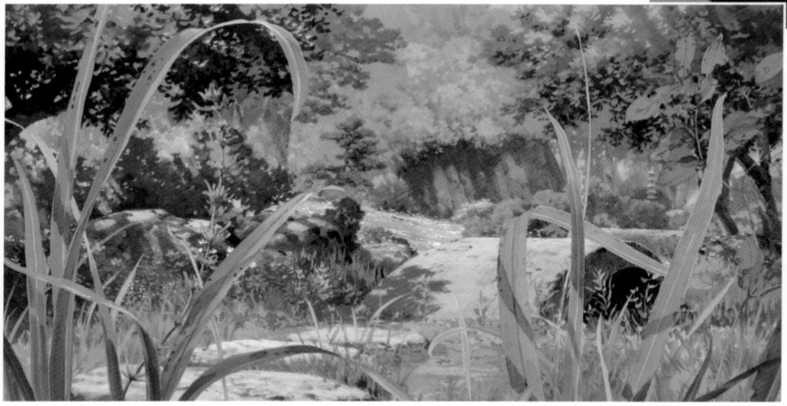

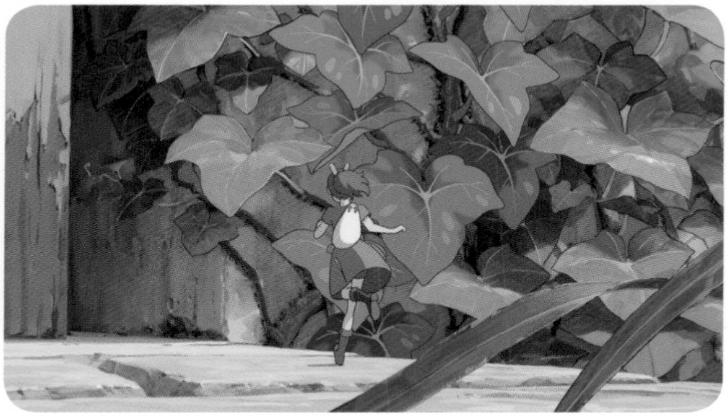

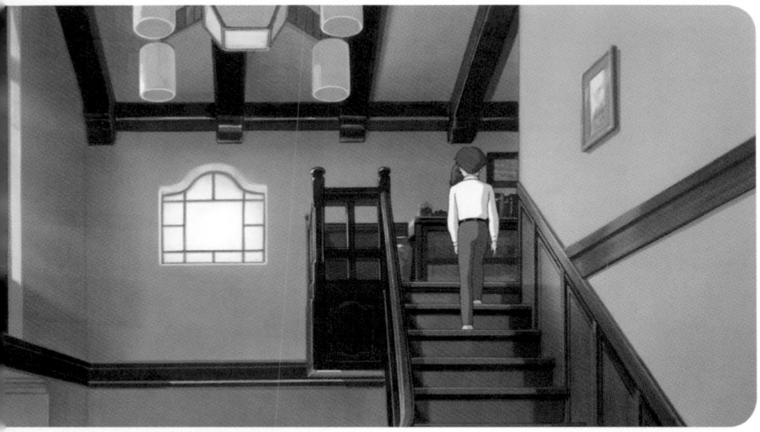

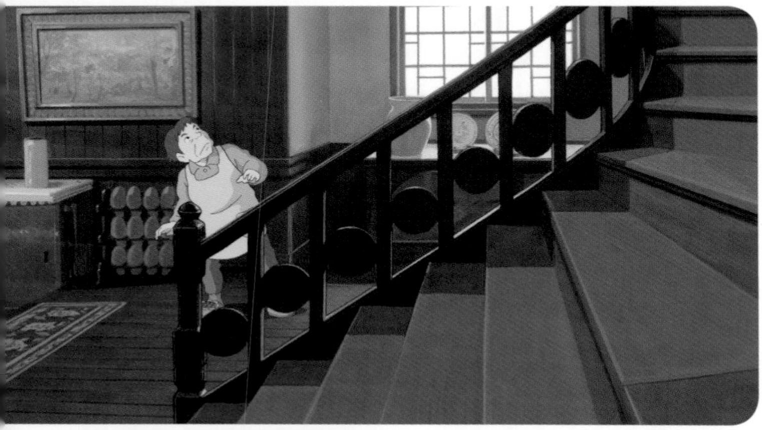

Hara watched as Shawn went back inside the house. He looked disappointed.

Hara waited until he was back in his room. Then she locked his door and hurried to the kitchen to make a phone call.

"Hello, Squeaky Klean? Could you get out here right away?

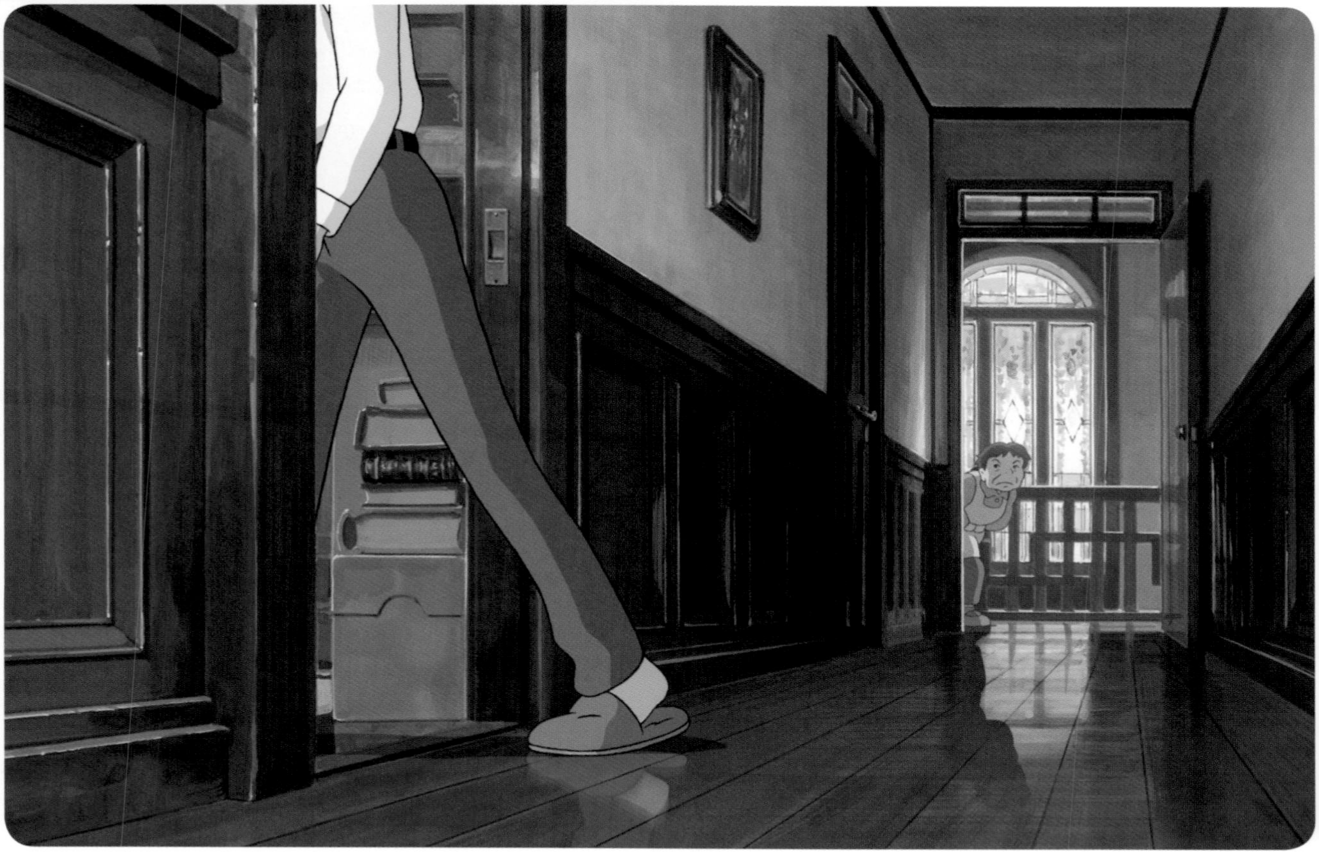

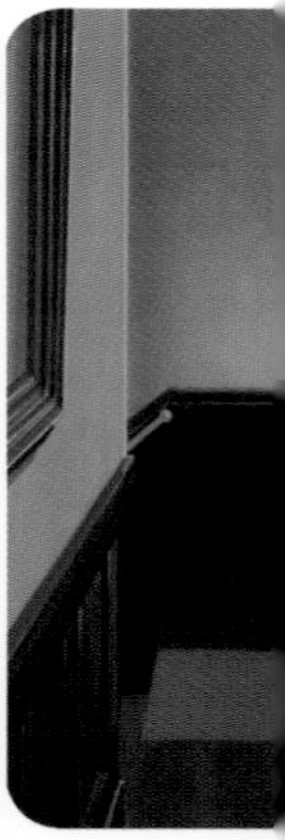

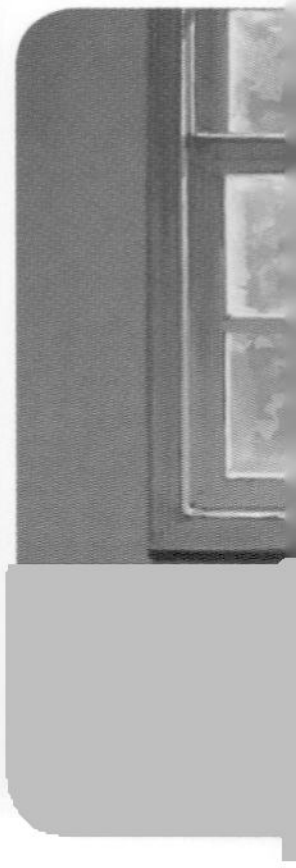

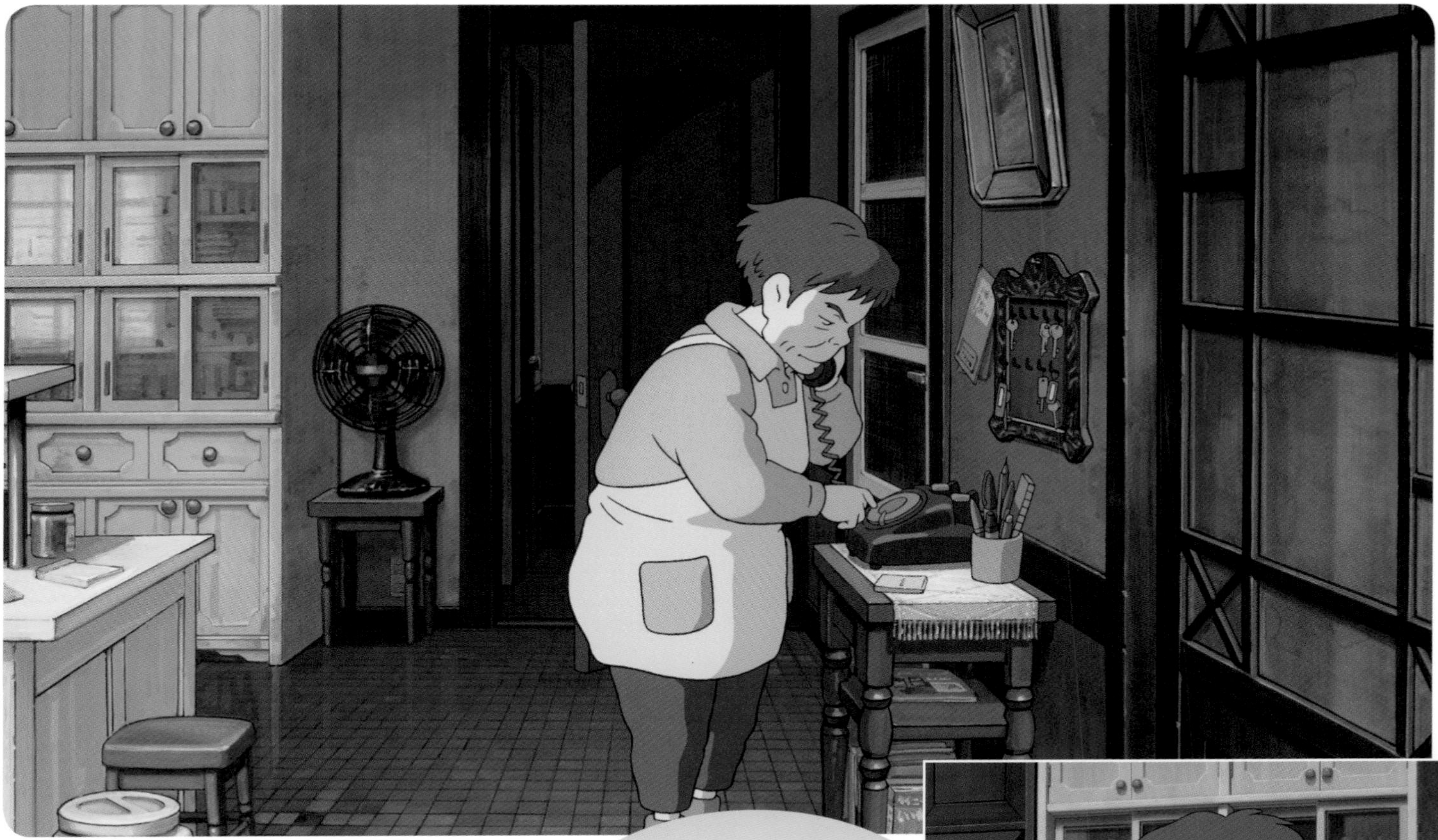

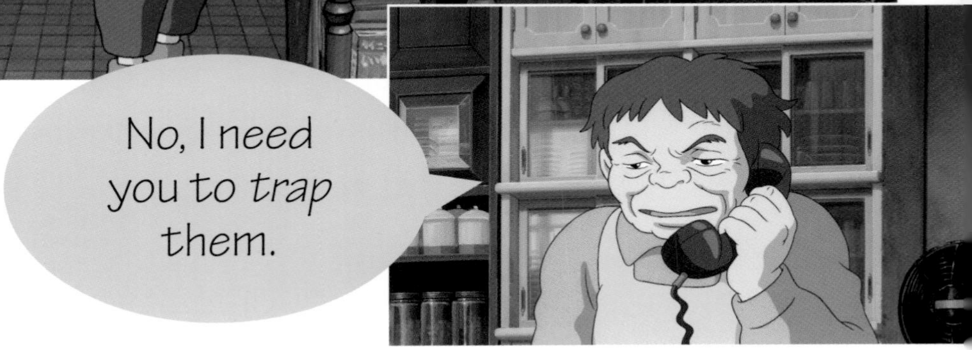
No, I need you to *trap* them.

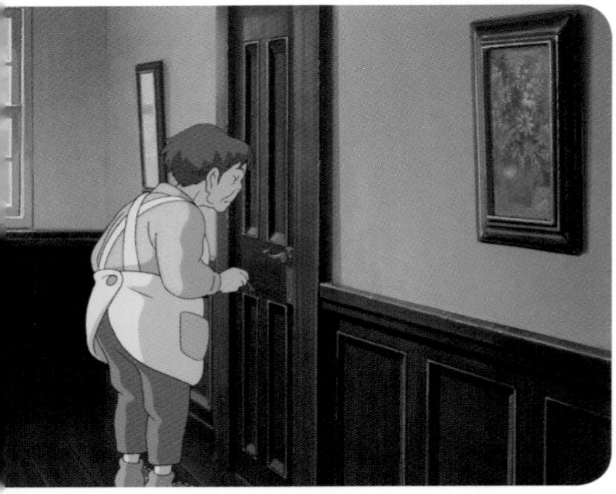

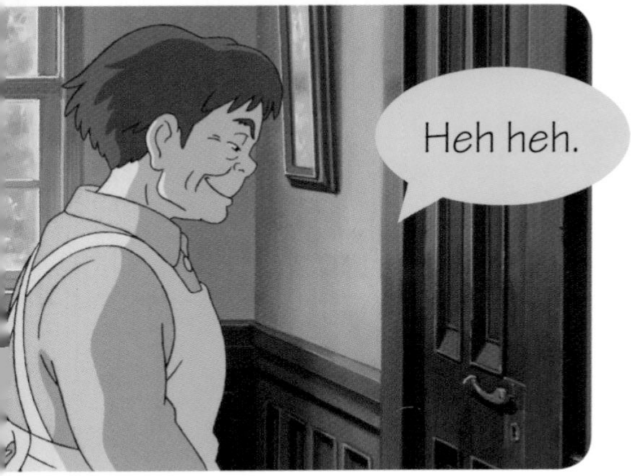
Heh heh.

"I have a very unique pest problem," Hara said.

"Is it mice?" asked the person on the phone.

"Oh, much worse than mice," Hara said.

"You want 'em exterminated?"

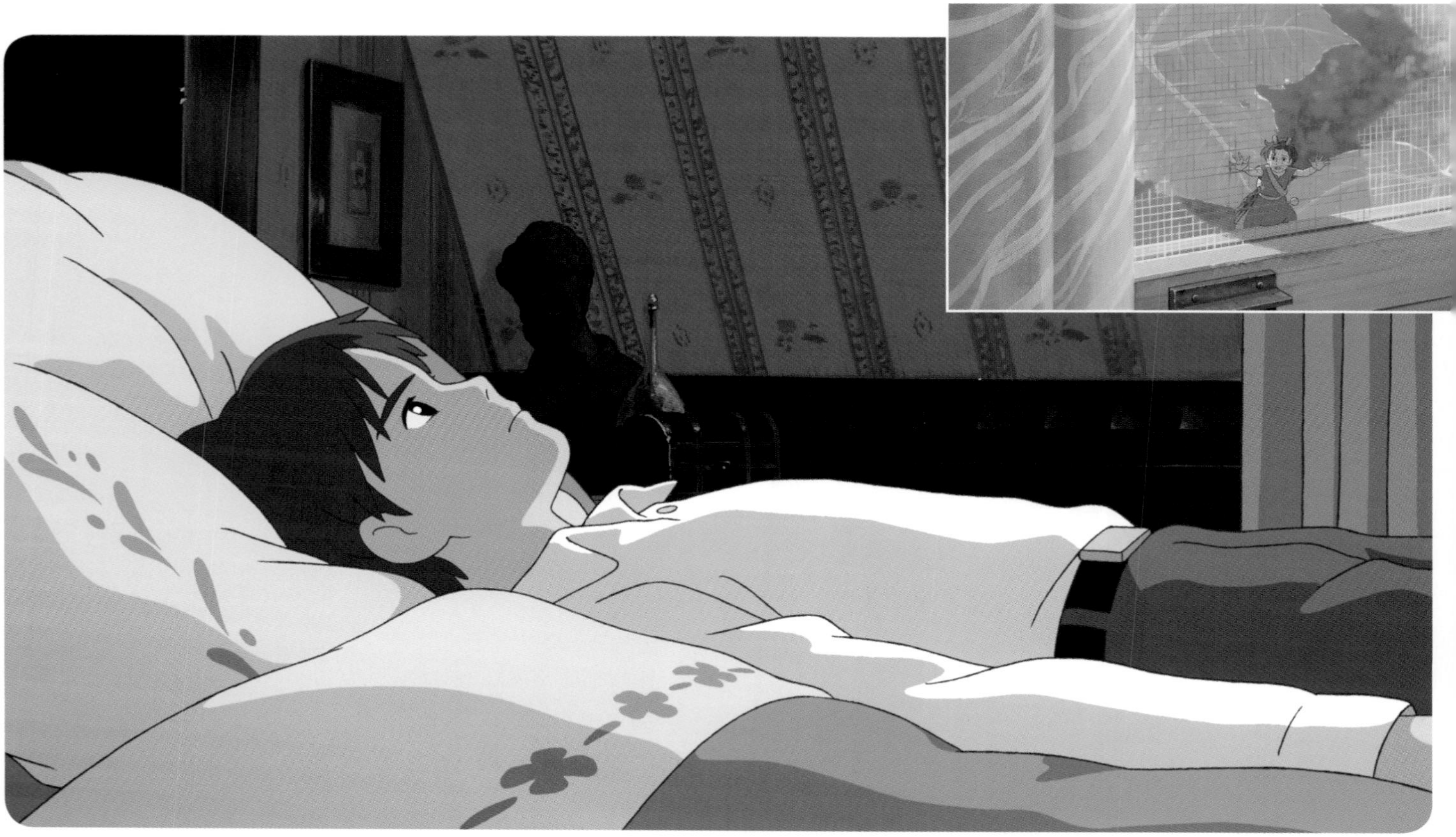

Shawn lay on his bed, staring up at the ceiling.
The truth was, he did not want to die.

"Shawn, Shawn!" Arrietty called at his window.

At the sound of her voice, Shawn quickly opened the screen.

"My mother's missing! Someone took the roof off. I think a human bean got her!"

Overcome with grief, Arrietty broke down in tears.

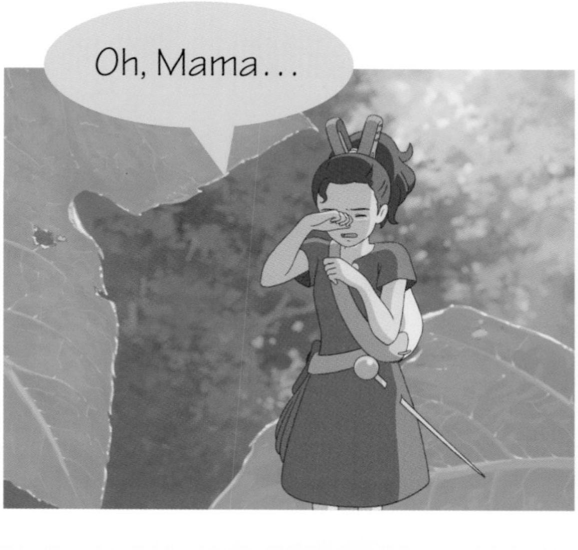
Oh, Mama...

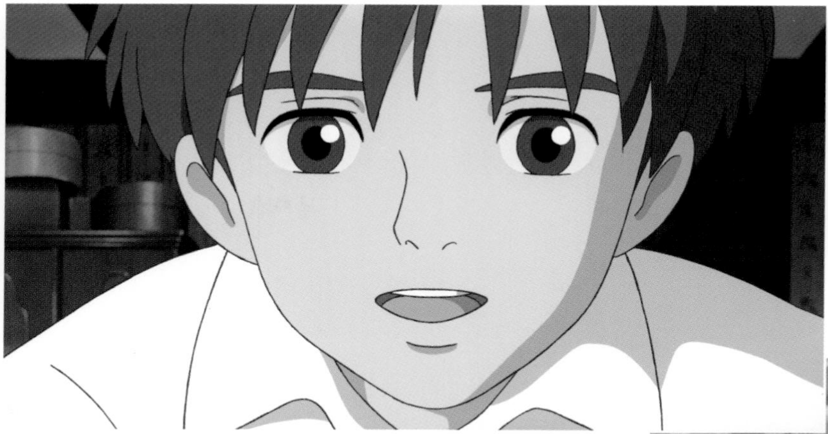

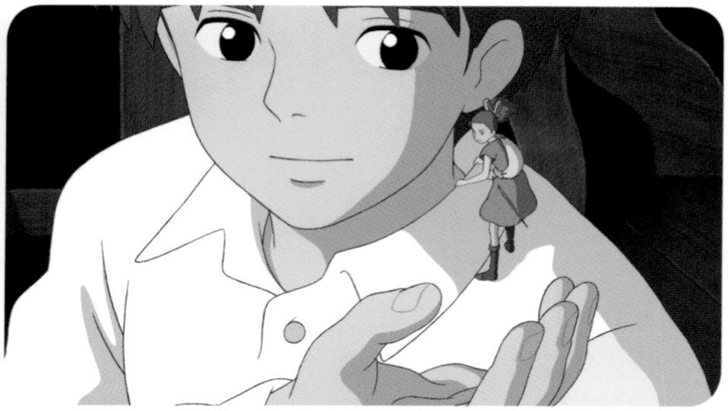

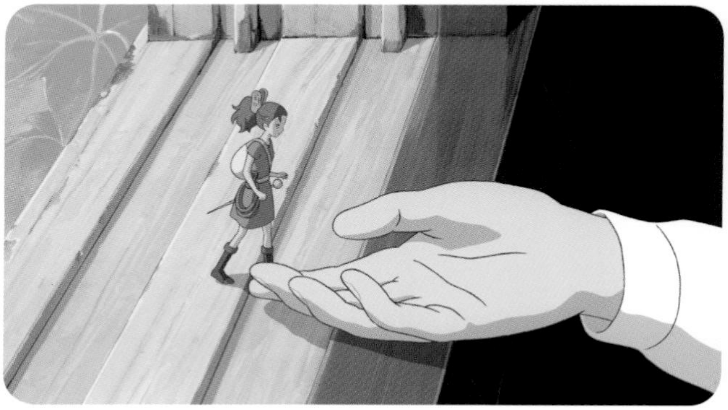

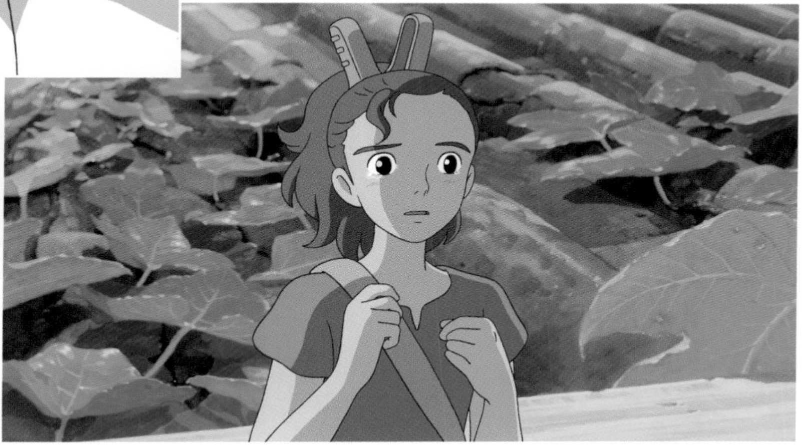

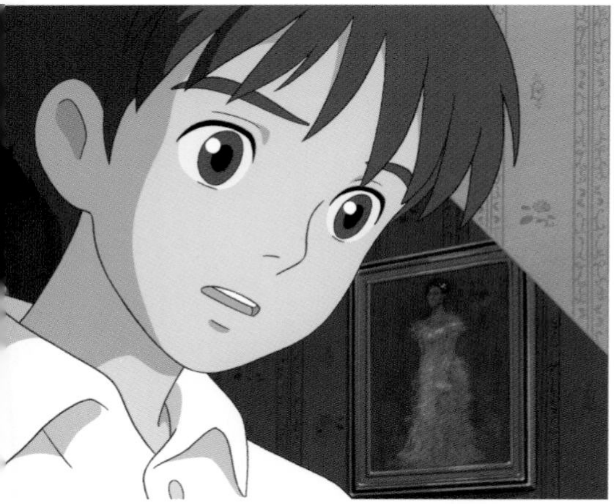

Shawn held out his hand.
"We will find her," he said.

Arrietty stepped onto the palm of his hand. Shawn lifted her onto his shoulder and tried to leave the room—but the door would not open.

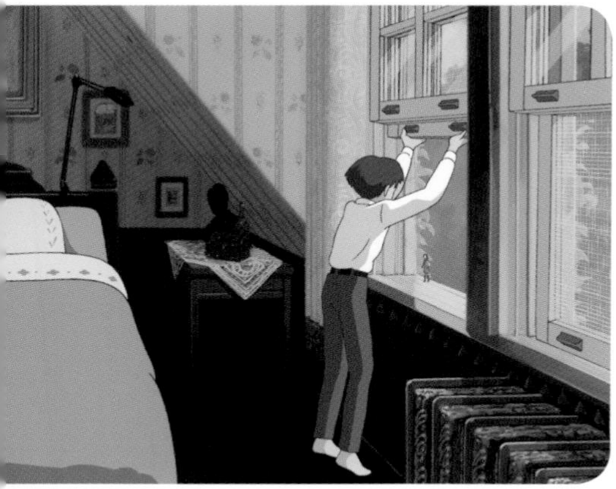

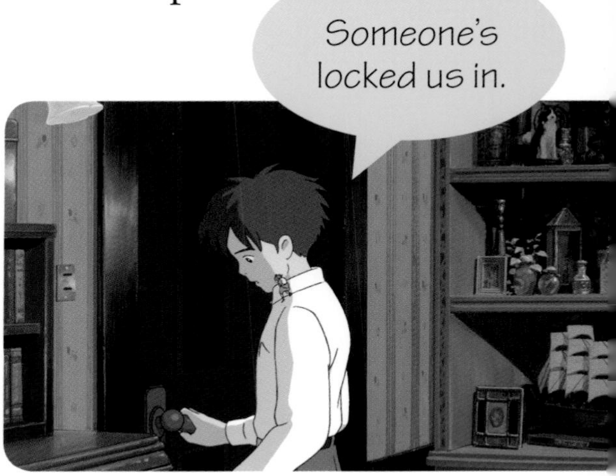
Someone's locked us in.

"There's a room next door. Hold on tight," said Shawn.

He climbed through the window onto the roof and held on to the wall as he tried to reach the next room.

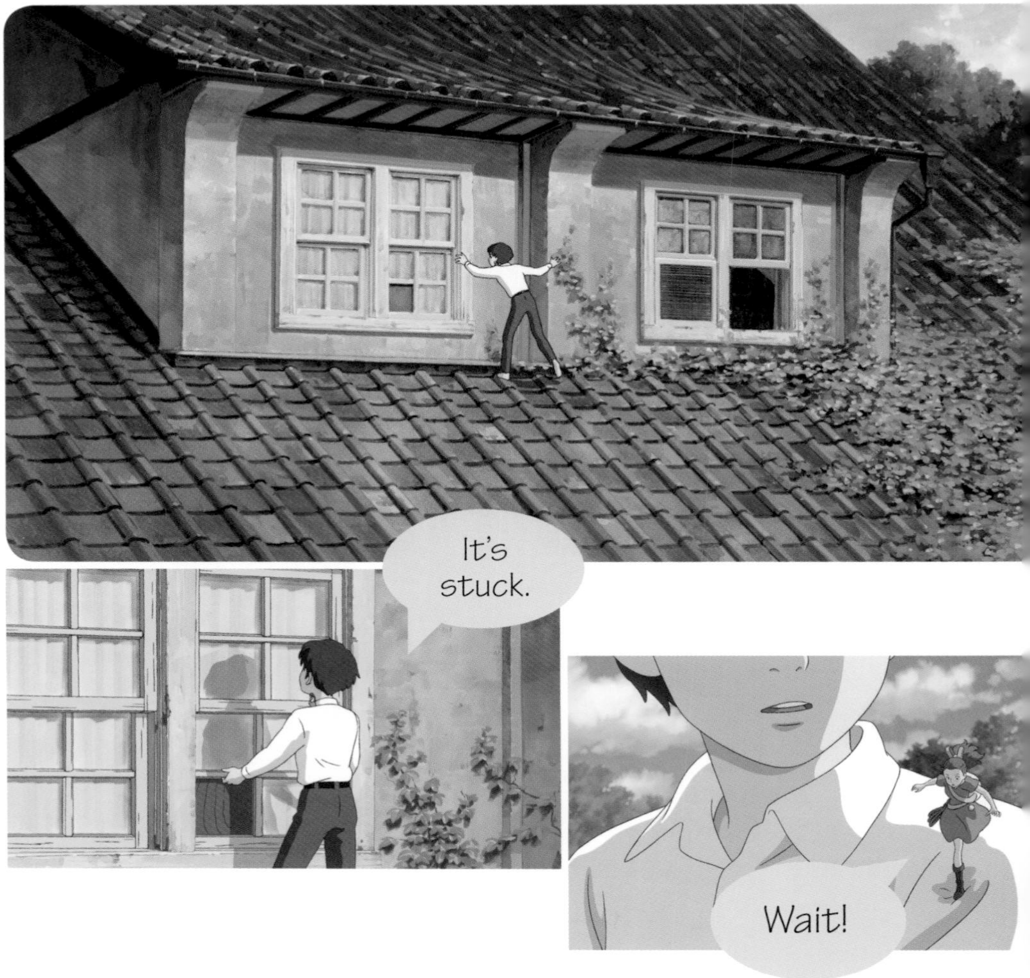
It's stuck.
Wait!

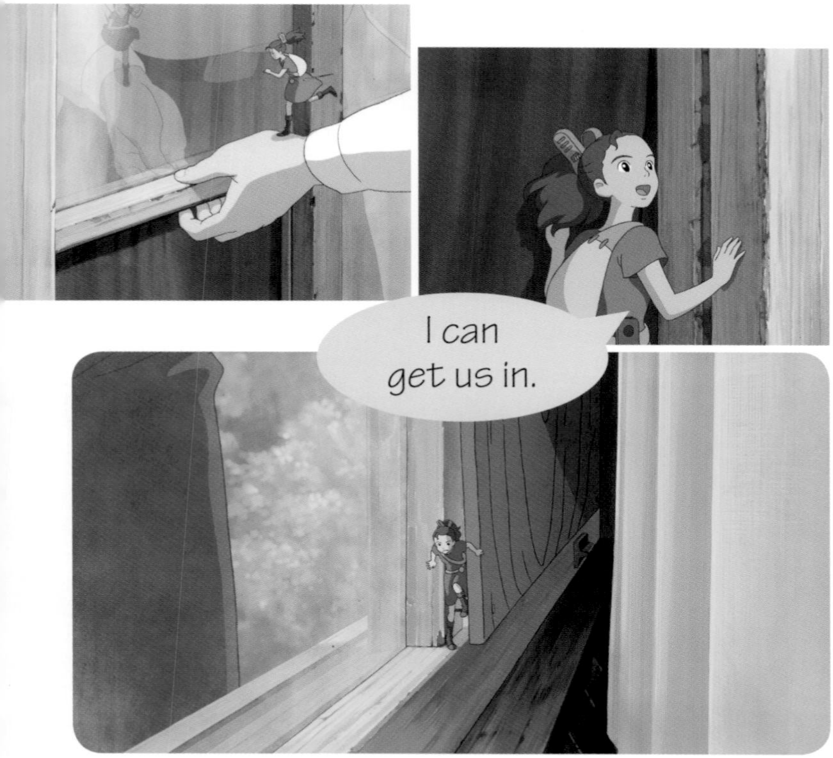
I can get us in.

But the windows to the next room were boarded up.

Arrietty climbed down from Shawn's shoulder and squeezed through a gap between the board and the window frame.

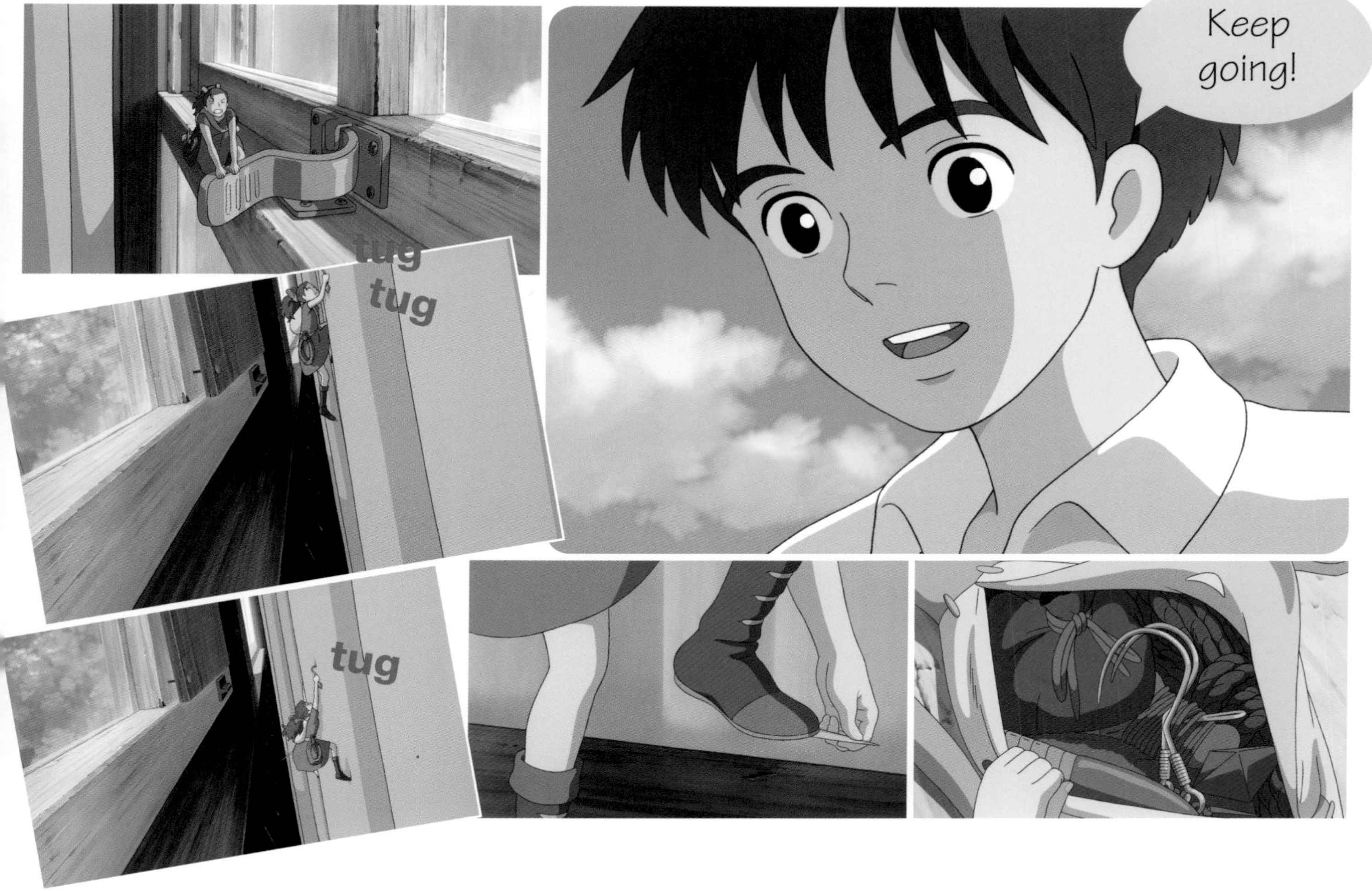
tug
tug
tug
Keep going!

Then she took a pair of earring hooks from her bag, pulled out the metal spikes in her shoes, and started climbing up the curtain.

Shawn watched in amazement at her strength.

Arrietty unlocked the window.

When Shawn opened it, Arrietty jumped on his hand and swiftly climbed back up to his shoulder.

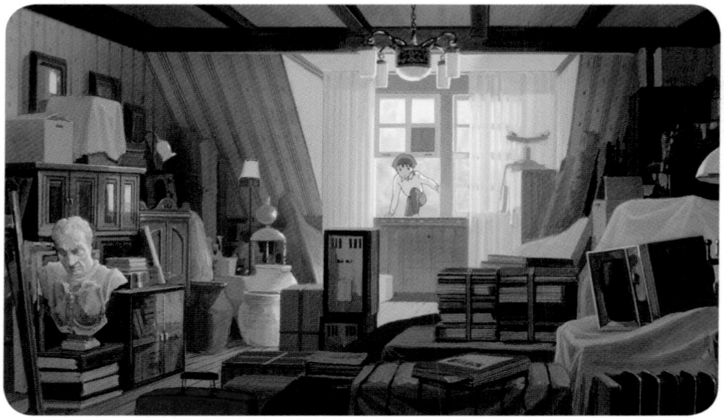

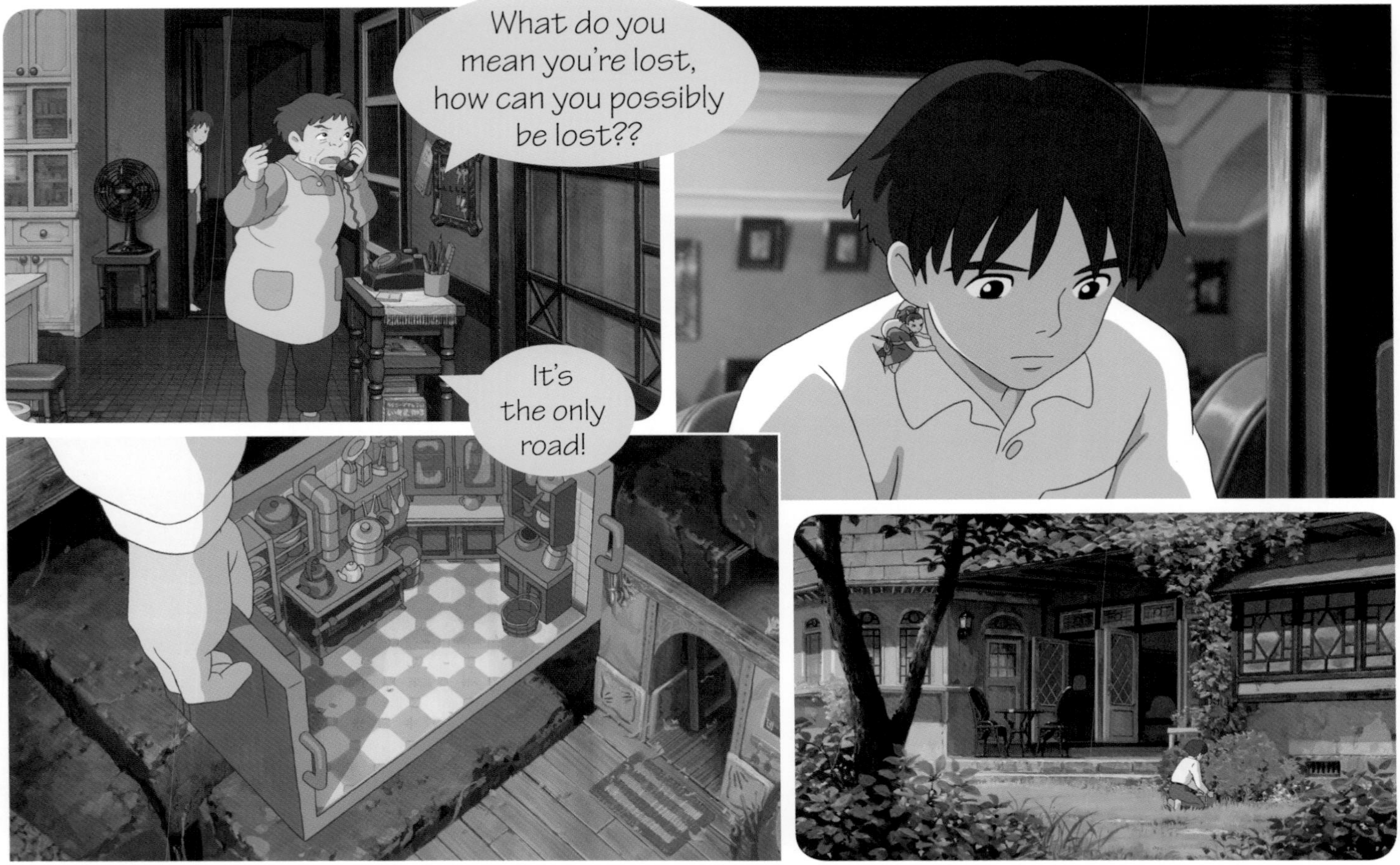
What do you mean you're lost, how can you possibly be lost??
It's the only road!

Shawn went down the stairs quietly. Hara was talking on the phone in the kitchen.

He went to the living room and opened the door in the closet floor.

"Hara must've found your home," he said.

Flap flap flap. The sound of Hara's slippers was getting close.

Shawn pulled out the dollhouse kitchen and snuck outside. He hid it in the bushes and hurried around the yard to the kitchen door.

He was painfully out of breath from the effort, and beads of sweat rolled down his face.

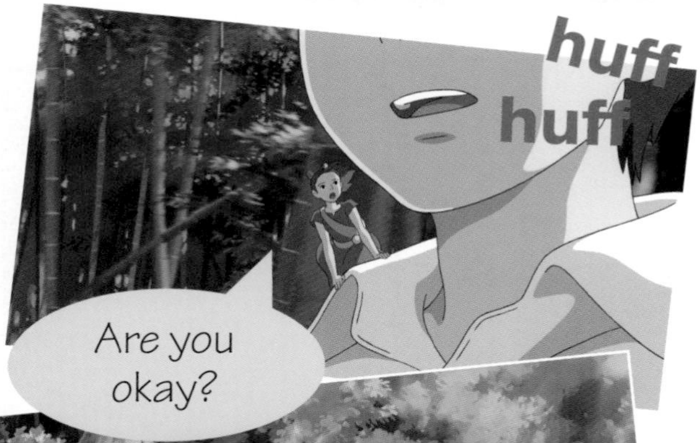
huff
huff
Are you okay?

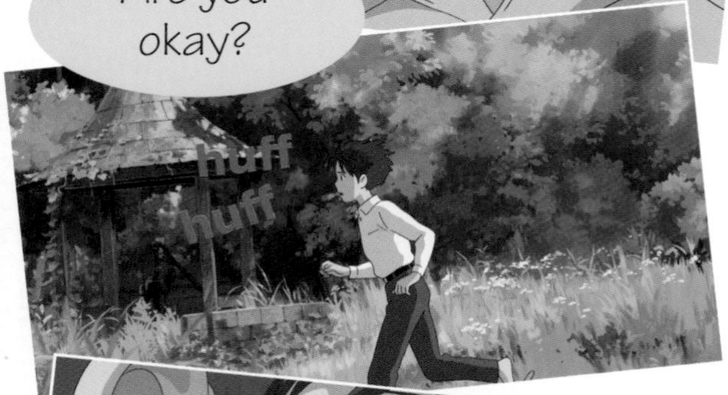
huff
huff

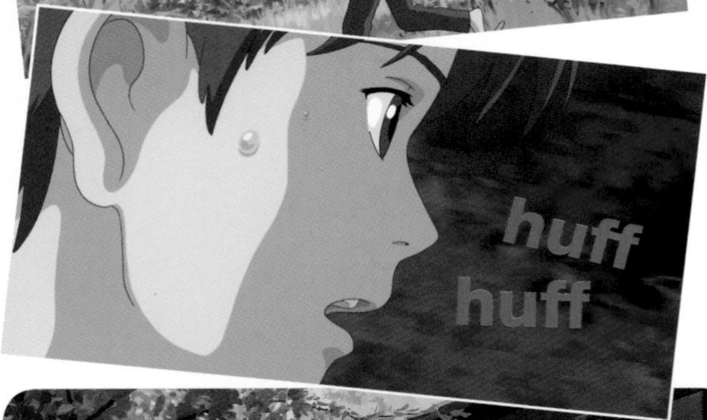
huff
huff

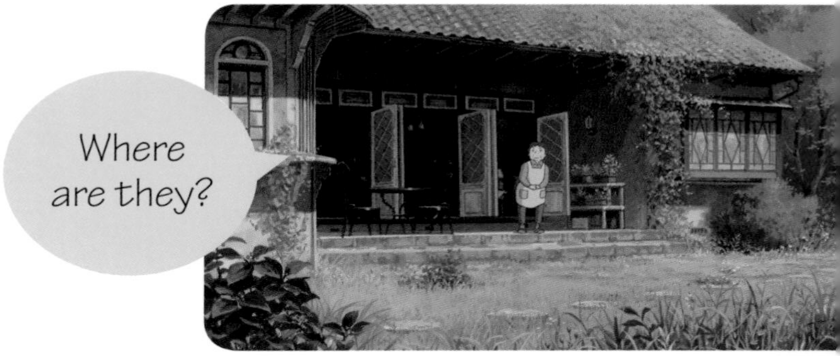
Where are they?

Shawn went into the kitchen and looked through cupboards and drawers, but he could not find Homily.

Flap flap flap.
Hara's footsteps!

Arrietty quickly hid in a cupboard.

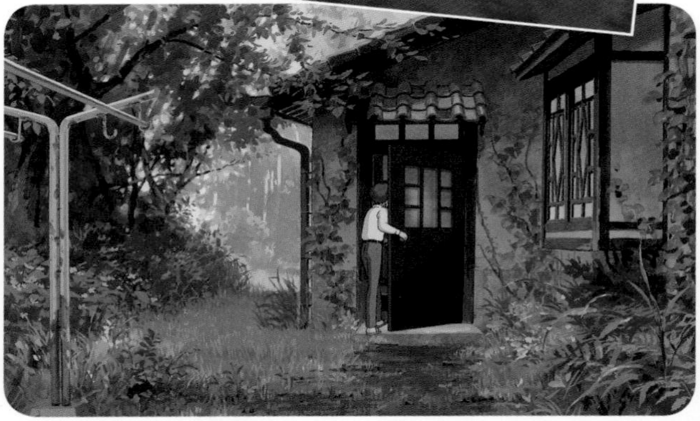

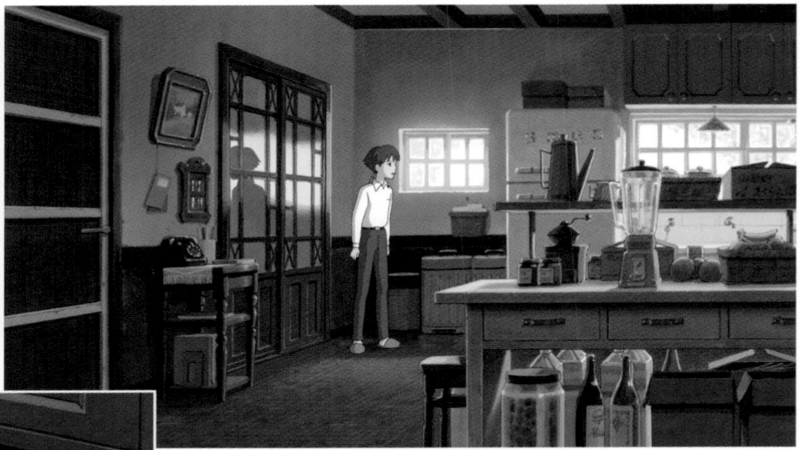

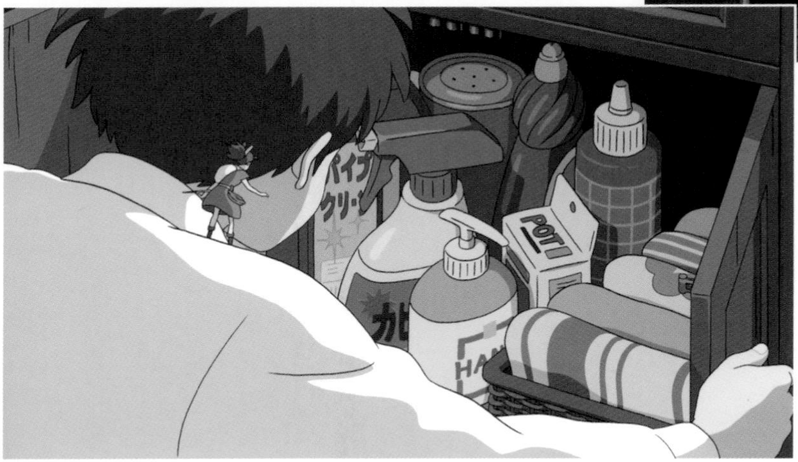
POT

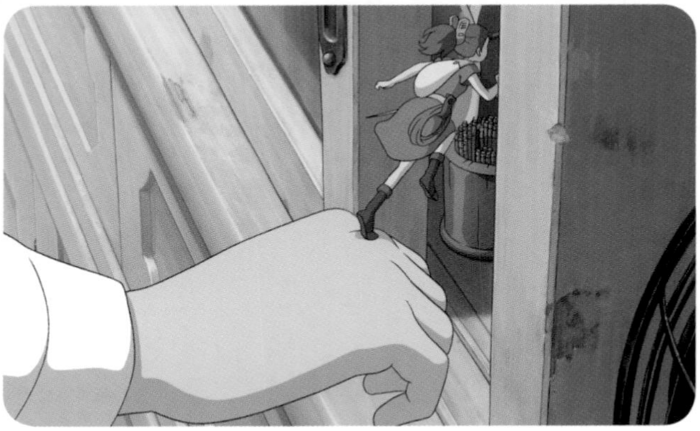

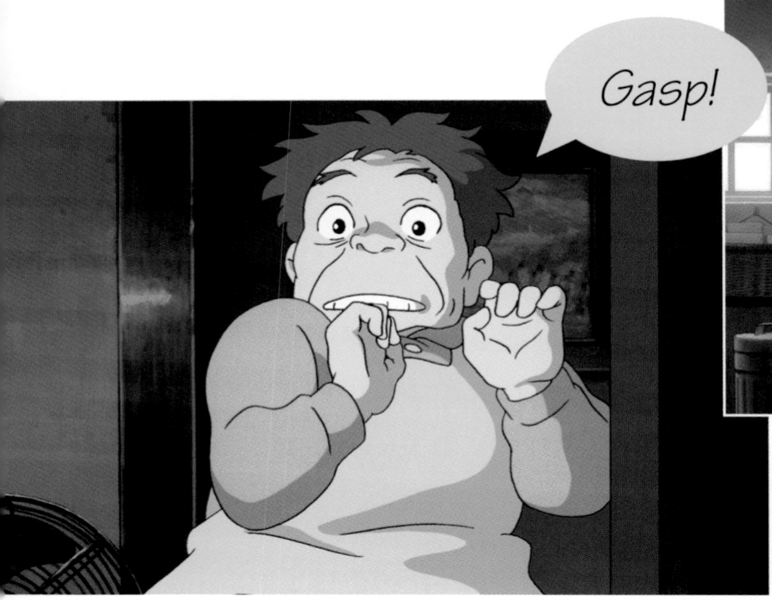
Gasp!

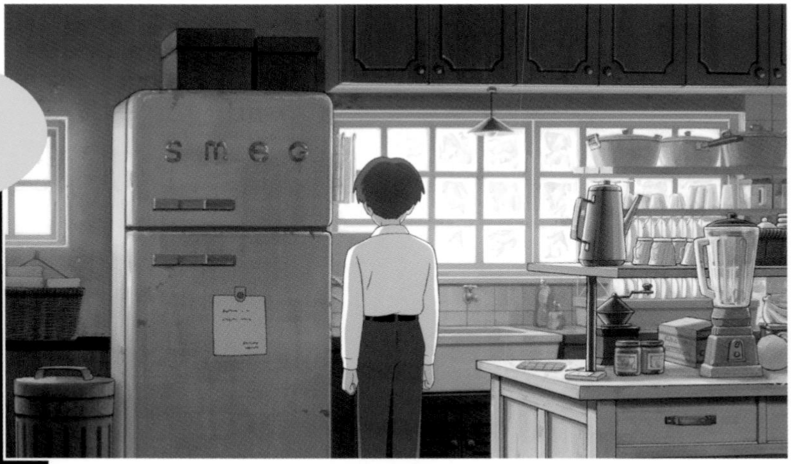

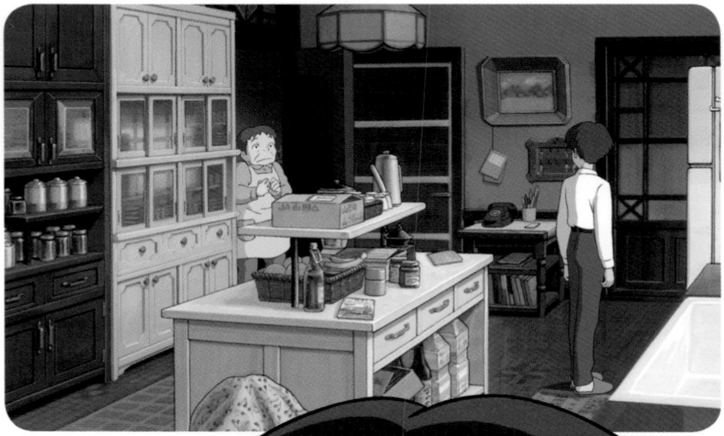

Hara hummed cheerfully as she entered the kitchen but was shocked to see Shawn standing there like a ghost.

"But…but…how did you…?" she stammered.

Shawn acted innocent. "Hara, could I have some warm milk?" he asked.

"Okay, wait just a minute," she replied.

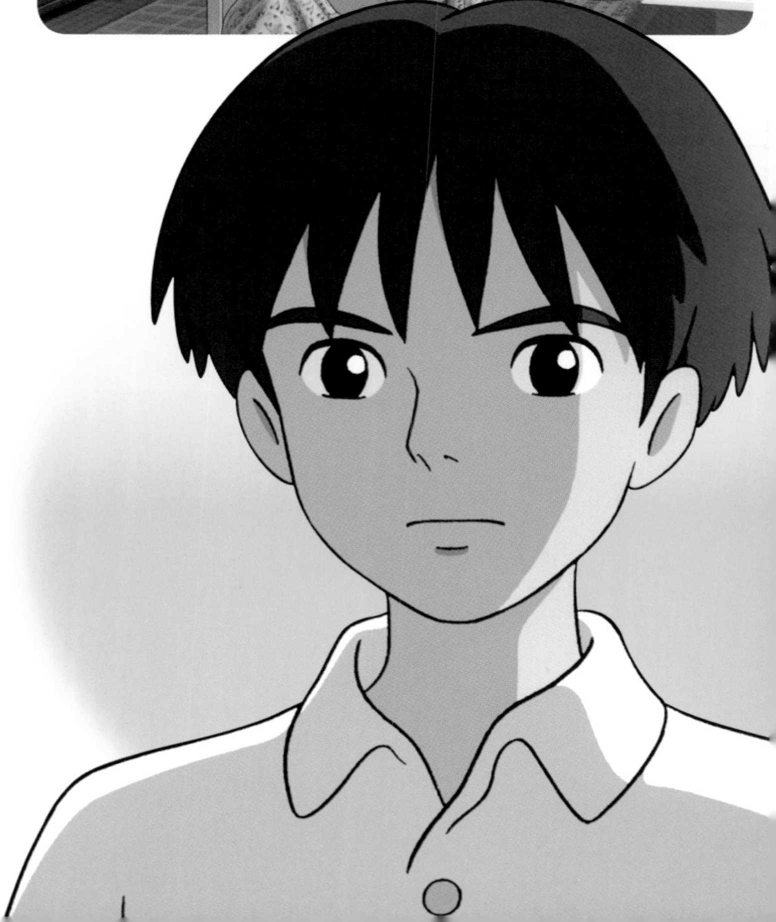

Hara kept eyeing the pantry. Shawn realized that Homily must be inside. He stood in front of the china cupboard. Behind his back he pointed to the pantry so Arrietty would see.

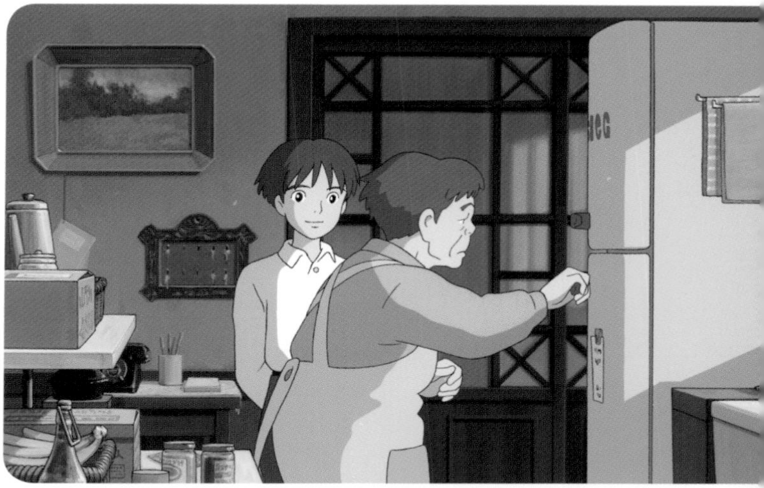

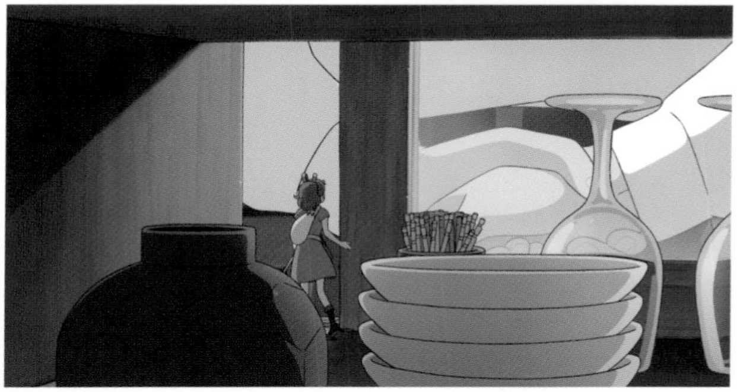

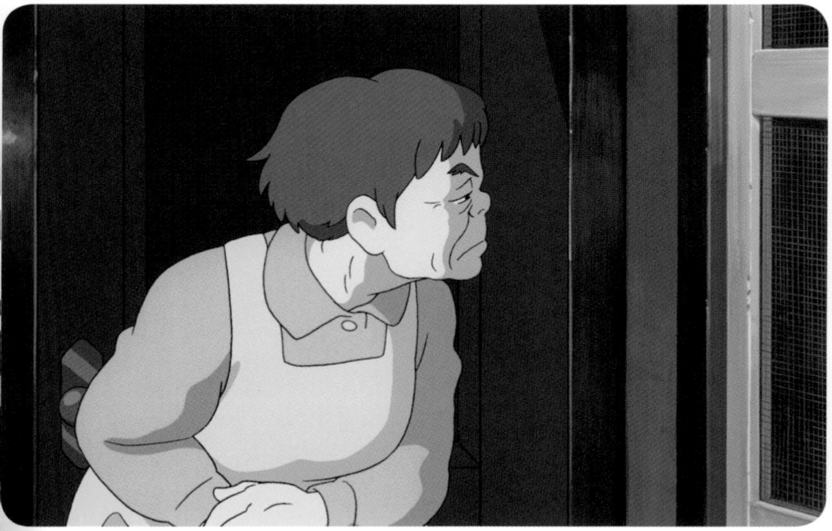

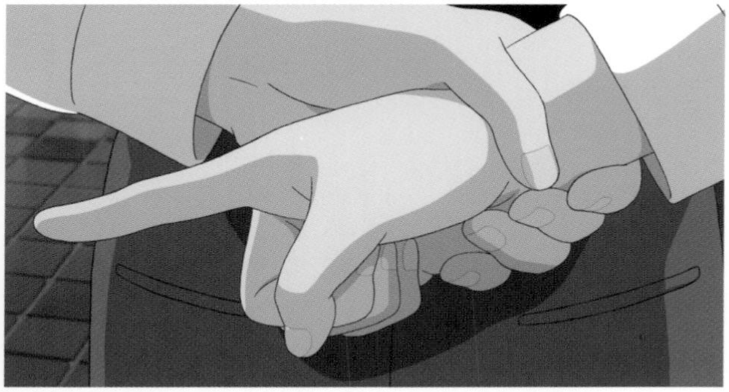

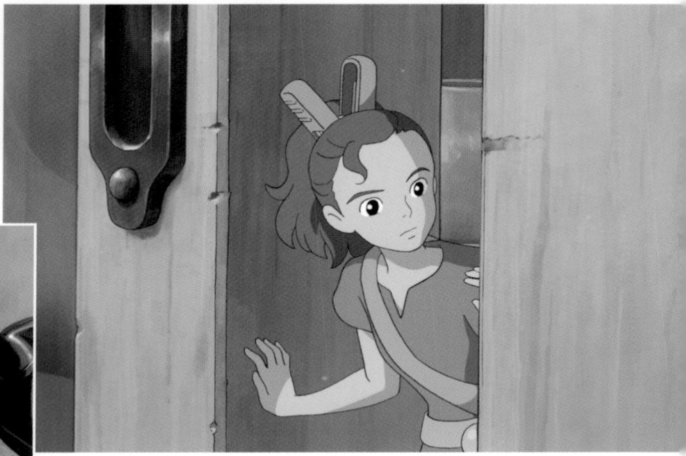

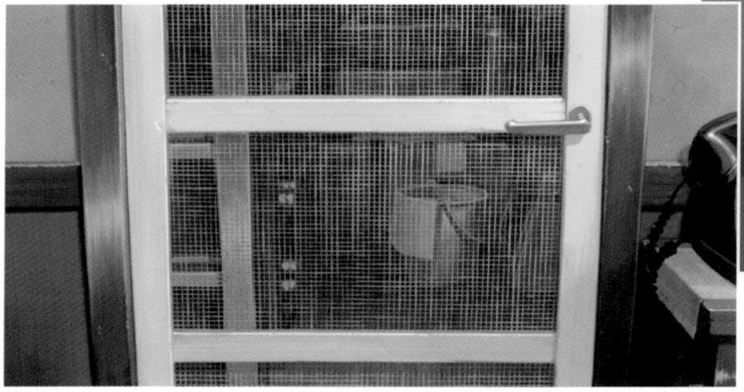

While Shawn kept Hara busy, Arrietty went to the pantry. She squeezed in through a tear in the screen.

"Mother!" Arrietty called as she climbed a ladder looking for Homily.

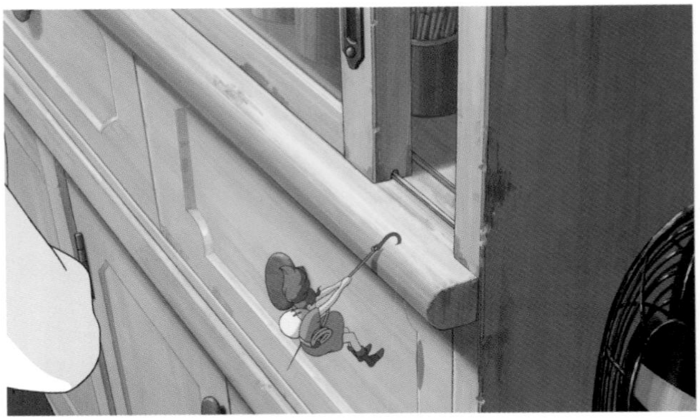

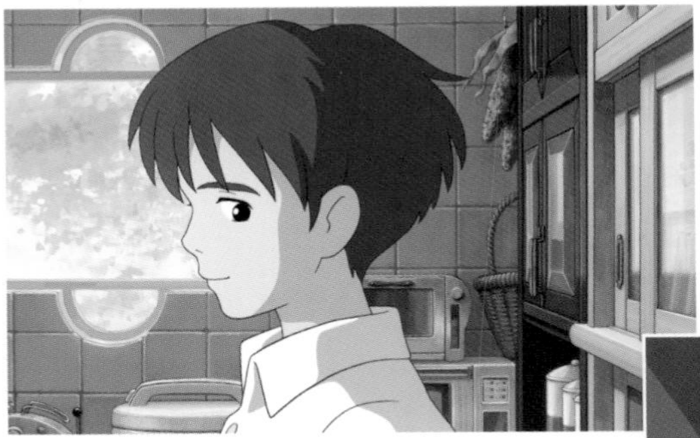

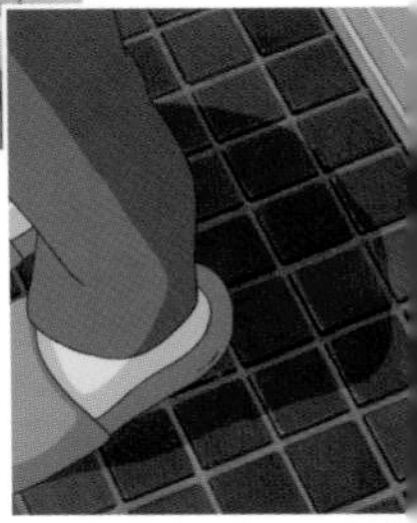

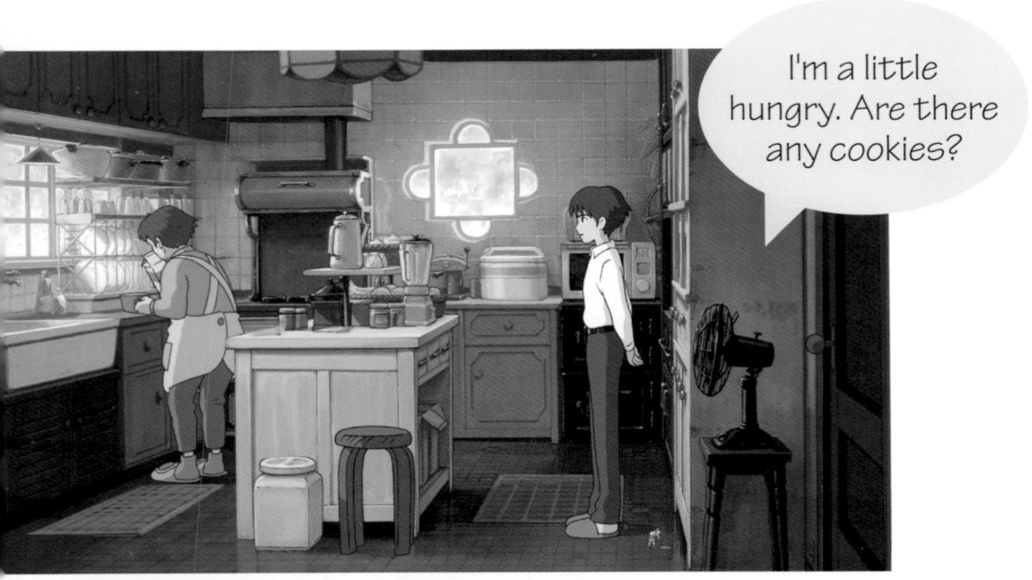
I'm a little hungry. Are there any cookies?

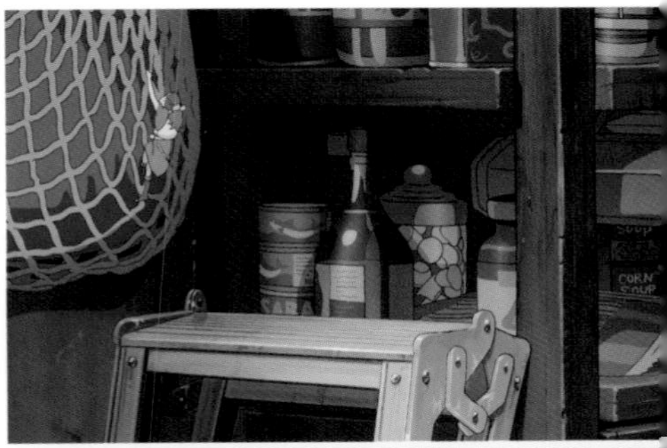

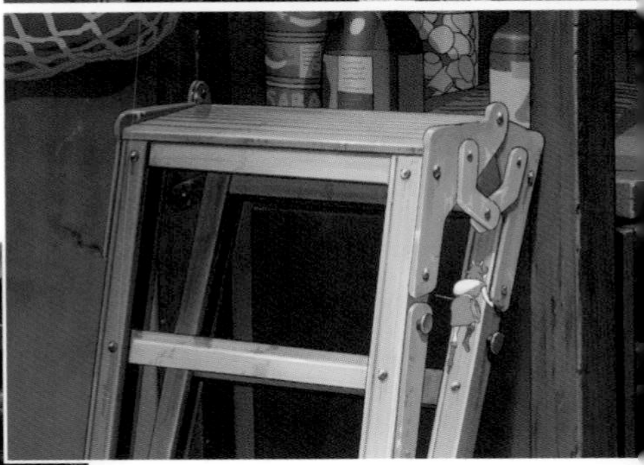

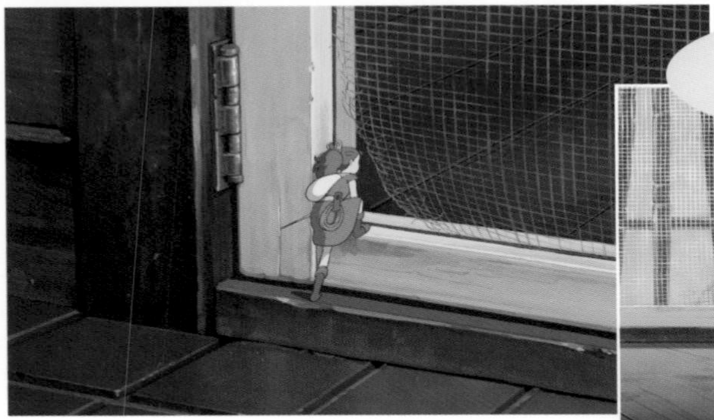

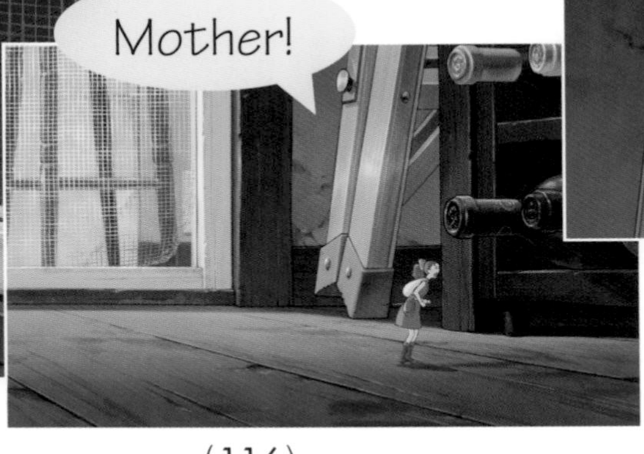
Mother!

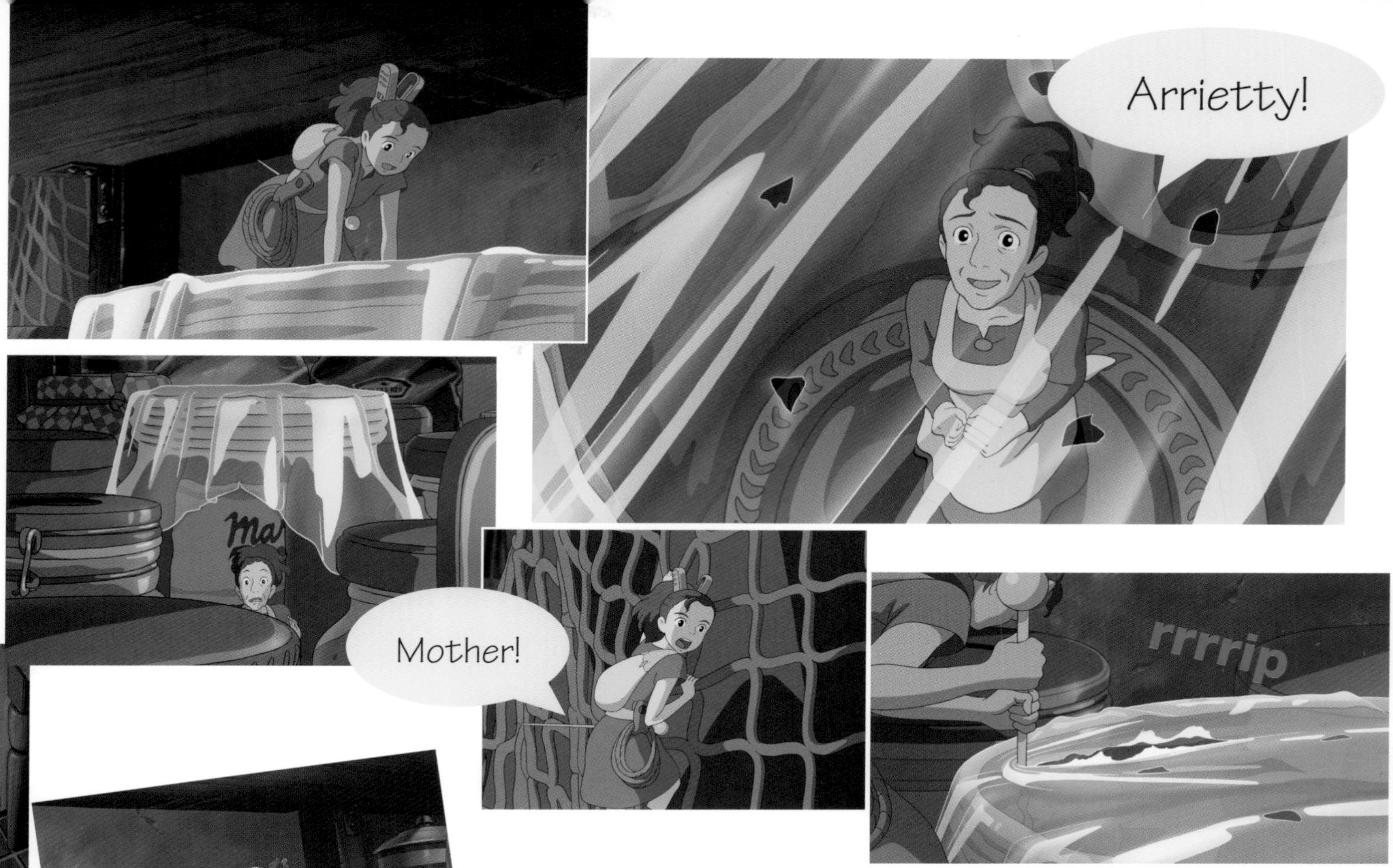
Arrietty!
Mother!
rrrrip

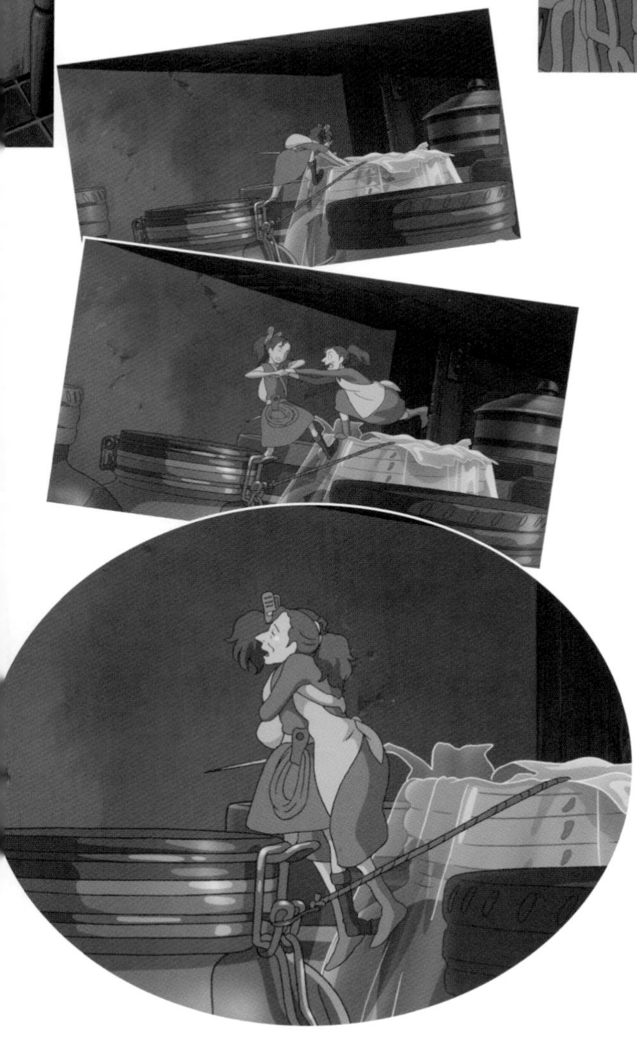

From above a small voice called out, "Arrietty..."

Arrietty climbed up a shopping bag to get higher. Then she spotted Homily in a jar in the back of the pantry. With her pin-sword, she sliced the plastic covering the jar and freed her mother.

Ding dong.

The doorbell rang.

"Oh good. There they are. They finally found the road," said Hara.

When she left the kitchen, Shawn peered into the pantry.

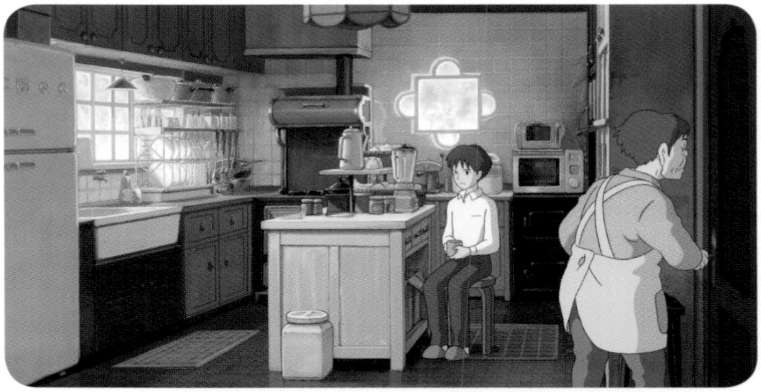

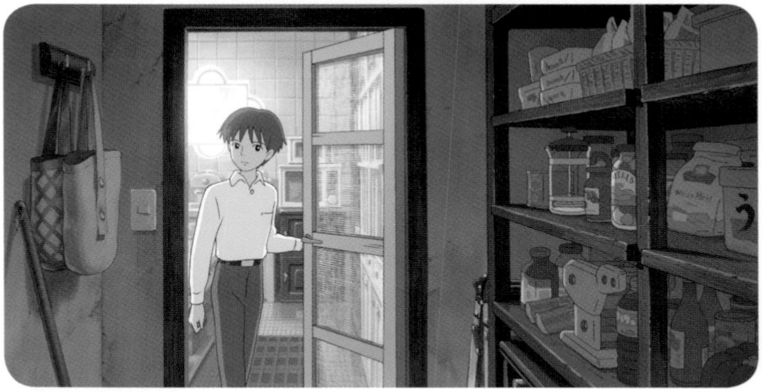

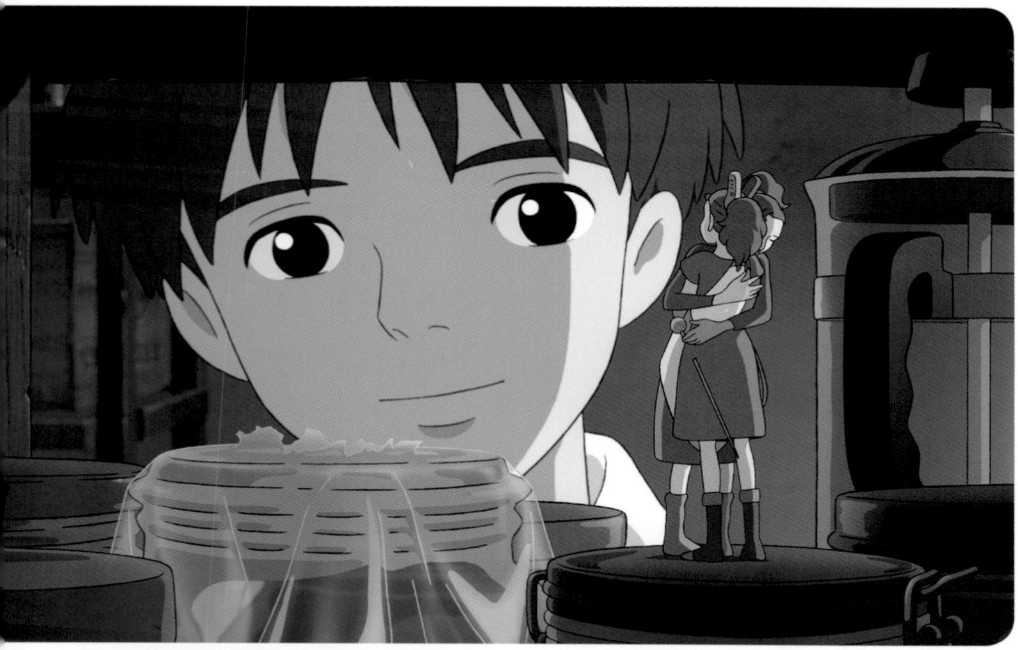

As Arrietty and Homily hugged each other, Homily noticed Shawn.

"Whaa! Another bean!"

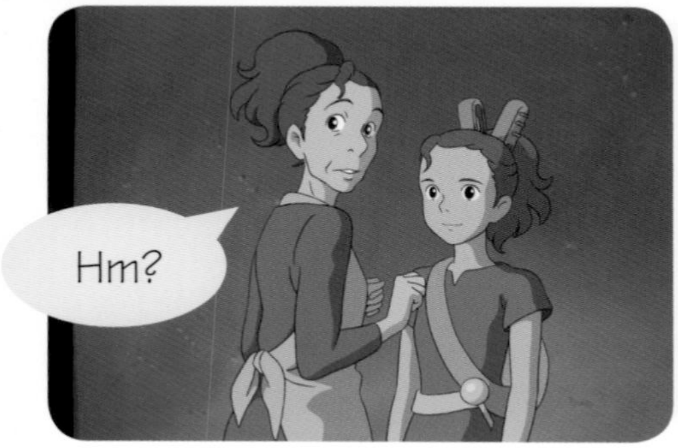
Hm?

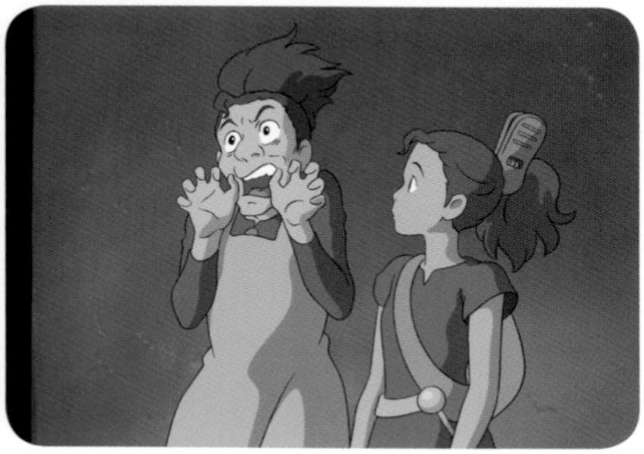

Homily panicked and dove for cover behind a jar.

"It's okay, Mother," Arrietty said, looking at Shawn.

Shawn returned her gaze with gentle eyes.

Arrietty helped her mother to the wall, then left after a final glance at Shawn.

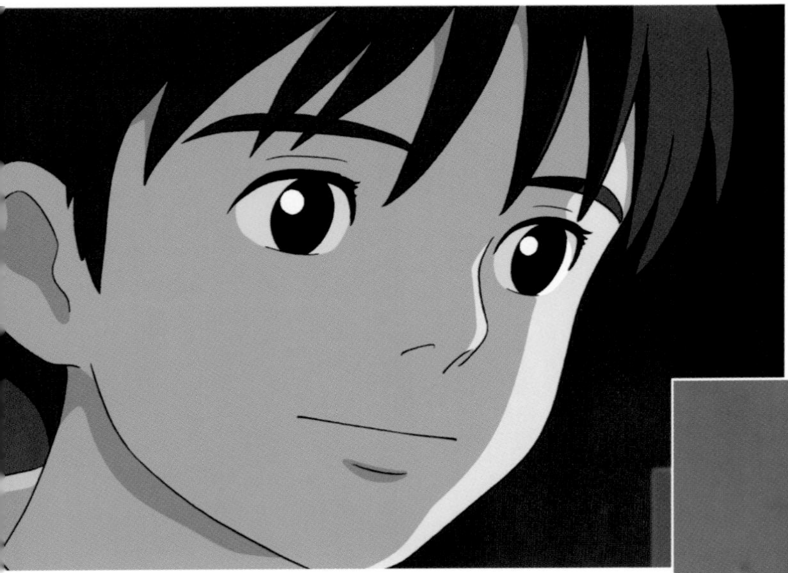

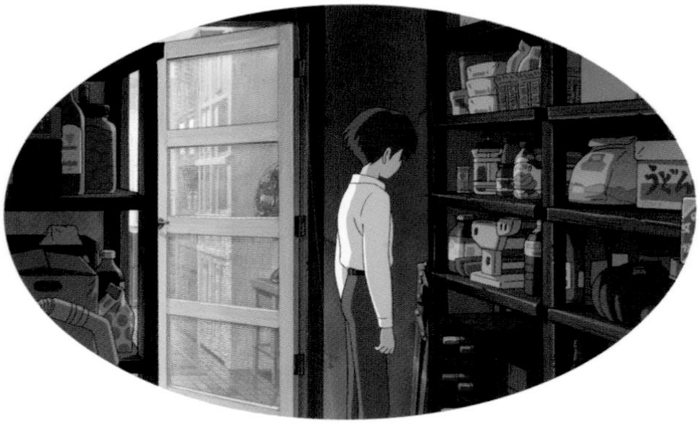

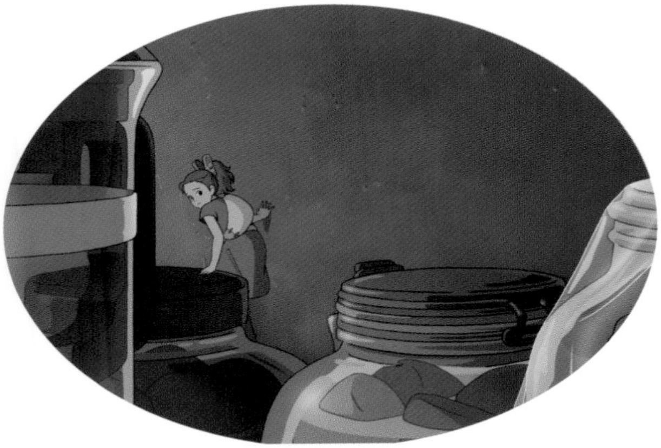

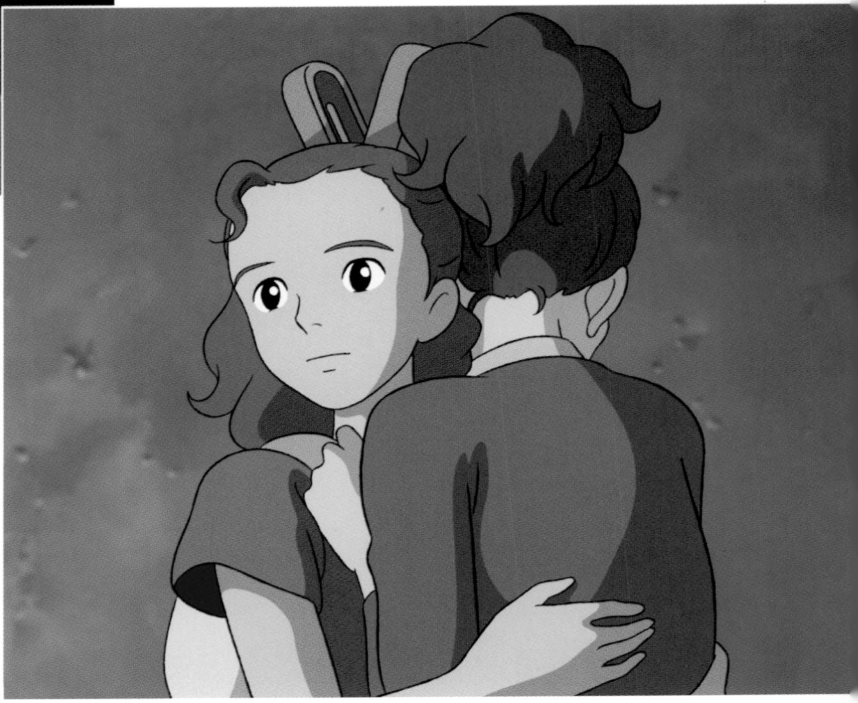

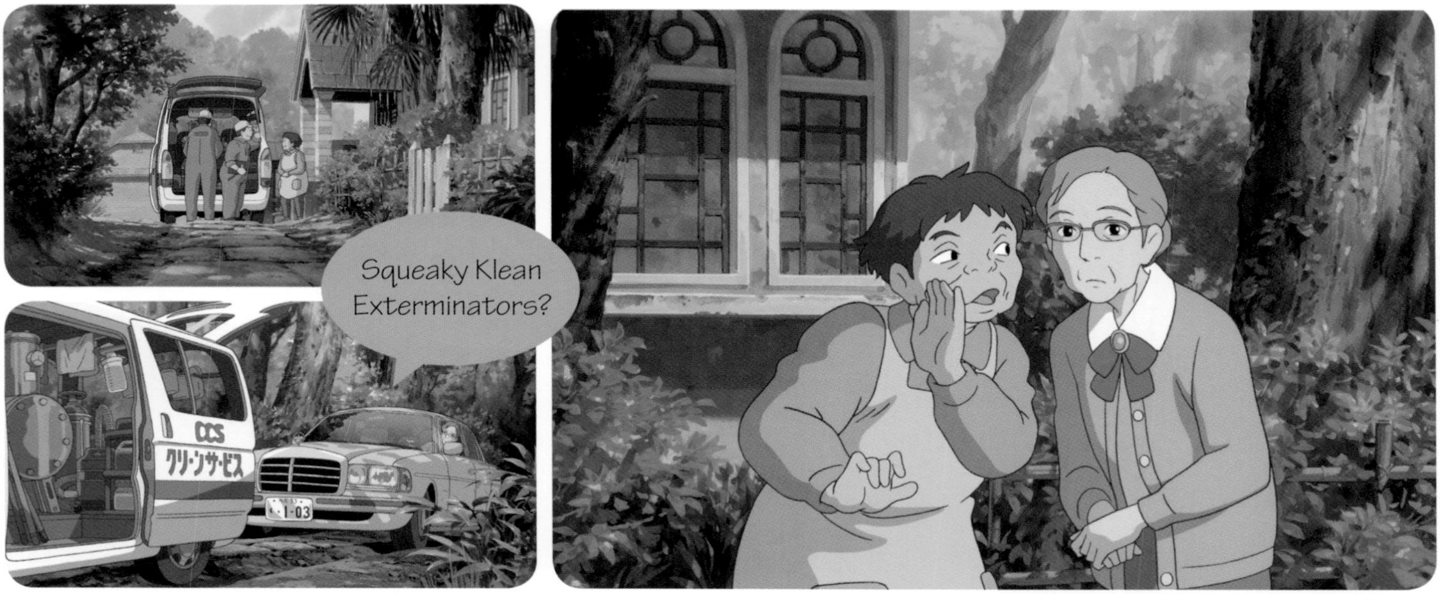
Squeaky Klean Exterminators?

Just as Hara was greeting the pest control workers, Jessica returned.

"Hara? Hara! What's going on here?" Jessica demanded.

"It's finally happened!" Hara exclaimed. "I found the little people!"

"Little people?"

Hara nodded then lowered her voice and added, "Yes. And what little robbers they are."

While Hara and Jessica were occupied, Shawn retrieved the dollhouse kitchen from the bushes, and took it into the house.

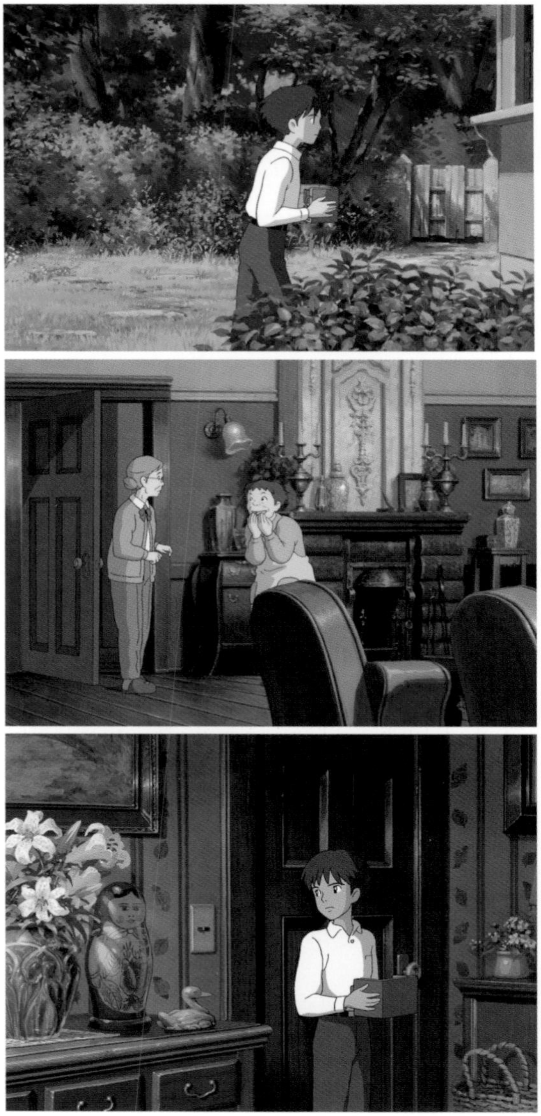

"I wouldn't have believed it," Hara said, "but I saw it with my own eyes."

She led Jessica to the living room and opened the closet door.

"And they have a whole house full of things they've stolen."

"Hara, what are you talking about?" Jessica asked.

"All these years you thought I was losing things—but it wasn't me," Hara cried. "It was them!

"You'll see when I show you," added Hara triumphantly as she lifted up the door in the closet floor.

"This is their nest..."

Jessica peered down and saw a jumbled heap of bricks, rags, dried grass and an empty bottle.

"Looks like a pile of old junk to me," she said.

"WHAAAT?!" Hara cried. She leaned forward and dug around in the mound of trash.

"I'm sending the exterminators away, Hara," Jessica said.

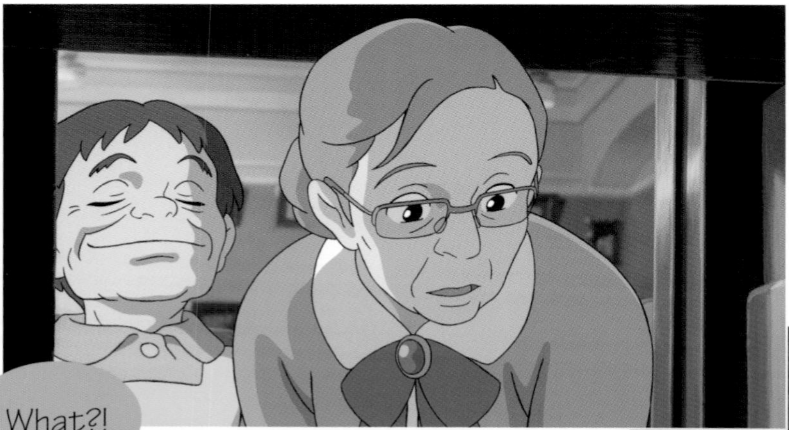

Hara panicked. "No! No! Wait just a minute!"

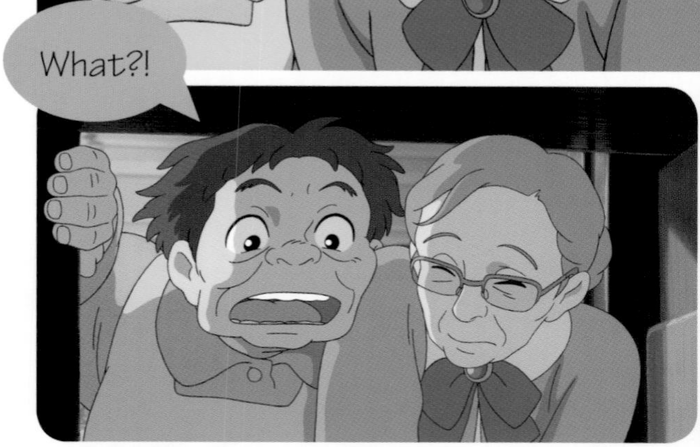
What?!

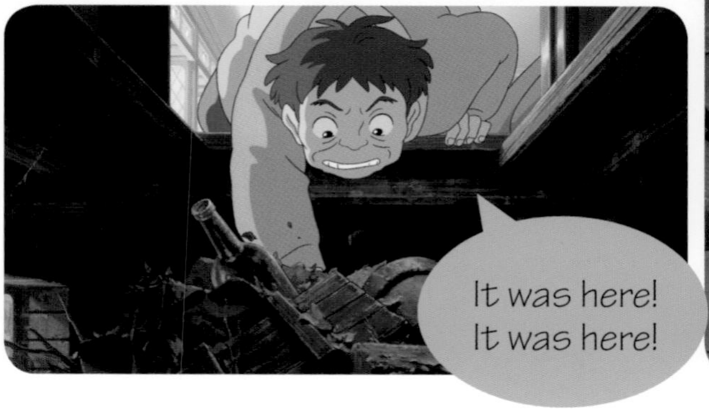
It was here!
It was here!

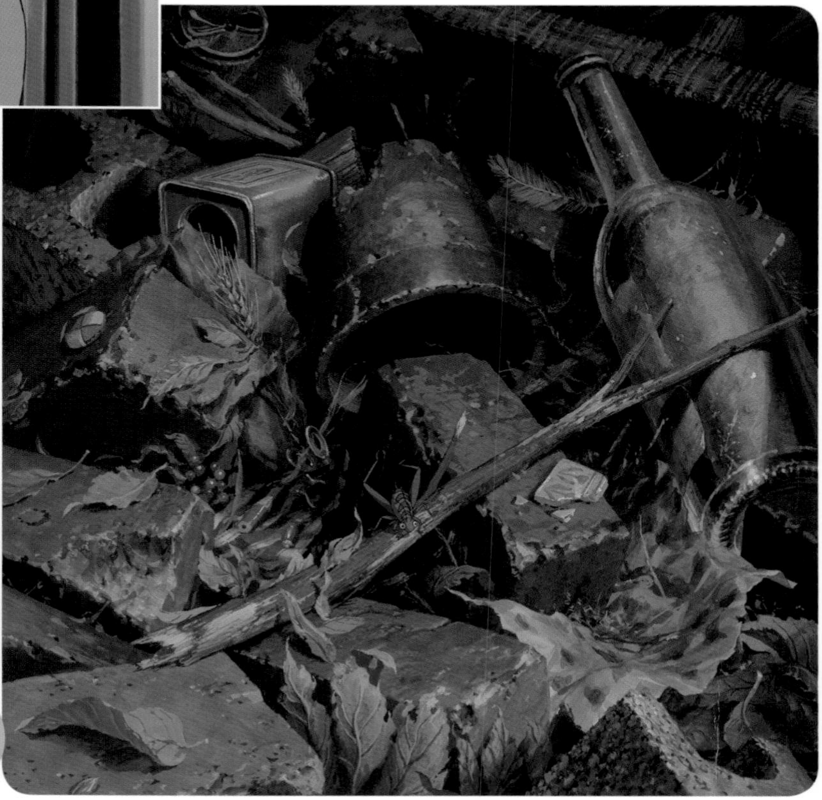

Still there.
Perhaps you need some time off.

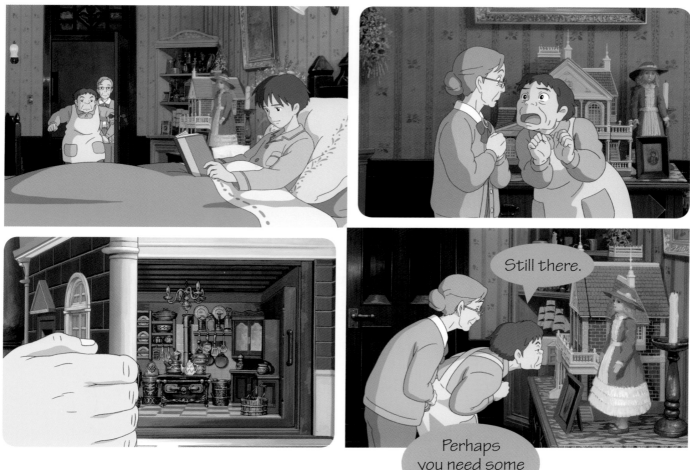

She brought Jessica to Shawn's room.

"Hello, Shawn! Can we come in for a minute?" Hara called from behind the door.

"It's open," Shawn replied.

When they entered, Shawn was in his pajamas, reading a book in bed as if he had been there all along.

"You'll see. Those little thieves stole the tiny kitchen," Hara said.

She peered into the dollhouse to find…

…the kitchen in place.

Shawn kept calmly reading his book, pretending not to notice the commotion Hara was making.

"Wait! Wait, I can prove it!" Hara cried.
"I've got one of them in a jar!"

Hara glared at Shawn, then thudded out of the room.

As Jessica turned to leave, she smelled something. "Is that fresh herbs?"

Jessica looked into the dollhouse and picked up the teapot.

She lifted the lid and saw one small mint leaf. It was still wet.

Poor Hara. I think she's finally gone bonkers.

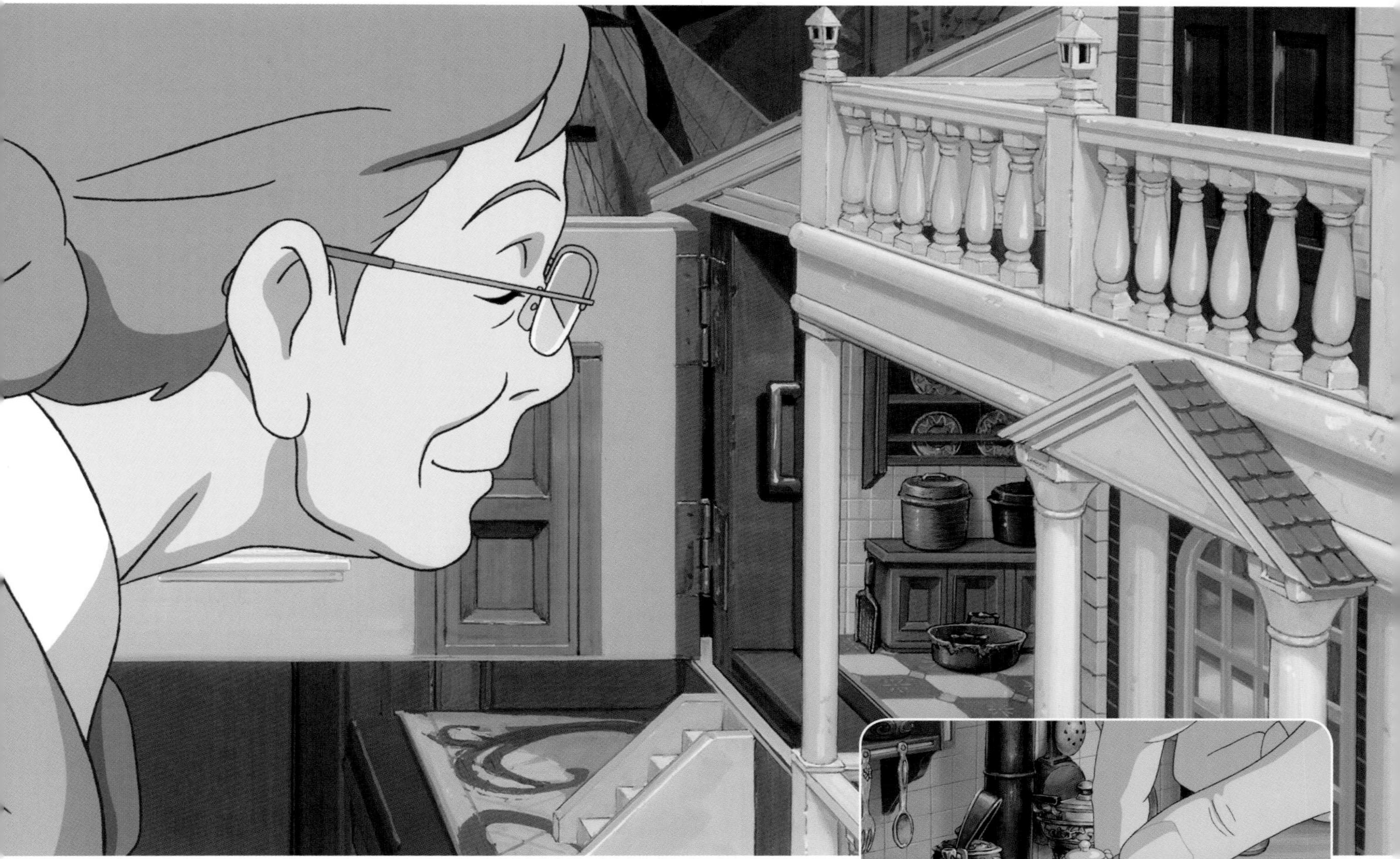

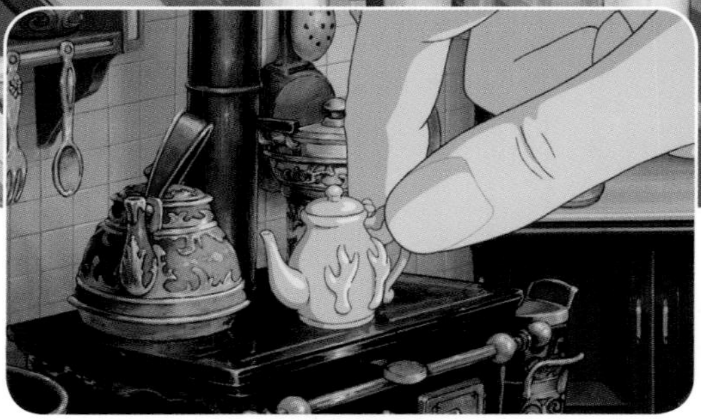

“Someone’s been making tea!” said Jessica. Her eyes sparkled with happiness.

“It’s just as my father told us! There really are little people living here.”

“Yes, there are,” said Shawn with a lonely smile.

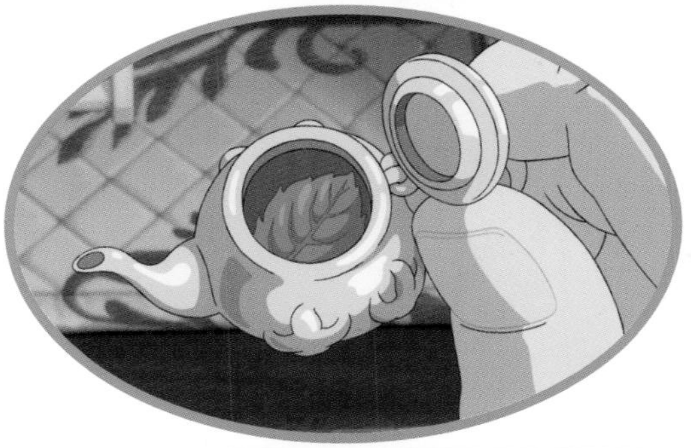

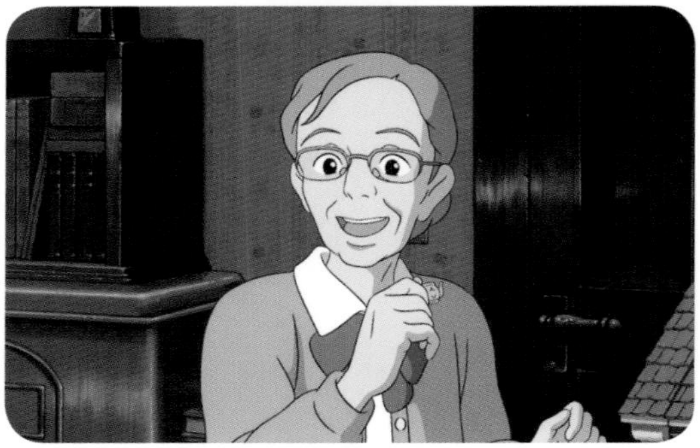

"Your mother really should be here to see this. She waited so long for proof that they exist."

"But they're not thieves like Hara said," Shawn said. "They're just Borrowers."

"What?" asked Jessica, looking up.

Shawn composed himself and replied quietly, "I mean... they must be very frightened. I just—hope they're still here."

Jessica looked at Shawn and nodded deeply.

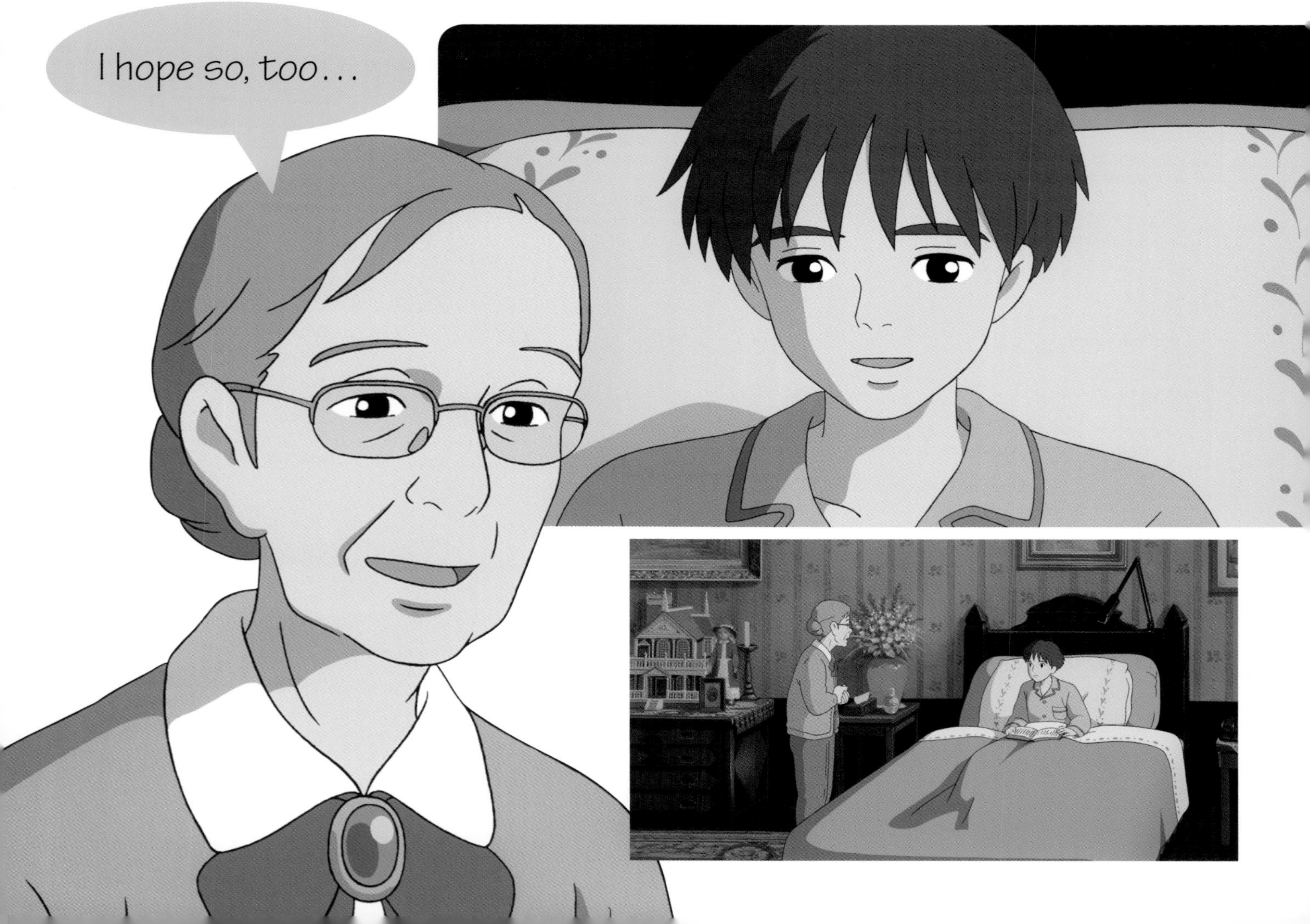
I hope so, too...

Hara ran to the pantry. The jar she had trapped Homily in was now empty.

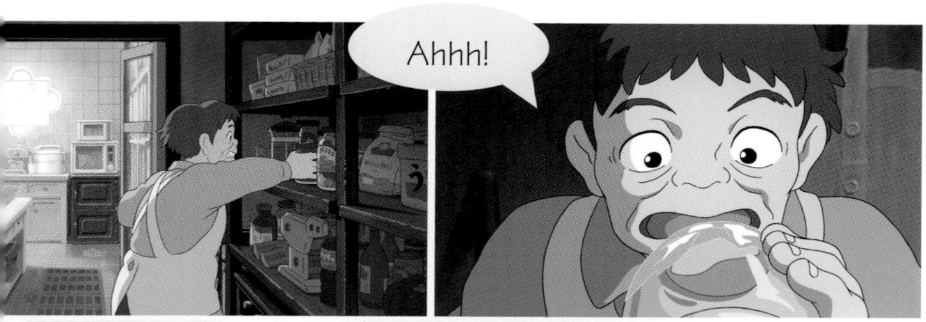
Ahhh!

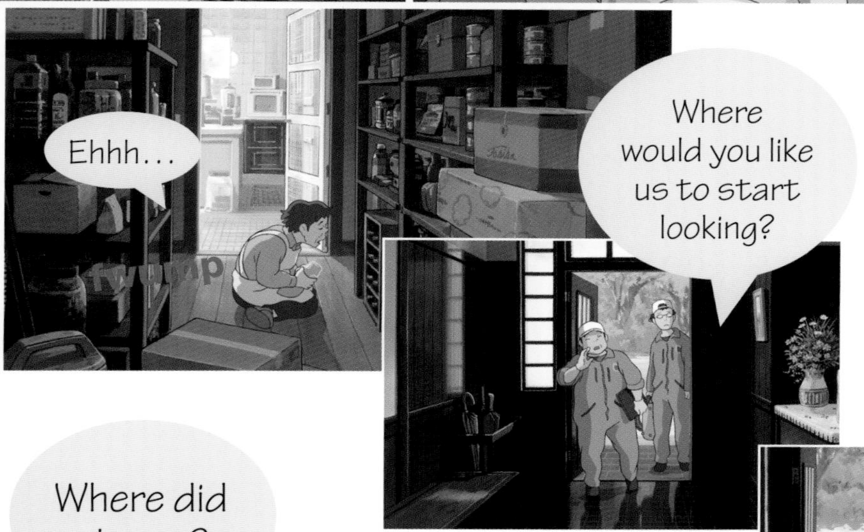
Ehhh...
Where would you like us to start looking?

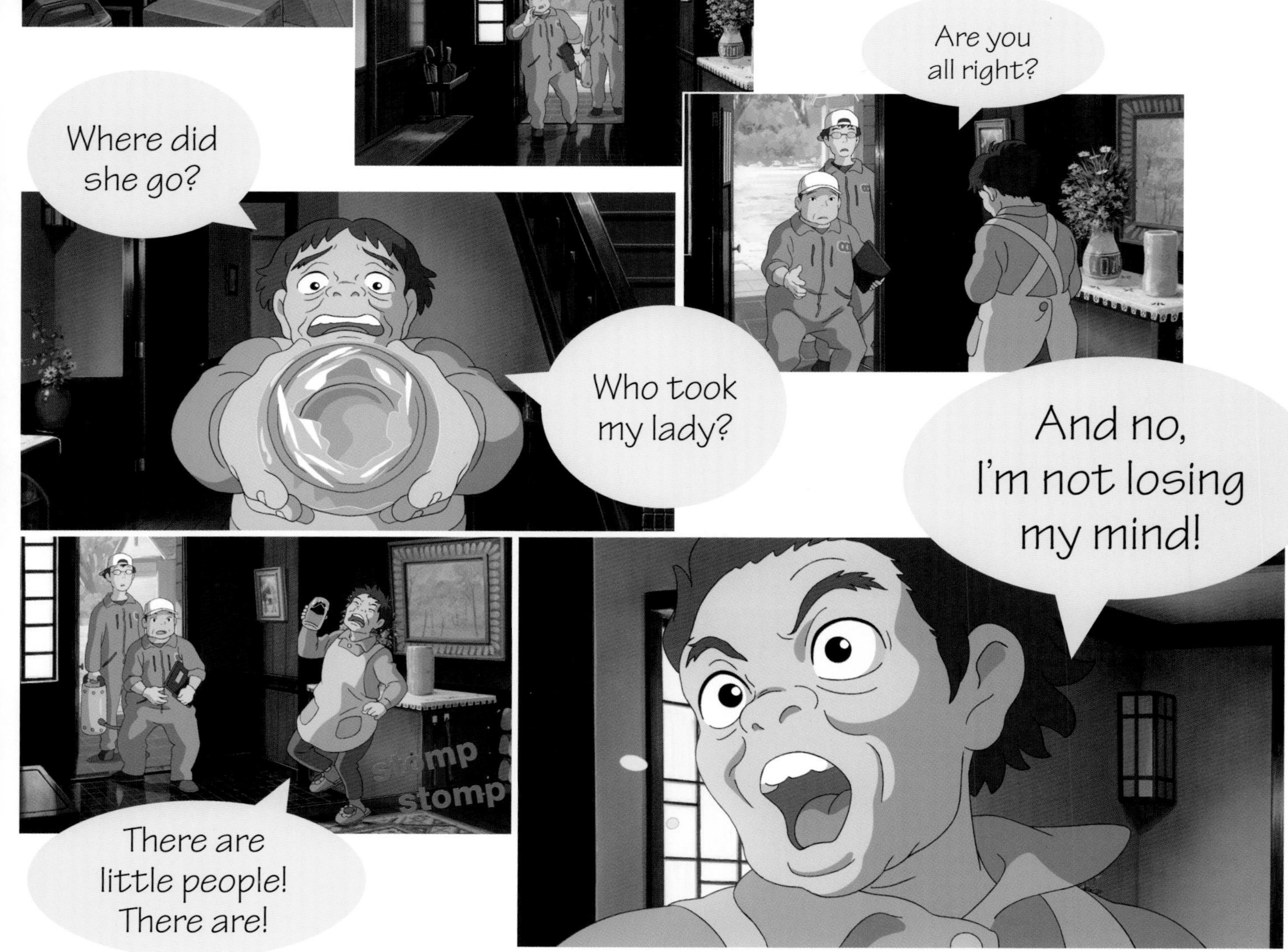
Are you all right?
Where did she go?
Who took my lady?
stomp
stomp
There are little people! There are!
And no, I'm not losing my mind!

A New Journey

That night, Arrietty and her family walked away from their home by the light of the moon.

"If I collapse…
leave me behind…
with my teakettle…"
Homily panted.

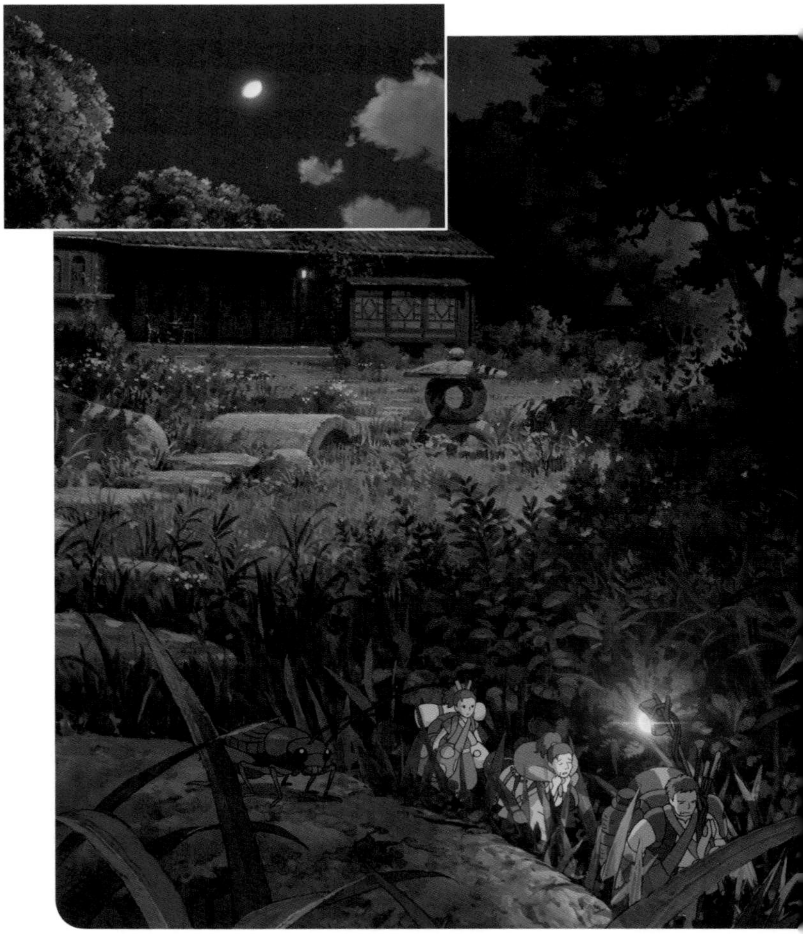

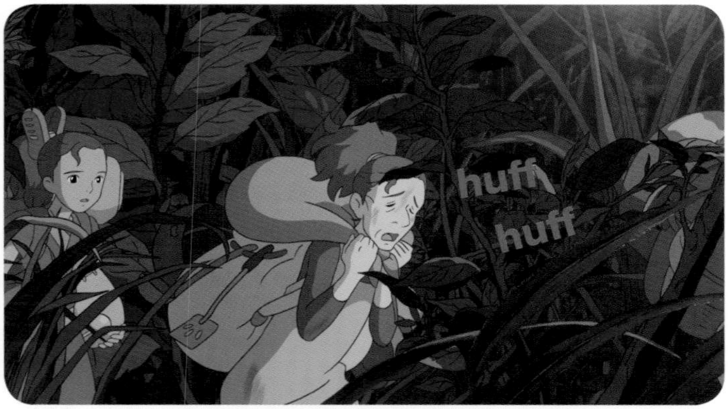
huff
huff

Pod turned back to look at her. "You're doing great," he said. "It's just a little further until we break to eat."

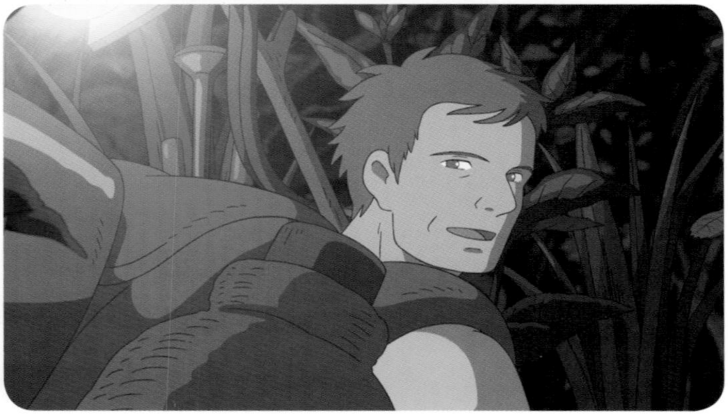

"Can't we just head back?" Homily pleaded. "We can live with the rats in the compost heap."

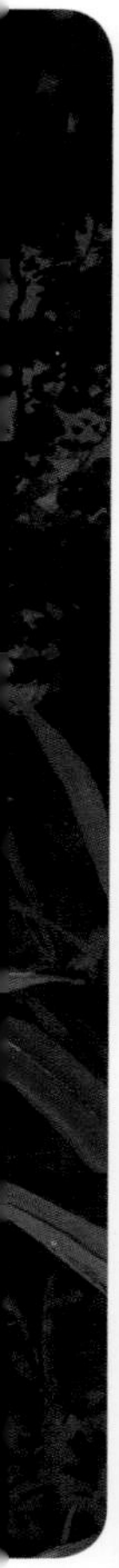

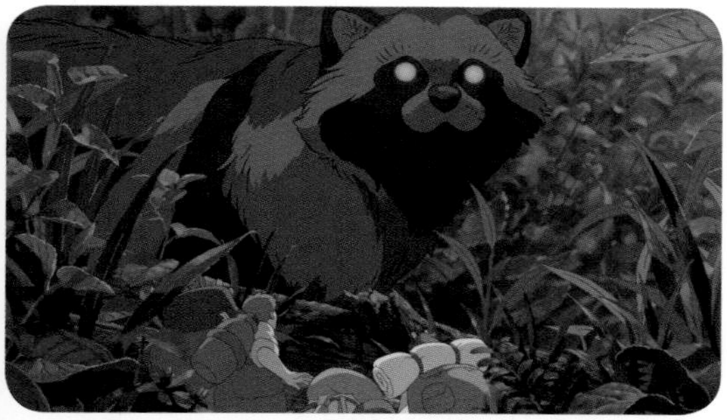

The family rested in an unused gazebo. Pod made a fire and warmed some cheese and bread.

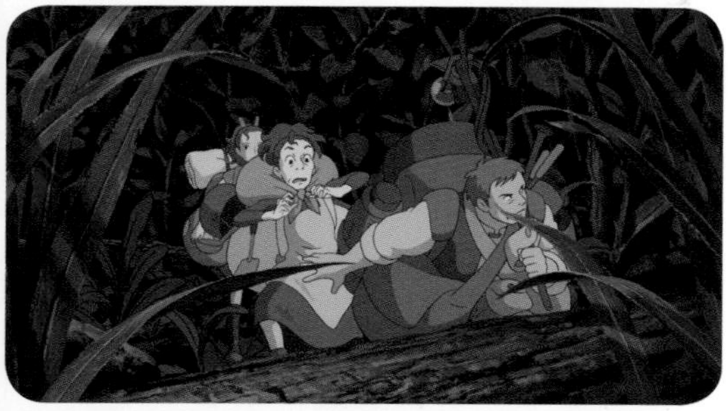

Arrietty hung her head and remained silent.

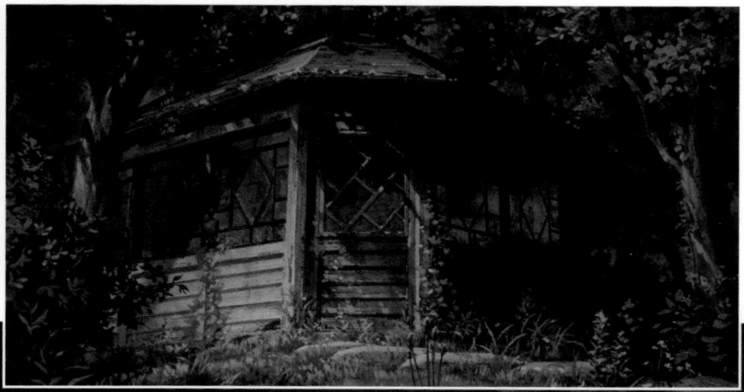

"Arrietty," Pod said. "You really should eat something. We're going to be walking at least until morning."

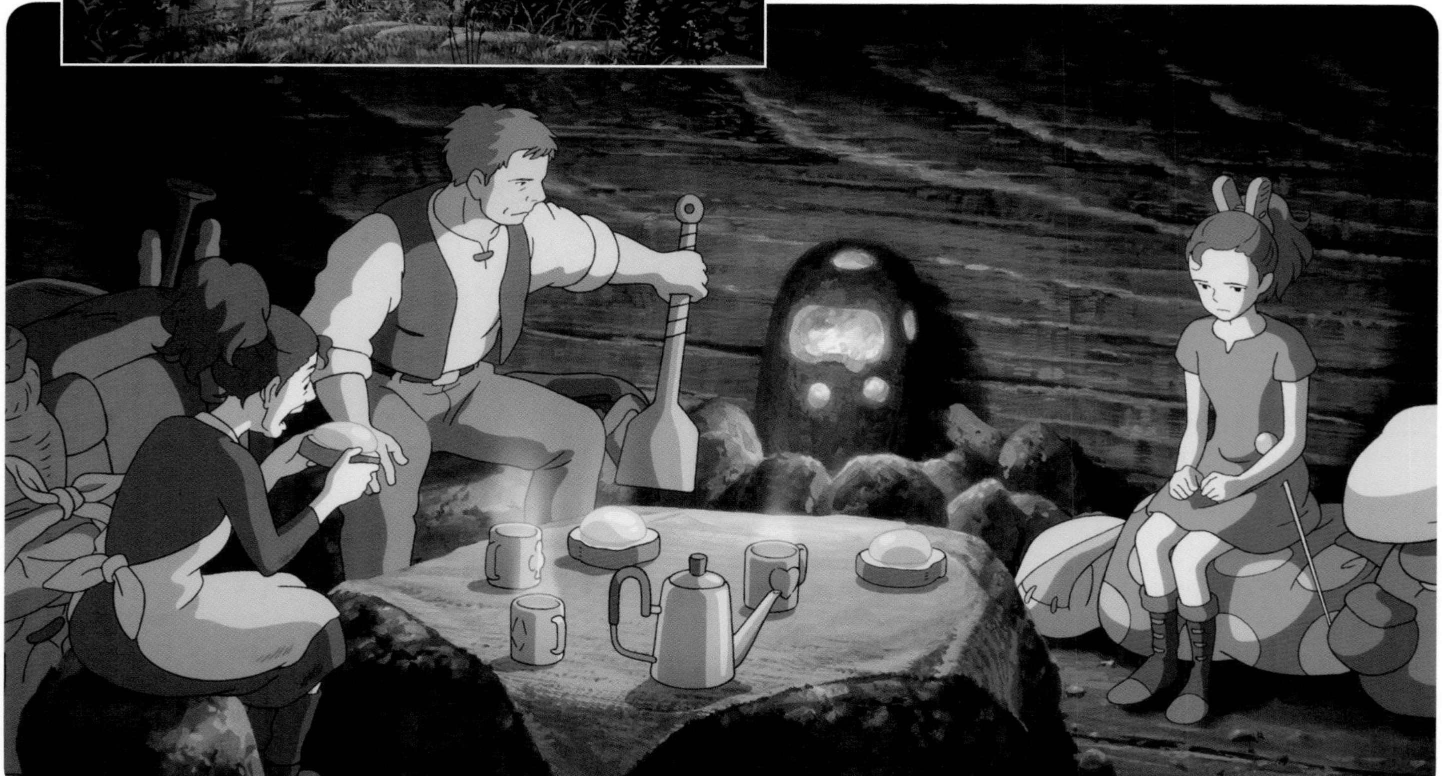

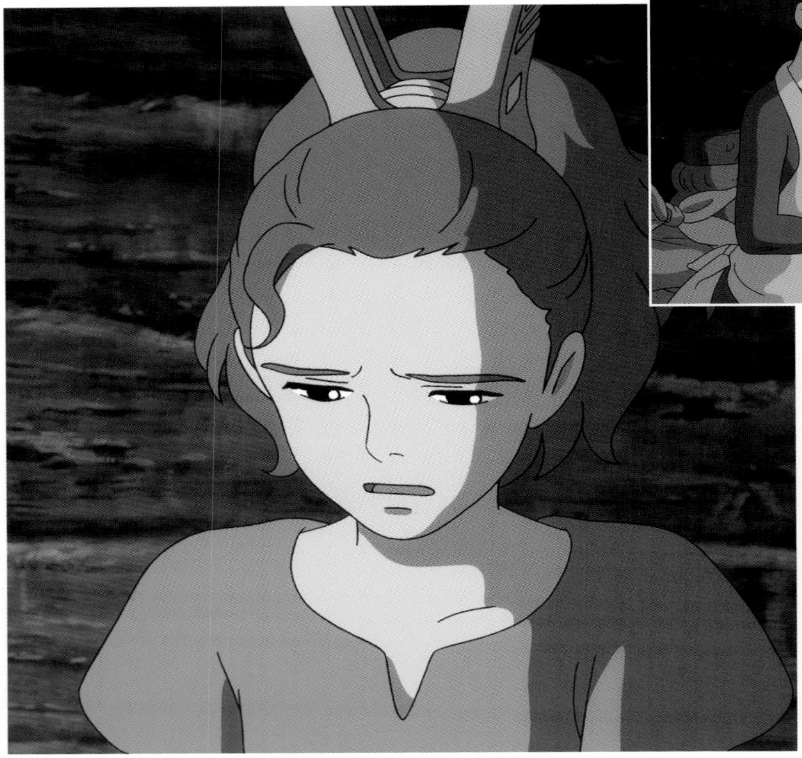

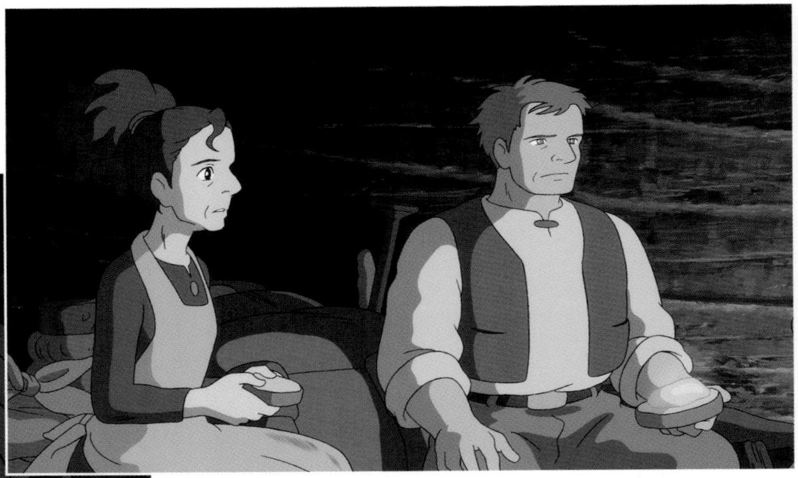

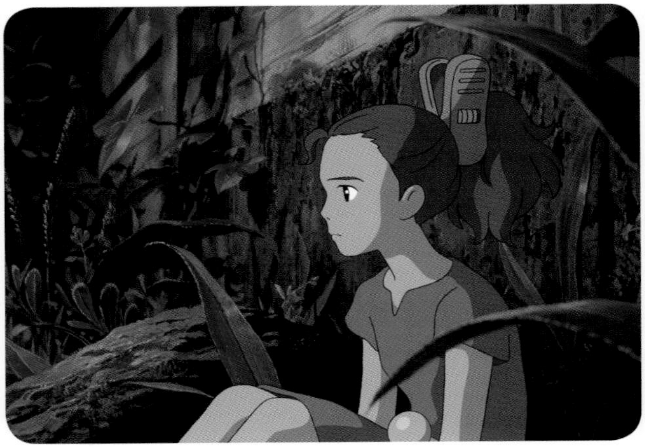

"I'm so sorry," Arrietty managed to say. "I feel like, maybe it's all my fault that we had to leave such a wonderful house."

"That's in the past," Pod said.

Homily smiled too. "We'll make another wonderful home. The three of us, together."

Arrietty gave a small nod. Then she slipped outside and sank into her own thoughts.

Suddenly, Arrietty saw a pair of eyes shining in the darkness. She braced herself—it was Nina the cat.

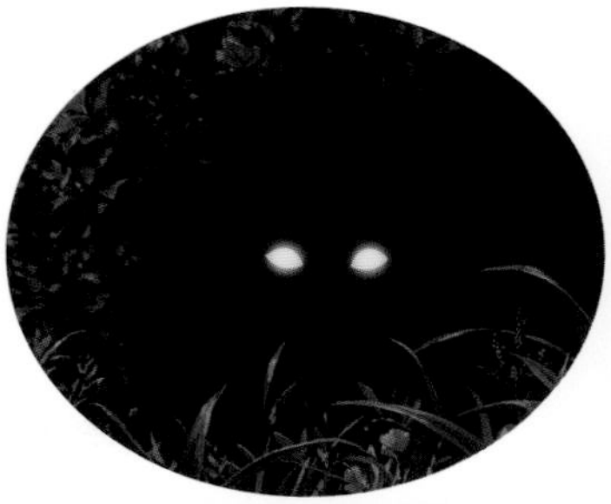

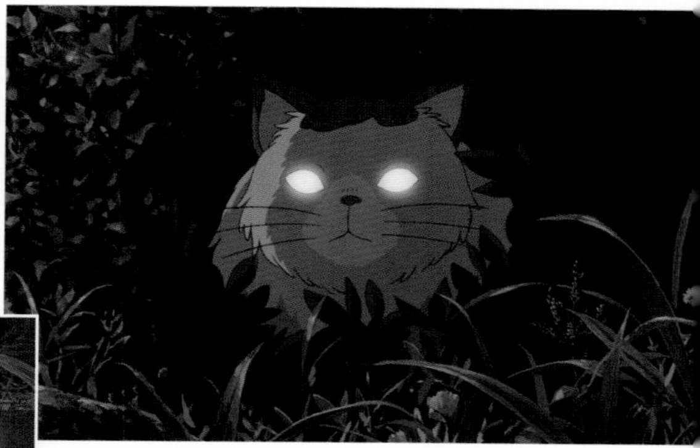

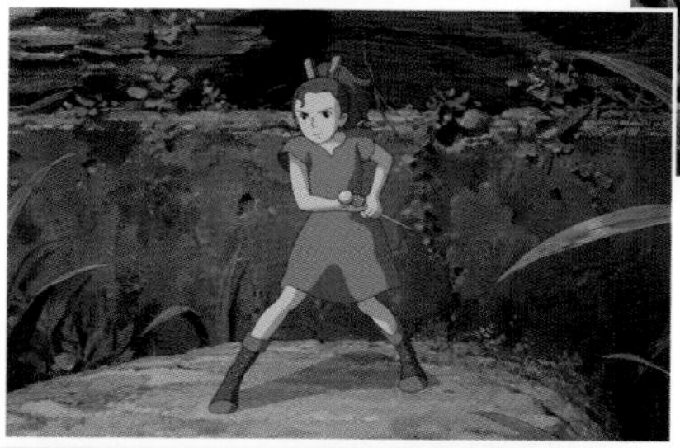

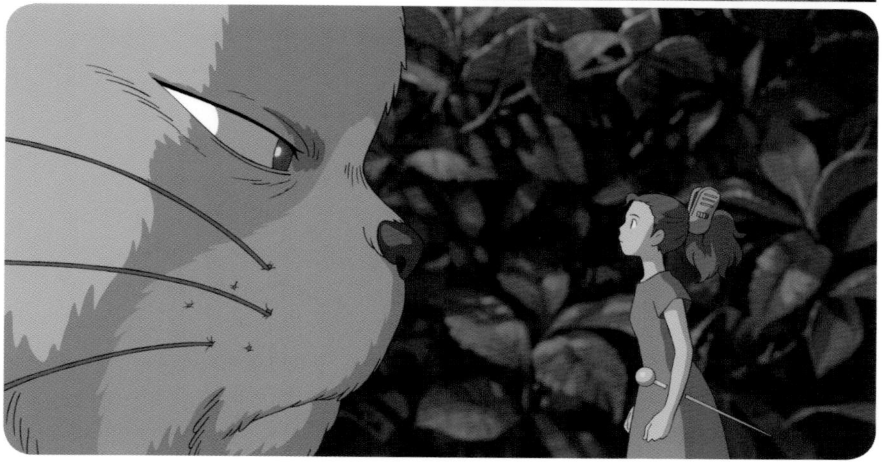

Arrietty gave Nina a long, meaningful gaze. Nina returned Arrietty's gaze and blinked slowly as if to say, "I understand." Then the cat turned and sauntered back to the house.

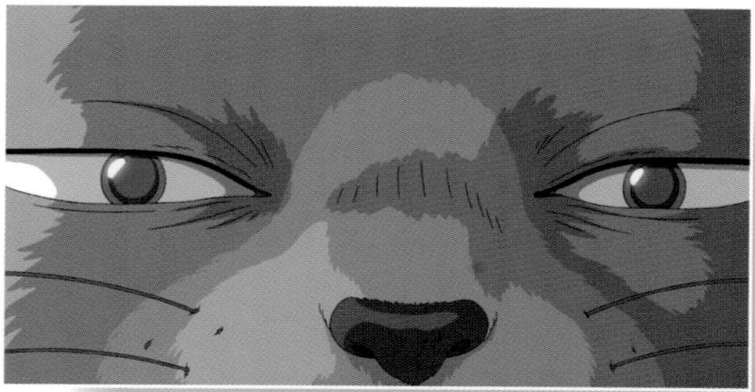

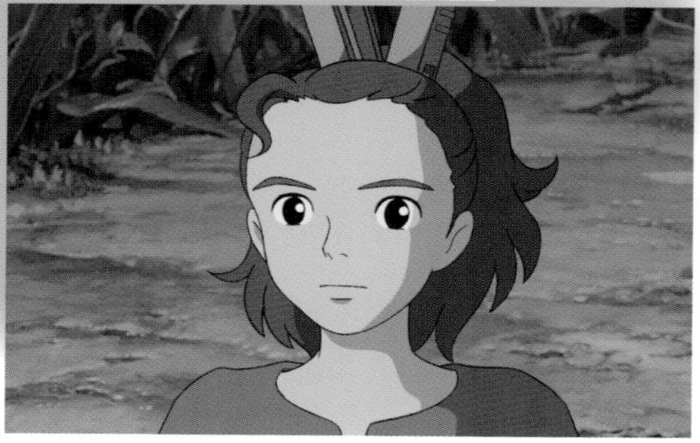

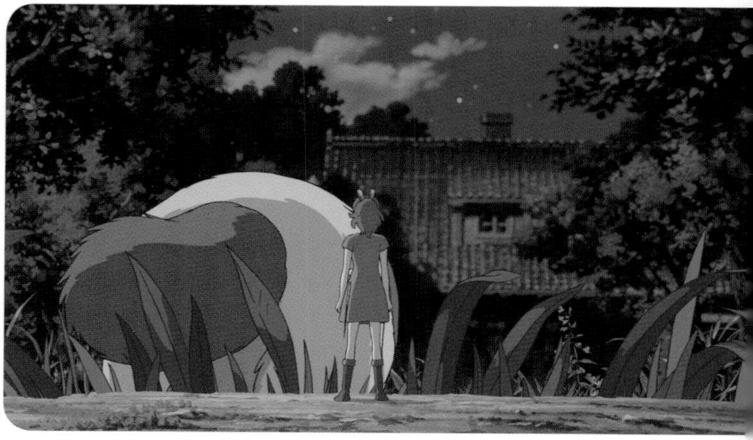

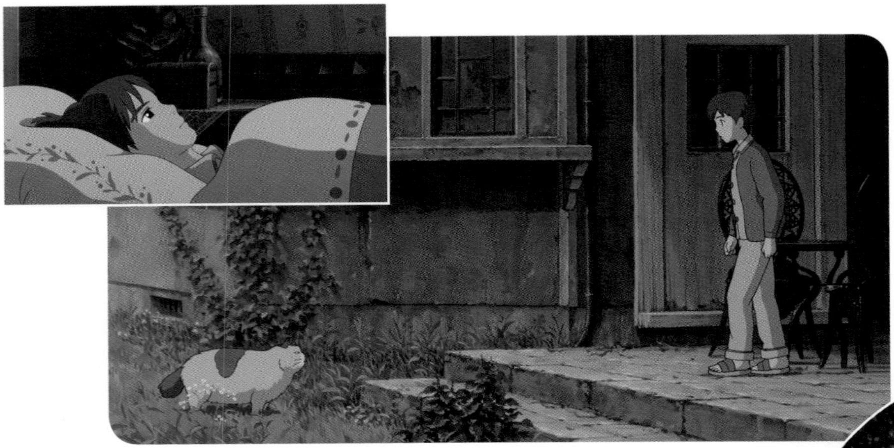

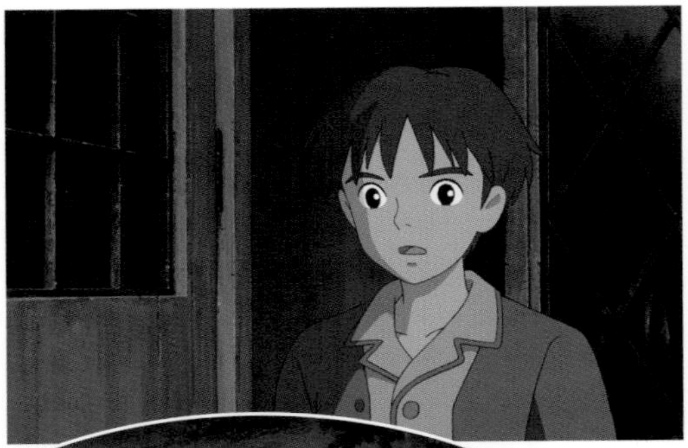

Shawn woke suddenly. He went to the moonlit patio where Nina was waiting.

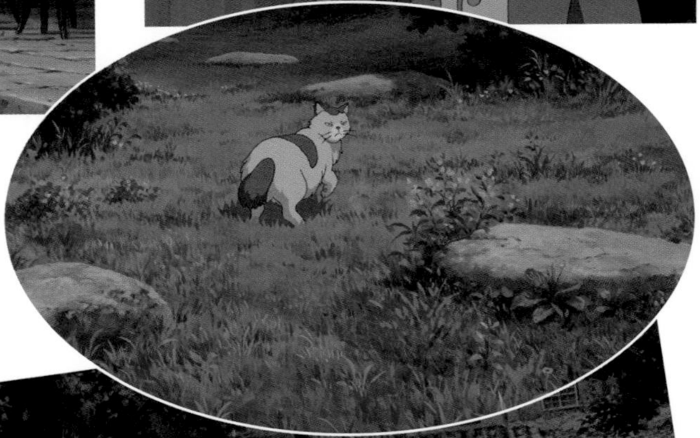

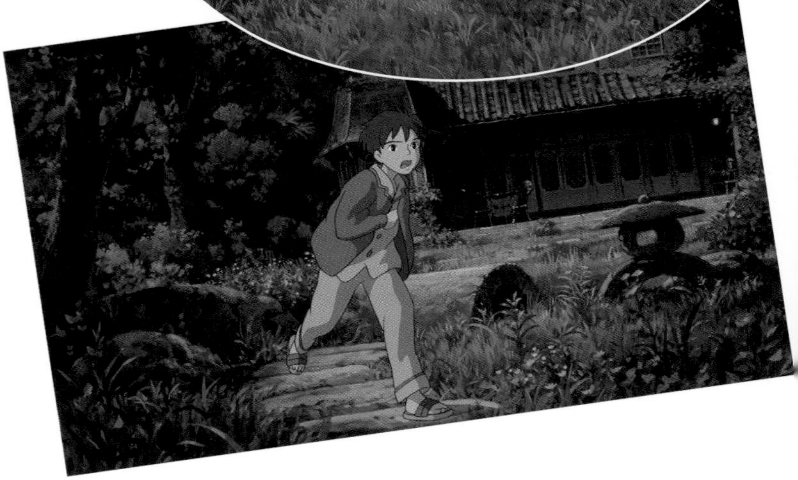

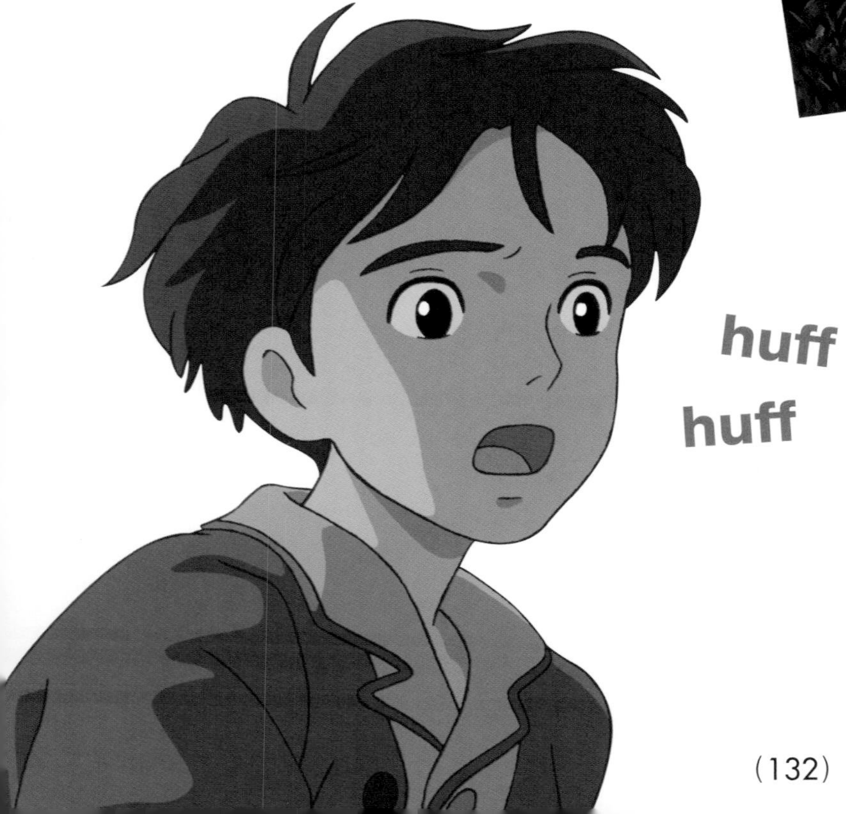
huff
huff

When Shawn approached, Nina walked away then looked back, as if beckoning Shawn to follow.

Shawn broke into a run and followed Nina.

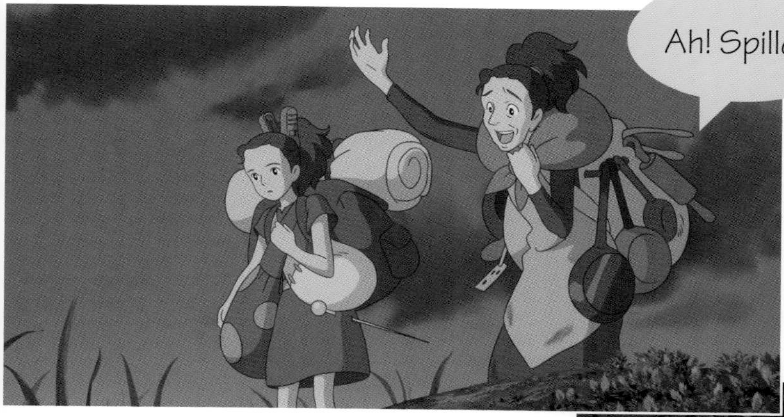
Ah! Spiller!

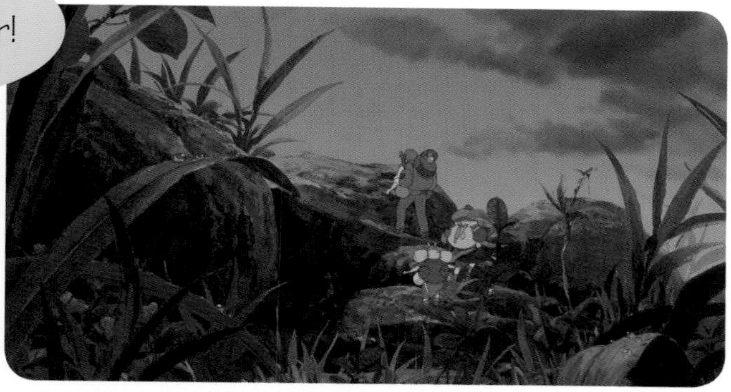

Arrietty and her family walked all through the night. Finally they reached the river where Spiller was waiting.

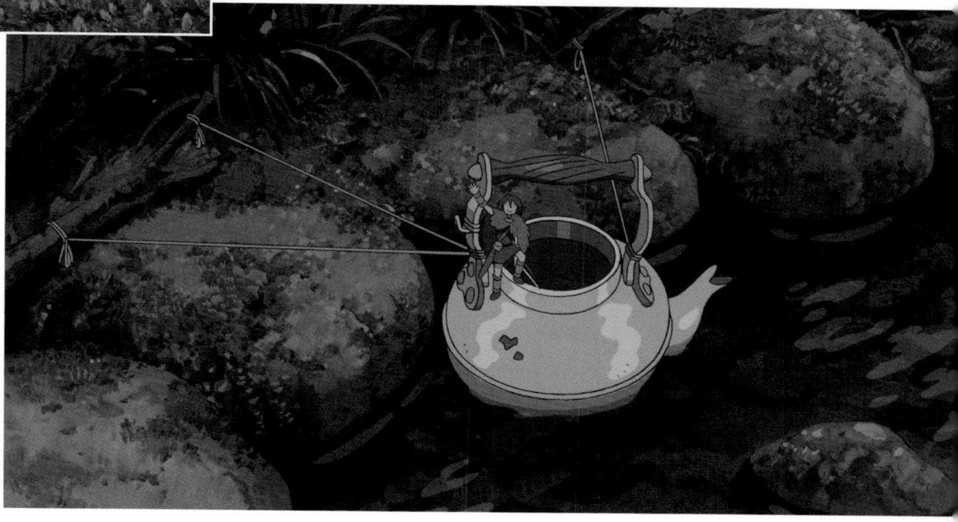

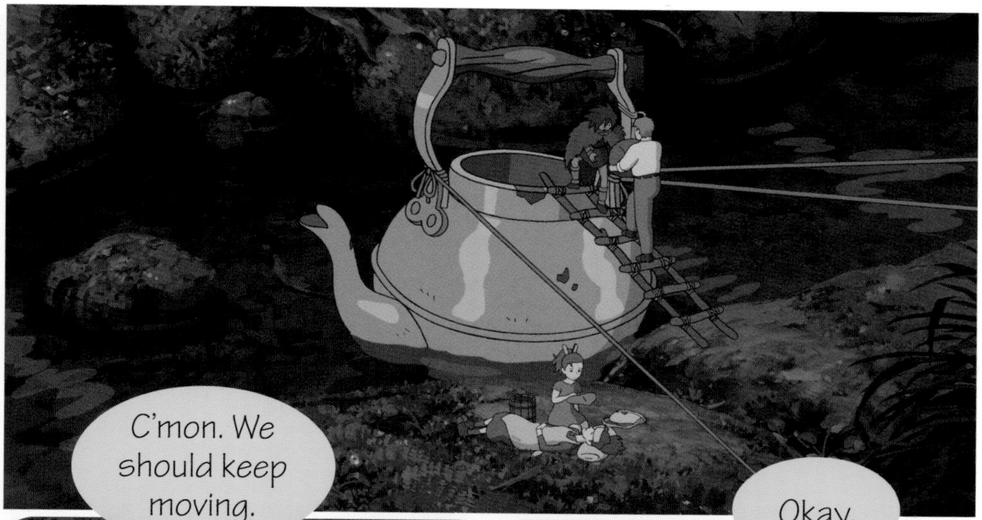

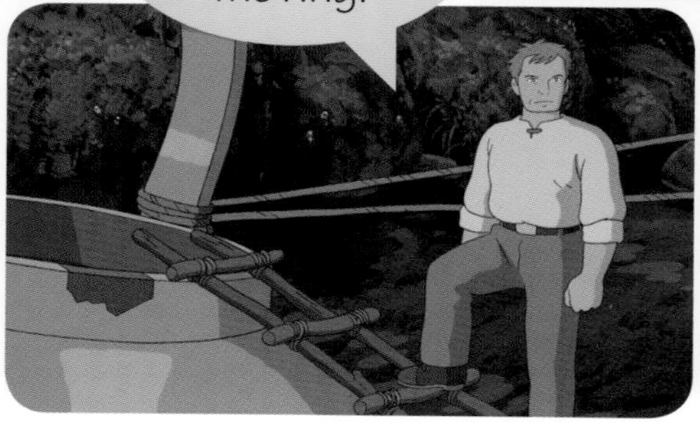
C'mon. We should keep moving.

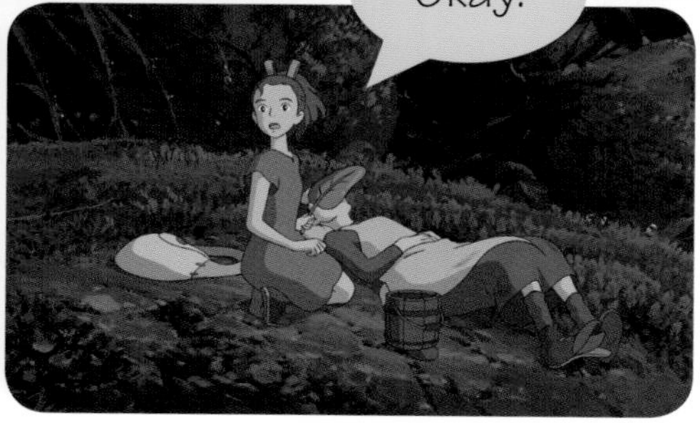
Okay.

Homily was exhausted. While she rested, Pod loaded their belongings into the kettle that they would use as a boat.

When Shawn reached the river, the sky was already beginning to lighten.

It was hard for him to breathe, and his body heaved with effort as he urgently searched for Arrietty.

He drew a deep breath and shouted, "Arrietty!" as loudly as he could.

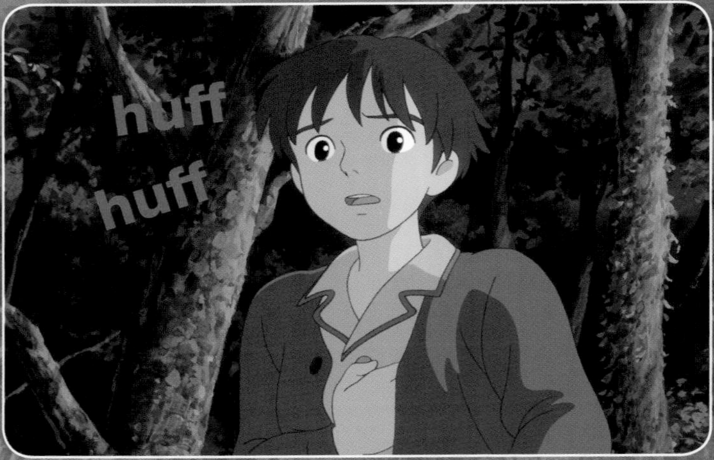
huff
huff

Arrietty was about to get into the teakettle. At the sound of her name, she looked up. She leapt off the teakettle, clambered up the rocks and hurried toward Shawn.

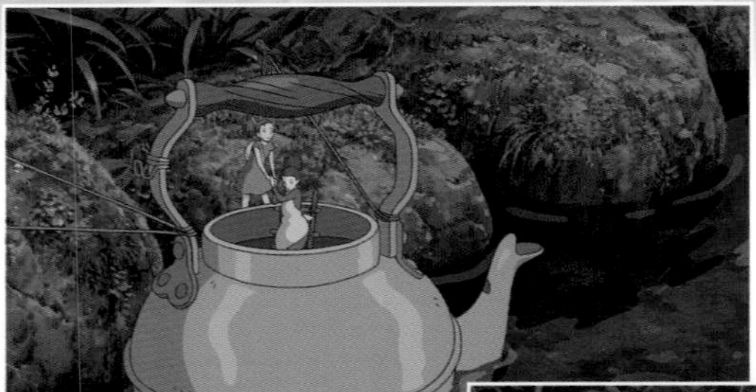

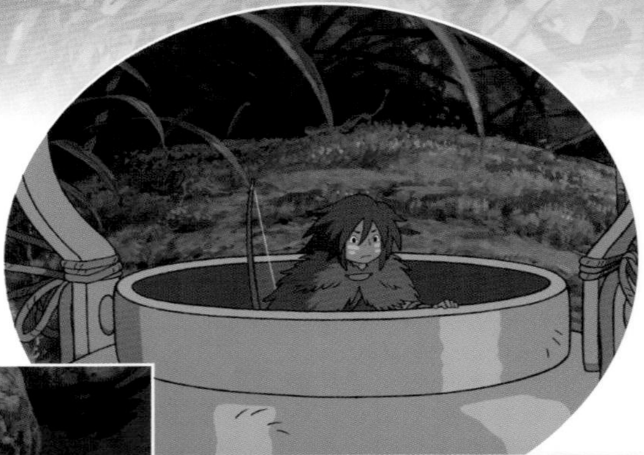

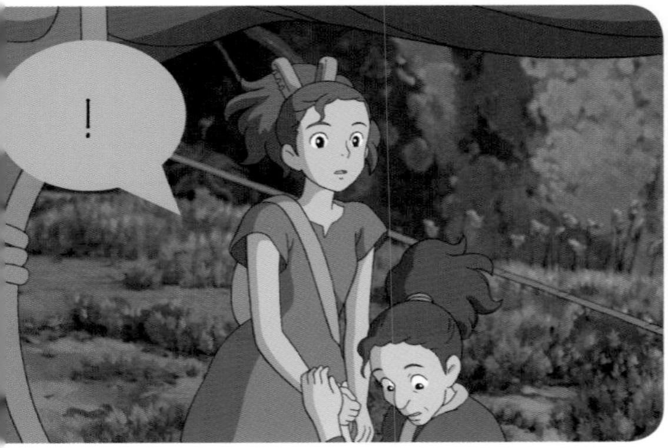
!

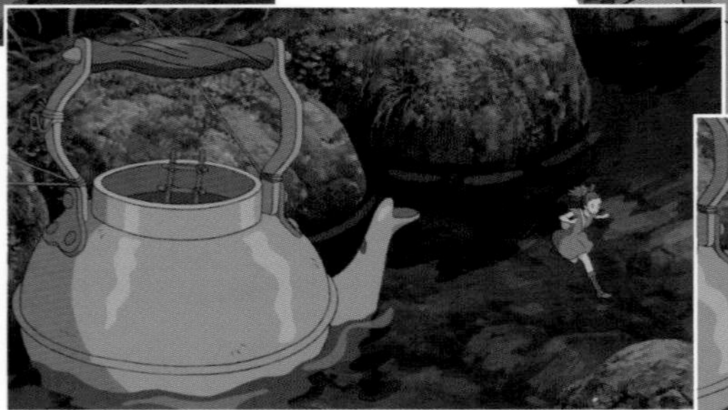

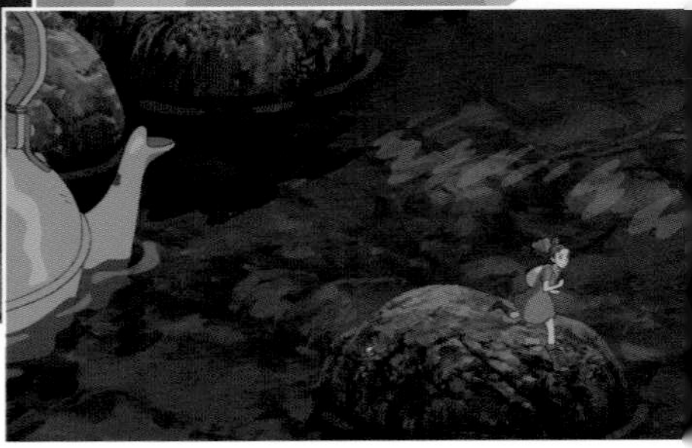

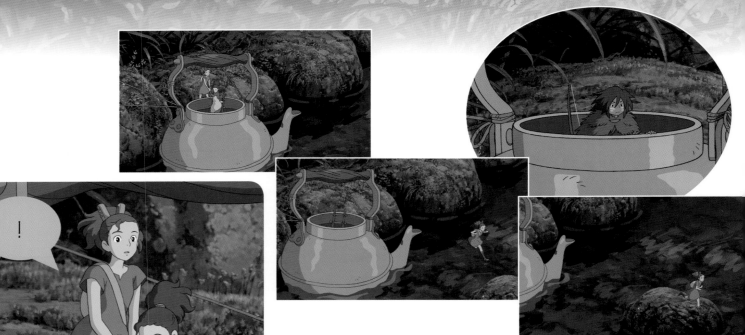

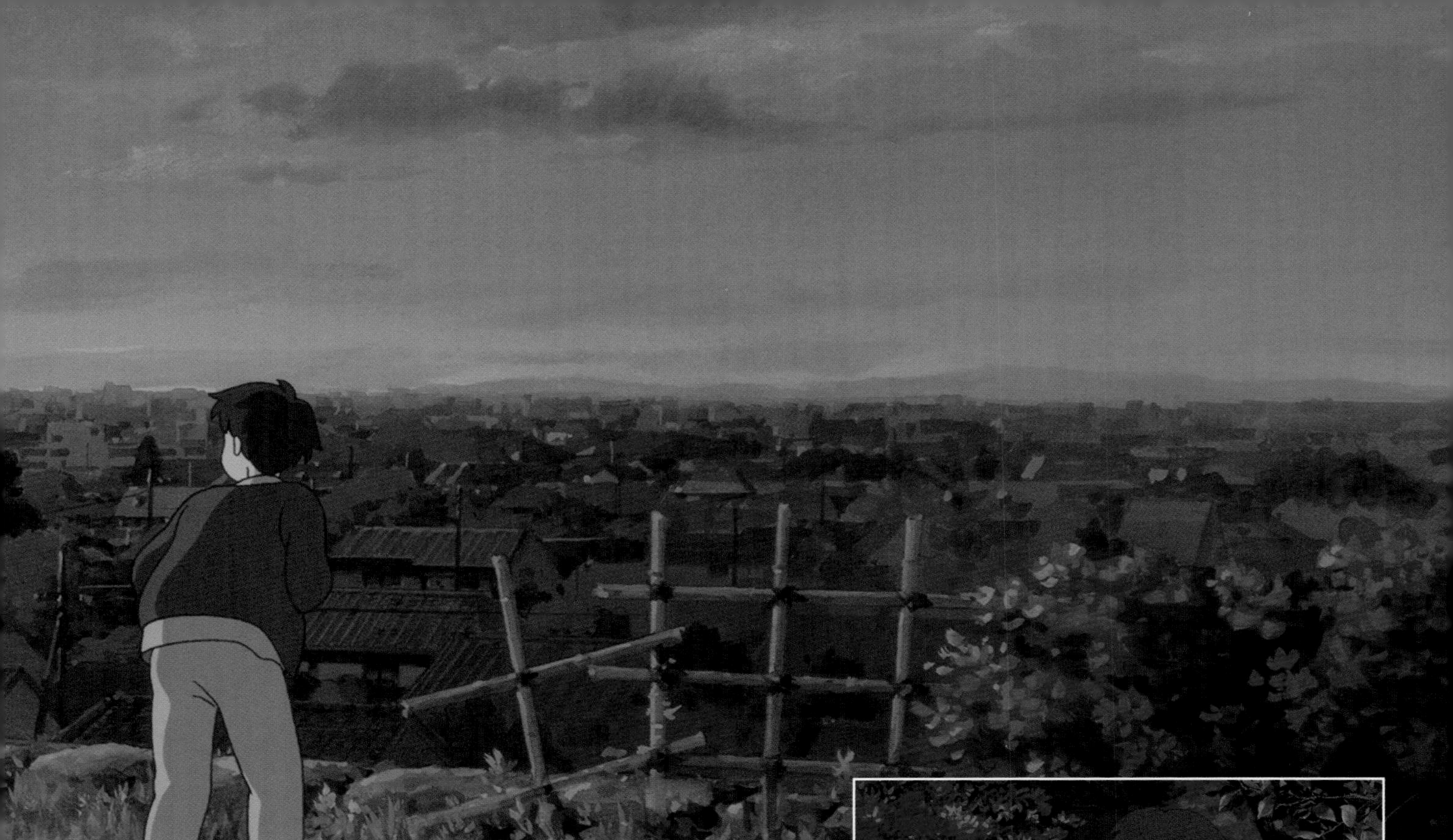

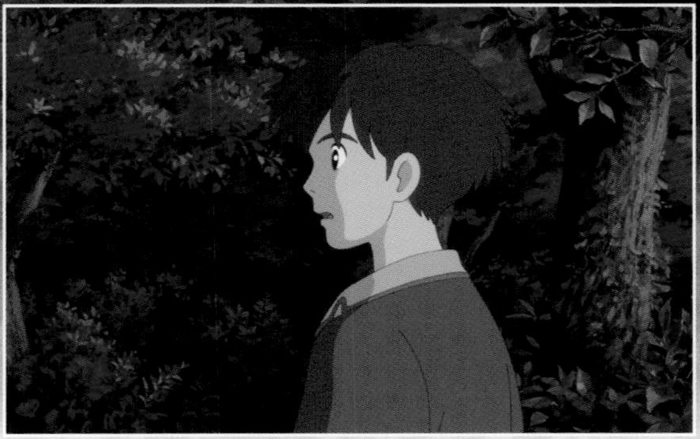

Shawn had given up. He was just about to leave, when…

“Shawn.”

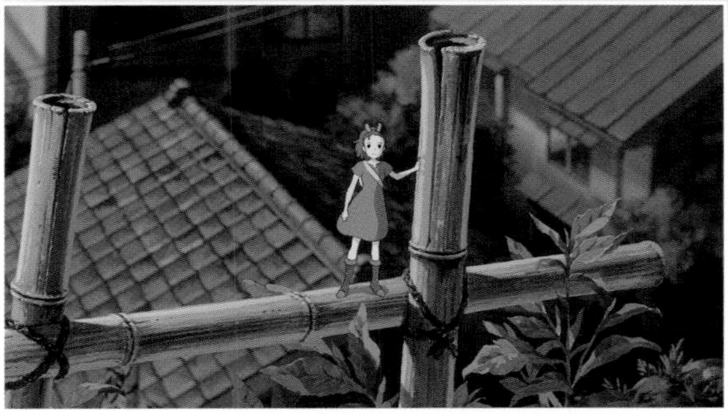

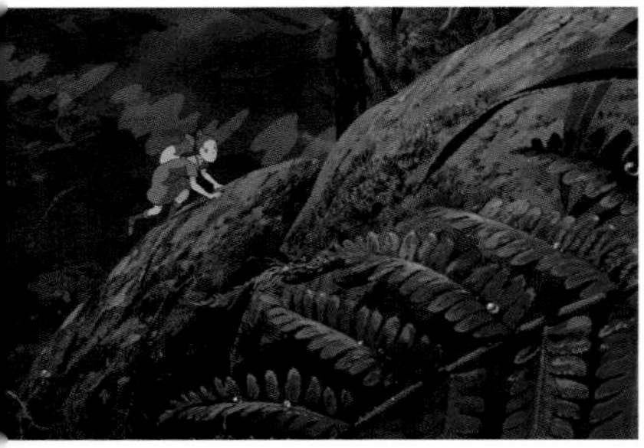

He turned toward the voice and saw Arrietty standing on a bamboo trellis.

“Arrietty!”

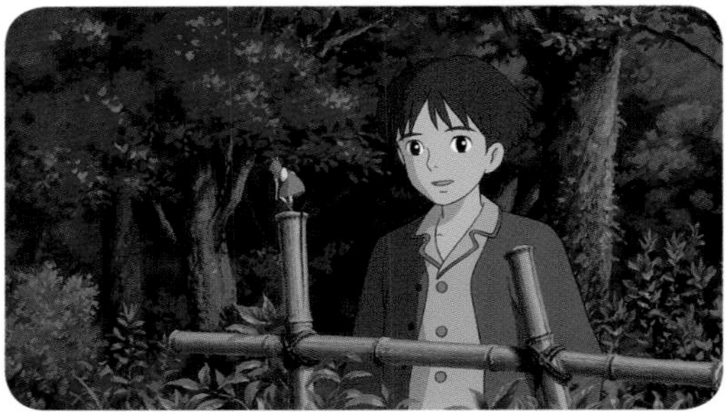

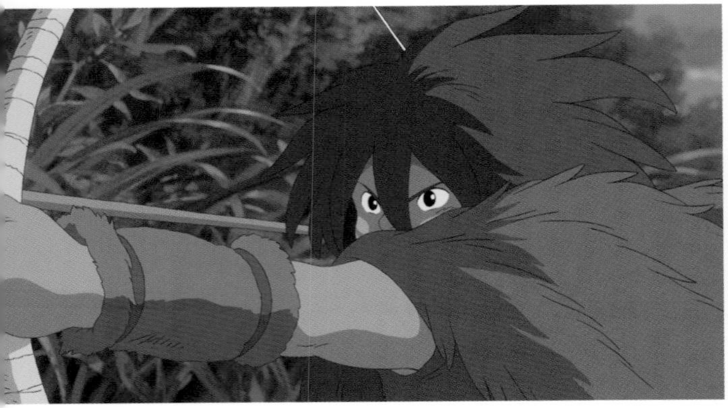

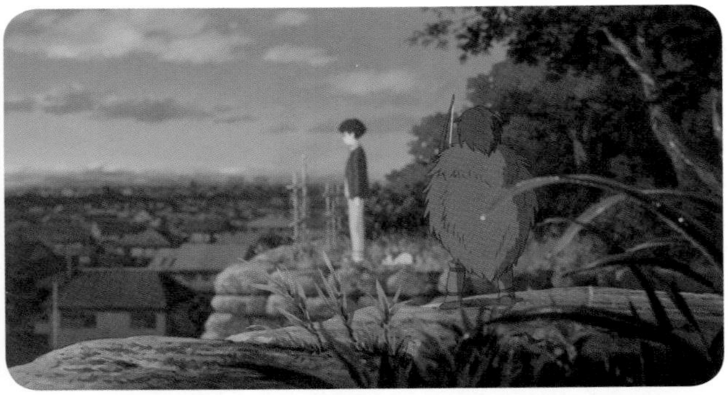

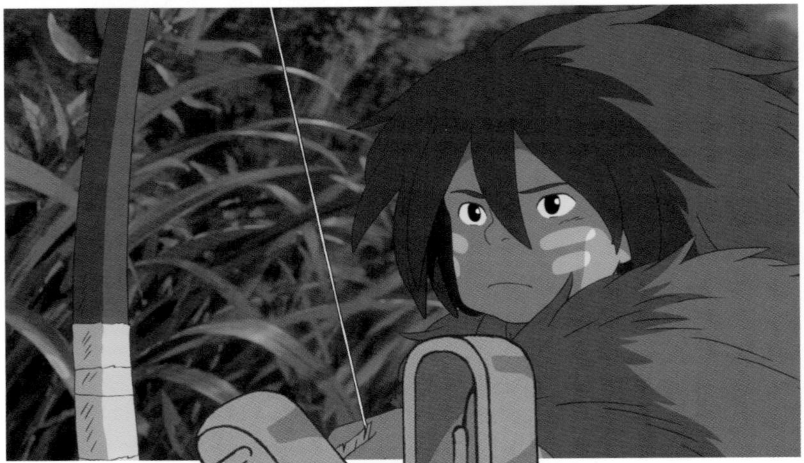

Worried about Arrietty, Spiller had followed her. At the sight of a human, he swiftly readied his bow.

He aimed at Shawn and drew the bow all the way back, but then relaxed his hand without releasing the arrow.

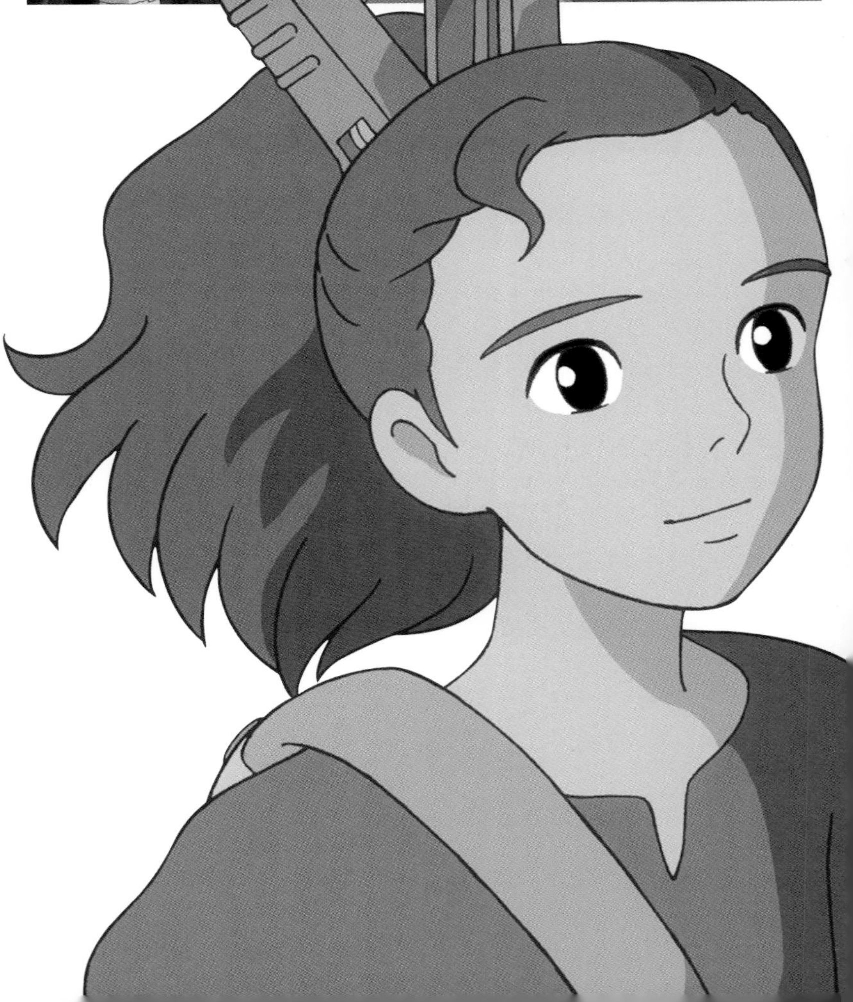

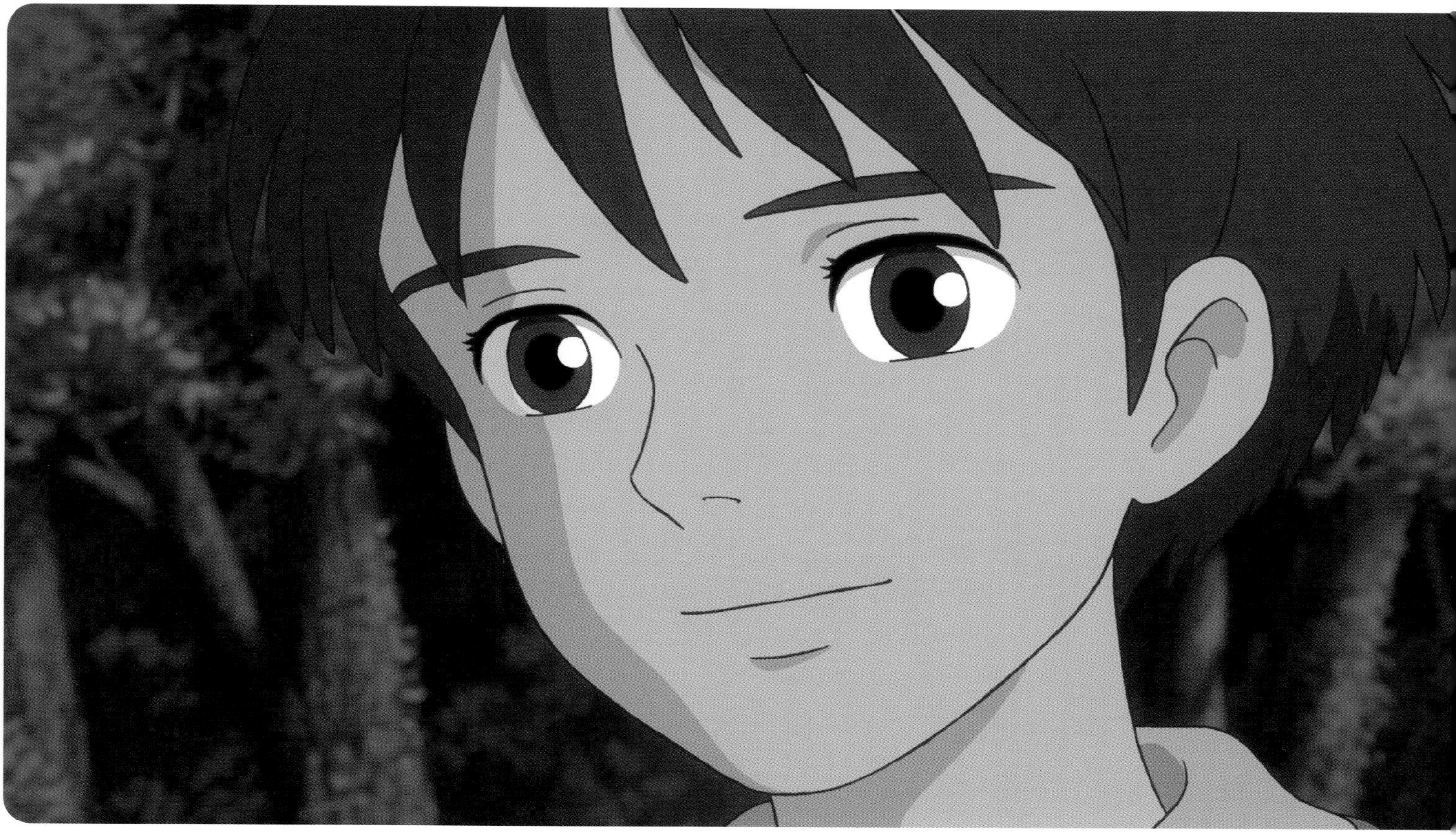

Shawn and Arrietty gazed at each other warmly.

"We have to leave," Arrietty said.

"I...I brought you something," Shawn said.

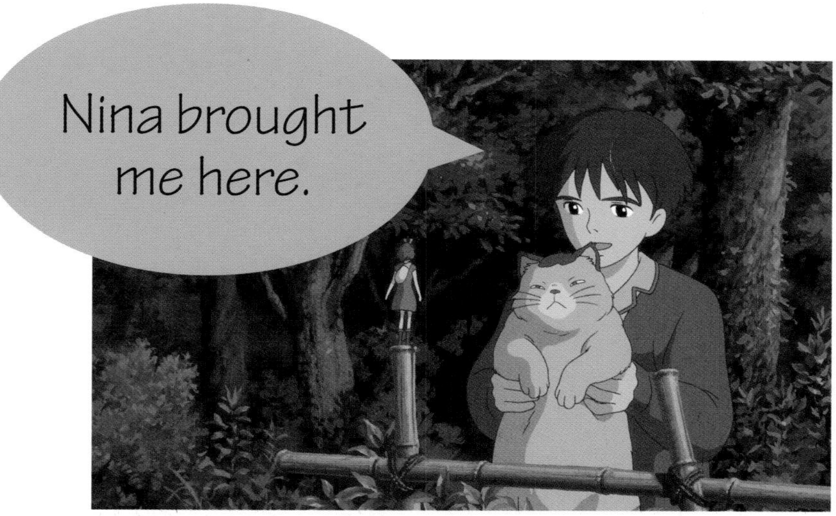
Nina brought me here.

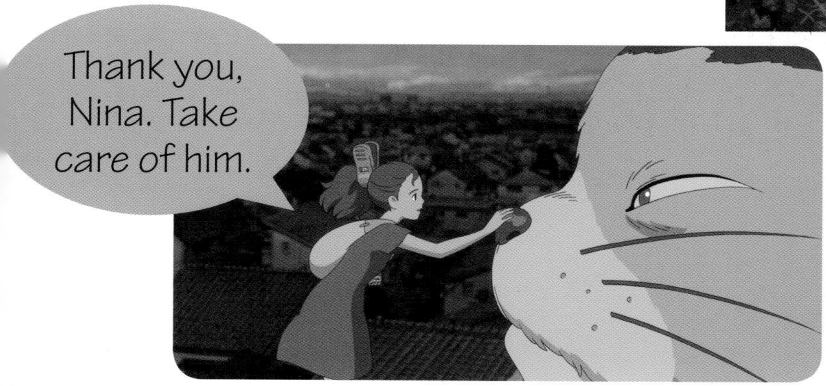
Thank you, Nina. Take care of him.

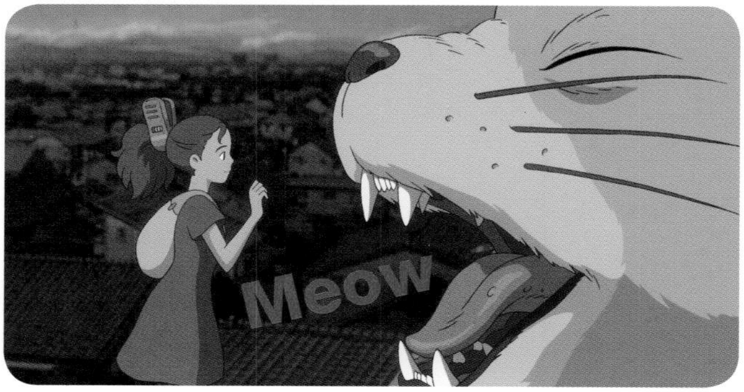
Meow

"Think of it as a gift from one friend to another," Shawn said as he unwrapped a sugar cube from a handkerchief and handed it to Arrietty.

"Thank you, Shawn." Arrietty accepted the sugar cube and put it in her bag.

To the east, the sky was growing bright. She could see Spiller going back down to the river.

"Well—I have to go. When is your operation?" Arrietty asked.

"Tomorrow. But I'm not scared…

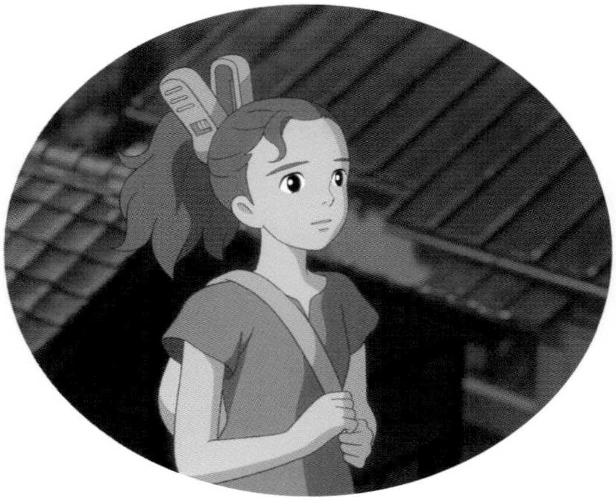

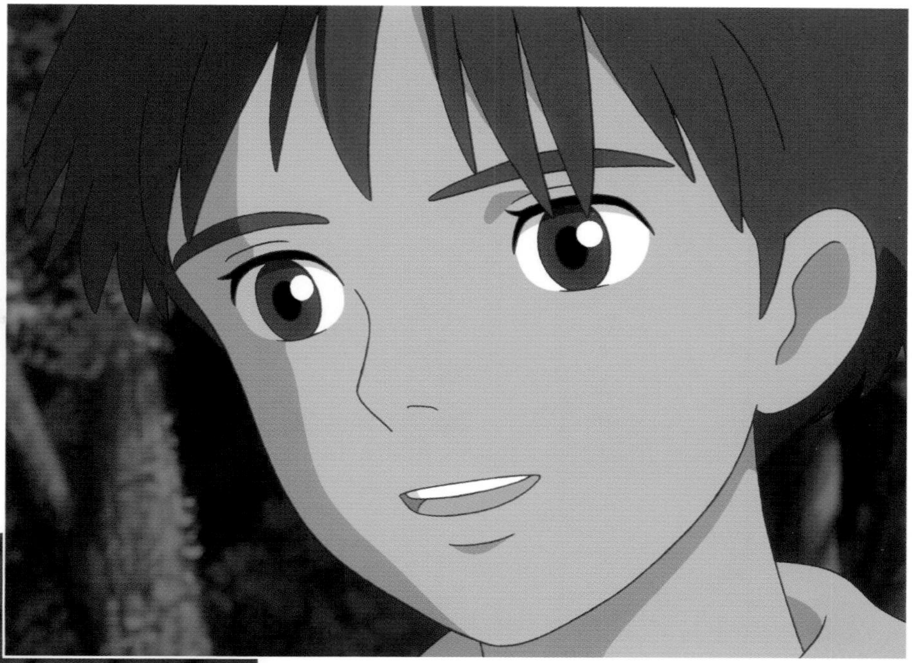

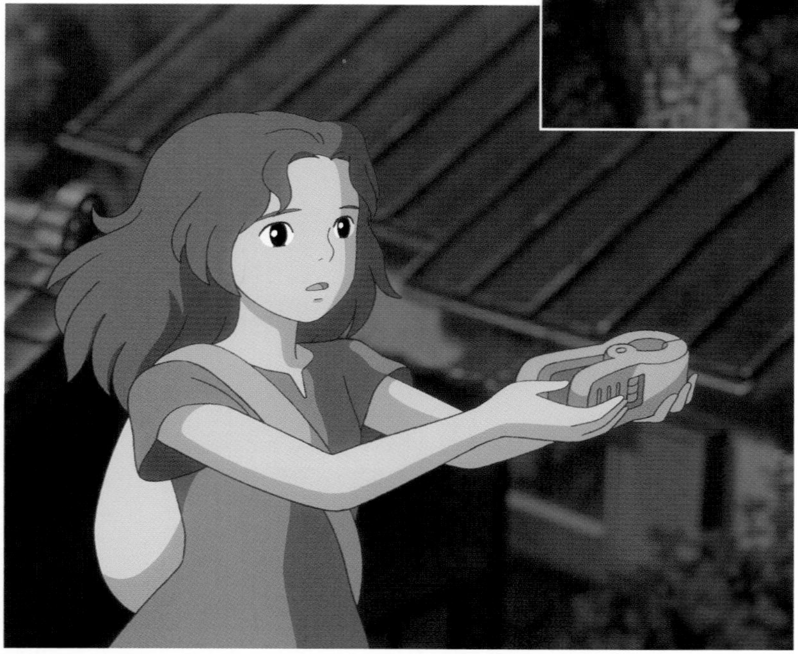

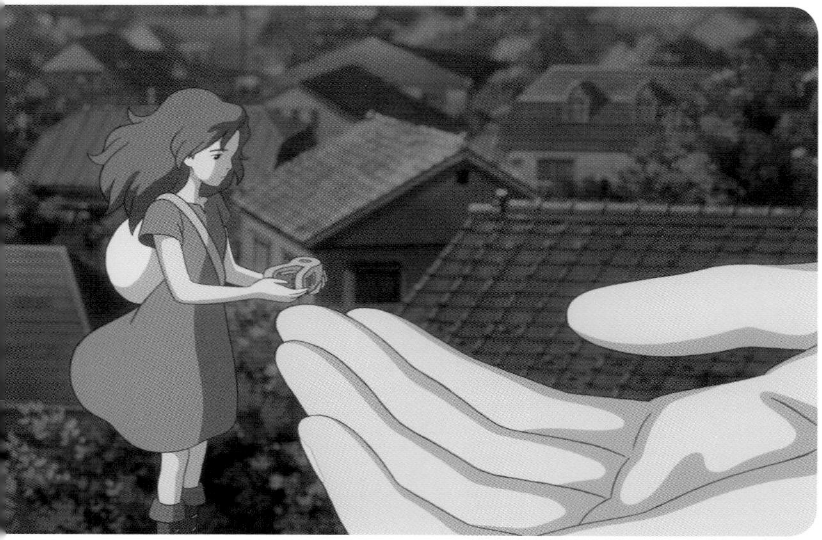

"...because someone taught me how to be brave."

Shawn smiled gently.

Full of emotion, Arrietty removed her hair clip and offered it to Shawn.

"So you'll remember me," she said.

"How could I forget you?"

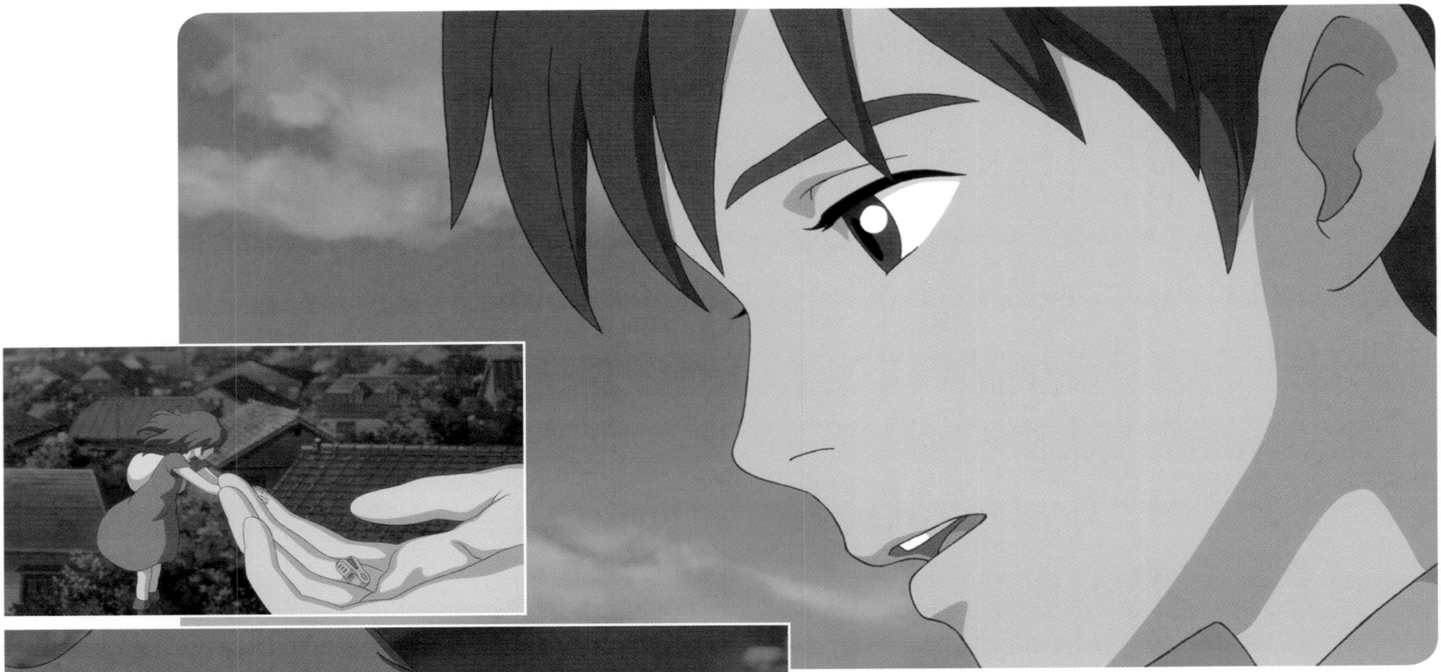

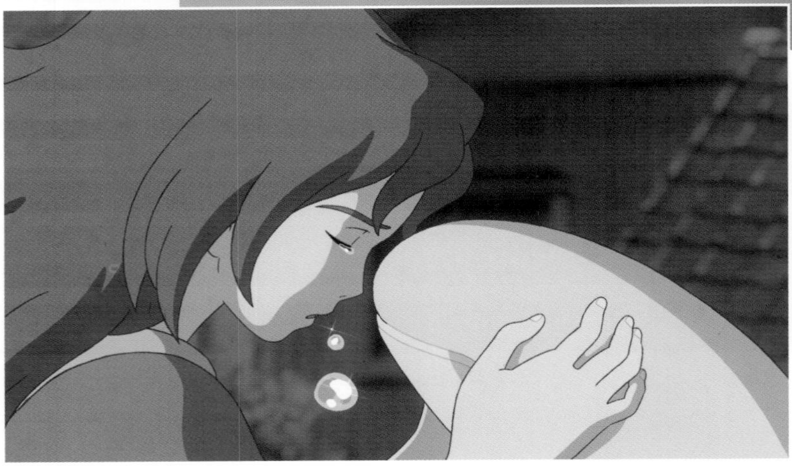

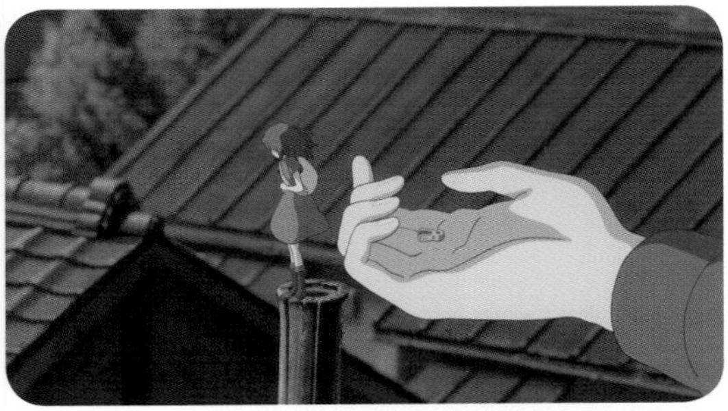

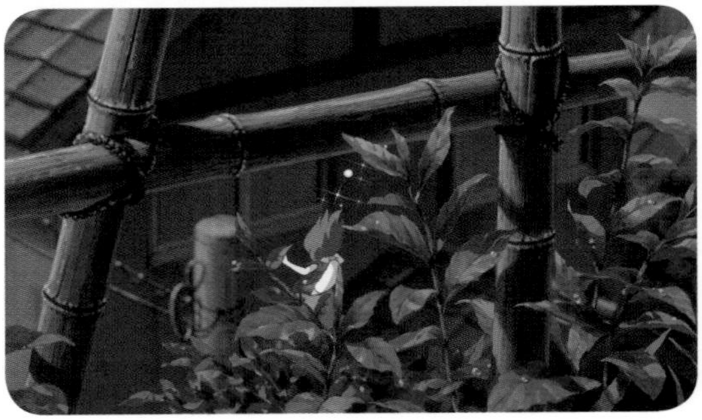

Arrietty grasped Shawn's finger with her hands and brought it closer.

"You looked after me after all."

"Arrietty..."

"I hope you...have a happy life. Goodbye, Shawn."

As Arrietty hopped down from the bamboo trellis, her teardrops glittered.

“Arrietty, my heart is strong now, because you’re in it. And you always will be. Forever.”

A fresh dawn was breaking.

Shawn held Arrietty’s hair clip gently in his hand as he looked out at the golden morning sun.

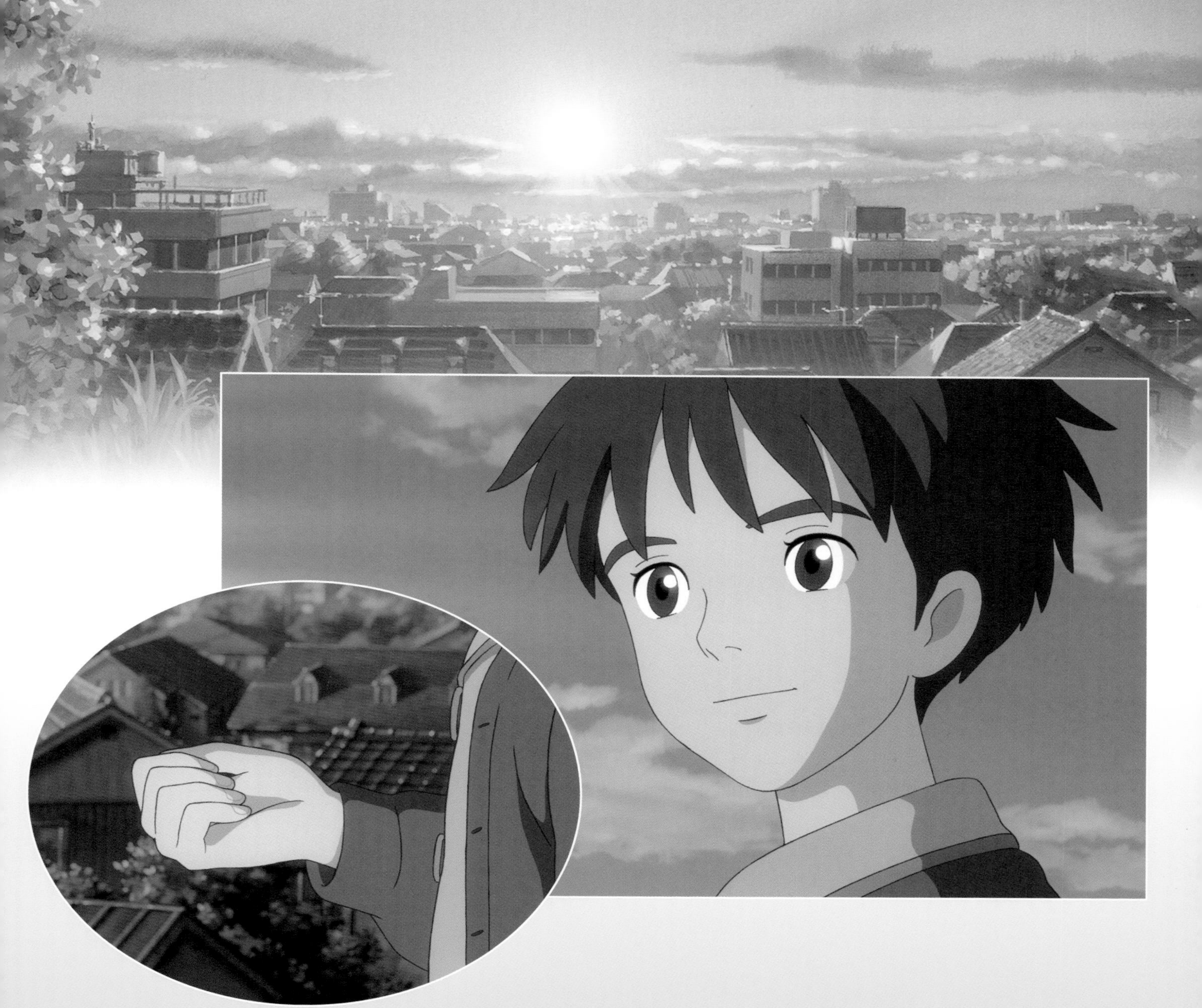

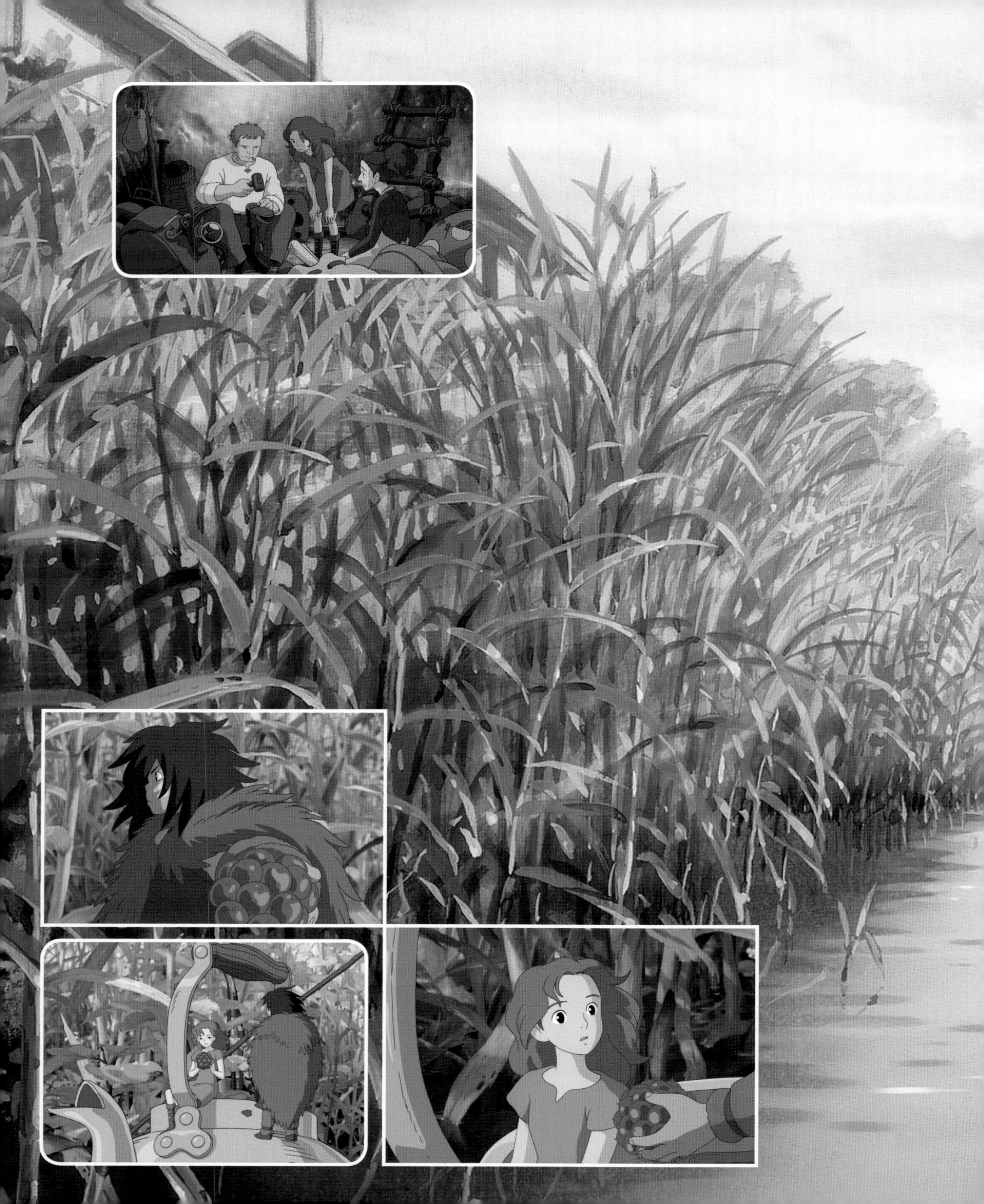

And the teakettle and
its four passengers
drifted down the river
toward a new life.

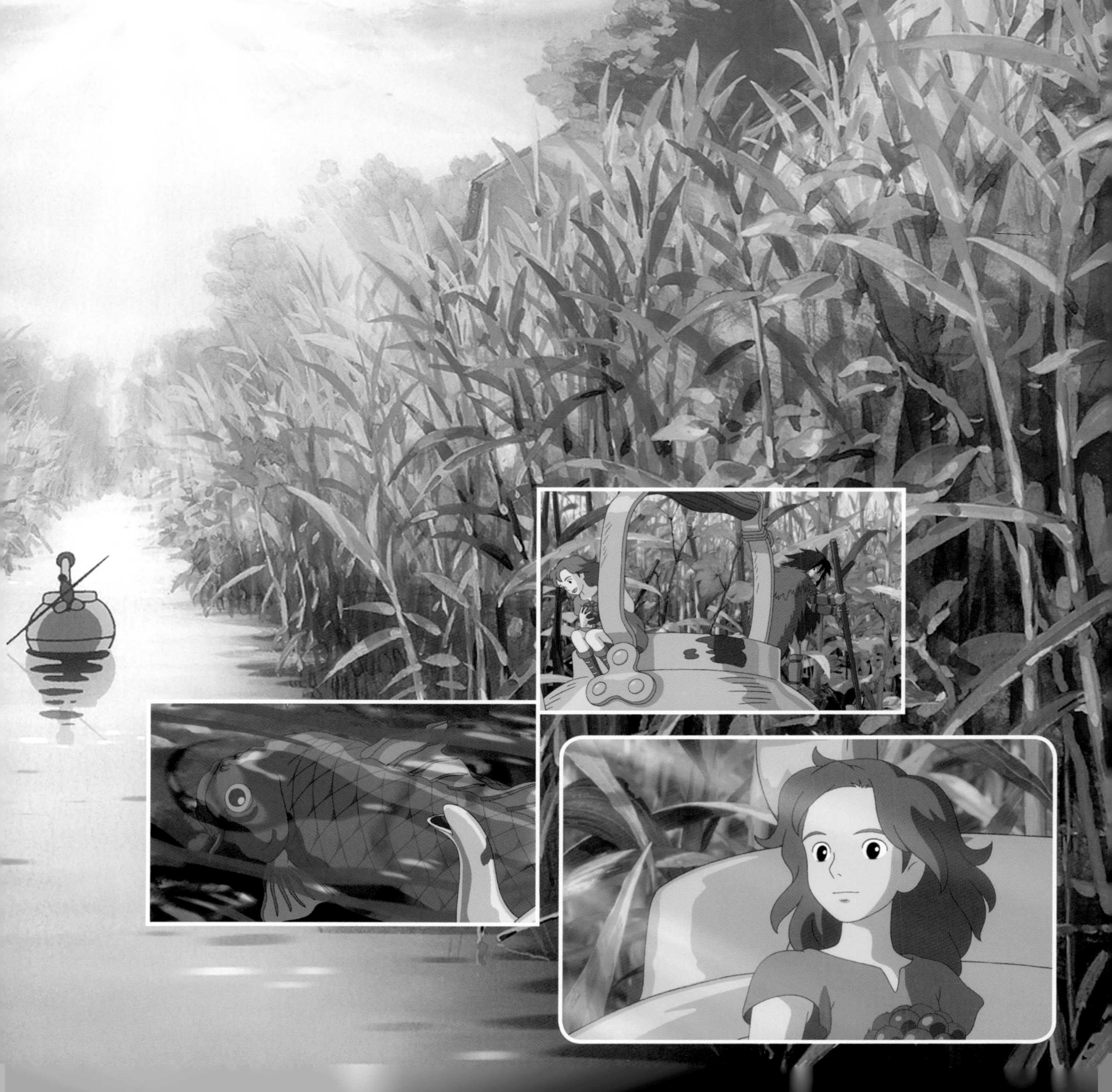

The Secret World of Arrietty
Picture Book

Planning by Hayao Miyazaki
Based on *The Borrowers* by Mary Norton
Directed by Hiromasa Yonebayashi
Original Screenplay by Hayao Miyazaki and Keiko Niwa
Translated from the Original Japanese by Rieko Izutsu-Vajirasarn and Jim Hubbert
English Language Screenplay by Karey Kirkpatrick

English Adaptation/Naoko Amemiya
Design & Layout/Fawn Lau
Editor/Traci N. Todd
Sr. Director, Editorial Production/Masumi Washington

Karigurashi no Arrietty (The Secret World of Arrietty)
© 2010 GNDHDDTW
All rights reserved.
First published in Japan by Tokuma Shoten Co., Ltd.
The Secret World of Arrietty title logo © 2012 GNDHDDTW
All other English translation © 2011 VIZ Media, LLC. All rights reserved.

Printed in Singapore

Published by VIZ Media, LLC
295 Bay Street
San Francisco, CA 94133

10 9 8 7 6 5 4 3 2 1

First printing, January 2012

www.viz.com